Audio Post-Production in Your Project Studio

Casey Kim

THOMSON
™
COURSE TECHNOLOGY
Professional ■ Technical ■ Reference

ISBN-10: 1-59863-419-4
ISBN-13: 978-1-59863-419-8
Library of Congress Catalog Card Number: 2007903973
Printed in the United States of America
08 09 10 11 12 TW 10 9 8 7 6 5 4 3 2 1

Publisher and General Manager, Thomson Course Technology PTR:
Stacy L. Hiquet

Associate Director of Marketing:
Sarah O'Donnell

Manager of Editorial Services:
Heather Talbot

Marketing Manager:
Mark Hughes

Acquisitions Editor:
Orren Merton

Development Editor:
Cathleen D. Small

Project Editor/Copy Editor:
Cathleen D. Small

Technical Reviewer:
Eldad Guetta

PTR Editorial Services Coordinator:
Erin Johnson

Interior Layout Tech:
ICC Macmillan Inc.

Cover Designer:
Mike Tanamachi

Indexer:
Kelly Henthorne

Proofreader:
Chris Small

THOMSON

COURSE TECHNOLOGY

Professional ■ Technical ■ Reference

Thomson Course Technology PTR, a division of Thomson Learning Inc.
25 Thomson Place ■ Boston, MA 02210 ■ http://www.courseptr.com

Acknowledgments

I'd like to extend a special thanks to the following people in no particular order: Mom and Dad, my two sisters Cindy and Wendy, Dazey Mitchell, Tom Chandler and Dark Red Audio, Amanda Morris, Patrick Ortiz, Breyde Bentley, Nate Howell, Cathleen Small, Orren Merton, Brad Cazden, Evan Bluetech, and everyone else who has ever given me a chance and or fostered my education/obsession with music.

I'm also thankful for computers, caffeine, eye drops, comfortable chairs, pajamas, the hours between 12am and 5am, 432 Hz, hand puppets, and the encouragement and understanding of my friends and family.

About the Author

Casey Kim began her education in classical music more than 20 years ago as a wind and double reed player. Her love of music drove her to learn to play ever more instruments, including guitar, bass, drums, and piano. Her ex-plorations of different genres, from alternative rock to underground electronic, ultimately led her to the production chair. Casey has spent the past 10 years working as a musician, composer, and digital audio post-production engineer, composing and producing music for film, television, multimedia, and video games. After serving internships with various studios and production houses, she established her first audio post-production project studio in 1999. She was heavily involved in the production and development of M-Audio's sample content series: ProSessions 24, ProSessions Producer, and ProSessions Premium Instruments. Casey currently owns and operates the Diavola Sound Workshop (www.diavolasoundworkshop.com), a full-service audio-production company based out of Los Angeles, California.

Contents

PART II
MIXING AND MONITORING IN THE PROJECT
STUDIO   51

Chapter 4
Don't Console Me   53

Chapter 5
Software Tools for Digital Mixing   59

Chapter 9
Three Sides to Every Story: Monitoring in the Project Studio 183

PART III
EFFECTS FOR DIGITAL AUDIO POST-PRODUCTION 205

Chapter 10
Rack in a Box   207

PART IV
MASTERING IN THE PROJECT STUDIO   289

Chapter 13
Mastering Audio in the Digital Age   291

Chapter 14
Software Tools for Mastering   301

Chapter 15
Mastering Techniques for the Project Studio   329

PART V
PROJECT STUDIO BUSINESS   367

Chapter 16
Operating Your Project Studio   369

Chapter 17
Resources   393

Index. 433

Introduction

Audio Post-Production in Your Project Studio is a comprehensive guide to the world of audio post-production as it applies to a real-world project studio environment. It focuses on DAW (*Digital Audio Workstation*) techniques using software programs and plug-ins to get professional-quality results. Chances are that if you're reading this introduction, you've already had some kind of experience in audio recording and you are looking for more information about how to make those recordings sound better either for personal satisfaction or to start making money with your production abilities. This book will explore everything from audio post-production applications and techniques to getting work and understanding the business side of operating a successful project studio.

What Is Post-Production?

Post-production occurs in the making of audio recordings. It's a general term for the stages of production that occur *after* the actual audio-recording process has been completed and *before* its relative project can be considered finished. Audio post-production processes may include audio editing, adding effects, conforming volume levels, sound design, audio mixing, or audio mastering, to name a few. Whether it is for an audio CD, a multimedia application, a movie, or a television program, audio post-production will take place before the recording is ever broadcast to the general public.

When Is Post-Production Necessary?

If your audio recording is intended for a commercial purpose, such as a record, a multimedia application, a film, or television, post-production is *always* necessary. Even audio recordings produced for private use can benefit from the use of post-production techniques. Audio post-production makes the recording sound more professional and contributes to a positive overall listening experience.

How Project Studios Have Changed Post-Production

It used to be that in order to edit performances and arrangements, major studios and post-production houses had to take a razorblade to the 2" tape from the recording reels and physically cut out the sections they wanted to keep, and then tape them back together to get perfectly edited tracks of audio. They would run racks upon racks of outboard hardware processors that applied effects such as reverb, compression, equalization, distortion, and modulation to an original piece of recorded audio. The audio would be routed through any number and combination of these effect processors, and then routed back into a recording console and "printed," or re-recorded, to tape so that the effects could be heard.

The downfall of this process is that once you've effectively printed the effects to tape, they become a permanent part of the recording. Allow me to illustrate: The average "old school, tons of gear, reel-to-reel" studio recording is composed of different audio signals that are isolated onto individual tracks so that later, the levels can be blended to produce a well-balanced mix. Suppose one of the tracks in this average studio recording contains a dry, or unaffected, vocal take. When you play back all the tracks at once, it is painfully obvious that the vocal take stands out in a way that interferes with the continuity of the overall mix. The engineer then decides that, in an effort to make the vocal take less obtrusive, some reverb should be applied to it. To achieve this, the isolated vocal take is routed to a reverb effect unit, then back into the console and re-recorded onto another reel. If, upon listening to the affected vocal, it is decided that the wrong reverb was used or that too much reverb was used, the controls on the reverb unit will have to be adjusted, and the process of routing and re-recording the audio signal will start all over again.

With the availability of digital audio software and hardware that, in the right hands, can produce studio-quality results, more and more musicians and engineers are assembling all-in-one audio production studios in their homes (in garages, bedrooms, or even storage sheds!) that are completely based around computers. Computers that are specifically designed for audio production are generally referred to as *DAWs*. And studios designed around DAWs are typically referred to as *project studios*.

Project studios and computer-based DAWs have drastically changed the way that audio post-production techniques can be executed. Now, effects can be applied, unapplied, adjusted, and reapplied with a few keystrokes. Performances can be edited, arranged, and rearranged to perfection with the click of a mouse. Processes that used to take an engineer countless hours of manual labor to complete can now be carried out in a fraction of the time from the comfort of your own home—and, on occasion, in your pajamas.

What You'll Find in This Book

In this book, you'll find:

- An overview of how the introduction of project studios has changed audio post-production.

- An in-depth look at audio post-production techniques, such as audio editing, mixing, using effects, monitoring, and mastering, tailored to the project studio environment.

- An introduction to the different types of software used in digital audio post-production.

- A comprehensive look at effect plug-ins used in digital audio post-production.

- Ideas and suggestions for making better-sounding audio recordings using post-production techniques in your project studio.

- Expert tips and tricks.

- The basics of frequency and audio properties.

- Audio post-production dos and don'ts.

- A realistic look at what it takes to start and run a successful project studio.

- Charts, diagrams, glossary terms, and other resources that can be used as a quick reference in any studio.

Whom This Book Is For

Whether you're an experienced musician just getting into production, a first-time project studio operator, or a hobbyist curious to learn more information, *Audio Post-Production in Your Project Studio* will serve as a worthy companion in your quest for knowledge. It will also act as a handy desktop reference guide to a wealth of information about audio post-production as it relates to your studio environment. This book is for anyone with a software-based project studio who is interested in making better-sounding audio productions or enhancing his or her post-production skills.

How This Book Is Organized

Audio Post-Production in Your Project Studio is divided into 17 chapters across 5 sections. Each chapter has a specific focus on a particular topic relative to the section containing it. The initial chapters are structured to provide general information and to introduce concepts and terminology that are discussed in greater detail in later chapters. The entire book can be used as a reference, but if you are new to audio post-production, it's a good idea to read through the chapters sequentially. Although the book doesn't refer to techniques that are exclusive to any particular software, *all* audio post-production techniques contribute to the end result of an audio project. No single technique can stand alone, and it is important to understand how one affects the other. This book is designed as a place to start. It will help you develop a good foundation with effective practices that you can immediately put to use, and it will take you all the way to obtaining professional-sounding results using the tools at your fingertips.

Audio Editing for Project Studios

1 Stretch Me, Tune Me, Bounce Me...

Audio editing will make up a sizeable slice of your post-production skill pie. You'll be surprised by how much editing actually takes place in the average recording. In fact, these days there is no such thing as a commercially released recording that *hasn't* been edited in some way. The primary reason is this: No matter who the performer is, not every performance will be 100-percent perfect. You will encounter the occasional out-of-tune, or out-of–time, note and multiple takes that need to sound like a single, seamless performance. Then again, sometimes a part of a performance is just *so* perfect that you'll want to use a copy of it again later in the project. With a little digital editing (or sometimes a *lot* of digital editing), you can resolve sonic inconsistencies that keep a recording from sounding professional. If you've ever wondered how Rockstar Band A made such a great-sounding record when the band's live show sounds like a pack of wild monkeys with broken thumbs, chances are a good amount of editing went into the project.

Post-production employs a great number of tricks and techniques that can help you clean up a performance so that it serves its purpose for the greater good of the mix. And that is really the whole point. Some consider editing a performance to improve upon the actual delivery as cheating. I can certainly respect that perspective. Being a musician, I have a great deal of integrity when it comes to my own music. I could never imagine someone altering my original performance to make it something that it's not. However, I expect a bit of cleanup to be done. As a post-production engineer, it's not your job to get a good performance out of a player or a singer. Leave that to the producer. It's your job to work with the sonic material provided by your client to make the best-sounding production possible.

If you're a composer who generates all the audio for your projects from your own studio, you'll do your fair share of audio editing as well. Original compositions require editing just like any other project. The primary difference is that you will have total control over all of the original audio material. This will hopefully eliminate the variable of third-party recording engineer bloopers. The process includes using loops to get good takes or to repeat frequently used patterns, reducing noise, and correcting sonic artifacts. But what exactly *is* audio editing?

What Is Audio Editing?

Audio editing is applying a series of techniques during post-production that will alter the original audio, or *source material*. Editing your audio prior to mixing will clean it up and give you a clean slate of pristine audio signals you can mix. Editing typically happens before you start mixing, but if you're also the composer, you might do both at the same time. Before editing, you might notice that a performance contains vocals from multiple takes that have been strung together in an obvious way, pops and clicks at the beginning and end of instrument takes, ringing overtones, and other various sonic blemishes that may have occurred during the initial recording session. When you're finished editing, the only thing you should be able to hear is nice, clean, natural-sounding audio signals with no noticeable inconsistencies.

The literal definition of audio editing is "the process of taking recorded sound and changing it." So technically, if you've ever created a mix tape by taking audio from multiple sources and "dubbed" them down to a single cassette, you've been involved in some form of audio editing. Under this definition, you could consider sound design an advanced form of editing, though a complex and intricate one. Editing encompasses several different actions, such as cutting and pasting; fading and cross-fading; adjusting gain, timing, and pitch; and reducing various unwanted sounds. Because "editing" is a blanket term for so many different processes, I'm inspired to dedicate an entire chapter of this book to the fine details of editing audio. Chapter 3, "Software-Based Editing Techniques," offers a more in-depth look at some of these detail-oriented practices.

Sound Design versus Audio Editing Sound design and audio editing employ many of the same techniques to achieve their goal. The primary difference between the two is the goal. Sound design is additive. It's usually a creative pursuit to develop original sounds, specific auditory effects, and landscapes that will usually be combined with preexisting audio. Audio editing, or *sound editing*, is subtractive. It's more like trimming the fat—removing unwanted noise from preexisting audio signals and making them cleaner.

Bouncing *Bouncing* is the technique of consolidating multiple audio tracks down to a single track. Suppose you have eight separate tracks to work with, but you need six more. You could bounce the initial eight tracks down to two tracks, thus freeing up six tracks on which you can record new audio signals.

Professional audio editing is an important first step in the post-production process. As anyone in professional audio production will tell you, the devil is in the details. They really couldn't be more right. No single thing creates a great-sounding recording. An excellent recording is typically composed of many small details all rolled into one great sound. The average music listener may not be able to describe *exactly* what makes a recording more professional-sounding because it's not *exactly* anything. It's the contribution of many small details that serve the bigger picture.

To Edit or Not to Edit... An excellent performance is the single most important thing in the professional audio equation. Producers and recording engineers work directly with artists or talent to get good source material. They know that if a performance will require a great amount of editing in post-production to sound passable, the artist probably should just do it again. Does that mean the artist will? Not necessarily. Because technology allows us to adjust the volume, timing, pitch, duration, and various incidentals on any part of a performance, it can be a little too easy to say, "That's good enough. We'll get it in post."

It takes a good ears, meticulous attention to detail, a boatload of patience, and *lots* of practice to be a good audio editor. I once spent nearly a year doing nothing but editing artifacts from audio files in my own project studio. Sure, my social skills suffered a little, but I have a great soda pyramid and stellar editing chops to show for it. Audio editing is a key part of the post-production experience. It is an extremely useful skill that makes other audio production tasks faster and easier. The more proficient you are with audio editing techniques, the better off you'll be.

Know Thyself Nothing sounds better than a great singer on the right microphone. Even a great singer on the wrong microphone is considered acceptable source material in most cases. But a poor performance on a great microphone still has the disadvantage of being a poor performance. We're not miracle workers. The best thing you can do is to know the limits of your tools and abilities so that when you receive source material, you can be realistic about what can be resolved with editing and what can't.

How Project Studios Have Changed Audio Editing

Allow me to provide a brief overview of the history of audio editing. It used to be that music was never edited. Bands would record with all members playing at the same time, in the same room, using a limited number of microphones. If someone screwed up, the entire band had to play the entire song over again. There was no fading the end of a song, overdubbing instruments or vocals, or correcting timing or pitch. Essentially, a live performance was immediately pressed to a record.

What was great about music before editing came into the picture was that you really had to know your craft. You could also feed off the energy and ideas of the other players in the room, which gave the recording its own unique sound.

Then the overdub came along. Overdubbing is the technique of adding additional recorded material to a previously recorded performance. With overdubbing, sound recording could be done in multiple parts. You no longer had to try to nail the performance in a single take. Using overdubs, you could specify at what point in the previously recorded performance you wanted to begin recording, and the engineer would punch you in or begin recording when you specified. Along with over-dubbing came the ability to bounce tracks. As you'll recall from earlier in this chapter, bouncing is the technique of consolidating multiple audio tracks down to a single track. Consolidating tracks was a pop-ular technique used to make room for even more overdubs.

Engineers soon began doing more advanced audio edits by actually unraveling the reel-to-reel tape and physically cutting it apart with a razorblade to assemble the best performances from multiple takes. Tweaking a musical performance to perfection was the work of many expensive engineers with good ears and eyes, as well as steady hands.

The problem with these more primitive forms of audio editing was that they were extremely destructive. If you cut tape, there is no turning back. Unless of course you made a copy....

Audio editing as we know it used to be available only to marketable performers on big labels with deep pockets. At the time, only a min-imal "big budget" demographic of the musical community reaped the rewards of professional editing. The ability to cut and edit tape, remove unwanted noise, cross-fade performances, and loop tracks was not available to the rest of us, which meant that the majority of musicians were limited in their ability to produce a high-quality recording on their own. But that is a condition of the past.

We are now able to quickly turn out professional-quality results from our project studios. Many of the recordings heard on the radio and in film and television are edited and produced *entirely* in project studios. Processes that used to take hours upon hours can be accomplished in a

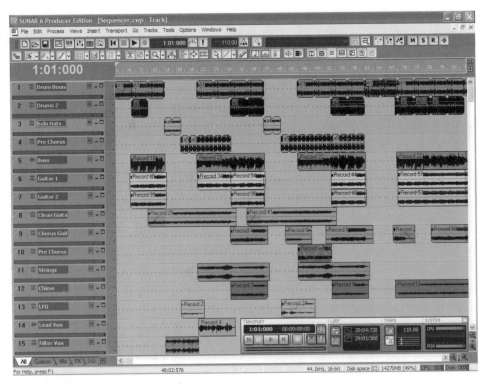

Figure 1.1 Cakewalk SONAR 6.

matter of minutes. These days, powerful sequencing software, such as Nuendo/Cubase, Pro Tools, SONAR, and Logic, or wave editors, such as WaveLab and Sound Forge, have made editing and arranging a perfect performance just a few cost-effective clicks away (see Figures 1.1 and 1.2). Using personal computers, professional audio software, and some know-how, we can perform complex nonlinear audio editing processes quickly and easily from the comfort of our own homes.

Nonlinear Editing In digital audio, all editing is done in a nonlinear fashion. This basically means you can modify any element of the project at any time without affecting any of the other elements in the project.

The term *nonlinear* refers to the ability to move elements freely within the timeline of the project.

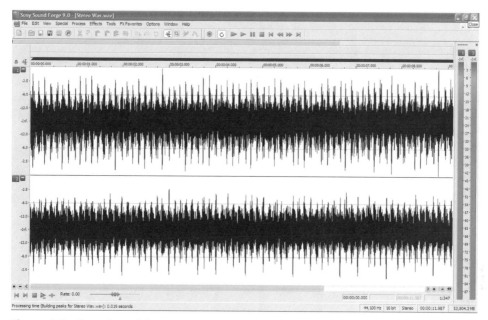

Figure 1.2 Sony Sound Forge 9.

The ability to digitally edit audio in the project studio has somewhat leveled the performance playing field of the music industry. Now "Joe Acoustic: Coffeehouse Legend" has many of the same tools available as John Legend does. In many ways, the advent of the project studio has made the music business both more competitive and more accessible. But try not to overestimate what you can accomplish immediately in the project studio. Just like splicing reel-to-reel tape, it takes a certain amount of skill to assess an editing challenge and resolve it.

Now that we've discussed the role that audio editing plays in the wacky world of post-production, let's take a look at some of the software tools you'll want to get to know.

2 Tools for Digital Audio Editing

When it comes to digital audio editing, it's important to know what your available tools are. In this chapter, we'll chat about wave editors, or *sample editors,* and how they are different from audio sequencers (which will be discussed a bit later), and I'll provide an overview of the common software tools used to edit audio.

Wave Editors

There are two main types of applications that you will use in your everyday audio-production endeavors—wave editors (or sample editors) and multitrack sequencers. A *wave editor* is a program used for designing, editing, and mastering audio. A *multitrack sequencer* is a program used for recording live audio, sequencing MIDI, arranging, and mixing. In many ways, wave editors and sequencers are similar; they have many features that overlap. For instance, you could use either a wave editor or a sequencer to edit, design, or master audio. However, you may find that a wave editor will have features and functionalities that are geared toward these specific tasks, making them easier and more efficient to perform.

Audio software for digital audio workstations (or DAWs) has come a long way. Software developers are doing their best make multitrack audio/MIDI sequencing and arranging applications your one-stop shop for everything from recording live audio and sequencing MIDI to scoring film and editing audio. But sometimes, just because a software program is *capable* of performing a particular task, that doesn't mean that it's the *best* tool for the job. When you need to really focus and work with a single audio file, a full-featured wave editor is ideal.

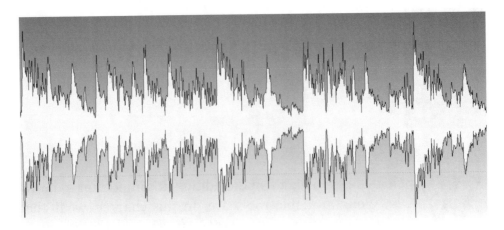

Figure 2.1   Peak and valleys of a waveform.

When cleaning up field recordings, crafting sounds for a video game, converting an audio track from a CD to an MP3, or mastering the final mix of a song, you will most likely turn to a trusty wave editor for a quick and painless execution, instead of a multitrack sequencer with all its bells and whistles.

Wave editors show audio in a visual context on your screen. This visual representation is called a *waveform* or a *wave*. Waveforms express a series of digital samples that make up an audio file. When multiple samples are viewed as a group, the shape of the waveform will be expressed as a series of peaks and valleys. The peaks represent the loudest amplitude dynamics of an audio file. The valleys are the amplitude climbs and descents that occupy the space between the peaks. Figure 2.1 shows the dynamic peaks and valleys of a mono waveform.

Wave files have become the standard for visually representing sound. The waveform of an individual instrument looks quite different from instrument to instrument. And a waveform that represents an audio file of the sum of many instruments, such as a final mix, will look drastically different from that of a solo instrument. In fact, these waveforms look so different from one another that shortly after you begin working with these visual representations, you will be able to identify what type of instrument a particular waveform is and whether it's sustaining, percussive, dull, or harmonically rich, just by looking at it. The waveform of a guitar, piano, or vocal may have lots of peaks

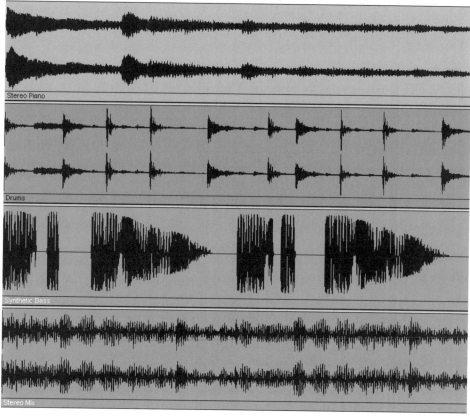

Stereo Piano

Drums

Synthetic Bass

Stereo Mix

Figure 2.2 Different strokes for different folks. Notice how different instruments and their dynamics and characteristics can affect the way a waveform looks.

and valleys, while the waveform of a bass or a synthesizer may appear to have fewer peaks and valleys. Figure 2.2 shows the individual waveforms of a piano part, a drum part, a bass part, and a stereo file that has been mixed down from multiple audio sources.

Wave editing programs (sometimes called *digital audio production suites* or *mastering suites,* such as Sound Forge, WaveLab, and Peak) also offer extensive features and tools for sound design and mastering. You can process audio in simple ways, such as altering the length of an audio file, applying customized fades, and changing volume. Or, you can do more drastic processing, such as treating audio with effects, creating audio projects composed of multiple audio files for burning to a CD master disc, syncing music to video, and mastering audio, which is an involved process that we'll get into later, in Chapter 13,

"Mastering Audio in the Digital Age." For now, let's discuss common features that are found in most wave editing programs.

Common Features

Although all wave editors and mastering suites look different and have different ways in which you access their functionality, often they perform common tasks and have a standardized set of tools for doing so. In this section, we'll discuss features that are found in most wave editors.

- **Auditioning.** A wide range of playback options is available for auditioning your audio. Beyond the normal transport functions, you can select or highlight a specific range of the audio phrase and hear it played back at a different speed or pitch. Or, you can hear the rest of the file played back with the highlighted section excluded, which comes in handy when you are trying to decide which version of the audio to use. On some programs, you can even set up two different sets of outputs to which to send the audio, so you can make quick A/B comparisons between two different sets of monitors just by pressing a hot key or a customized keystroke.

- **Analysis.** Wave editors provide many ways to analyze an audio file. These analysis tools provide a visual representation of the audio you're analyzing so you can easily determine where there might be issues with equalization, phasing, level, panning, unwanted noise, and audio artifacts in an audio phrase. You can even analyze just a small section of the audio phrase if you wish. Use these tools before you start editing your file so you can get a better idea of what you want to fix. Most wave editors also provide an option to generate audio signals for doing a room analysis that can help you set up your speakers for an optimal monitoring environment.

- **Editing.** All wave editors allow you to process audio in a number of different ways. You can normalize (or increase the volume to its maximum level without distorting), or you can make smaller gain adjustments to the entire file or parts of the file. You can customize fading for any part of the audio file to ease the transition into or out of an audio phrase, or you can combine two files and create a cross-fade to get them to blend together in an aesthetically pleasing way.

Most wave editors are compatible with all kinds of third-party effect and processing plug-ins that can be used to process your audio in different ways, as well as many built-in tools for time stretching, pitch correction, noise reduction, audio restoration, and removing audio artifacts.

- **Formatting.** Wave editors are compatible with many different file types. You can import almost any kind of audio file known to man —even the audio from DVD tracks in some cases! Furthermore, you can save an original file as a wide variety of different file types, create MP3s, export a stereo track as separate left and right mono tracks, and even convert multiple files to another file type. You might want to consult your software documentation to see exactly which formats your application supports, though I'd be very surprised if any file types are *not* supported.

- **Batch processing.** Batch processing is when you change the attributes of many different files at the same time. Suppose you have 100 wave files that you need to convert to MP3s. You also need to put a prefix that identifies the project in the file name for all 100 files. You can open up the batch processor and tell it which files need converting, what file type to convert them to, and what prefix you need added to the file names. Then, with a single click of your mouse, *voilà*! All your files will be converted and formatted just the way you want them. In most wave editors, you can also batch process files with the same effects, which brings us to presets....

- **Presets.** You've been designing a sound for hours, trying to get it just right. You've used 10 different plug-ins, all with custom settings. You really like the way it sounds now, and you decide that you want to affect 30 other files in the exact same way. So, you save your individual plug-in presets. You're probably thinking, "Well, what good does that do? I still have to pull up those 10 plug-ins and presets 30 different times to process those other files. Why can't I just do that in my audio sequencer?" Here's why: Now that you've saved all of your individual plug-in presets, you can save a global preset that contains all 10 plug-ins, with all their settings exactly the way you want them. Now you can tell the batch processor which files to process and which global presets you want to use to process them. Then, with a single click of the mouse…well, you get the idea.

In the end, you'll find that wave editors are capable of far more than you imagined—perhaps far more than you'll ever use. But there is no denying that they can be very powerful tools and they can play an important role in your studio if you take the time to really understand them. Next, we'll discuss some of the more popular wave editors used in project studios today.

Sony Creative Software Sound Forge

Sound Forge by Sony Creative Software is used in many professional environments for manipulating audio (see Figure 2.3). Praised for its ease of use and range of features, Sound Forge has become an industry standard for audio editing and sound design on a PC. The latest version (currently version 9) supports 24-bit audio, multi-channel editing and processing, 5.1 surround format exporting, and the simultaneous use of more than 40 VST and DirectX plug-ins. And, because Sony

Figure 2.3 Sony Creative Software Sound Forge.

Creative Software also develops ACID, Sound Forge includes tools for creating Loops for ACID. Sound Forge also supports a wide variety of different file types, including multiple video formats, so you should never have trouble with the files your client gives you for editing.

For more information about Sound Forge, please visit www. sonycreativesoftware.com.

Steinberg WaveLab

WaveLab is a wave editor and mastering suite developed by Steinberg, the makers of the popular audio/MIDI sequencing applications Nuendo and Cubase (see Figure 2.4). WaveLab is an all-in-one solution for high-resolution audio editing, restoration, sound design, and mastering. WaveLab 6 operates on a 32-bit floating-point audio engine for optimal use with all VST and DirectX plug-ins. It comes with many audio analysis tools, nearly 30 integrated plug-ins, and a built-in database for organizing your audio files. It also uses an "audio montage" feature that allows for simultaneous editing across several tracks and burns Red Book, replication-ready CDs.

A full list of WaveLab's features can be found at www.steinberg.net.

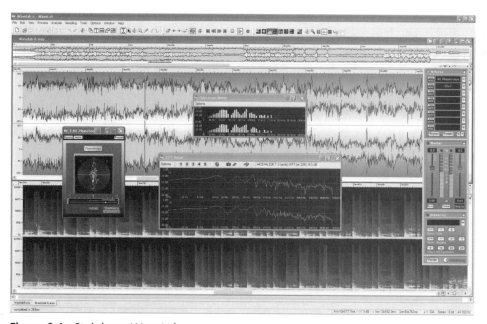

Figure 2.4 Steinberg WaveLab.

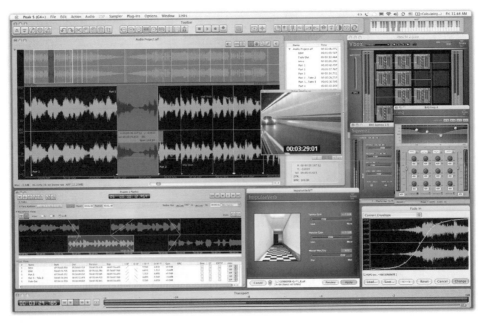

Figure 2.5 Bias Peak.

Bias Peak

Bias Peak is a longstanding industry standard for Macs (see Figure 2.5). It's used by sound designers, mastering engineers, web designers, and podcast producers alike for audio editing, broadcasting, and mastering audio. Peak 6 has a plethora of integrated features for authoring podcasts, such as voiceover ducking (which dynamically lowers music levels during voiceovers) and direct podcast uploading tools. Peak also features iTunes integration that allows you to quickly export audio documents or playlists and drag and drop audio files between iTunes and the Peak playlist. It also burns CDs, supports 24-bit, 96-kHz audio resolution, comes with more than 40 effects processors, and can run as many third-party VST and Audio Unit plug-ins as your computer can handle.

Visit www.bias-inc.com for more information.

These are the most popular programs used in audio editing, but they aren't the *only* ones used. Just because everyone says that they're the industry standard, that doesn't mean that there aren't other competitive programs available. What is important is whether they produce the results you desire. Chapter 3, "Software-Based Editing Techniques," will give you a better idea of how you can use wave editors.

3 Software-Based Editing Techniques

In this chapter we will discuss many different techniques that are commonly used in professional digital audio editing. Each technique discussed in this chapter will become a building block, a tool, or a weapon in your audio-editing arsenal that will help you solve complicated audio equations. How do you clean up a noisy audio file? What can you do to help extract a good performance from a singer or a drummer having a slightly off day? Although the techniques alone may seem simple, the combination of a few of these techniques will help get the production where it needs to be. Let it be understood that audio editing can't take the "suck" out of a poor performance, but it might make it less noticeable.

The techniques we'll discuss are best learned through first reading and understanding what they're for, and then putting them into practice in your own projects so you can hear the effects they produce. There is nothing wrong with reading this chapter all the way through before you open up your wave editor or sequencer and try some of these techniques, but it may be less overwhelming—especially if you're new to audio editing—to read a section, then learn how to execute it in your application before moving on to the next technique. I cannot stress enough the importance of becoming familiar with the editing tools that are available in your chosen software application and exactly what they do. The more you know about them, the easier it will be for you to get them to do what you want them to.

Cutting, Copying, and Pasting

Just as they are used in text files and spreadsheets, so are cutting, copying, and pasting used in audio editing. In reference to audio, the terms take us back to the days of 2-inch tape and console-only styles of recording. Engineers in professional studios would literally cut the 2-inch tapes of the performances with a razor, then copy, paste, and arrange the parts by hand. This was common practice for drums and vocals. When the artists achieved the perfect chorus, often it was cut and pasted into *every* chorus. Up until about 1996, this occurred in big-budget productions; it took a very seasoned and patient professional with lots of mistakes and years of botched edits under his belt to accomplish this.

These days, we can select a scissors tool in a wave editor or software sequencer, and a single mouse click will cut the chosen audio track, creating a section of audio that is independent from the original and can be pasted to another location anywhere in the project timeline. Cutting, copying, and pasting are a few editing techniques that have been made simpler through technology. Not to mention, the ability to hit Undo an *unlimited* number of times has taken the fear out of what used to be an extremely destructive editing process.

Beyond creating perfect choruses, we can use cutting and pasting to fix and adjust a wide variety of performance problems in an audio track. Suppose, for instance, the singer coughs in the guitar break. Somewhere in the break, that season's flu will always linger in the background of the project. With digital editing, you can zoom into, or magnify, that section of the song, cut out the piece of audio where the cough resides, and delete it altogether, thus creating a cough-free performance.

Cutting and pasting also allows you to actually *make* better takes. I know this may sound ridiculous to some people. And obviously, if you have to edit a billion vocal tracks together just to get *one* good verse, the singer should probably just sing the part again, but often in post-production, you don't have the option because the recording session is long over. Sometimes a singer may overdo a loud, irritating consonant into the microphone, which results in an unpleasant dynamic on the vocal track. By copying and pasting, you could easily extract the same word from another chorus and replace the outstanding word or even the consonant itself. Similarly, if a drummer is pounding the snare drum all the way through a chorus, and then he suddenly gets a hand

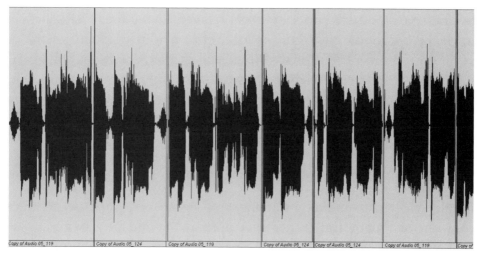

Figure 3.1 A vocal track with multiple cuts and copies to create a perfect take.

cramp, which in turn causes a few hits to be quieter than the others, you could use cut, copy, and paste to replace the low-velocity hits with harder ones so that the part doesn't lose its intensity and so it maintains consistency throughout. These techniques are used all the time to construct better performances and make cleaner recordings. Figure 3.1 shows an example of a vocal track that has had multiple cut and copy edits applied to it.

Time Correction

Time correction is a difficult topic to discuss in print. Basically, this is the process of lining up audio using reference points and fixing any timing issues that might exist within an audio file. The reference points can be the project tempo; the project timeline, which can be expressed in a number of different ways (Timecode, Bars+Beats, Seconds, or Samples, to name a few); or the drum parts that were played by a drummer. With digital audio editing, you can magnify an audio part and compare it to the drum track or one of the other timing references, and then adjust it so that it sounds perfectly in time.

In music, time is liquid. It's important to understand the musical style that you're working with to make sound judgments about what timing corrections will work for the good of the project. A vocal that sits just behind the drumbeat can seem very relaxed and loose. Such a vocal might be appropriate for jazz or folk, but obviously not for metal. A vocal on top of the beat or slightly ahead of the beat can seem anticipated and aggressive, which might work for something like punk rock, where it is important for the vocalist to sound excited and bursting with angst. Make sure you know what your client wants before you make any drastic timing corrections.

Sometimes, the actual performance can get in the way of clarity. Music is a form of communication. Words, note choices, and phrasing are usually written to make a statement of some sort. Suppose a singer runs out of breath and truncates a note at the end of a phrase. This is like writing a sentence without a period. Just as a copy editor would correct the sentence by adding a period to complete the statement, so would an audio editor use time stretching to complete a musical phrase. You can usually find a way to make the sustain of the truncated note last a little longer by using the tools or plug-ins in your DAW software. This will help "complete" the statement by making the timing of entire phrase feel correct to the listener. Many software programs offer time stretching as an option in the menu, but there are also many other effect plug-ins and software programs that can assist with time correction, such as Serato Pitch 'n Time, Synchro Arts VocalALign, Ableton Live, or Celemony Melodyne.

It is entirely possible to align background vocals word by word, stretch drums into perfect time, and make a performance seem mostly flawless. Granted, if the original audio was properly recorded, you shouldn't really have to. In digital audio, the more you process an audio file, the more it gets bent out of shape. For example, it is easier to speed up audio than to slow it down. Compressing the timing of an audio file to make it faster will typically go unnoticed in context to a listener. But stretching time to slow audio down can get a little tricky. I'm not saying it can't be done, but the opportunity to accumulate sonic artifacts in the form of a "warble" or maybe a drop in pitch is much greater. It might sound obvious to the listener that the phrase of audio was slowed down. Realize that when you're compressing audio to make it faster, you're working with the audio that you already have. When you're stretching audio to make it slower, you're actually trying to make the audio last longer than it really does. It's like trying to fill a 16-ounce glass all the way to the top using only 8 ounces of liquid.

Time stretching is a great tool and an important part of audio editing when used effectively. However, be careful and proceed with caution. It is easy to overdo time correction on some instruments and voices. And each time you stretch an audio file, its audio quality will inevitably be reduced. Listen to what sounds natural while still getting the point across. Listen for artifacts and problems. Using this tool sparingly and appropriately is the executive call of the post-audio engineer.

Another thing that's important to remember is that just because everything is perfectly in time and lined up to a grid or beat, that does not make it perfect music. In older recordings that everyone loves, listens to, and uses as templates for "perfection," the drums often rush a little, guitars may play on top of the beat, and vocals and bass may drag a little behind. Sometimes a big "perfect" hit is one in which the drums are on the money, the guitars or horns are a hair early, and the bass is slightly late. Use the people around you as a barometer, because once you've had your head in a project for a while, you might lose objectivity and push too hard for perfection on a minute level, rather than seeing the big picture. Also, remember that time is liquid; even in the most precise musical forms, such as electronic music that is composed using mostly MIDI around a tempo grid, not everything in relation to timing is perfect.

Pitch Correction

It cracks me up how often pitch correction is discussed in the world today. Everyone on Earth, audio professional or not, seems to be aware of an "expensive studio trick" called auto-tune that magically makes below-average singers sound like radio-quality performers. This particular technique of pitch correction has become so popular that it was even parodied on *The Simpsons*. However, auto-tune is not the only type of pitch correction that is used in audio production.

Here's a lengthy definition for you: *Pitch correction* is the process of manipulating the approximate frequency or pitch of a monophonic vocal or instrumental performance that is either sharp or flat of the intended note. This is done so that the performance is perceived as being "in tune" within the context of the other audio elements that make up the musical composition in which it resides. Pitch correction is typically and most effectively used for spot treatments on a flat string bend in a guitar solo or a singer who pushes out a note a bit sharp. With the right know-how and pitch-correction tools, you can even move the frequency of a note more than a few semitones and thus change the note entirely.

Sometimes, pitch correction is used as an effect rather than as a tool. I'm sure you've heard the effects of pitch correction blanketed over an entire vocal. Cher's dance anthem of yesteryear, "Believe," is a perfect example. I think it's safe to say that such an effect was a production trend for vocals in the late 1990s and has pretty much run its course, with few exceptions. Regarding our discussion on pitch correction, I personally do *not* believe in life after love.

Pitch correction is used every day on many kinds of instruments, and not just vocals. Often strings, horns, and woodwinds are hard-tuned in a mix. Pitch correction is used to make everything more harmonically exciting in this regard. The theory is based on the idea that the more the instruments are in tune in an arrangement, the thicker the harmonic layers will be. Often in pop music, pitch correction is used on bass guitar. It helps correct a lot of the intonation issues that are inherent in stringed instruments. Tuning lower-frequency instruments in an arrangement will help set up the other instruments in the higher frequencies to have a solid reference point for pitch.

There are two common misconceptions when it comes to pitch correction. The first is that because a performance is perfectly in tune, it must be perfect. The second is that all popular music is perfectly in tune and in key. Both of these statements couldn't be more false. Although absolute pitch is fixed and defined by precise measurements, your ears are not. The history of music typically defines the way pitch is perceived by the human ear. In fact, most music prior to 2000 involved no hard tuning at all. People always had to "earball" (as opposed to "eyeball!") music into acceptable tune.

A good rule of thumb for tuning is that if it sounds good, it is good. If you pitch corrected every guitar solo bend, vocal harmony, and bass note, music might actually lose a lot of the quality we like about it. For example, guitar solos are usually very sharp due to vibrato and bending. If we pitch corrected them as we do with vocals, the solo would actually sound flat and funny to most listeners. As humans, we are set up by our listening history to hear things that are out of tune in a certain way. Even the way that the equal temperament theory works on piano is slightly out of tune. I cannot imagine how funny something like the Rolling Stones would sound all perfectly pitch corrected. Sometimes the looseness of tuning leads to an edgier, freer sonic aesthetic. So just be careful. It's possible to grossly overdo it with pitch correction, which can only result in what people would perceive to be an artifact of a poorly executed technique. Just as we discussed with time correction earlier, go for tuning that sounds natural and free.

Equal Temperament Theory Equal temperament is a tuning system used to keep all the key signatures of western music "equally in tune." Prior to Bach, musical notes on a piano could only be "perfectly tuned" to one scale at a time. So if we tuned our piano to the key of A major perfectly, a key like E flat major would be horribly out of tune. (Unless of course we retuned the entire keyboard to E flat before performing in the new key—talk about time-consuming!) So in western music, every note of the scale is relatively close enough in pitch for all different key signatures to sound good without retuning. Though you may notice some minor tuning discrepancies (especially if you have perfect pitch or deal with percussion and fretted instruments), it works fabulously for the 12-note/12-scale needs of western music. Basically, the equal temperament system keeps all the keys in tune by having each key make small tuning sacrifices for the greater good of the tuning in general. This is a very "forest for the trees" approach that our forefathers took toward fixing the tuning dilemma. Otherwise, piano players would be more like harmonica players and would have one piano for each key.

Antares Auto-Tune, Celemony Melodyne, Serato Pitch 'n Time, and Waves Tune are the software programs and plug-ins most commonly discussed in reference to manipulation of pitch in digital audio. Although they are grouped into the same category, they don't all do the same thing. Each one has its own application. For example, Antares Auto-Tune is a plug-in that is used specifically for manipulating the pitch of an audio signal in real time so that you can audition the effects of it as it's working. Melodyne is more effective for creating vocal harmonies and developing vibrato unity from an original performance. You *can* use it for standard pitch correction, but the sound that Melodyne outputs has a different, less transparent characteristic than real-time pitch correction plug-ins. We will discuss these types of programs and plug-ins a bit more later in the book (in Chapter 11, "Software Tools for Effects").

Cross-Fading Edits

After doing so much audio slicing, time aligning, scooting, and editing, you may wonder how to get rid of some of the inherent artifacts (such as zero-crossing pops) and spacing weirdness and how to get a smoother-sounding wave edit overall. Usually the best (and easiest) process is one that all wave editors have, called *cross-fading*.

Cross-fading is blending two different audio elements together in an audibly pleasing way by reducing the amplitude of the element that is ending, or fading out, and increasing the amplitude of the element that is beginning, or fading in. Most software editors allow you to have total control over the amplitude levels and the position at which the cross-fade will occur. It is almost always necessary to cross-fade overlapping audio files. This cleans up the soundscape, leaving it clear of pops and digital black (the sound of no audio present). Most editors/sequencers also allow you to fade in and fade out the file at the end of phrases where no audio is present at all, thus avoiding any nasty or abrupt sonic transitions.

Another way that cross-fading is used in post-production is in the case of editing music for a film, where you might be transitioning from a slow song's string outro into an upbeat montage number. You would

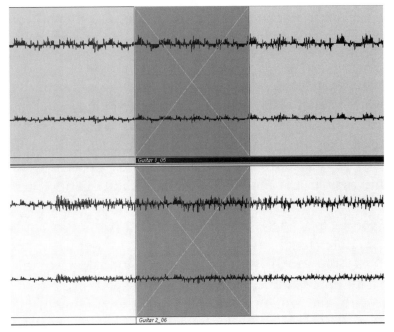

Figure 3.2 A typical cross-fade.

probably use a large cross-fade to eliminate dead space and make the two numbers segue seamlessly. Figure 3.2 shows what a typical cross-fade might look like.

Removing Audio Artifacts

An audio artifact is essentially unwanted sonic material. Artifacts can usually be identified as pops or clicks that are heard during playback of an audio phrase. When any kind of aggressive processing or editing is done to an audio file, such as time stretching, cutting, and pasting, audio artifacts have the potential to be created. Some artifacts are easy to deal with; others you may not be able to completely work out in post. Removing a simple pop or click at the beginning or end of a file is much less complex than trying to remove a pop in the middle of a solo vocal take.

Understand that a phrase of audio typically does not have any silence in it. Therefore, when editing, if you cut an audio file, you are disrupting a constant audio signal. During playback, when the cursor of your software editor/sequencer reaches the edit you made, you might hear an artifact as the audio ends abruptly. This is because of something called *zero-crossing*.

In relation to audio, we refer to silence as *digital black*. A zero-crossing is the point at which digital black becomes an audible audio signal (or where an audible audio signal becomes digital black). For example, suppose you're working on editing a bass part. You decide that you want to keep only the first four bars of an eight-bar bass part. So you cut the audio file right in the middle and discard the last four bars. You hit Play, and the four bars of bass play back, but as the section of audio ends, you hear a pop where it was edited. If the transition going from an audible signal to digital black (or vice versa) is too abrupt, an artifact will probably occur. The best way to correct this type of artifact is to apply a quick micro-fade to the end of the truncated bass part where the artifact exists, so that the amplitude of the signal is reduced to silence gradually. In doing this, you ensure that the audio of the existing four bars of bass exits at digital black and, subsequently, that the pop that was caused by the abrupt exit has been eliminated. Figure 3.3 shows an audio file that has been magnified to illustrate what an artifact looks like before and after correction. The top file has a zero-crossing artifact at the beginning. The bottom file shows what the correction would look like.

Artifacts may not even really jump out at you as the post-audio engineer *until* you solo up an instrument, and suddenly, it's Pop City. It's more difficult to detect these in drums, but with instruments such as bass, keyboards, vocals, and guitars, these types of artifacts are usually loud and quite annoying. Also, the more tracks you have starting and stopping in the same places, the more you can have a cumulative artifact effect.

Suppose you were to edit about four instruments playing together to make a verse. You chopped (cut) the beginnings and endings of all four wave files together. Then you pasted a copy of these instruments right next to the original to extend the verse. Normally, you would experience the World Series of Pops at the starting and ending point of each newly edited audio file. Additionally, the more compression you are

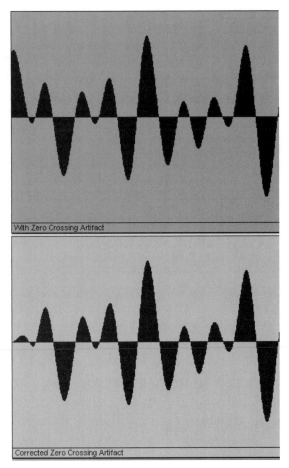

With Zero Crossing Artifact

Corrected Zero Crossing Artifact

Figure 3.3 A corrected zero-crossing—before and after.

running on the tracks in post, the more you will excite the artifact. You might not even notice the sonic blemishes on a snare track until you go to final mixdown and you add a compressor plug-in to take some of the "snap" off the snare drum. Next thing you know, the snaps and pops have become louder and more pronounced. Right about now, you're probably thinking that the compressor has ruined the track. This is not the case; you've just made the artifacts significantly louder by compressing them to the same dynamic as the audio. Usually, these can be eliminated by zooming deep into the edited part to perform a micro-edit that will correct the amplitude levels at the beginning and end of the audio files to gradually fade out (or in) to silence. Figure 3.4 shows what a cumulative artifact effect might look like.

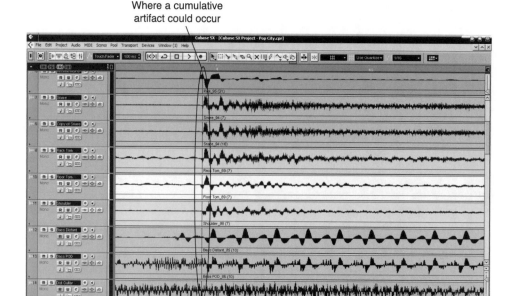

Figure 3.4 The road to Pop City. Even if you can't hear an individual artifact in a full mix, multiple tracks with uncorrected artifacts can lead to an audible problem.

Unfortunately, artifacts can also be created by your audio interface or the operation of your DAW itself. Quite possibly the *worst* kinds of artifact, these can occur during the initial recording of audio material and during audio mixdowns. These types of artifacts are almost unavoidable in the digital project studio. Everyone will experience them at least once. I've heard $200 audio cards make them and $2,000 audio cards make them. Unlike zero-crossing artifacts, these cannot be seen in the visual representation of the audio signal, and they usually happen right in the middle of an audio file, which makes them more difficult to remove.

For the post-audio mixer/engineer, these artifacts are next to impossible to deal with. They are often caused by recording audio for long periods of time without saving a project, doing multiple takes with track management issues, using heavy effect processing, or even having audio card manufacturer driver issues. They can even occur if you don't have enough RAM in your computer to run multiple processes. Suppose you're recording 8 tracks of live drums and you're monitoring 16 tracks of other audio at 24-bit, 96-kHz resolution. This is a lot of audio processing for even the most pimped-out DAW to deal with. It's also a perfect scenario for an artifact to occur. If you are the recording engineer, you might be able to minimize the chance of experiencing real-time artifacts by bouncing only the necessary tracks (16 tracks, in this case) to a stereo mix. In most scenarios, it's a lot easier for a CPU to manage only 9 tracks of active audio (8 for recording, 1 for monitoring) than it is for the CPU to manage 24. You could also increase the I/O buffer value of your audio interface and optimize your DAW's settings to assist in freeing up your computer's resources, making more RAM available to process audio and take you further away from experiencing CPU overload.

Some quick tips for removing these types of artifacts are as follows:

- **Replace it.** If you had a nice, clean version of the chorus in which the words "happiness and love" didn't have a pop or click in them, you could try copying the same words from that pop-free chorus and using them to replace the original. Sometimes, a piece of pristine audio can be copied to somewhere else in the project, and suddenly there's a pop in it! This might be one of those cases where the computer just had a fraction-of-a-second hiccup, and an artifact was created. It happens, so don't be afraid to re-edit and use a clean section of audio to replace the problematic audio.

- **EQ it.** Another way you might be able to eliminate a system-generated artifact like this is by separating the affected area of audio and reducing the gain of a narrow band of EQ in which the pop exists by adjusting the Q settings. Figure 3.5 shows an EQ with a narrow Q setting. This would be a viable option for a popping guitar or bass, perhaps. This technique is not recommended for vocals because nearly any EQ change on a vocal will drastically change its tonality. Sometimes these artifacts are so small and instantaneous that no one will even hear them in the full mix. Most artifacts really are only fractions of a second, so there's a bit of wiggle room for what can be done to work them out.

- **Listen to it.** Sometimes you won't even be able to hear a pop in the overall mix, so make sure you audition the problematic part in context before making any drastic corrections. If a guitar has a little

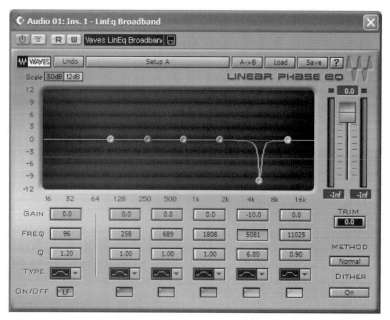

Figure 3.5 An EQ treatment with a narrow Q setting to reduce an isolated band of frequency that will assist in eliminating an artifact that occurs in the middle of an audio file.

pop, but it's during a part where everyone else in the band is rocking their faces off, correcting the pop might not be a worthwhile use of your time. Or, if a vocal artifact occurs when the hi-hat is doing a lift beat, you probably don't have to worry about a small, unnoticeable pop. If a compressor is exciting an artifact and making it more audible, you could also use automation to reduce the level of compression during just that *tiny* segment of audio when the pop occurs. Remember, we're talking about fractions of a second here, and the good news is that the listener is not usually listening for pops.

There is also a time to be extremely cautious about making sure *all* artifacts are eliminated. In the case of editing audio samples for library music and sample CDs, you have to make sure that every file in the library is pristine because it will eventually be used by you or someone else to produce a commercial piece of music. And people don't spend good money on stock audio sample libraries just so they can spend time cleaning them up. Another scenario in which you would want to be careful about removing artifacts is in a section of music where an instrument is soloed or the instrumentation is sparse. You can bet that an artifact would stand out of that sonic landscape like the Statue of Liberty stands out of the New York Harbor.

Another important thing to remember is that you shouldn't drive yourself nuts looking for little pops and clicks. If you can't hear them in the final mix, chances are they are not a big fidelity-crushing deal. You definitely want to minimize their effects, but they exist in *every* digital recording. I've even received professionally produced sample series drums that have zero-crossing pops in them, as well as pro tracks from big Hollywood studios with artifacts all over the transitions. The fact is that no one could really hear them *in context*. Although you should make sure all of your audio editing is as clean as possible, don't spend so much time hunting and killing artifacts that it compromises the timeline of your project. It is possible to be so meticulous that you never really finish any projects and you spend too much time just cleaning up noise. Remember, you are a sound engineer, not a dishwasher.

Noise Reduction

Noise, like an artifact, is unwanted sound. But where an artifact occurs in fractions of a second, noise is typically persistent over the duration of a phrase of audio. Typically, the noise you wish to reduce comes from excess frequencies in the EQ spectrum, the electronic properties of the recording equipment used to capture the original audio, and/or signal processing of effects. Because the post-production or mix engineer rarely has control over recording the original audio tracks, you keep your fingers crossed that the recording engineer knew what he was doing and has minimized the amount of noise captured on a recording. And if that fails, it's up to you to resolve any noise issues in post-production. The following sections detail the most common types of noise you might encounter on your post-production adventure.

Preamp and Microphone Noise

In a perfect audio world, everyone would have an SSL console and noise-free Neve preamps. Everyone in this perfect world also would have perfectly isolated rack gear, great microphones, top compressors, and no electrical and grounding issues in their project studio environment. Not!

Truth be told, as a post-audio engineer, you will get a lot of tracks that come from someone's $200 Mbox recorded with a $100 dynamic microphone with the gain cranked all the way up on the preamp. There's nothing inherently wrong with $100 mics and budget-conscious preamps, but they take significantly more work to get a good, clean sound in post, and most already have an above-average noise floor to begin with.

Noise Floor *Noise floor* is the measurement of the signal created by the sum of all noise sources and unwanted sound. The level of your noise floor is essentially the quietest you will ever be able to record an audio signal. Some audio recording interfaces have microphone preamps built into them that create a low level of noise. Ideally, your preamps should make as little noise as possible because a preamp that generates a high level of noise will contribute to raising the overall noise level in your recordings.

The microphone used on a recording itself produces noise. Mics are modified and reengineered all the time to boost and scoop certain wanted/unwanted frequencies to affect the fidelity of the source that will be recorded through them. I hear this most commonly with dynamic microphones used on drum kits. Kick drum mics are heavily boosted in frequencies that excite the high and low end of a kick drum.

Low-end preamps can be a prominent culprit for noise. The more you turn up the gain on a preamp to get the input signal loud enough, the more your tracks will swim in an ocean of background hiss. Sometimes operational noise can be caused just because the mic is plugged in. Even if you have a pretty decent preamp, the more you crank the gain and raise the noise floor, the more operating and residual noise and hiss you will pick up.

Track Hiss

The most common type of noise that needs to be minimized is hiiissssssssssss. If you are old enough to remember listening to music on cassette tapes, you know exactly what I'm talking about. Strangely, a lot of low-end preamps and soundcards (even with high bit and sample rates) have a tendency to generate the same type of noise once their gain knobs have been turned up. Another culprit for bringing out tape hiss is compression. Because compression equalizes and limits dynamics, pushing all levels closer together, the hiss can become horribly amplified once an audio signal has been compressed.

Sixty-Cycle Hum, Grounding Issues, and the Dreaded Hard Drive

Sometimes the very equipment and tools we use to produce music can create noise. Unless you have silent hard drives, never use guitars with single-coil pickups, or have a studio that was custom-built for optimum power performance, you're bound to encounter one or more of these noise issues.

Sixty-cycle hum, or *ground hum,* is an audible oscillation of frequency that exists at about 50 to 60 Hz, depending on the electrical configuration of the building in which you're operating your studio. The hum often has heavy harmonic content and multiplies itself, creating a second harmonic that is audible at 100 to 120 Hz in the form of a low-frequency rumble. It can typically be heard in things such as speakers, guitar amps, and the analog outputs of a computer or audio interface.

Electrical hum in a studio is picked up via a ground loop. In this situation, an amplifier and a console or computer will typically be a distance apart from one another. Both items are grounded via the main grounding pin in the power connector and are also connected along a different electrical pathway via a shielded cable. Because these two pathways do not run parallel, an electrical circuit in the shape of a loop is formed. You can run into the same situation with guitar or keyboard amps and the mixing desk or PC. I've even heard of grounding issues related to a person's refrigerator being on the same electrical circuit as all of his studio equipment. To resolve this, people often have to get a "ground lift" switch to break the loop.

A more dangerous but frequently used option is breaking the ground off the power plug used at the mixer, computer, or guitar amp. I do not—repeat, *do not*—suggest sacrificing the ground integrity of your computer, speaker, or amplifier's power supply. I've had a lightning bolt strike right outside my studio and jolt the computer's power completely off. Chances are, if my computer hadn't been grounded, there would have been no way to protect it from getting fried.

Now, here are some ways to make quick work of unwanted noise on an audio track.

Noise Gates

The easiest and most efficient way to eliminate the types of unwanted sonic material that a microphone or preamp will make is a noise gate. Do you remember going to an amusement park as a child and not being allowed on a rollercoaster ride because you had to be at least 4' 10" to get past the guy taking the tickets? A noise gate works a bit like waiting in line for a rollercoaster. Before you scratch your head at this analogy, allow me to define the parameters of it. Suppose you represent park management. The people passing through the line represent an audio signal, and their height represents their decibel level. People taller than 4' 10" represent a loud signal, and those shorter than 4' 10" represent a quiet signal. The guy taking the tickets (let's call him Bob) represents the threshold of the noise gate. The rollercoaster itself represents the master outputs of your audio software. You, the park management, tell Bob, the threshold of your noise gate, that he can't let anyone shorter than 4' 10" pass through to the rollercoaster. So he observes as he takes tickets, and anyone not up to the height (or level) requirements is not allowed to pass, while those that do can go through to the rollercoaster. This is how a noise gate basically works. You tell the threshold what minimum decibel level is allowed to pass through the noise gate and be heard through your master outputs. The noise gate then "observes" the audio passing through it and keeps any signal that is that is quieter than the decibel level you defined from passing through to the master outputs. Unwanted noise typically exists at a very low decibel level. So you could set the gate's threshold to a decibel level that is slightly higher than the noise itself, and the gate would allow everything but the solo noise in the audio signal to be heard. When a noise gate allows an audio signal to pass through it to the main outputs, it is considered to be open. When no sound is passing through it, it's considered closed.

A good rule of thumb for gates is to adjust the sensitivity threshold of the gate first, then adjust the opening and closing speed of the unit or plug. With this technique you cannot *completely* eliminate *all* noise, but when the singer is not singing or the drums are not being struck, you can definitely just cut down the amount of hiss, operating noise, and background noise present. This is a common practice used on tracks that might contain electric guitar amp noise or headphone bleed. Gates are not the same thing as noise-reduction plug-ins. Although they do reduce noise, they do so only when no wanted signal is present. If you have a guitar part with a rest in it, a gate would reduce noise during the rest. A noise-reduction plug-in would reduce noise over the entire guitar part, *including* the rest. I'll discuss more about common parameters found on noise gates and other plug-ins during the plug-ins overview in Chapter 5, "Software Tools for Digital Mixing."

Reducing and Adding EQ

Adding and subtracting EQ from the right frequencies by an appropriate amount can work wonders in many situations where excess hiss can be heard in the audio material. When you have an audio file that contains hiss, activate the EQ on the channel strip for the track or add the equalizer plug-in of your choice as an insert on the track. Create a −6-dB reduction (with about a 3.0 Q setting or larger) anywhere in the higher end of the frequency spectrum. Then, lower the frequency gradually and listen carefully to find out where the troublesome hiss seems less obvious. When you find the frequency where the reduction appears to have the most effect, adjust the value of the Q control to make the frequency range of the reduction wider until the hiss has been reduced to your satisfaction without compromising the quality of the rest of the audio. Figure 3.6 shows what a subtractive EQ curve for reducing low-end rumble might look like.

You might lose some of the tonal characteristics of the instrument in the noise-reduction process. You may notice the track just doesn't pop

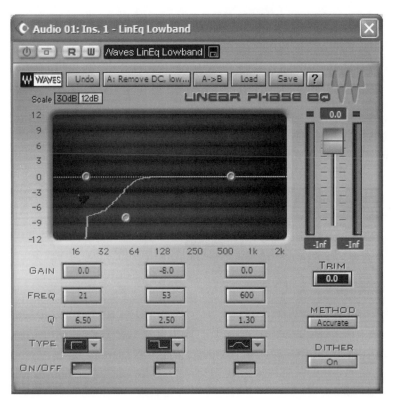

Figure 3.6   Subtractive EQ for removing noise.

as much or have the clarity it used to. This type of EQ fix is a double-edged sword because you have to be careful not to reduce so much of the higher frequencies that the audio loses its brightness and shimmer. Though you may be reducing noise, you may also be reducing clarity and the overall good sound of a track.

An option that works well on stereo mixes to resolve tone that has been dulled by noise reduction is to put some of the EQ back in after the reduction has taken place. On a mono track, you may want to use a harmonic exciter plug-in to regain some of the lost clarity. However, I would not recommend reducing or adding a lot of aggressive EQ on organic instruments, because it can cause the original audio to sound unnatural. Six decibels or more is considered to be a *lot* of EQ in most cases. It might be a good idea to keep an original copy of the files you are working on as a reference to help make sure you're not compromising the track with too much noise reduction or EQ compensation. Although many DAWs offer an unlimited number of Undo options, you can never really be too careful. Sometimes the noise is just part of the way an instrument sounds, so be sure to use your best judgment and intuition to know what's good or bad and how much is too much or too little.

Noise Reduction Plug-Ins

Plug-ins designed for reducing unwanted noise are a great way to save some time and take the guesswork out of the noise-reduction process. They analyze the various frequencies in the audio material and create a noise profile that determines where in the frequency spectrum the noise lives. Different EQ adjustments that help reduce noise for different scenarios are compiled into equalization algorithms that are generally accessed like plug-in presets. So when you go to a noise-reduction plug-in and choose a preset for tape hiss or 60-cycle hum, you're actually applying EQ reductions to several different problematic frequencies at once. Depending on which frequencies are being removed, the noise-reduction process can cause the audio material to sound dull. To remedy this, most noise-reduction plug-ins will give you the ability to enhance the audio signal by adding level to complementary frequencies.

The basic controls on noise-reduction plug-ins are typically very simple. There is one fader for reducing noise, one fader for enhancing the signal, a display window, and a button that tells the plug to analyze the signal. A good rule of thumb for working with noise-reduction plug-ins is to start with a preset for the type of noise you're trying to remove, and then make manual adjustments until the desired effect has been achieved. Make aggressive adjustments at first so that you can hear the effect they have on the audio signal, and then ease them closer to being appropriate. Remember, part of the beauty of digital audio is that you can always hit Undo and start over again.

Following are some good starting points to ensure your studio is free of hum:

■ **Get a qualified person to install your power.** This sounds like a costly expenditure, but it's a lot less expensive than you might think. If your studio is in a house or a freestanding structure, an electrician can typically wire adequate power in a spare room or garage in two to three hours, depending on the electrical setup in your building. This ensures you'll get enough proper power to run everything in your studio. It is ideal to have at least two outlets that are on a separate circuit from the rest of the house to avoid ground loop issues. It may cost a few hundred dollars in labor and parts, but if your studio is active, it'll pay for itself in the hours you might have spent scrubbing unwanted electrical noise out of your audio tracks. Besides, proper wiring also reduces the risk of fire hazards.

- **Get a power conditioner/regulator and a battery backup.** Most people are aware of a company called Furman and their line regulators. Line regulators are an inexpensive way to ensure you're getting adequate regulated power and to reduce noise. They are also a relatively low price to pay to make sure you have the right amount of power all the time. Power is typically inconsistent. The power in your dwelling is fluctuating even as you read this sentence. The way these regulators work is that they act as a central processing stage for power between your electrical outlets and your equipment. No matter how inconsistent the power that flows out of your electrical outlets is, it's fed into the regulator, conditioned, and output at a consistent voltage level, reducing the risk of power surges due to improper electrical wiring. When there is a surge of power fed into the regulator, it stores the excess voltage internally and applies it to the output when the input voltage is low, thereby equalizing it and outputting consistent power. Most power conditioners and voltage regulators are designed with musical applications in mind and are insulated to keep ground hum and 60-cycle hum to a minimum.

A good battery backup, or UPS (*uninterruptible power supply*), is nothing short of a fantastic idea for project studios. I can only think of a few things that are worse than having your computer shut down abruptly and without warning during a windstorm or some other power-threatening weather. You can damage your computer, ruin your hard drive, and throw hours of work (or even a client's project) straight to the wind if you don't take the appropriate measures to protect yourself from unpredictable power interruptions. In the event of a blackout or brownout, using a UPS in your power chain will give you a good 20 to 30 minutes to complete your current task and shut down your DAW properly. There are even some devices that function as both a UPS and a power conditioner. Though at present we're discussing noise and power issues, power backup is definitely a noteworthy topic.

Final Thoughts on Noise Reduction

Truth be told, wherever there is audio being recorded, *some* noise will always exist. No matter how large or insignificant the amount, if you have cables, microphones, and a computer bringing them all together, there will be noise. As a post-production engineer, you want to reduce this noise and keep tracks as clean and pleasant-sounding as possible, but again, don't drive yourself mad with every little hum, crackle, and hiss. Just as I mentioned earlier regarding artifacts, they really only matter if they are making an audible difference in the mix.

Although a mix will sound louder and cleaner with reduced noise, EQ, and gating, there's no reason to stress out about a guitar with a tiny bit of 60-cycle hum or a compressed vocal with a tiny bit of excited background hiss. Again, sometimes this noise is part of the way an instrument sounds. Believe it or not, what a lot of people hear as warm, good, and clear is in fact noise and distortion. So don't be afraid to let a little of that bit of color do its job. Don't go removing so much EQ and gating so tightly that people are distracted by the effect of the reduction.

To this day I can still hear the squeaky kick drum pedal on Led Zeppelin's "Since I've Been Loving You." It seems louder to me each time I hear it. Have you ever noticed it? Did anyone you know ever hear the song and say, "They should have taken the high end out of the kick drum?" I doubt it. I also can still hear the tape hiss as loud as the keyboard/organ part at the beginning of Boston's "Foreplay/Long Time." If the engineers then would have pulled out a bunch of EQ from these tracks, they would not be as clear or sound the same. Sadly, I think only the true "audio nerds" ever took notice of these little things. In some circles, it is even believed that these nuances make these recordings more likeable.

What I'm trying to say is that in the digital medium, it is easy to get carried away and do the music a disservice by trying to reduce the amount of noise aggressively. Use some of these tips to clean up a mix a bit, but try to remember to enjoy the tracks as if you were a first-time listener. Chances are, if your track doesn't start with 30 seconds of ground hum, the listener won't mind and will enjoy the music for what it is.

Understanding and Using Loops

In today's musical climate, looping audio is a popular studio technique. Many different genres, such as hip-hop, electronic, and pop, take advantage of loop-based production techniques. A *loop,* for anyone who doesn't know, is a repeated musical phrase of a predetermined length (usually 4 to 32 beats). This term originated in the early days (the 1970s) of dance and rock recording. When a recording engineer got one small section of rhythm section tracking that just grooved more than the rest, he would often cut the small section from the tape and tape it back together, making a piece of mended tape that resembled a loop. Then the engineer would record that tape loop on a two-track machine, usually employing a broomstick or some other round stick-like object (PVC pipe was popular) to hold one end of the loop while the piece played over and over on the tape head of the tracking machine. Then the rest of the dance track was created over the looped audio, and the track always ended with a fade-out. Disco was really the first music to totally employ looping audio.

Today, the technique of using loops is much simpler. No sharp objects are involved. There are two primary ways that loops are used in audio production: musically and technically. When I say that loops are used musically, I mean that looping audio phrases are defined by the artist and used over and over again as a part of the composition. For example, hip-hop and rap tracks are often eight-beat drum patterns or instrument sequences that are looped repeatedly throughout the entire song as other loops and instrumentation are layered through different parts of the composition. Electronic music is similarly structured with varying levels of complexity. This is what is considered to be *loop-* or *pattern-based* music production. I often use loops in this capacity when I'm sketching out song ideas for a client or a particular genre in which loop-based production is employed.

Almost all sequencers and wave editors have looping abilities, but some programs and stand-alone machines stand above the rest for working with loops. Ableton Live has limited audio-editing capabilities, but is perfect for loop-based sequencing and altering the timing of preexisting audio so that loops can be played back at virtually any tempo. With Ableton Live you can time-stretch, pitch music up and down, quantize, and align beats in real time. It is very musical and intuitive and can even be used in the context of a live performance (hence the name). Ableton Live will be mentioned in greater detail later in Chapter 5.

A hardware favorite for creating and working with loops is the Akai MPC series sequencers. The primary advantage to the MPCs is that they have triggers/sample pads on the surface that allow you to interact with the unit like an instrument. Drum samples, instrument samples, or audio loops can be user-assigned to each trigger and played in real time by physically tapping the pads with your fingertips. On the MPC series sequencers, audio isn't represented in the same visual way as it is in software. It's more like a gigantic drum machine where you can enlist sounds and sample libraries from external sources and layer them together. The latest models even have built-in CD burners so that you can create a loop-based masterpiece and print it directly to a disc for listening.

So what does the post-audio project studio need to know about loops, looping, and loop-based software? This is the part where we talk about the second technique I mentioned. When you use looping in a technical way, you are using it like a tool to accomplish a particular task. In audio post-production, you can use the loop or cycle function to audition a part over and over again as you listen for something that might need to be corrected. A good example of this would be something like defining the volume level of a vocal on a verse. You keep listening to it, and some parts seem much quieter than others; some parts seem too loud. By setting up the loop points, or cycle markers, in your editing program and using the loop function, you can listen to an isolated section of audio while making minor volume changes to the wave file as the verse plays over and over. You could solo up the vocal as it's looping and listen to it with just the rhythm section to make sure the vocal phrasing is in time, or you could listen to it up against a solo instrument that might be a pitch reference. Listening to a small audio section as it loops is also good for making minor adjustments to individual parts that help get the audio to that magical place where everything just makes sense and is equal in volume and tonality. Listening to the parts looping section by section can allow you to get smaller sections of audio under control as well. If a bass note pops on beat 3 of measure 44, it's a lot easier to have measure 44 loop as you correct the problem than it is to reset the cursor every time you make an adjustment and need to hear your changes played back.

The loop function is your friend. I often set up loops during mixing and then switch monitors to hear the same part on different speakers. Or I'll apply different real-time effects and alter them all in real time without interrupting the playback. An important factor that should be considered here is your computer's RAM use while applying effects to a looped section in real time. Most DAW software programs have a CPU usage meter. Use it! Looping audio won't be much good to you if you're running at 80-percent CPU usage before you even get started. If this is the case, see what you can do to free up some resources. Raise your buffer size, freeze some tracks, deactivate any plug-ins that are not in use, and, if all else fails, buy more RAM. The ability to preview audio in looped sections is a timesaver in audio post-production. In my own experience, I've found that it's worth doing what you can to make it work for you.

Editing Dos and Don'ts

In music as well as post audio, there really aren't any hard and fast rules. This section can be summed up as good habits to form for editing audio. Here are some helpful hints I may have covered briefly or not at all in the previous sections.

- **Eliminate things that detract from the listening experience.** Many times people go too far with audio editing, especially if the person is new to the editing process and feels the need to take his new-found power to the maximum level. Suddenly, the craft, creativity, and engineering techniques that go into processing audio become the feature. It's not a contest to show people how neat or cool you are and what nifty stuff you can do with editing. Your job is to enhance the listening experience and not take away from it.

Many times small adjustments are necessary in post. But it's not your job to turn a rock into a gemstone. That's the artist's or the producer's job. Many times people have sent me post-production projects for which I have created two versions. The first is a heavily edited "what I think we should do" version; the second is a series of minor adjustments and basic cleanup services. The second, less effected version has won out almost every time. Artists often get very attached to the way the music sounded when it left their hands, and sometimes they lose the objectivity to hear it any other way. I have been guilty of this with my own music in the past. That being said, keeping it as simple as possible while improving the listening experience goes a long way.

- **Make sure fades and transitions sound natural.** I hear a lot of projects where the cross-fades and transitions on vocals or drums are absolutely *nasty*. I've heard vocals that have been edited in a way that *no one* is physically capable of singing. I've heard toms that should ring out abruptly disappear right when a chorus starts. The basic guideline here is to edit and make the necessary changes to make everything in the tracks sound natural. And yes, quite often this means more work may have to go into fixing or editing the tracks. Sometimes it's better to spread a vocal over three tracks and do the necessary edits and effects for each individual track. Just be careful not to go overboard.

- **Reduce noise, clicks, hiss, and clipping.** Noise, clipping, and background levels of hiss will only make your track sound worse and less professional. Do everything you can to eliminate these, as we discussed previously. Use gates and editing to chop out the noisy areas. Make sure you don't have audible pops and clicks from zero-crossing and bad edits. Make sure you don't have any plug-ins producing hiss or processing noise while the track is running without sound or audio present. A good thing to do is to listen to all tracks, or all your "money tracks," soloed up. Hear every edit and effect and make sure everything is clean. By *money tracks*, I mean vocals, drums, guitars, or anything up front in the mix. Removing a little pop on a track of keyboard ear candy that plays for three seconds on top of the 80 tracks of audio already running may not be the best use of your time if you can't hear it in the mix. Listening to each track, even once, with no other audio playing is to your benefit. You will probably discover many things you didn't hear before when the entire mix was playing. The last thing you want is to hear a track in its final, unchangeable format and realize that a click you neglected to fix has been amplified so much that every time it sounds, it sets off the Clapper to which your studio light is connected. So, again, be careful. Do your best to correct obvious editing problems, but pick your battles when it comes to cleaning and fixing the little things.

- **Watch out for artifacts.** Processing audio alone can cause an array of artifacts. Also, bouncing down a final edited mix can make things a little funky if the computer is doing heavy, real-time processing. Suddenly, a vocal stretch may sound warbled and effected because of a compressor. Auto-tune could have made some real-time error and might not get all the way up to the correct pitch, or it might just sound glitchy once the bounce is complete. Keep your wits about you and watch out for things as you listen to *every* final edited bounce. There may be artifacts popping out that you never heard before, so you'll have to correct and perform another audio mixdown. Everyone in this business of audio post-production has made the mistake of not listening back to the last bounce at least once. The next thing you know, you're on the phone with the artist or label, and you realize the CPU went critical during the mixdown process and the last 60 seconds of the song are a blast of granulated noise. This is the kind of mistake that only happens once. If you ever experience it, you just might be so traumatized that you and your children (and their children, and their children's children) will always be sure to listen to a final mix all the way through before sending it off.

- **Back up *all* of your audio files.** If you are doing intensive audio processing, it's a good idea to keep all the original files. Often, after I've got all of the client's audio compiled into one project and all the audio events are in their correct positions, I'll save the project, then make a copy of the project and make my changes there. That way, I've always got a blank canvas to return to, just in case. You don't want to modify a bunch of files and make new versions of them without ever being able to revert to an original. Or, before making any drastic changes, you can duplicate the track you're working with, apply your changes to the copy, and deactivate the original so that it's always there in case you need to replace a botched "it seemed like a good idea at the time" irreversible edit with an untainted copy of the original. For instance, suppose your ears are burned out. You've been listening to the same track for hours on end, and in a moment of temporary insanity, you make a very bad decision to alter the vocal timing because it's bothering you. You get up the next day, listen to the track, and it just feels and sounds awful because of all the tweaking you did. At this point, you'd want to start from the beginning. Your backup copy of the project will do the trick—or, if you've spent a considerable amount of time on it already and you just want to start over with the vocal, a copy of the original vocal will work.

Another problem that can occur is that a project within any software may be bogged down with hundreds of audio files from edits. The computer passes through every edit as if it were an independent audio file. If there are 200 edits, the computer might try treating them as 200 separate audio streams that become stacked in the audio buffer as they play back, overlapping one another and increasing resource usage. The computer is thinking and working so fast and in such great detail that it may struggle to keep up. This can create playback issues, which can lead to audio driver and software crashes. This, in turn, could lead to losing a whole lot of hard work. This is basically file loss due to CPU overload. The point is to do whatever you can to keep the original audio files that a client provides preserved *somewhere*. External hard drives are great for this. I have several external hard drives for different purposes in my studio, one of which stores *only* original file content that I receive from clients.

■ **Make sure audio files are properly organized.** In audio post-production, there are few things that are more important than being able to find all your work, original files, and edits, as discussed a moment ago. The best way to do is this is to stay organized from the get-go. When you start a project, know what location you're saving it to on your hard drive, which folder, and where the information is being stored. Often, when post-audio people aren't paying attention, the drum tracks end up on one hard drive and the cymbals on another. When the edits from day two are saved in your My Pictures folder, you have a cluster you-know-what on your hands, where nothing is found and nothing can be played back because the software says the file is missing. If you listen back to tracks on a project and you end up using computer drive searches to locate files that you may or may not have named properly, you're in trouble. Having to locate your audio files due to an improperly organized project can be extremely time-consuming. Another downside to a lack of organization can be if the software has to draw the audio in the project from too many different places at once. This, too, can cause problems due to CPU overload. Having said that, different software programs handle audio files in different ways. Be sure to find out what type of file organization is recommended by the developer.

Does all that sound like a mess? Good, because it is! I made some of these same errors in the beginning, and once you know better, they're really just errors of laziness. Nothing is worse than deleting the wrong project folder, only to find that the current project you're working on no longer has any guitar tracks. Make project folders, make song folders, and put them on a predetermined drive. Make sure when you bounce or save edits, you name and rename files and tracks properly, such as "lead vocal," "vox harm 1," and so forth. This will save you an infinite amount of time in the long run, and it really equals a couple seconds of clicks and a minute's setup time. I look over my old drives and projects now, and I feel sad that I may never hear the proper bass edits in "Lost Cause" ever again because I foolishly saved the bass bounce in the wrong song folder—a hastily deleted song folder because I never wanted to hear "Folk Singer Band's less-than-amazing power ballad" ever again. Shall we move on to the mixing primer?

Mixing and Monitoring in the Project Studio

4 Don't Console Me

The days of mixing audio projects on enormous studio mixer consoles with a billion flying faders and enough blinking lights to induce seizures in small animals aren't necessarily gone, but for many musicians recording their own music, this type of mixing environment isn't realistic. These days, do-it-yourself musicians working in project studios are more likely to use software mixers or spend a few hundred bucks on a control surface than they are to rent a studio with an engineer for what some would consider a small fortune.

Mixing is both science and alchemy. There is a great number of constant audio principles that must be adhered to, but at the same time, there is an infinite number of variables and rules that you can bend and sometimes break. I don't want to scare you, but audio post-production is like solving an algebra problem for which the answer is already given to you. You must determine what the variables are in order to complete the statement. The answer is generally defined as a professional-quality audio project. Now you just have to figure out what it will take to equal that definition. Mixing is an equation *within* that equation.

You can use many different tools to help you resolve these equations, but the tools alone are not enough. Anyone can be schooled in the technical ins and outs of general audio production, but that doesn't mean that person will be great or even good at it. It's especially difficult when you're the guitar player and you want a rippin' guitar solo to be as loud as possible so the listener can really experience it. Ultimately, though, you have to know what your available tools are and how to use them effectively, and then train your ears and learn trust them. Objectivity and good decisions that benefit the project as a whole will make the difference between a good mix and a bad one.

This section will cover an overview of mixing, and then focus on mixing for different media, setting up an efficient software mixing workspace, and taking an in-depth look at different software tools, mixing techniques, tips, tricks, and the hows and whys behind them. We'll even explore monitoring audio in your project studio environment. Let's begin!

What Is Mixing?

Mixing is the art of balancing relative volume, frequency, spatial divisions, and the dynamic content of a number of different audio sources. It requires that you know your way around the software interface of your mixing program, but it also requires that you make "sound" judgments when it comes to how loud or quiet an audio source should be in the mix, where to pan it, or what frequencies to boost or cut. The general goal is to consider all these variables and combine the audio signals in a way that is pleasing to the ear.

The basic goal of mixing is to provide listeners with the correct interpretation of the audio presented to them. If the desired effect of the music is scary and ethereal and the listener hears ambient and pretty, you may need to rethink the way certain elements are mixed to get the right idea across. Mixing is a psychological process to some degree, and at times it is a guessing game. You need to have experience with what audio gives the listener the proper emotional cues to interpret it.

How does Pink Floyd's *The Wall* makes us feel and why? People are often drawn to music that makes them feel a certain way, and they are likely to listen to other music that reminds them of that feeling. So if the music is meant to express something specific and you can't seem to make the statement you want, chances are a lot of other music out there had the same goal. Find some and figure out what makes it feel that way. Then, apply some of those concepts to your own mix.

It's important to understand that it's really up to us as post-audio professionals to make that call. Listeners deal in the end product, which is a good and bad thing. Like the TV commercial says, "You never get a second chance to make a first impression." Well, you never get to hear a mix for the first time twice. You wouldn't want anyone to think your

Metallica-esque shred fest sounded thin and wimpy, and you wouldn't want your simple folk ballad to sound aggressive and harsh, so proper mixing must be employed at all times to get the point across.

Another consideration is that to the average listener, final presentation and fidelity are integral parts of the experience. In commercial audio production, fidelity goes hand in hand with content and composition. Our ears use reference points for the way we think things should sound. The average listener is trained by CD-quality audio and accepts it as a standard for fidelity. Anything less is unprofessional. With the prominence of MP3s, we've become accustomed to accepting them as a compressed version of that standard. Even if the ear can't discern exactly what the audible difference is between high-resolution MP3s and CDs, listeners know that their favorite song will sound better on CD than on its compressed counterpart.

Fidelity *Fidelity*, for all intents and purposes, is a fancy word for audio quality. Webster's dictionary defines it as the "accuracy with which an electronic system reproduces the sound or image of its input signal." In the old days, "high fidelity," or simply "hi-fi," meant that the audio material the term was used to describe was of high, or highly accurate, reproduction quality. "Lo-fi," or "low fidelity," meant that the referenced audio was of low reproduction quality. The sound of music being played from an old vinyl record would be considered low fidelity. The same music transferred over to a compact disc would most likely have better fidelity than the original record, but probably lower fidelity than a modern recording.

In digital audio we generally strive for pristine, high-quality audio, or good fidelity.

All things considered, a mix can make or break a final product. And though a good mix cannot make badly written or poorly performed music stellar, if the source material is recorded well, it can do positive things for the listening experience and perceived professionalism of the recording. I cannot tell you how many times I've heard amazing sounds and compression jobs on *terrible* bands and artists. On the flip side, many great musical pieces (Bruce Springsteen's "Nebraska" comes to mind) suffered from less than professional recording practices and were able to rise above the fidelity because the music was just so amazingly personal and good. The goal is to create a healthy balance. Make the best of each mix and project, and try to make the correct audio decisions to improve the overall quality of the final product.

Before you begin mixing, you may want to do a little fidelity research. Prior to starting any new project—be it mixing, tracking, or mastering—I listen to a few CDs of benchmark recordings for that style. I listen to the details and EQ. I take the perceived loudness, pans, spatial divisions, and perspective for each song into account. I make notes of subtle differences in mixing from track to track.

Every style of music has its own inherent mixing guidelines. As a quick example, if you are mixing a hip-hop track, the bass and low frequencies will be *far* different from those of an up-tempo rock song you mixed days earlier. Typically, the boomy low end of hip-hop kicks would make a horrible mess of a rock track. "Why?" you might ask. "Can't rock kick the bass just as hard as hip-hop?" The short answer here is no. Hip-hop is typically much slower than rock, and the notes can resonate more and last longer. If each rock kick drum had the frequency and resonance of a hip-hop kick drum, you would have a migraine and a destroyed car stereo after about 30 seconds of listening.

For these reasons, it is always a good thing to do your research and learn the sonic reference points. How compressed is a folk music vocal? How much low midrange is in jazz guitar, and when is it too much? All these style-indicative factors will be part of each mix, so do your best to familiarize yourself with them.

How Project Studios Have Changed Mixing

Once upon a time, it was not crucial for a musician to know anything about what happens after the recording session is over. An independent musician who wanted his or her audio project mixed had to pay for time in a professional studio and pay a mixing engineer by the hour to sit in front of a large console and help mix. Many leather couches were sat on, much mineral water [*or insert other beverage type here*] was consumed, and all was good. A great number of large professional studios have since turned to the convenience of software, using tens of thousands of dollars worth of high-end Pro Tools HD systems…and they still charge the big bucks for the mineral water.

Lucky for us, the growing number of project studios has driven hardware and software manufacturers to make more professional-grade audio recording products affordable. So now, instead of renting a studio and hiring an engineer, people who go to big audio production studios can pay us to do the work instead! On the flipside, musicians have more tools accessible to them, so they can learn about audio production and they don't *have* to go to the expense of outsourcing audio production projects. Don't get me wrong; I'm not discounting the work that large studio production houses can do. They have dedicated, almost scientifically designed studio environments and trained staff with lots of experience and loads of gear to get the job done. It takes a lot of time, effort, and dedication for an individual to learn how to make recordings sound professional, but with enough experience, education, and the right tools, it *can* be done.

As it applies to project studios, mixing has primarily changed in the tools that are used to achieve the same results that the big studios get. Huge studio consoles used for mixing different audio sources have been replaced by powerful mixing software that can perform all the same functions, such as level adjustment, panning, equalization, and routing. Instead of having an engineer run around patching cables to route effects, you can manage all your effect inserts and sends by clicking a menu. In the '80s, studio mixing consoles started using automation by way of motorized faders to control volume, bus, and auxiliary levels. Automation can now be achieved by literally drawing the value using a visual interface and your mouse. Also, most software sequencer/mixing programs allow the integration of MIDI tracks that can control software synthesizers or hardware instruments; these programs allow such MIDI tracks to be mixed and manipulated just like audio tracks. Essentially, audio software has taken the manual labor performed by three or four engineers and put the functionality of a full-blown production studio into one convenient little box—your computer.

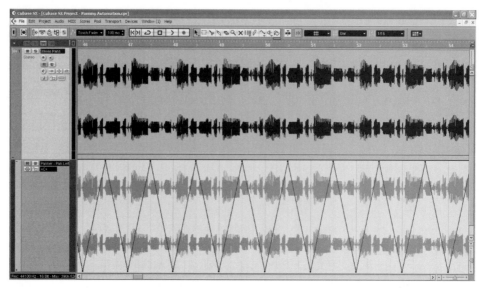

Figure 4.1 What the described panning automation might look like in Cubase.

What Is Automation? *Automation* is the technique of operating the functions of your software mixer without continuous hands-on control. Basically, you define parameters and values of an operation that will change over the timeline of your project, and then you are able to hear the effect of those changes every time the project is played back without having to manually alter those values.

Suppose you're working on a song and you want a particular audio event to pan back and forth during the verses. You can define how far left or right you want the event to pan, for how long, and when, all by using automation to set the values. See Figure 4.1 for an example of what this automation might look like.

This is just one example of how automation can be used. Typically, mixer functions, software synthesizers, equalization, and effects can all be controlled using software automation. Refer to the manual for the software program you are using to find out whether it is capable of automation and what automation can be used for.

---

5 Software Tools for Digital Mixing

S oftware mixing employs a number of different tools. Your sequencing/mixing software will act as the base of operations for your mix. In conjunction with a combination of different software effect plug-ins and utilities, you'll be able to get a well-balanced mix that is ready to be mastered.

In this chapter, we'll discuss different software programs and plug-ins used for mixing and get familiar with the general functions of a software mixer.

Choosing a Software Sequencer for Mixing Digital Audio

A *software sequencer* is a program that manages digital audio as multi-track events. Each audio source is assigned to its own track and can be affected by the functions within the program. All software sequencing programs perform basic mixing functions. They allow you to mute and solo tracks, write and activate automation, adjust volume and pan settings, manage the routing of insert and send effects, as well as name and organize your tracks to accommodate the way you work, to name a few functions. A good sequencing/mixing program is the core of your project studio.

Choosing the right software is an important decision. Often, project studios are designed entirely around what software will be used. Different sequencers have different user interfaces (UIs) that all have different appearances. Sometimes the location of editing tools or the way the software handles plug-ins will differ, but they all do basically the same thing—manage audio (and usually MIDI).

When I first started using digital audio software, I used a program that I got for free from a software developer that shall remain anonymous.

It worked fine. It did everything I wanted it to, and I really had no complaints about it. Then one day, a friend told me that there was another software out there that was quickly becoming an industry standard. He went on and on about how much it had improved his workflow and how good the audio engine sounded. So I gave it a shot. I don't dispute that there was a noticeable difference in the sound quality, but although there is always a natural transition period and learning curve in changing platforms, I never quite got the hang of this program's software environment. What was I supposed to do now? I didn't want to use a software interface I didn't like just because it sounded better, and I didn't want to go back to the software I *did* like using because now I knew that something was missing from the quality of the audio. After much experimentation with different sequencers, I found one that was intuitively laid out. Everything was where I thought it should be. I never even had to pick up the manual for it. I still use this program to this very day, and I regularly hear that others did not find it as easy to use as I did. The bottom line is that what works for someone else might not work for you, and vice versa.

Some software sequencing programs have more bells and whistles than others. Some are perceived to have better-sounding audio engines that affect the way your project sounds overall. Some cost a great deal more than others. What software you use is really a personal preference, but know that the *wrong* software program can hinder productivity and, in some cases, *creativity*. My advice is to take a moment to realistically consider your needs and budget. Do some research, download some demos to try them out, and then narrow your choices from there. The moral of the story is: When it comes right down to it, choose a software program that makes the most sense to you.

Now, let's take a moment to briefly discuss a few of the more popular software programs used for recording, editing, and mixing. Chapter 17, "Resources," contains a direct feature comparison of all the programs discussed.

Digidesign Pro Tools

Pro Tools is a digital audio workstation software program by Digidesign. It was one of the first programs to offer 16-bit/44.1-kHz

CD-quality multitrack digital audio editing on a personal computer. Now offering 24-bit and up to 192-kHz resolution, Pro Tools is regarded as the industry standard for music production, post-production, and TV and film scoring. You will find it used in almost every major studio or post-production house in the world.

Digidesign offers three different types of Pro Tools systems that cover the needs of audio professionals and hobbyists alike: Pro Tools|HD, Pro Tools LE, and Pro Tools M-Powered.

- **Pro Tools|HD.** This is Digidesign's professional-level digital audio recording system. HD systems use PCI or PCI Express cards to perform audio processing on DSP chips to reduce the CPU load on your computer's internal processor. It also uses proprietary TDM plug-ins in the same way. HD systems are offered in three primary configurations: HD1, HD2, and HD3. The differences between the three core systems are processing power and software options. The more money you spend, the more power and software options you will have. In addition to the core systems, Digidesign offers a broad range of hardware interfaces, such as A/D, or analog-to-digital converters; D/A converters (bet you can't guess what those are); MIDI and analog I/Os; and control surfaces that work seamlessly with Pro Tools software. If you're seriously considering purchasing a full-blown Pro Tools|HD rig, unless you are already familiar with all the available options and systems, it is *highly* recommended that you do a *lot* of research and consult a professional (not necessarily a salesman) regarding an HD configuration that meets your needs. The different options can be rather confusing if you don't do your research.

- **Pro Tools LE.** Pro Tools LE systems are consumer-level digital recording packages. *LE* designates that the included software is the little brother, or "lite edition," of the Pro Tools software environment. Instead of using PCI cards to handle the workload, LE systems use the internal CPU of your computer to process audio. This will not tax your system any more than running any other type of digital audio program. Another difference is that the LE software has a limited track count of 32 tracks, versus the 192 tracks available in Pro Tools|HD. Also, Pro Tools LE supports two-channel (stereo) output only. In the Pro Tools software family, only HD offers multi-channel surround-sound output.

For hardware, LE systems are based around FireWire and USB connectivity, which gives the added bonus of mobility. There are currently three different hardware options—the 003 audio interface/control surface, the 003 Rack, and the Mbox. (However, you can probably still find the previous 001 and 002 models second-hand and save a few bucks.) Pro Tools LE software is locked to Digidesign's hardware, meaning that if there is no Digidesign hardware present, the software will not launch.

If you want to get into the Pro Tools software environment, but you can't afford tens of thousands of dollars to get an HD system, LE just might be the way to go. Pro Tools LE project files are also compatible with Pro Tools HD software should you decide to upgrade or move to a studio that is running HD. Pro Tools LE is often used to produce professional-quality commercial projects and would be a great choice for any project studio.

■ **Pro Tools M-Powered.** M-Audio is a business unit of Digidesign that manufactures of a variety of "pro-sumer" digital audio workstation products. In April of 2005, they released Pro Tools M-Powered (see Figure 5.1). M-Powered shares about 95 percent of the features that LE has and is locked to select M-Audio audio interfaces.

For more information on Pro Tools, please visit www.digidesign.com.

Steinberg Cubase/Nuendo

Steinberg Cubase is a cross-platform (PC and Mac) digital audio program for composition, recording, editing, and mixing (see Figure 5.2). Steinberg first released Cubase (then called *Cubit*) back in 1989 for the Atari ST. It quickly gained popularity over other available sequencers of its time due to its superior Arrangement window. Now in version 4, Cubase is designed primarily around music production. Its MIDI and deep sample editing capability are held in high regard in the DAW community, so if you use a lot of virtual instruments or you need to make meticulous micro-edits, this might be one to look at.

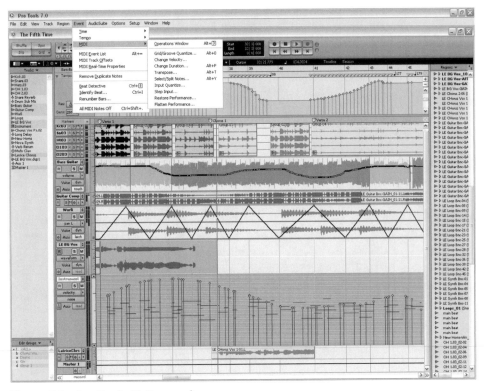

Figure 5.1 Pro Tools M-Powered.

Cubase is capable of up to 24-bit, 96-kHz audio resolution and has a 32-bit floating-point audio engine. It handles audio and MIDI, offers 5.1 surround mixing capability, supports ReWire and VST plug-ins (both of which will be discussed a bit later in this chapter), and limits your track count only to what your computer can handle. It *does* support video formats, but Cubase is more of an audio post-production program. Its big brother, Nuendo, was designed to be the video post-production powerhouse.

32-Bit Floating Point 32-bit floating-point resolution, as it applies to a software's audio engine, means that DSP (*digital signal processing*) will always occur at a higher resolution than the audio data was recorded at. As opposed to *fixed* resolution, which conforms DSP to a fixed bit rate, *floating-point* automatically adjusts for DSP processing *up to* 32-bit.

Figure 5.2   Cubase 4.

Not all effects or VST plug-ins are created equal. Some operate at a higher bit resolution than others. As you add more VST instruments and effect plug-ins to your project, the mathematical equations the audio engine has to make in order to conform the DSP resolution to a fixed bit rate become increasingly more complex, and you may sacrifice sound quality. Thirty-two-bit floating-point assists in resolving this issue by allowing your audio engine to compensate for variable bit-rate operations caused by the use of digital signal processing.

Nuendo and Cubase are based on the same 32-bit floating-point audio engine, but Nuendo was developed around video post-production. It is capable of performing all the same functions as Cubase, but it has added features for working with video. It is capable of up to 24-bit, 192-kHz audio resolution, offers 10.2 surround mixing capability, and comes with a plethora of video post-production plug-ins and video management features.

For more information on Steinberg Nuendo and Cubase, please visit www.steinberg.net.

Apple Logic Pro

Logic Pro is a MIDI sequencer and digital audio workstation that is well respected among electronic music producers for its audio quality and integrated virtual instruments and effect plug-ins (see Figure 5.3). Logic was introduced in the late '80s by a German software company called Emagic. Back then, Logic was available for both Mac and PC, but in 2002, after the release of version 5, Emagic became part of the Apple Corporation, and Logic has since become available to Mac users only.

Audio Units *Audio Units* refers to a Mac-specific system-level plug-in architecture that is provided by Core Audio and is used by applications such as GarageBand, Soundtrack Pro, Logic Express, Logic Pro, Final Cut Pro, and most third-party audio software developed for Mac OS X.

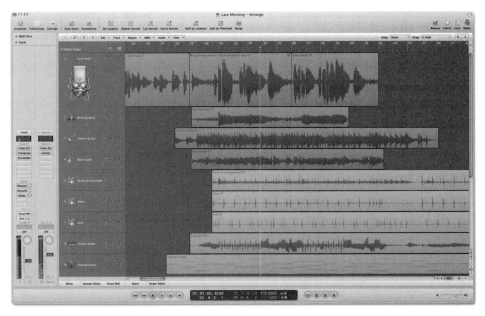

Figure 5.3 Logic Pro 8.

Logic Pro features a 32-bit floating-point audio engine that is capable of up to 24-bit, 192-kHz audio resolution, a deep sample editor, up to 7.1 surround mixing capabilities, 70 built-in effect plug-ins, 34 virtual instrument plug-ins, and Apple Loop support, which allows correctly formatted loops to be played back at any project tempo. Apple Loops also let you to access and classify your audio loops by descriptors such as key, tempo, instrument, and mood for easy integration into your Logic Pro project. Apple Loops will also be discussed later in this chapter.

For more information on Logic Pro, please visit www.apple.com/logicpro.

Cakewalk SONAR

SONAR is a PC-only, all-in-one, digital audio and MIDI workstation in Cakewalk's professional software line that can be used for recording, editing, mixing, and mastering (see Figure 5.4). SONAR's popularity has grown exponentially (especially with film and television composers) due to the improved audio engine (over previous versions), new enhancements to the user interface, and ease of use. It is worth

Figure 5.4 Cakewalk SONAR 7.

mentioning here that SONAR is also capable of using and generating ACIDized WAV files. Although most sequencing programs can *read* ACIDized WAV files, they can't create them. I will discuss ACIDizing WAV files in the "ACIDizing" section.

Now in version 7, SONAR has a number of impressive features, such as ACT (*Active Controller Technology*), which dynamically remaps effect, mix, and instrument parameters to hardware controllers, and Audio-Snap, which allows the quantization of audio. In addition, Cakewalk is very responsive to user feedback. If you submit a feature request, chances are you'll see it in the next update or version. To date, SONAR 7 is the only major DAW on the market that offers full beginning-to-end 64-bit internal processing, a 64-bit audio engine, a 64-bit mixer, and 64-bit Windows support.

See www.cakewalk.com for more information about SONAR.

Other Tools

In addition to your sequencer, there are a number of other tools that can help improve the productivity of your workflow. You'd be amazed by how much time you can save by using specific formats and little helper utilities that allow you to stretch an audio file to the tempo of your project or rename 50 files with the click of a button. Both you and your clients will appreciate these little gems.

ReWire

ReWire is a software protocol that was developed by Propellerhead for syncing and transferring audio or MIDI data between two computer applications in real time. It allows two separate applications to run in tandem while sharing remote functions and transferring data.

It works like this: The first ReWire-capable application launched is the *ReWire host*. The second ReWire-capable application launched is the *ReWire slave*. ReWire automatically initiates communication between the two applications. The transport functions of either application behave as a set of global transport controls for both applications. In other words, if you activate Play on the transport of one application, both applications will play. But wait; that's not all! You can also send MIDI data out of your host application and trigger a software synthesizer in the slave application, then use the automation in your host sequencer to manipulate the soft synth and hear the effect of the automation during playback. You can even print the output of the synth to an audio track inside your host sequencer. Pretty neat, huh?

ReWire has become somewhat of a standard in digital audio, so nearly every major digital audio application supports it. The best part is that you don't even have to buy ReWire. It's automatically included in the installation of all ReWire-compatible software applications. In the latest version, ReWire 2, you can stream up to 256 channels of audio and 4,080 individual MIDI tracks between applications. ReWire is a great way to seamlessly integrate features from different software programs into one useable workspace.

For more information on ReWire and ReWire-compatible software programs, please visit www.propellerheads.se.

ACIDizing

ACIDizing is method of preparing an audio file so that you can alter the timing and pitch by inserting meta information or data tags into the existing audio. ACIDized files can come in handy when you're working on a project in an ACID-compatible sequencer and you want to use a loop or audio phrase that has a fixed tempo or pitch. Almost every sequencer these days can read and use the time stretching and pitch information encoded in ACIDized audio files, but there are only a handful that can generate it. The most common are Sony Creative Software ACID and Cakewalk SONAR.

ACIDizing is a precise procedure. If a file is not properly ACIDized, you will not be able to change the pitch or stretch the timing of the file correctly, which will result in audio artifacts. To ACIDize a file, you must first be using a program or utility that can create ACIDized files. Second, you must determine the key of the audio in the file, then enter the correct key in the appropriate field in your software program. That's the easy part. Next, you have to look and *really* listen to the audio file to determine where the transients are and place a time-stretch marker at the beginning of *every* major transient. (And when I say "major transient," I mean the transients that fall on major beats and any medium-sized spikes that lie between subdivided beats.) These markers help the software calculate what to stretch and how far to stretch it. The space between the markers is the actual audio that will be stretched. If there are too many beats and/or major transients between two markers, that section of audio will not be stretched correctly and might sound as if it's either faster or slower than it should be when you attempt to play it back. There are some utilities available that claim they can batch ACIDize multiple audio files, but the results can often be questionable. You're better off taking the time to do it correctly than taking your chances with a shortcut, only to find out that you've got to go back and re-ACIDize all over again.

Transients When you are working with digital audio software programs, audio is represented graphically. As mentioned earlier, these graphical representations look a bit like mountain ranges with peaks and valleys. Each peak is considered to be a transient. Wherever a transient falls on a beat is typically a good place to put a marker when ACIDizing. Figure 5.5 shows what a properly ACIDized file might look like.

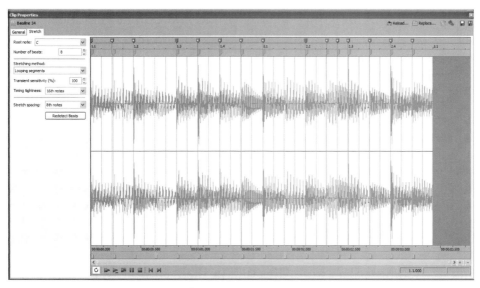

Figure 5.5   A properly ACIDized file.

ACIDizing is a nondestructive process, which here means that ACID-izing a file doesn't alter the original file in such a way that it can't be used just like a regular un-ACIDized file.

Rex Files

Rexing is another means of preparing an audio file with a fixed tempo to be time stretched. Rex files were originally developed to work with hardware samplers. Then later, a module called the Dr. Rex player, found within Propellerhead's Reason, would serve as the software equivalent. The Dr. Rex player can read the "slice" marker informa-tion inside a Rex file and play it back at whatever tempo the host pro-gram designates. Rex files can only be generated using a program by Propellerhead called ReCycle.

When you create a Rex file in ReCycle, you insert what are referred to as *slice markers* at the beginning of each transient. Whenever you place a slice marker, just like ACIDizing, the audio between two markers will be stretched to fit the host application's tempo. But unlike ACID-izing, which writes the additional time-stretch and pitch information over the top of the existing file without changing the file itself, Rexing actually divides the audio into separate audio events. Because of this, it is critical that you place your slice markers only where there is a zero-crossing at the beginning of the transient. As I discussed earlier in the book, the amplitude at the beginning and end of an audio file *should* always be absolute silence or digital black; otherwise, you'll hear a pop when the cursor leaves digital black and the audio file begins to play. After all your slices have been defined, you can save the altered audio as a new .rex file that will be compatible with all programs that have Rex support. Figure 5.6 shows the proper placement of slices in ReCycle.

Rexing works well on audio files that are composed of percussive instruments, and it's great for extracting one-shots from an audio file, but due to that zero-crossing conundrum I just mentioned, it isn't as effective at sustaining instruments such as pads or strings due of the absence of zero-crossings entirely.

Major sequencers from Cubase to Pro Tools can import and use the time-stretching features of a Rex file in their native project windows. You can, of course, also use the Dr. Rex player in Propellerhead's

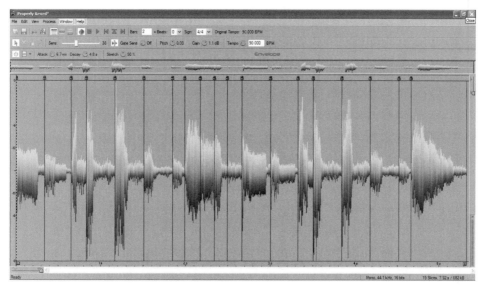

Figure 5.6 A properly Rexed audio file.

Reason to play back Rex files. Additionally, Propellerhead's Reason is ReWire-compatible, so you could also run Reason alongside your sequencer as a ReWire slave and access Rex files (among other things) that way.

Apple Loops

Apple Loops are yet another format that allows for pitch change and time correction of an audio loop with a fixed tempo. An Apple Loop is basically a WAV or AIF audio file that has the metadata written on top of it. As with the other formats, you can specify the original pitch and placement of time-stretching markers, but Apple Loops bring a little something extra to the table with the ability to insert additional information, such as scale type, author, genre, instrument, and descriptors such as whether the audio in the file is composed of single instruments or an ensemble, whether they're acoustic or electric, whether they're dry or processed, whether they're cheerful or dark, and more.

Figure 5.7 shows the Apple Loop Utility's interface window. Furthermore, you can use these descriptors to search through your audio files using the loop browser in Logic Pro, GarageBand, or Soundtrack for easy organization. Need an acoustic guitar that is dissonant and dark with a delay effect on it? Just indicate the parameters you want the file

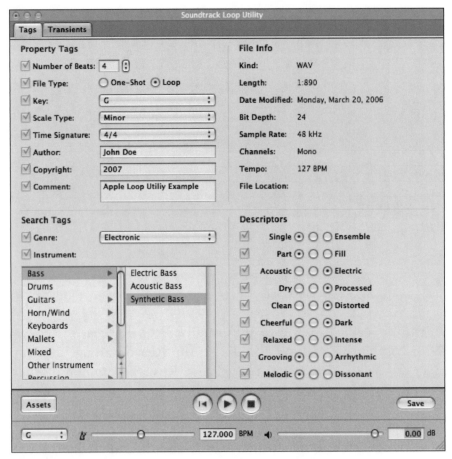

Figure 5.7 The Soundtrack Loop Utility used for classifying Apple Loops.

to have, and the loop browser in your Apple Loop–compatible software application will show you all the Apple Loops that fit into those parameters. The categorical information that Apple Loops contain can only be read by compatible software programs on a Mac. Actually, any audio program that supports the AIF format can import and use an Apple Loop, but if the Apple Loop format is not supported, the additional metadata will be ignored.

Ableton Live
Ableton Live has been my life preserver and has saved me many times from drowning in a sea of deadlines. It's a loop-based audio+music production program that allows improvisation and the manipulation of audio elements in real time (see Figure 5.8). One of its more unique

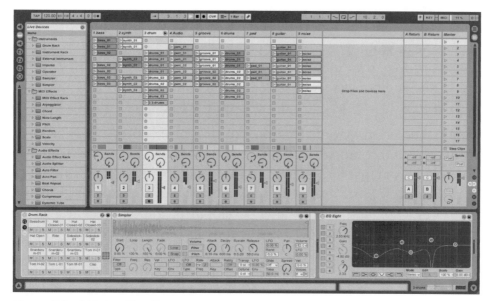

Figure 5.8 Ableton Live 6.

features is that it has what Ableton calls the *Elastic Audio Engine*. The Elastic Audio Engine allows you to treat audio with a fixed tempo as if it were an elastic band, hence the name. You can stretch the audio to follow the tempo of your project, regardless of what the audio's original tempo was.

Imagine that you're working on a composition for a client in your preferred sequencing program. You're almost finished, but you feel that the chorus needs a little something extra. You know that you have an audio loop in your library that would fit perfectly. So, you proceed to import the audio loop into your existing audio project. You place it in the chorus and begin playback. As the cursor approaches the newly supplemented part, you anticipate how the loop will harmoniously accentuate the other audible instruments in the mix. When the moment of cursor impact arrives, you shriek in horror because the loop you've imported is completely out of sync with the rest of the song.

This is where Live's Elastic Audio Engine comes in handy. At this point, you can launch Live to run alongside your host sequencer. This will automatically initialize ReWire communication between the two programs, allowing them to sync tempo and transport functions as if they were one application. Now you can import this "perfect loop" to where the chorus would start in the timeline of Live's arrangement window and begin playback. This time, when the cursor hits the chorus, the audio loop plays perfectly in time from Live as the rest of the audio plays from your sequencer. In actuality, the process I just described takes about half as long to execute as it did to read.

Don't be deceived by organization. Ableton Live is perfectly capable of producing a professional-sounding audio recording from start to finish. The only reason that I've referred to Live as a *tool* rather than as a *multitrack sequencer* is because 1) it can be a quick way to flesh out ideas and create quick compositions for later development, and 2) it can be a *highly* effective timesaver as a ReWire slave to your host sequencer.

For more information on Ableton Live, please visit www.ableton.com.

Utilities

No matter what type of post-production projects you encounter, it will always work in your favor to save time where you can. Spending hours renaming files to accommodate the needs of a particular project or searching your entire 300-GB hard drive to locate a single sound is hardly productive when the same task can be carried out in moments with the click of a mouse. There are a vast number of utilities available that may not even have been developed for digital audio, but that will help you carry out tedious busywork with the greatest of ease. I suggest that, at the very least, you employ a file management program and batch processing utility.

File management programs can help organize your sound files by making them searchable. They'll also allow you to enter notes about the file, classify it with different descriptors, and then search for them using those descriptors. This is an extremely efficient way to keep your sound files organized so that you can easily locate them later. File management may not seem important right now, especially if you're just starting your project studio, but wait until you're too busy to sleep. You'll appreciate it much more!

One of the most useful utilities in my studio is a batch renaming program I downloaded for free. There have been occasions when a client has wanted every single file to have an underscore in place of a space or to have the date, project name, or number at the beginning or end of every file name. Some clients require the file names to be formatted in a *very* specific manner because of the way they intend to use them. And in some cases, clients don't even realize it until the project is halfway finished! A batch renaming utility makes quick work of such a task and allows you to spend the time you saved on more lucrative endeavors.

Exploring Mixer Functions

As mentioned earlier, every software sequencer has its own personality. They all look different, and one may have a few features that another doesn't. However, in order for the concepts of digital audio to be understood, basic functionality for all software sequencers has been standardized. So whether you're switching platforms or entering digital audio from an analog background, the mixer in your software sequencer should look pretty familiar.

In this section, I'll be discussing the common features that all typical software mixers have and what they're for. If you've got a reasonable amount of experience with software sequencers, you can probably skip this section, but for those who are new to the world of DAWs, this section will serve as a primer in basic mixer functionality and will set you up for Chapter 8, "Mixing Techniques," later in the book. Before you move on, please take a moment to examine the software channel strip shown in Figure 5.9.

The section of your software mixer in which *most* activity will take place is the channel strip. When you create a new track in a project, a channel strip will automatically be generated for it. Every button, fader, and indicator on the track's channel strip will either directly affect the track or provide information about the state of the track wherever the cursor is located in the timeline.

Here are the basic features you will find on almost every channel strip in every software mixer:

■ **Level fader.** The level fader controls the volume of the track. This should *not* be mistaken for the volume of the individual audio events on the track itself. A new track's fader level will default at

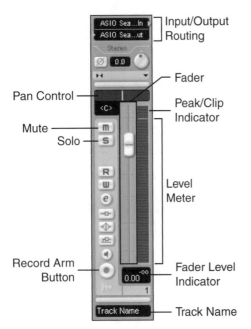

Figure 5.9 A standard software mixer channel strip.

−0 dB, or zero decibels, and is relative to the volume of the audio on the track, which means that just because the level fader is set to −0 dB, that doesn't mean that the audio on the track is as loud as it can be without distorting.

- **Fader level indicator.** The fader level indicator is a feedback field that is typically located in a small window just below the fader. It provides feedback as to the current position of the level fader. The fader level indicator expresses decibel levels as integers. For example, −1.5 equals one and a half decibels below 0 dB.

- **Level meter.** The level meter is a graphical representation of the audio level. It is typically shown as a narrow window to the right of the level fader. Inside the window is a column of bars that increases in height the louder the audio signal gets. If the track is a mono track, there will be a single column in the window. If it's stereo track, there will be two columns that represent the left and right channels. The color-coding that is used to represent the loudness of an audio signal may vary from sequencer to sequencer. Sometimes, the color will transition from a light blue, indicating a quiet audio signal, to a bright green/yellow, indicating an acceptably loud audio level. But the color red *always* means that the audio signal is clipping, or that the level is so loud that it's in danger of distorting.

- **Peak/clip indicator.** The peak indicator lets you know when the audio level is clipping. It lights up red when the software "thinks" the audio is distorting. I say "thinks" because the software is not always right. Remember, *you* are the brains of this operation. If you don't hear distortion, there probably isn't any, but until your ears are trained, you can use the peak/clip indicator as a guide. You can reset the peak indicator by clicking on it. You can then bring the level fader down until the peak/clip indicator is no longer triggered during playback.

- **Channel/track name.** Every software sequencer has a field in the channel strip to enter the name of the track. It is *usually* located at the bottom of the channel strip and is linked to the track name shown in the arrangement view. If you change one name, you change them both. I cannot stress enough how important track organization is. When you get into projects that have 40-plus tracks and you have to change the volume of one of the keyboards, will you remember whether it was on track number 27, 9, or 32? Or was it track 15?

- **Mute.** Typically signified by the letter M directly on the button, the mute function does exactly what it promises—it mutes the track so that it cannot be heard during playback. This is useful when you want to audition a part of a project with certain elements removed from the mix. You can also use mute to find a problematic needle in a haystack. Suppose you're listening to the playback of your mix and you hear a pop or a hiss, but you're not sure where it came from. You can isolate the track on which the problem exists by systematically muting tracks until you find the culprit. Sometimes, if I am unsure whether a track is loud enough, I'll mute it to see whether I can hear an audible difference between when it's muted and when it's not. This can help your ears discern the role that the track actually plays in the mix. And I bet you were wondering why I needed a whole paragraph to explain the mute function.

- **Solo.** Always marked with a letter S, the solo button allows you to isolate a track during playback. You can also solo a selected number of tracks to hear back an instrument group without the rest of the audio in the project. If you want to hear the lead vocal track apart from the rest of the mix, it's much more efficient to solo just the lead vocal than it is to mute every track *except* the lead vocal. Like the mute button, the solo button can assist in identifying problems such as frequency clashes or phasing between two (or more) audio sources.

- **Pan control.** The pan control is generally located at the top of the channel strip. It is used to control how far left or right the audio on the track is positioned in the stereo field. The pan control on a new track typically defaults to dead center in the mix, meaning that the audio on the track will play back in both speakers at equal volume levels. If you take the same audio track and move the pan control to the left, you will be able to hear the audio move with it because it will become more audibly prominent in the left speaker than in the right. Keep in mind that the pan control doesn't usually change the volume of the audio; it just changes its position on a lateral left-to-right plane. Using the pan control to move certain audio elements to the left or right will help you develop a stereo image or a widened perspective in your mix. It can also help eliminate clashing elements of a mix by allowing you to "move" them out of the way of one another. Figure 5.10 shows what a well-balanced mix might look like when different audio elements have been panned to create a stereo image.

- **Record arm button.** The record arm button uses the universally recognized symbol of a single red dot to identify itself on the channel strip of a DAW software program. You may notice that the same red dot is used to identify the record function button on the main transport. Although these buttons are connected, they are not the same. The record function button on the transport actually begins capturing audio or data when it is activated. The record arm button on a track lets the software know that when the record function button is activated, it should capture audio or data only to the tracks on which the record arm has been enabled.

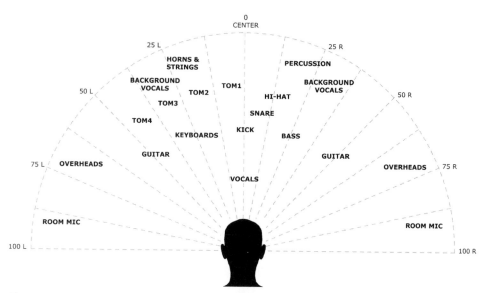

Figure 5.10 The left and right positions of audio elements across the stereo field.

■ **Input/output routing.** The channel strip also gives you access to routing options for the track. The routing options are usually accessed through two drop-down menus that provide the available choices for the track's inputs and outputs. It can be a real timesaver to set up the typical input and output configurations you know you'll use for the majority of your projects and save them as a template project in your software sequencer. That way, when you begin a new project, you can just open the template and get right to work.

That covers the basic features you will find on any software mixer. There are a few other features that are common to all sequencers, but don't necessarily reside on all software channel strips, such as input monitoring, phase switch, trim level control, read/write automation, and bypass buttons. If your channel strip has any of these features, you can refer to the software manual for specific information about them.

Plug-Ins

Plug-ins (a.k.a. *plugs*) are your friends. Each one is a tool that will help you get a little closer to that golden sound you're working to achieve in your productions. There are hundreds of quality effect plug-ins available for compression, reverb, delay, noise reduction, equalization, effects, and more. Although two reverb plug-ins may have the same purpose —applying reverb to an audio signal—they may not execute the process in the same way, which will ultimately make a difference in the way the post-processed audio will sound.

It's true. Most software sequencing programs have an equalizer built into the channel strip and come with a few plug-ins for treating audio with compression or reverb. You might be thinking, "If my software already has these features, why do I need external plug-ins?" If the built-in EQs, compressors, and reverbs are delivering the desired result on everything you treat with them, and you don't see any real need for improvement, then maybe you don't need any more plug-ins. But in reality, this is probably not the case. Although there is nothing wrong with the stock plug-ins that ship with your software sequencer, you may discover that a third-party plug-in is a better tool for a particular job.

Third-party plug-ins can offer a lot to the mix and the mixer. Different plug-ins treat different input signals in different ways, which gives them their own characteristics, or "color." Some plug-ins are revered *because* they color sound. And some are designed to emulate vintage hardware processors, mimicking the interface aesthetic, unique tonal characteristics, and everything else. On the flipside, the antithesis of color is when a plug-in is considered to sound transparent. When we say that a plug-in is *transparent,* it means that when we use it to affect an audio signal, it produces an accurate-sounding result without adding any additional coloration or tonal characteristics.

A great way to discover what third-party plug-ins will work best for the applications in your mixes is to put different plug-ins to the test in a "Pepsi Challenge." Try several different plug-ins. Download demos and samples, read magazines, visit audio forums, do some research, and hold a listening preference shoot-out with your ears. Use the plug-in's presets to get familiar with common settings and develop reference points for different types of instruments and applications.

Quite honestly, you'll probably be able to find a purpose for every processing plug-in that you try. Some of the plug-ins will be used frequently. Others may only be employed a handful of times because they'll do the trick for very specific scenarios. Some audio production engineers use only a specific set of plug-ins that they feel work for everything, and others collect every plug-in available just so they have them if they ever need them.

A few plug-in manufacturers are worth mentioning, such as Waves, Universal Audio, Unique Recording Software, and McDSP. They can be pricey, but if you're running a serious production studio, they just might be worth the money to you. No matter which plug-ins you choose, if you don't understand them inside out, they won't be worth anything to you. So invest some time in really getting to know your tools.

Because this is a section on tools used for software mixing, I'll present different types of processing plug-ins that are commonly used in audio production, and I'll review common control functions and average uses for each. In Chapter 6, "Different Types of Mixing," we'll discuss basic principles, some not-so-basic principles, and practical applications that will help you use these tools more effectively.

Plug-In Formats

All right, before we move on, I'd like to briefly discuss plug-in formats. A *plug-in* is a computer program or software module that communicates with a host program—in this case, your digital audio software—to grant access to its functionality and features. These two programs must speak the same language in order to communicate. This language is the plug-in format. Originally, digital audio software developers created their own plug-in formats for what I imagine to be one of the same reasons that you can't play a PlayStation game on an Xbox.

Ahem . . . ask yourself if this has ever happened to you. You're reading an article of an interview with a famous mixing engineer, and he drops the name of a plug-in that he uses all the time in his studio. Now you're curious. You go to the Internet and look up the plug-in manufacturer's website to see whether you can download a trial version to check it out. And as you read, your curiosity turns to confusion, then sadness, and finally anger because this golden plug-in is only offered in two formats—neither of which your software is compatible with.

Steinberg created Virtual Studio Technology (VST), Microsoft is behind DirectX, and Digidesign developed RTAS and TDM. These days, most digital audio software programs can use multiple formats, and most effect plug-ins are offered in all of these popular formats, so compatibility with new plug-ins isn't *that* big of an issue in most cases. However, it's good to know that DirectX is PC-only, Audio Unit is Mac-only, and VST can be used on both. RTAS and TDM can be used on both Mac and PC as well, but for Pro Tools *only*. The sequencing software you choose will most likely support one or more of these formats.

Another plug-in-related tool is called a *wrapper*. Usually developed by a third-party, wrappers are basically plug-in format converters that allow you to access plug-in formats with which your host software isn't natively compatible. For example, Pro Tools doesn't support VST plug-ins, but a VST to RTAS wrapper could allow you to access a VST plug-in in Pro Tools.

Wrappers were born of necessity. Before DAW software could use multiple plug-in formats, and effects and instruments were offered in only a limited number of popular formats, a wrapper was a great way to use a "must have" plug-in without having to change software platforms. I've seen wrappers work flawlessly on some systems, but crash repeatedly on others. They are not supported by the manufacturers of the plug-ins you're using them on, so if you *do* encounter a problem, you probably won't be able to get any help from the plug-in manufacturer. FXpansion offers two types of wrappers—VST to RTAS and VST to AU. Even though there is a great deal of cross-compatibility between plug-ins and digital audio software applications, a demand for wrappers still exists because Logic Pro and Pro Tools still don't support VST plug-ins.

Equalizers

Equalization (EQ) is generally used to treat the individual audio sources in a mix so that the appropriate frequencies of particular instruments and audio elements are either increased or reduced to support their position in the overall frequency spectrum of the mix. If you're mastering, you'll use EQ after the mix is complete to increase or reduce frequencies that may be lacking or too prevalent in the final mix. An important distinction to make is that when you're applying an EQ in mastering, you're trying to make the final stereo mix as pleasing to the ear as possible by balancing the levels between relative frequencies. When you're using EQ for mixing, you're affecting only *one* audio element in an effort to avoid frequency conflict with other audio elements in the mix. Just like any other type of processing, keep your wits about you. Only reduce or add what you need to. And unless you're going for an inorganic sound, try to keep everything sounding as natural as possible.

There are two main types of equalizers that you might find yourself using in audio production—a *graphic equalizer* and the more common *parametric equalizer*. A graphic equalizer allows you to adjust the addition or reduction of fixed frequencies only. Think of a graphic equalizer like the bass and treble on your home stereo. The EQ controls are labeled as *Bass* and *Treble*. When you turn the bass up, you perceive that the music booms with low end. When you turn the treble up, you can hear that the vocals, guitars, and other instruments that exist in the higher end of the frequency spectrum become clearer (or, when reduced, muddy). You know that the typical bass boost occurs at about 90 to 100 Hz because that's where the boom lives. With a graphic EQ, this frequency is fixed, so even if you wanted to, you couldn't change what frequency the bass boost is actually affecting.

A parametric equalizer is much more flexible than a graphic equalizer is. It not only allows you to adjust bass and treble, but you usually also have control over two additional bands of frequency: low-midrange and high-midrange. Already, you've got more options for shaping the EQ curve... but wait! There's more! Parametric EQs also allow you to adjust the frequency that each band affects. So if you want your bass boost to happen at between 120 and 130 Hz for some reason, you can adjust the frequency range that the bass band of your parametric EQ will affect.

Different EQs from different software companies really can be just that "different." On a track-by-track, source-by-source basis, one EQ may work great on drums, but sound brittle and harsh on vocals. So try a lot of different EQ plug-ins. You'll probably be able to find a use for every single one down the line. Personally, I prefer EQs that do not use visual aids for referencing the frequency spectrum. I like to listen and turn virtual knobs, like those of an analog mixer, and change the settings until I *hear* the sound improve. Sometimes if I'm stuck in my basic channel strip EQ, my ears may be fooled by the graphic representation of the stock equalizer. I may fool myself into thinking I'm altering a signal too much or not enough just by seeing the visuals. Conversely, I may be using the visuals of another EQ in order to remember the shape of the kick drum's equalization "starting point" from a few weeks ago. It's really a case-by-case basis, and the third-party EQs definitely can add something unique to the mix.

Hearing versus Seeing Because digital audio gives you the ability to see EQ as a graphically represented curve, all too often you can allow yourself to forget that it's more important to hear how the EQ is affecting the audio than it is to see it. What's worse is that you can become dependent on the way an EQ curve "looks."

If you're new to digital audio, using visually represented EQ is a good idea until you get more familiar with the way it all works and sounds. But don't let your eyes do the job that your ears should be doing. I highly recommend that at some point, you become well acquainted with an EQ that forces you to rely solely on your ears.

Figure 5.11 shows an EQ plug-in with a visual interface, and Figure 5.12 shows an example of an EQ that will force you to exercise your ears.

We'll get pretty in depth about frequency fundamentals and understanding EQ in the next chapter, but here is a glossary of sorts for common controls and terms that you will encounter when working with EQ plug-ins:

- **Frequency bands.** All equalizers divide the frequency spectrum into *bands,* or ranges of frequency. You will typically be provided with low, low-mid, high-mid, and high frequency bands as reference points for adjustment.

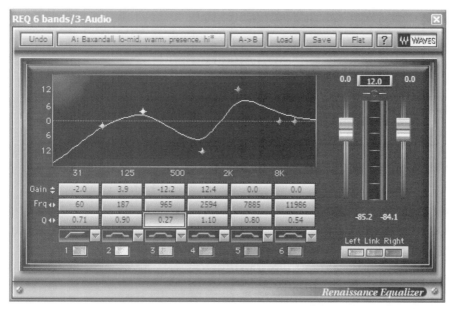

Figure 5.11 A visual EQ.

Figure 5.12 A not-so-visual EQ.

- **Q or width.** *Q*, sometimes referred to as a *width*, allows you to reduce or expand the range that a frequency band affects. If you need to apply EQ to only 90 to 100 Hz, you could adjust the Q of the low-frequency band so that it affects only the frequencies between 90 and 100 Hz, and nothing else. This gives you more specific control over smaller ranges of frequency.

- **Gain.** You should be very familiar with the concept of *gain* by now. The Gain control on an EQ band allows you to increase or decrease the level of the frequencies being affected by the corresponding band. This value is expressed in decibels using positive and negative numbers.

■ **Filters.** *Filters* are the method by which the EQ is affected. Filters have different shapes that either repress or allow only certain frequencies to pass. There are four main types of filters: high-pass, low-pass, band-pass, and notch. High-pass filters reduce bass frequencies and allow the frequencies in the upper end of the spectrum to pass unaffected. Low-pass filters do the opposite by reducing high frequencies and leaving the low end untouched. A band-pass filter allows a specific range of frequencies to sound while repressing all others. And a notch filter allows for the adjustment of a very narrow range of frequencies without affecting those outside of the specified range. Figure 5.13 shows an example of these different equalization filters.

■ **Bell.** A *bell* refers to a shape used to affect frequency on an equalizer. It's defined as an EQ that has a peak in its response. If you're looking at an equalizer plug-in with a graphic representation of frequency, it would be a lone bump in the EQ curve. The range

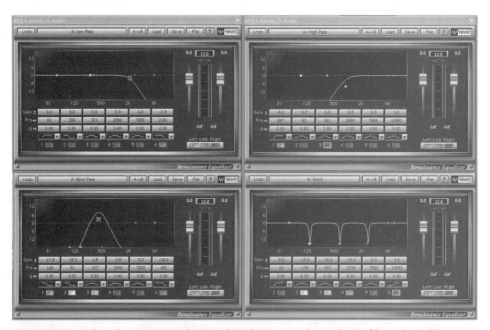

Figure 5.13 What low-pass, high-pass, band-pass, and notch EQ filters look like.

Figure 5.14 An EQ curve with a low shelf and a bell in the high midrange.

of frequency that the bell shape affects is narrowed or widened by the Q value within the relative frequency band.

■ **Shelf.** A *shelf* is another EQ shape that is used on either the high end or the low end of the frequency spectrum. A shelf will affect from the value of the set frequency all the way to the extreme end of the range. For example, a high shelf with a value of 10,000 kHz and a +2-dB gain increase would increase the gain of the frequencies between 10,000 kHz and 20,000 kHz by +2 dB. Figure 5.14 shows an EQ curve with a bell in the high-mids and a low shelf.

Dynamics

Compressors and limiters are the most common types of plug-ins used to control audio dynamics. They can effectively "sculpt" the varying levels of an audio signal and make the relative volume more even and under control. A *compressor* reduces the dynamic range of the signal, making softer sounds louder, louder sounds softer, or a combination of the two. A *limiter* makes sure that the signal never exceeds the user-defined output level, which avoids clipping even after other plug-in devices have been added to the signal chain. The use of this "dynamic duo" will contribute greatly to the professional quality of your recordings.

Common control features for dynamics plugs include:

- **Threshold.** *Threshold* determines at what decibel level the compressor takes effect over the audio signal. Signal levels that are above the user-defined threshold are affected by the compressor, but signals below are not affected.

- **Ratio.** *Ratio* sets the amount of gain reduction that will be applied to signals that are above the threshold level. This value is expressed as *x:y*. So if the ratio is set to 5:1, it means that for every 5 dB the input signal is increased, the output signal will increase by only 1 dB. Subsequently, if the input signal is increased by 10 dB, the output signal will increase by 2 dB.

- **Attack.** *Attack* determines how quickly the compressor will respond to the audio signals above the threshold. This value is typically expressed in milliseconds. A long attack allows more of the original signal to sound before the compressor affects it, but an attack of only a few milliseconds will be compressed almost immediately.

- **Release.** When the signal drops below the threshold level, the *release* is used to set how quickly it returns to its original gain level. This value is also expressed in milliseconds.

- **Makeup gain.** When you compress an audio signal, some level will be lost. *Makeup gain* is used to increase the gain of the output signal to compensate for the volume loss.

- **Soft clip.** *Soft clip* is basically a compressor's built-in limiter. When activated, it "softly" begins limiting the audio signal when it exceeds about −6 dB. Soft clip is a feature found on many compressors, but not all of them.

- **Classic/Complex.** The *Classic/Complex button* on a compressor toggles between two modes (Classic mode and Complex mode) that have different attack and release settings. Classic mode has fixed attack and release times. Complex mode intelligently adapts the attack and release times to the actual audio signal. The Classic/Complex mode is a feature that is commonly found on multi-band compressors used in mastering. While this feature exists, it is not found on *all* compressors.

- **Soft/hard knee.** *Soft knee* and *hard knee* refer to how quickly the signal transitions from no gain reduction to full gain reduction. Basic compressors normally use hard-knee compression, meaning that the compressor will not affect an audio signal until it has reached the set threshold level. This transition can sound abrupt to a listener, but it is useful for when you want to compress a signal for effect. Hard-knee compression is more susceptible to "pumping," or unnaturally affecting, an audio signal. When used deliberately, it can provide perceived loudness to the signal.

  Activating soft knee causes the compressor's ratio to increase gradually until it reaches the threshold level. Once it reaches the threshold level, the full user-defined compression ratio is applied to the signal. This smooths out the transition from zero gain reduction to full ratio, making it less obvious to the listener.

Make note of where the aforementioned features are located on the basic compressor in Figure 5.15 and the multi-band compressor shown in Figure 5.16.

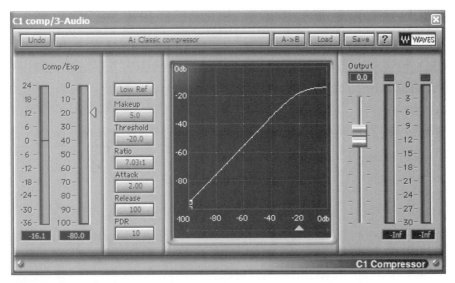

Figure 5.15 A basic compressor.

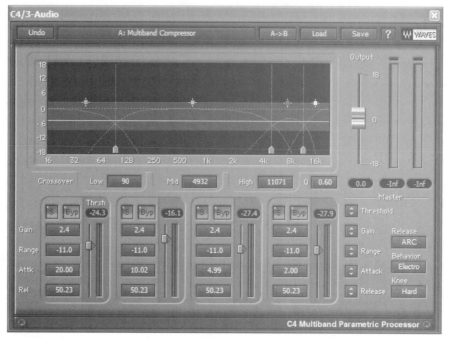

Figure 5.16 A multi-band compressor.

Reverb

Reverb plug-ins supply space, distance, and perspective to a mix. Almost all reverbs come from a plug-in of some kind these days. A truly superb reverb requires a serious sound-processing engine that often isn't present in the audio engine of a standard software sequencer. Even reverb plug-ins—especially ones with extensive preset and impulse response libraries—can be extremely taxing on system resources. Like everything else, reverb can be used as a tool or abused as an effect. But the best post-audio engineers use these plugs to create a spatial environment in a mix. Often, this effect, like compression, requires a light touch. When you've used it appropriately, people may not be able to perceive that it's there at all.

Basic reverbs emulate common spaces, such as bathrooms, plates, churches, or snare rooms. Convolution reverbs are a bit more complex in that they use scientifically measured impulse responses from real acoustic environments (concert halls, cathedrals, and so on) to produce accurate-sounding, detailed reverb. As the post-audio engineer, you may need to decide what kind of space the music or instruments live in and use reverb to place them in their natural habitat.

Common control features on reverb plugs include:

- **Room size.** *Room size* defines how big the simulated room environment is. To create a drastic spatial effect, you would use a large room. To give something a more intimate, up close and personal sound, a small room would be appropriate.

- **Reverb time.** *Reverb time* determines how long the reverb will resonate. In a real-world scenario, this would be affected by how reflective the walls in the room are. Know that the longer the reverb time, the more difficult it will be to keep the reverb under control in the mix. This parameter, in combination with reverb size, damping, and pre-delay, will define the properties of the virtual room.

- **Pre-delay.** *Pre-delay* is how far the sound source is from the walls of the virtual room. It's measured in milliseconds by how long it takes for the audio signal to travel from its source, bounce off the wall, and reverberate in your virtual environment. If the pre-delay value is set to 2 ms, it will be two milliseconds before the first reflections are heard. Pre-delay is the parameter that provides depth and is a big part of what keeps reverb algorithms sounding natural.

- **Damping.** *Damping* can be used to create diffusion, or the level of sound absorption in a virtual environment, by simulating room objects or wall coverings that affect sound reflections. This is effective when you are trying to realistically simulate a particular type of space for dialogue and/or sound effects to live in.

- **Mix.** The *mix level* controls the balance between the clean signal and the effect. Once you've dialed in the "perfect" reverb settings, use the mix control to add the appropriate amount of the effect to the dry signal so that the desired effect is achieved in the mix.

Figure 5.17 shows an example of a basic reverb, and Figure 5.18 shows a more complex convolution reverb.

Figure 5.17 A basic reverb plug-in.

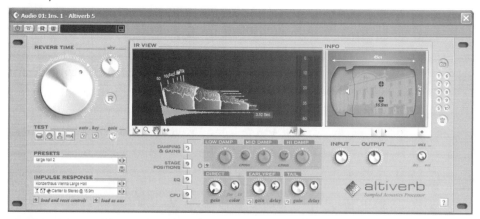

Figure 5.18 A convolution reverb plug-in.

Other Plug-Ins

So many plug-ins, so little time. EQ, dynamics, and reverb are just the basics and the most common types of processing used in the mixing stage. But there are many, *many* different types of plug-ins that you can employ for various uses.

There are plug-ins that you can use as tools to achieve pitch, timing correction, and noise reduction. Distortion plug-ins can do more than just make things sound nasty and dirty. By using a type of gain to overdrive a signal, you can enhance the harmonic richness, adding color and achieving a kind of analog, almost vintage-sounding warmth. Sometimes, if I'm working on a rock mix, and the vocal is sticking out because it's too clean or sterile sounding, I'll duplicate the vocal track and insert a distortion plug-in on top of it. Once I dial in a distortion that I like the sound of, I slowly blend it in with the clean vocal until it sounds just right in the mix.

Tube emulators are another type of dynamic effect that can add low-level distortion and create warmth for an audio signal. You can use de-essing plug-ins to control dynamics by taking the edge off of harsh consonants. You can use delays (with a light touch) to spread a vocal across the stereo field with subtle stereo delays, thus enhancing the stereo image and drawing more attention to the vocal in the mix. And then there is an entire array of effects that you can use more creatively and aggressively as effects rather than tools—some of which we've already discussed *as* tools.

You can use equalization filters for more than just creating frequency separation between different audio signals. You can make signals sound as if they were just recorded from an AM radio by using a high-pass filter where the frequency is drastically reduced, starting in the upper midrange. You can use delay aggressively to create ear candy by reinforcing an audio event with spatial repetition. Occasionally, I'll apply a delay to a snare-drum track using equal volume and note values so that the hits double up and it sounds as if it was played twice as many times as it actually was. A chorus effect adds short delays to the original audio signal, and then modulates the pitch of the delayed signals to create a doubling effect, adding dimension and making the signal seem wider.

You'll be amazed by what you can accomplish with a few good effect plug-ins. You never know what will work for a particular application. Don't be afraid to get creative when using effects—for effect or as tools. Try out a lot of different plug-ins. Find out what you prefer to use and why. You can save a lot of time if you can identify what effect will work so you can go directly to the one you know and trust.

So now that we've discussed software sequencers, different plug-ins that are commonly used in mixing, and the functions of a software mixer, it's time to get right down to it.

6 Different Types of Mixing

Before mixing any project, there are a couple of questions you want to ask yourself. First, what should you be aiming for? We briefly discussed how important it is to have a good idea about what the client is trying to express with his or her music. Although you have to work with what you're given, different types of music convey different ideas and feelings. As mixing and post-production engineers, we can help reinforce these ideas by producing an appropriate mix. Next, you must consider what is appropriate for the instrumentation. A cinematic piece that uses mostly orchestral instruments will obviously be mixed differently than a rock project would. Are you aiming for realism or effect?

Orchestral and Symphonic Mixing

When mixing an orchestral piece, you are most likely going for realism. If you're creating or mixing a symphonic piece in your project studio, it is most likely a virtual orchestra. Not all virtual orchestras are created equal, and there are many things to consider when it comes to making a virtual orchestra sound realistic.

Reverb types should be appropriate for the piece. A big reverb would not work well on a string quartet, and a small room would not be appropriate for an 80-piece orchestra. Also, you'll want to use the same reverb room type for each section or instrument. Think of how strange an orchestral piece might sound if the French horns were in a nice concert hall, but the strings were in a bathroom…. This is an extreme and completely unrealistic example, but it's helpful to understand the concept of relative space in a mix. Once you've chosen an appropriate reverb type, just use varying mix levels of it to simulate proximity. Spatially, the percussion and bass instruments are on the outskirts of the orchestra, while the instruments that voice higher notes are closer to the conductor. You may want to keep this in mind when applying reverb. Also, many virtual orchestra instruments have reverb or ambience effects built right into the application. Using the provided reverbs in these instruments will take some of the guesswork out of selecting the *right* reverb, but you still have the choice to use a third-party reverb if you wish.

If you're going to use it at all, go easy on compression with symphonic music. Orchestral music is naturally very dynamic. Too much or inappropriate compression can blur the distinction between naturally soft and loud passages, as well as mask the subtle nuances of the instruments. You may actually do a disservice to the composition as a whole by using compression at all. Trust your ears on this one. If it sounds better without any compression whatsoever, then don't use any.

Panning is kind of up in the air for mixing an orchestral piece. Some would say that you want to be sure each instrument section is panned appropriately for where it would exist, as if you were standing in front of a real orchestra. But know that there are many, many different ways that an orchestra can be arranged. A real orchestra might be laid out much like one shown in Figure 6.1.

Unfortunately, when used too literally, this method doesn't really work in a full-spectrum stereo field. Imagine sitting in a large movie

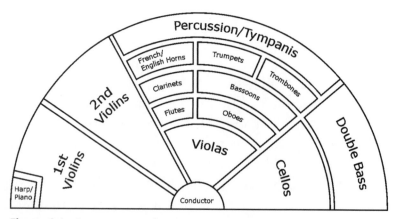

Figure 6.1 A common orchestra stage setup.

theatre watching an epic masterpiece that has a very dynamic orchestral score. If the basses are panned hard right, as they might be in a real orchestra, the people sitting on the left side of the theatre may not be able to hear them very well—or at all. What's worse is that the effect will be lost altogether.

Remember that one of the goals in mixing is to achieve a well-balanced mix, no matter what the style of music. One way to do this for a symphonic mix is to narrow your stereo field. A regular stereo field allows you to pan an audio signal anywhere between the extreme panning positions of 100 Left and 100 Right. By restricting the stereo field of a symphonic piece to something more like 45 Left and 45 Right, you will be able to maintain the relative positions of the instruments and sections, while still providing a balanced mix to the listener, no matter where he or she is sitting in the theatre. So go ahead and pan your orchestra realistically, but use a limited stereo field. Classical music recordings often rely almost solely on a stereo mic configuration that is positioned around the conductor stage. This mic configuration picks up the entire orchestra and the room ambiances as a whole, so even instrument sections that are sitting hard left or right will be all over the mix due to room reverberation. Understand that unless a signal is panned *hard* left or right, some of the signal will exist in both the left and right channels, but in varying degrees. This can be illustrated if you solo an audio signal and slowly pan it to the left (or right). The farther you pan a signal to favor any one channel, the less of it you will hear in the opposite channel…but it *is* still there.

Here are a couple of things to remember:

- First, instruments that produce higher notes should probably be panned closer to the center because they will stand out of the mix if they are panned too far to the left or right.

- Second, any solo instrument that plays a melodic phrase should also be panned closer to the center, even if its native instrument section is panned farther away from center. This will draw more attention to the solo instrument and keep it from seeming out of place, while making it audible to the entire audience.

Applying some of these ideas to your symphonic mix should help you get closer to the orchestral mixing Zen you're working toward.

Mixing Bands

This is where all your hard work as a lifelong music listener will finally pay off. This is where the answer to the question "What are we going for?" becomes *really* important. When you know what your client wants, do your homework. Listen to different albums that sound the way your client wants his or her project to sound and take note of what it is about the mixes that makes them sound that way. Pay attention to the way certain elements are panned or how much reverb is on the snare and lead vocal. Take some notes. When you're ready, try some of what you heard on your client's mix. Things such as reverb, compression, and EQ will be used to shape the source material into a controlled yet natural representation of the performance.

Mixing a band is somewhat similar to mixing an orchestral piece in that you are trying to create a realistic audio representation of a band as if you were seeing it live on stage. The primary center elements are drums and lead vocals. Bass is typically slightly left or right of center, guitars are doubled on the left and right, keyboards can be panned wherever they sound appropriate and don't compete with other instruments that occupy the same frequencies, and background vocals are usually off to the left or right of center. This is typical, but again, there are many different ways for a band to be arranged.

When it comes to reverb, know that no matter how "dry" something sounds on a commercial recording, it almost always has *some* reverb applied to it. Reverb provides space for the music to exist. Ever notice how Def Leppard's "Pour Some Sugar on Me" sounds as if it's on a big stage in a huge stadium, even though the studio album was obviously *not* recorded that way? If your band project is going for a big '80s sound with a lot of space, you're going to use bigger reverb rooms. If it's an acoustic project, you probably want to use a smaller, more intimate-sounding reverb.

Reverb can be used to blend obtrusive elements into a mix and also to create perspective. As an example, other than listening to what each vocal is singing, how might you make the distinction between a background vocal and a lead vocal in a mix? If you imagine a band on a stage, where would a background vocalist stand in relation to the lead singer? A background vocal will usually be panned left or right of center and will be at a lower volume so that it doesn't fight the lead for attention. It will typically also have more reverb applied to it than the lead vocal, in order to provide the perspective that it is farther away from the lead, or more in the background. (Hence, why they're called "background vocals.")

People often underestimate compression. Virtually everything in a band mix gets compressed. Distorted guitars, acoustic guitars, bass, drums, and vocals all get varying levels of compression. These days, everything in pop or rock music is loud—compression can help even out a performance by making the extreme loud and soft parts more equal in volume, but in a natural way, without losing the subtle tonal characteristics. If the individual tracks are more even, they will be easier to sculpt into an even-sounding mix. Compression can make whispering the same volume as screaming, so that it doesn't get lost in the mix but it still sounds like whispering.

Because not everyone can play an instrument with perfect consistency from note to note, guitars and bass are compressed to keep them under control so that, again, notes don't get lost and so the listener isn't surprised by any obvious volume inconsistencies from note to note. Drums are often compressed for punch, which allows them to cut through the mix and be heard consistently throughout the track.

Now that I have cited all these uses for the miracle of compression, heed this warning: Be mindful with compression. Make tasteful decisions in how much compression is applied to anything. If you use compression correctly, the listener won't be sure that you've used it at all. And if you use it incorrectly, you risk the sonic integrity of elements within the mix, or even the mix as a whole.

Equalization is typically used to provide frequency separation in a rock mix. With so many instruments competing for the same frequencies—such as bass guitar and kick drum for low end, or multiple guitars and vocals fighting for mid range—a mix can become sonically cluttered if you don't use EQ to carve out a place for each instrument to exist and do your best to eliminate the competition.

You'll find that every instrument has its role and inherent frequency in a mix. While no two instruments are alike, bass guitars and kick drums always produce a lot of low end, guitars and vocals always produce a lot of mid range, and so on. When you first start working with EQ, it's important to understand how boosting or cutting certain frequencies will affect a type of instrument. You might want to pull a solo guitar or vocal into your sequencing software and insert an EQ plug-in. Activate the high mid band of your EQ, narrow the Q setting, and then turn up the gain. Figure 6.2 shows what this will look like.

Now begin playback and listen as you adjust the frequency of the EQ band in real time. As the EQ boost you just applied moves across the frequency spectrum, notice how the original audio is affected. This is a great way to get familiar with the way EQ affects different types of instruments and audio signals. I suggest that you start working with EQ presets or create your own presets that will work for vocals, guitars, bass, and so on, and then tailor them for each mix. You'll find that when instruments are properly and appropriately equalized, the entire mix will have much more clarity.

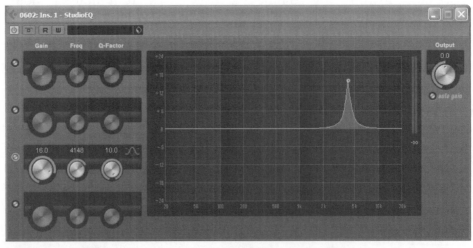

Figure 6.2 An EQ with a narrow Q setting.

Electronic Music

I'm going to keep this short because *most* electronic composers will not look to an outside source for post-production. When it comes to mixing, electronic music is a bit of a different animal. Like a guitar player uses a guitar as an instrument to create music, an electronic musician uses computers and synthesized elements as instruments to create music. The process of creating electronic music is as much of an art as the music itself. Often, electronic music is created by one or two individuals who meticulously craft sounds into a complete composition. Post-production is part of that creation process. So unless you are an electronic composer, the type of post-production work you might do for an electronic composition will probably be limited to mastering, at best.

While the same underlying goal of a balanced mix exists, elements within the composition are often mixed for effect. Electronic music is somewhat of a more flexible playing field because there are no set rules. How do you mix an electronic song for realism? You just don't. Even organic elements, such as strings, vocals, or drums, can be placed pretty much anywhere across the stereo field as long as different elements don't clash sonically and the end result is perceived as a pleasant and well-balanced listening experience.

Sound Effects

Sound effects (or *Foley*) are most commonly used in post-production for movies, television shows, and video games. For these purposes, again, the target should be realism. Even with unrealistic sounds such as laser fire or alien dialogue, certain unchangeable sonic properties, such as proximity and environment, can help make them seem more realistic. What size (environment) is the room in which the laser was fired? From what direction was it fired (proximity)? Placement (panning) and space (reverb) are the two primary considerations for mixing sound effects.

It's important to remember that all sounds exist within a spatial environment. Our ears are not limited to hearing just a sound itself, but also all the detailed characteristics of the sound. If you hear a car backfire, even if you don't see the actual vehicle, you can tell from what direction it came and whether it was nearby or off in the distance. If you were standing on the sidewalk to the right of the road, facing the street, and the car was driving past you as it backfired, the sound of the backfire might be panned from the left to the right. It would probably also be quite loud. If it backfired while driving on the rim of the Grand Canyon, it would have a monstrous echo that you could simulate with a huge reverb and decaying delays. Whenever you're working with sound effects, ask yourself, "Where does the sound exist in the stereo field?" and "What space (or environment) does it live in?" These kinds of details can help make sound effects appropriate for a given purpose.

Dialogue is usually compressed so that quiet words don't get lost and can be clearly heard by the listener. It typically is louder than ambient sounds or music—unless of course it is background dialogue that is meant to supplement the environment in which the main dialogue is being spoken. And of course, if any reverb is applied, it should be appropriate for the space.

These days, the use of sound effects goes far beyond the Foley used in movies, TV shows, and games. Sound effects are often used in music to suggest ideas and environments to the listener. If you listen to the beginning of "Jack's Cheese and Bread Snack" by Ott, before the music even begins, you'll hear what sounds like a person leaving a dance club or a rave, walking to his car, starting it up, playing music inside the car, and then driving away. In this instance, all the different sound effects were mixed for realism to give the user the auditory experience of leaving a venue. Using sound effects in this way draws a mental picture for the listener and sets him up for the music he is about to hear.

Sometimes, the sound effects themselves are used as musical elements. A traditional snare drum in a drum beat might be replaced with the sound of a breaking bottle. Or maybe a cinematic explosion could be used to accent the downbeats of a song. The applications of using sound effects as musical elements are too numerous to mention. When they are used in this fashion, realism may not be as important. Some forms of experimental music are completely composed of sound effects, or sounds derived from sound effects, and take more of an "electronic" approach to mixing in that the rules governing the position and proximity of musical elements for realism are pretty much thrown out the window.

Format Mixing

There are many different destinations for your work. You might be composing a short audio clip for a website, mixing a song for a movie, or preparing backing tracks for a live performance. Some of these scenarios have different sonic limitations related to playback quality or available frequencies. Although it's true that if a project is mixed well, it will sound good in any situation, there are a few things you should know that I will cover in the following sections.

Film and Television

Mixing for film is much like mixing for compact discs, except you typically get to work with more dynamic range with regard to volume. Try to mix with clarity in mind. Know that the audio will most likely be heard on home theatre systems and in movie theatres. Understand that in these situations, the full frequency spectrum is available to the listener, so truly, the higher the quality and the clearer the audio is, the better it will sound in this medium. Your audio will have the benefit of being delivered and heard as full-resolution, uncompressed waves, so you don't have to give much consideration to the idea that the sound quality will be degraded in its final format.

Movies (and *some* CDs these days) are often offered in two-channel stereo (left and right), as well as 5.1 surround (left front, right front, center, left rear, right rear, and a subwoofer). Television programs that are not movies are not typically mixed in surround because there is no way to tell whether a viewer has 5.1 capabilities. Surround mixing is a topic that really deserves (and has) multiple books all its own, so I won't go into much detail about it here. However, if you are working primarily on post-production for video in your project studio, it's a good idea to get well acquainted with surround-sound mixing techniques.

Video Games and Multimedia

Audio for video games is reliant on what the game's sound engine is capable of. When working on a game project, make sure you fully understand the sonic limitations of the sound engine that the game will use. Also be sure that you understand the format in which the audio needs to be delivered. Often, sound effects or audio will be compressed into MP3 format, which means any sound or music that is abundant in high frequencies will sound noticeably bad due to the narrowed frequency spectrum. (MP3 compression is explained later in this chapter in the section on sound quality.) One way to avoid (or at least reduce the risk of) high-frequency sonic "weirdness" when you *know* the audio will be compressed is to compensate by reducing the high frequencies in the final mix.

MP3 formats make a big difference in the data size of the final project. A standard two-channel uncompressed stereo wave file that is four minutes long equates to roughly 40 MB, whereas the same file compressed as an MP3 at 192 kHz is only about 5 MB. When it comes to web and multimedia projects, less data means faster loading times, so that the viewer isn't waiting 10 minutes to hear 30 seconds of audio. To keep the overall data size of multimedia or web projects small enough to load quickly, high-quality MP3s are the way to go.

Another format requirement that you might encounter when working with web or multimedia content is looping audio. As you can imagine, it is far more efficient for a small 500-KB piece of audio to loop repeatedly than it is for a lengthy 5-MB piece of audio to play in its entirety. Occasionally, when working with games, websites, and multimedia projects, you'll be asked to create audio content that is designed to loop properly. This will usually be a short phrase of audio that lasts anywhere from 4 to 32 bars (sometimes longer). These must be "perfect" bars so that when the phrase ends, it can begin again with a seamless transition that cannot be detected by the listener and that sounds like a single never-ending phrase of audio.

Live Applications

Have you ever seen a live band and heard strings or electronic sequences playing, but there are no string players or synthesizers on the stage? These bands are playing to what is referred to as a *track* or a *backing track*. Running tracks for live performances is a pretty common thing. The idea is to reproduce the sounds and instrumentation you heard on the album, *not* to trick the audience into thinking that the band can play something that they really can't. Think of how anti-climactic it would be to go see a band after hearing the album, and all the strings that make the chorus so big and beautiful are nonexistent in the live show. Unless the band can afford to hire a string section or a keyboard player for each performance, they will most likely run a track that will play the strings during the chorus so that the audience members don't end up looking at each other in total confusion.

Backing tracks are also used for singers who move around a lot during a performance. Many performers are persecuted by their audiences for using a lead vocal backing track because people think, "If you *can* sing it, then why *don't* you?" But consider for a moment how difficult it is to sing loudly and clearly, without losing your breath, while vigorously doing the Running Man. In the eyes of some, using a lead vocal backing track seems like cheating, but such tracks are used more often than anyone realizes, which is actually good news for us!

Mixing backing tracks means that you are essentially pulling out of the final mix any instruments that will be played by a real person in the live show. Also, in live performances, speaker systems are usually big, which means the left and right speakers will be pretty far apart. This could cause problems with musical elements that are panned too far left or right. To avoid potential problems, you may want to narrow the stereo field or mix entirely in mono, just as you would while mixing an orchestra. Otherwise, all the other musical elements should sound just like they sound on the band's album.

Depending on the method that will be used to play the track, you may be asked to mix and provide just a two-channel stereo version of the track. However, this means that whoever is running the track will not be able to change any of the discrete levels of the individual audio elements. Usually, you'll be asked to format this version so that it can run in a particular software program from a laptop on the stage somewhere. That way, the person who controls the playback of the track can tailor the levels themselves, as if they were mixing for live sound. You'll need to find out what program they'll be using and either know how to get around in that program or convert the track to a useable format for that specific piece of software.

Sound Quality

And now, a word on sound quality. I want to begin by giving you an understanding of how audio resolution is expressed. You probably already know that a compact disc is considered to be the digital audio resolution standard at 16 bit, 44.1 kHz—or 16/44.1k. The *16* refers to the bit depth, and the *44.1k* refers to the sample rate, or sample frequency.

For all intents and purposes, I'm not going to enter into an in-depth explanation of what a bit is. That would require a deeper level of understanding about binary code that relates to the topic of mixing like you relate to a third cousin, twice removed. But even a basic explanation has the potential to get complicated, so here we go.

In digital audio, because everything is recorded through a computer, audio is really just data. A *bit* is a basic unit of information storage on a computer. Broken down to its most basic form, audio data is a series of binary digits, or bits, that are expressed as ones and zeroes. (You saw *The Matrix,* right?) These binary digits are translated by your computer into the resulting audio. What's important to understand is that *bit depth* is the number of bits you have available to capture data. Theoretically, the higher the bit depth, the more digital headroom, or dynamic range, your recording will have.

You might be wondering how much audio resolution you can really get out of only 16 bits—or 16 binary digits—but the math isn't quite that simple. The resolution quality comes from a combination of the available bits. With 16 binary digits, there are 65,536 possible numerical combinations. Think of these combinations as resolution levels. The more possible levels you have, the better the resolution will be. The term *16 bit* means that there are 16 binary digits available to capture information, but it's a combination of these 16 digits that makes up the 65,536 possible levels available to record and store data.

As additional bits, or digits, are added to the equation, the number of levels, or possible combinations, doubles. So, if you are recording data at 24 bit, you should be able to get better data (or in this case, audio) resolution because there are 16,777,216 possible levels available to store the information. Now absorb all that and realize that we're talking about capturing data for only a ten-thousandth of a second, or more specifically, for one sample.

A *sample* is a measurement of time in which data occurs. The *sample rate* is the number of samples that occur in one second of audio. So if the sample rate is 44.1k, there are 44,100 samples that occur in one second—or, more simply put, 44,100 samples per second. If your sample rate is 96 kHz, then (you guessed it!) there are 96,000 samples occurring per second. The higher the sample rate, the better the audio resolution will be, which results in a more detailed sound…in theory.

Figure 6.3 shows the progression bit depth and sample rate over a period of one second.

Now, having said all that, a lot of people *think* they can hear the difference in bit depths, but in actuality, there aren't many people in the world who can *really* distinguish between 16 bit and 24 bit. There are even fewer who can hear the difference between 20 bit and 24 bit. The truth is that the human ear is only capable of hearing so much. Some people say they like the way 16 bit sounds better, and in some scenarios, they might be right. Others swear by 24 bit for more headroom, expanded available frequency, audio detail, and clarity. The eternal question is "16 bit or 24 bit?" If you do an Internet search for the term, you'll find many forums hosting heated debates on the topic, with opinions that go from one end of the spectrum to the other.

24-bit/96kHz									
Bits	1677722	3355443	5033165	6710886	8388608	10066330	11744051	13421773	15099494	16777216
Samples	9,600	19,200	28,800	38,400	48,000	57,600	67,200	76,800	86,400	96,000

16-bit/44.1kHz									
Bits	65536	131072	196608	262144	327680	393216	458752	524288	589824	655360
Samples	4,410	8,820	13,230	17,640	22,050	26,460	30,870	35,280	39,690	44,100
Seconds	0.1	0.2	0.3	0.4	0.5	0.6	0.7	0.8	0.9	1

Figure 6.3 Bit depth and sample rate calculations as they occur over one second.

Although 24 bit is becoming an industry-standard format, not everyone is completely sold on it. If you're planning to record at strictly 24/96k, make sure that you have plenty of storage capacity. Because digital audio recordings that are produced at 24/96k are literally more data than 16/44.1k recordings, they require two to three times more hard disk space.

CD Audio

As I mentioned earlier, the audio resolution of a standard compact disc at 16/44.1k is the digital audio standard. The properties of CD audio cannot be changed. The audio quality will always be 16/44.1k, and you will never be able to fit more than 80 minutes (74 minutes, in most cases) of audio on a commercial audio CD. Even projects that are produced at a higher resolution of 24/96k will be dithered down to 16 bit to be produced in CD format. This may be something else you want to consider when choosing a bit rate and depth with which to work.

Dithering *Dithering* is a process that takes place in the mastering phase of audio production. When you take a 24-bit audio file and reduce it to 16-bit for a compact disc, you're taking the same amount of data from the 24-bit version of the file and trying to squeeze as much of it as possible into 16 bits. It's a bit like trying to fit 24 ounces of liquid into a 16-ounce can; you can't get all 24 ounces in the can, but you can get most of it. In this process, the data is truncated or torn away to fit it into the smaller container, and the tearing scars cause some digital distortion. Dithering adds a small amount of broadband noise to the digital signal to help mask this digital distortion and smooth it out, making it less noticeable overall.

When you are preparing audio files to be pressed to a standard audio CD, the replication facility will usually ask for a master disc that is composed of two-channel stereo, 16-bit, 44.1-kHz WAV files, burned in a single session, or in *disc-at-once* mode, as an audio CD that is Red Book–compatible, meaning that it can be played in all regular CD players.

Some replication facilities offer mastering services, but you never really know what you are going to get. Just because a facility has a mastering engineer who can turn some knobs, that doesn't mean he or she will be the best person to master your client's disc. For best results, either have someone you really trust master the final project or, because this is a book about audio post-production, simply read on.

MP3s

MP3s have quickly become an audio format standard. With the advent of digital distribution services, more and more music consumers are buying entire albums online and downloading them in MP3 format. MP3s are a compressed form of a full-resolution piece of audio. When you encode an MP3, you're basically making a tradeoff between sound quality and disc space by reducing the bit rate of the original file and removing frequencies that are outside the normal human hearing range. If your MP3 has been encoded at too low of a bit rate, you will most likely encounter compression artifacts that are especially noticeable in the higher frequencies of a recording. At 128 KBps (128 kilobytes per second), you might be able to hear that the cymbals in a rock song have been reproduced with a kind of swishing or phasing effect. In fact, 128 KBps is a very common bit rate for music used in multimedia applications, even though the compression artifacts are noticeable. MP3s encoded at 192 KBps are usually high enough quality to eliminate most compression artifacts.

As a little experiment, grab a CD from your collection and choose a song from it that you think sounds great. Convert that song to an MP3 at 128 KBps, and then encode a second MP3 at 192 KBps. And if you're *really* curious, encode one more at 320 KBps. Listen to the song on your studio monitors in its full-resolution format directly from the CD. Then listen to the 128-KBps version and note how much different it sounds, and what *specifically* is different about it. Then listen to the 192-KBps version and so on, taking note of the audible difference between the bit rates. At a certain point, you probably won't be able to hear the difference between an MP3 encoded with a high bit rate and the original CD, but now your ears should be able to tell where that line is when it comes to MP3 compression.

I realize that this is a lot of information to absorb. And we're only about 40 percent of the way through! It is unlikely that anyone will ever know *everything* there is to know about mixing audio or audio production in general. Every musician, engineer, composer, or producer will tell you that they still learn new things about their craft almost every day. (And if they say they don't, they're probably lying.) I hope that you've gained some new and worthwhile information just from reading this chapter. We've still got quite a bit ahead of us, so take a break. Get a snack. Watch some TV, and then come back, and we'll get into some ways to help make the time you spend in the studio a little more efficient.

7 Organizing Your Digital Workspace

This entire chapter is dedicated to making your life easier and your workflow faster and more efficient. If your studio is a mess of cables, un-racked gear, and randomly placed hard drives all over the desktop, your ability to function as an effective post-production engineer could come into question. A client may begin to doubt your professionalism if you are constantly flipping through random windows, trying to locate the arrangement pane, looking for files that seem to be missing from a project, or searching for forgotten shortcut keys to execute what should be fairly simple actions in your software.

I recently produced a session and asked my engineer to find an audio file of a keyboard part from a previous project, import it, and apply a delay effect we used on a mix the previous month. Not only did he have no idea where to locate the keyboard file, but he didn't save the delay effect preset I wanted to use. When I asked him where the keyboard file could be, he replied, "It's just gone man." Had the engineer been properly organized, he would have known the exact (or at least nearly the exact) location of the missing file, and the delay preset would have been stored from the previous session. Having small details like this organized can save an unbelievable amount of time in the post-production process. Unfortunately, you may never know how much time it can save unless you make some of these organizational mistakes yourself. You'll have to trust me on this one.

Predefined project templates, common tracking scenarios, and easy file paths to locate files should be commonplace in the organization of your digital studio. Unless you plan to start fresh every session, as if you've never done a project or mix before, you may want to heed the words and warnings of this chapter. In the ideal situation, your producer/engineer should be able to go into your computer and easily find all the necessary tracks, files, and effects from previous endeavors with minimal confusion. Not only will this save you and others time, but a well-organized workspace with common configurations, routing, and templates plays to the professionalism and pragmatism of the post-audio engineer.

Obviously, each project will be a little different, but are you telling me you may never use an eighth-note delay at 120 BPM again? Or that there's no good reason to have a drum mixing template with panning positions, common reverbs, compressors, and tracks labeled "kick," "snare," "toms" (1, 2, and 3), and "overheads" (L and R) all in place? Little things like this can save you a great deal of time and show your clients that you're on the ball. You may be surprised at what organization will do for you.

File Organization and Storage

The first step toward getting it together is file organization and storage. Often, I have to dive into a client or producer's drive to find out where files are located, only to realize the client or producer is playing 30 tracks from three different drives simultaneously while accessing a temp file that was sent via email that for some reason is no longer part of the track. Sounds like a nightmare, huh? It pretty much is. So let's start by getting organized.

- **Project names.** Name all your projects properly—something both you and your client will recognize. Untitled 1023 is not an effective project name. There's a good chance you or an intern could erase Untitled 1023, thinking it's a mistake, the next time you clean up some hard drive space. If the artist or client has given a project a specific name, keep the name the same or use an understandable abbreviation of it as the title of the project file. If you and the client haven't decided on a title yet, name it something like Pearl Jam Style Song for TV Ad. With a title like this, there will be little confusion about what the track is. If I can't think of a title immediately, I use the client's last name, a song number, the date, and the version to

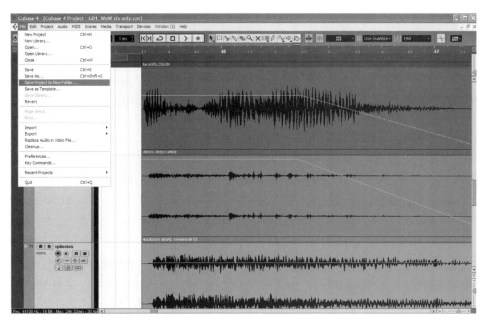

Figure 7.1   Self-contained project option in Cubase 4.

identify it. For example, I might use smith_song1_100507_v1. Each time I'm about to make a major revision to the project, I immediately save the project, changing only the current date and version number (such as, smith_song1_100608_v2). This helps me track revisions efficiently. Also, if I want to go back and start from before a particular revision, I can find the right project easily because everything has been well organized.

- **Project folders.** Make sure each project has its own project folder. Many software programs allow you to create self-contained project folders (see Figure 7.1). Saving a self-contained project puts all of the audio data and files into a single folder. The file paths are updated automatically to draw all audio information from this one folder. This also means that once a project has been saved as a self-contained project, you can move the project folder to another hard drive or even another studio, and it will work (using the same software on a different computer) without a hitch. Check out your software's manual to see what features are available for creating self-contained or bundled projects.

- **File locations.** When you save, bounce, and export files, take the time to figure out where the file is being stored. Nothing is worse than finding out you accidentally sent a perfectly bounced stereo drum track to a folder on the desktop that you ended up deleting later that night. When you hit Save, Bounce, or Export Audio, make sure you are sending the file to the correct project and storage folder. Many programs offer a default location for saving bounced files inside a folder that is specific to your current project. Just be sure to inspect the file path to be sure that the files are being saved in the correct project folder.

Track Templates

Possibly the most underutilized feature of many sequencer/software programs is the ability to create track templates. Track templates allow you to set up a project just the way you like it, with any type and number of tracks, configuration settings, routings, commonly used plug-ins, virtual instruments, and even key commands, and then save the template for future use. Templates can be useful for a great number of different audio applications. I've got a template that I use when I am trying to generate new musical ideas. It has a bass track, two guitar tracks, and a vocal track, all routed to record from specific inputs on my audio interface. It also has four MIDI tracks for drums, labeled as kick, snare, hi-hat, and cymbals. When I load this template, a basic compressor, a versatile reverb, and a virtual instrument for acoustic drums are also loaded. Whenever I want to start chiseling away at ideas, I choose this template and simply start recording. I estimate that it saves me about 20 minutes in setup time. Although 20 minutes doesn't sound like a great deal of time to be saved, it makes a big difference when I only have about an hour to spend on a new idea.

If you're recording 10 songs for a band, and the basic instrumentation is always the same, you can create a template of the first project that retains all of the track information, so that when you record the second song, you can open up the template and get straight to work. A template for adding sound effects to a video might include a video track; a ruler track that displays time in timecode rather than in bars and beats; and a compressor, a reverb, and an EQ plug-in that are set up as insert effects. There are a vast number of things for which you can create templates. If you haven't already, try to set up a template for the type of project you work on the most, and see for yourself how useful templates can be.

Folder Tracks, Subgroups, and Buses

Grouping similar things and organizing your project in small sections can also save you tons of time and work. One of the best things about working in the digital domain is the ability to organize materials while maintaining consistency and control. If you want synth2 to appear above synth1 in the track order, you can simply grab the track and move it without interfering with the audio. This makes it possible to organize your tracks into workable groups that make them easy to manage and negotiate.

Nowadays, you can organize all of your perfectly mixed common tracks into a single folder track and keep them neatly tucked away in a small corner of the project. This prevents accidental modifications to the individual tracks within the folder. Rather than sifting through the individual tracks, trying to get to other tracks, you can move them into a single folder track and consolidate your precious screen real estate. I find it useful to mix common elements and then move them to a folder track to improve track management within the project. This is common with drums, vocals and background vocals, multiple synths, keyboards, or multiple guitars. When I want to work on a particular group of instruments, I simply expand the folder track and work with only the instruments inside of it. A folder track may be called something different in your software program, such as a *group track* or something similar. And, some software programs don't have folder tracks for optimizing your workspace at all. Again, you'll want to check your software manual for specific nomenclature.

The most common form of organization utilized in post audio is assigning similar tracks to a bus or a subgroup (sometimes called an *AUX* or an *auxiliary track*). A *bus* is a master channel strip that governs multiple tracks assigned to it. If you were creating a drum bus, you would assign drum tracks 1–7 to a subgroup. The volume and

EQ found on the subgroup's channel strip, as well as its insert and send effects, would then globally affect drum tracks 1–7. When you've got a good drum mix going, this is a great way to make the drum kit louder or softer without affecting the volume of the drums in relation to one another. Now move drum tracks 1–7 into a folder track labeled Drums, and your drum track organization will be in good shape.

Linking Channels

As an alternative to using a subgroup, you can link channels together. Most software programs let you link any tracks you want together, so that the volume changes applied to one linked channel are applied to all linked channels. So if you link drum tracks 1–7 instead of assigning them to a subgroup, you can change the global volume of the drums by adjusting the volume fader on any linked track. The functionality of linked tracks isn't always limited to just volume adjustments, either. Some programs offer control over pan, sends, mute, and various other global parameters.

Key Commands

Key commands, sometimes called *hot keys,* help you execute all kinds of different processes easily within a software program. Hot keys are simply keyboard shortcuts (or a series of keystrokes) connected to a particular software program. The processes that the key commands execute usually take a significantly longer time to access if you click through the menu screens in a program. These days, there is a lot more to operating a software program with hot keys than just plain old Ctrl+C or Apple+V. In fact, in the current versions of most audio software programs, almost every process can be carried out with a series of quick keystrokes.

Some programs, such as Pro Tools, have predefined keyboard commands so that Pro Tools users will feel at home on any Pro Tools system. Pro Tools is such a popular software package for digital audio recording and processing that special keyboards are sold to help you navigate through all the commands. In my opinion, key commands are at their best when they are user-definable. It's really nice to be able to choose shortcuts that you'll remember time and again. Plus, you can take your key command set with you by copying the key command preferences file to any computer that has the same software installed on it. In my own key command setup, I use a backslash (\) to execute a fade out, a forward slash (/) to execute a fade in, and a less-than symbol (<) to reverse the audio signal. See how logical key commands can be? In a few short keystrokes, I can truncate an audio file, loop it, change the gain, fade the beginning, fade the end, and export it—all this in a fraction of the time it took to read this sentence.

It's a matter of preference as to which software speaks to you as an engineer, but some may make more sense to you than others on the hot-key front. When it comes to these useful shortcuts, don't be afraid to crack a manual or the online PDF file and get a list of your hot keys. Or, develop an entire set of shortcuts on your own. You may be surprised at how much time and effort you will save without sifting through the menu drop-down screens every time you need a bounce or something similarly simple.

Sends and Effect Presets

I consider one of the biggest timesavers in my post-audio applications to be the ability to store effect presets. Few things have been as useful to me as the instant recall of a common reverb or compressor setting that I've already spent an hour tweaking.

In mixing music or creating sound effects for video, you may find that one effect really works well for a track, and you want to use it on multiple sources. This works well with things such as reverb, delay, and chorus. Running any effect as a send effect that can be applied to multiple tracks in varying degrees is much more efficient than bogging down your CPU with multiple instances of the same effect on each track. Valuable system resources can be directed elsewhere in the project, whether it's getting more tracks, having a smaller audio buffer size, or running more virtual instruments. You are less likely to encounter system hiccups if you use send effects to make your projects run more efficiently.

When working with similar types of tracks that could benefit from similar effects, applying the same effect to each track individually is not something we'd consider to be mix-friendly. When it comes to making changes, you'd be making adjustments for each and every plug-in that has been used on each track. If you have three background vocal tracks that could all use the same type of reverb, no matter what software you're using, it's usually pretty easy to set up a single send effect and route all three tracks to it. Then, if you decide you want to change the reverb type or parameters, you can change the send effect only, and it will affect the reverb on all three tracks. You can even automate send effects. This gives you the ability to have a "room" set up with its own reverb type specifically for your background vocal tracks, a synced delay for multiple instrument tracks that create a complementary rhythmic delay pattern, or a compressor that makes drums and bass more cohesive without straining your machine.

Now that you've got your send effect set up, it's time to utilize the effects presets. Most plug-ins have an impressive library of different presets for different purposes. Although these are good to explore, over time you'll develop settings that are all your own. When you find that a golden combination of ratio, threshold, and attack on a compressor plug-in often works on acoustic drums or electric bass, will you be able to dial it in again?

In the old days, all processor and mixer settings were well documented on a pad of paper so that if the engineer had to walk away from the mix for a while, where he left off could be approximated when he returned to the mix. With digital audio, this is no longer an issue. Now you can dial in the perfect setting and save it as an effect preset. Sure, the settings may change a bit from mix to mix, but if you can call up a preset, you at least have somewhere to start. If you end up modifying the preset drastically, you can save it as a new preset, keeping the original and building your personal preset library.

Another advantage to storing your presets is that if you need to work in a different studio than your own, you can copy the folder to which you saved your presets and take them with you. As long as the same plug-ins exist on the computer in your destination studio, you'll be able to call them up just as you saved them.

Having several easily accessible presets for plug-ins you use all the time will save you hours of sonic tooling. I save almost every preset, no matter how small or insignificant an adjustment I've made. I name it the first thing that comes to mind, such as Death Metal Strange Panning Delay, so it will be easy to remember and identify if I need a delay of that type again. If I'm mixing for a female R&B singer and I get the reverb and compressor dialed in, there's no reason not to use that as a starting point for other singers of the same style. And I keep it in the preset menu because we may get more work from the singer or engineer in the future. So be smart and build a preset library!

In Living Color

Computer recording and sequencing software have made digital audio a visual experience. Not only do we use our ears, but we also use our eyes to keep track of what we hear. We can see audio visually expressed in great detail as waveforms. Some of the guesswork is taken out of using parametric equalizers with a little help from the graphic representations of the EQ spectrum.

Colorizing tracks is yet another way that modern technology has improved working with audio. Tracks or parts of tracks can be coded and visually organized by different colors. This allows you to differentiate between tracks just by looking at them. Some programs have a predefined color palette; others let you make all the decisions when it comes to painting your project window with all the colors of Lucky Charms and then some.

In my personal color application, all percussion and drum tracks are yellow. Yellow is the easiest way for me to clearly see waveforms and transients. The high level of contrast makes the typically black waveform images really stand out. Because percussion tracks have many visual spikes that generally outline the tempo of the song, it's important to see them easily while you're editing. I color keyboard parts bounced from MIDI that are in perfect time and performance and that are relatively low in the amount of transient peaks dark purple because the contrast isn't as important. It's not as important to see every detail in a track like this because it has less variance in the wave-form anyway. Also, I do fun things to remember what other track colors are. My best friend is a bass player. I make all my bass tracks powder pink because I know it upsets him. It's an added bonus that light pink is a high-contrast color against a black bass waveform. This helps when I'm trying to visually align to the drums. I make solo instruments red. Why? Because killer solos are "hot!" Duh…

Colors can also be used to signify when a sonic change is about to occur during the course of an audio project. I often make verses one color and choruses another. Intros, outros, bridges, transitions, and so on all get their own colors. This is useful when I am assembling arrangements in a project. I know that if I want to move the chorus, I need to grab all of the blue sections to see that the entire chorus has been moved and that important parts of the chorus aren't accidentally left behind, causing confusion later. This way, I can avoid things like, "How did that huge cymbal crash get placed in the middle of the verse?" Just by looking at the project, I immediately can see that a blue color-coded cymbal crash is sitting right in the middle of an orange section and that it needs to be moved to its appropriate place among the blue section.

Over time, I'm sure you will come up with your own code of colors for every purpose. Sometimes it's fun to be a little creative because music is supposed to be *fun,* right? And quite possibly the best thing about the vast color schemes in modern software programs is, of course, that they look impressive to clients! All joking aside, colorizing your tracks can have an impact on overall track management and project organization, though many of your clients *will* respond to the visual excitement of their projects shown in full color. Some musicians even naturally relate instruments or particular sounds and notes to different pigments in the color spectrum. They might really enjoy the fact that you can change the colors of the tracks to suit the instruments.

Track Names

Though this might seem simple and possibly redundant to mention after our recent discussion of file organization, track naming is its own animal entirely and deserves some dedicated page real estate.

In digital audio production, you are constantly copying, moving, duplicating, and bouncing tracks. You need to know exactly what audio material exists on each track so you don't get confused and accidentally make changes to the wrong track. It can be an easy slip-up to edit the lead guitars on one track when you really meant to edit the rhythm guitars on a different track, simply because they were named Audio 1 and Audio 2—or, more specifically, because they weren't named correctly.

In the past I have been guilty of neglecting my track names. In the beginning, you'll make this mistake at least once. Allow me to cite an example of how easy it is to overlook a seemingly minor detail. It's common for me to duplicate a vocal track twice. I'll apply a reverb on one to provide a little space, and I'll apply compression on the other to make the dynamic volumes more equal and give the overall vocal more presence in the mix. I use the volume fader of these affected tracks to blend in how much of each track I want to mix with the original signal. Often, when I want less reverb, as in the case of a verse vocal, I'll reduce the volume for that part only, using automation so that the reverb-affected track is barely noticeable. Then, I'm knee-deep in reducing the volume of what I *thought* was the reverb track for every verse. I hit playback, and as the verse sounds, I still hear tons of reverb, and the vocal seems washed out and buried in the mix. Why? I didn't rename the tracks, so the original vocal and the two duplicates were all named Audio 12. Because the duplicated tracks were identical copies of the original, there was no way to visually distinguish between them, and I inadvertently reduced the volume of the compression track, rather than the reverb track. After hitting Undo about 40 times, I was able to make the correct edits on the correct tracks. Had I just taken two seconds to rename the tracks as Lead Vox Verb and Lead Vox Compressed, the mistake never would have been made. It is worth the effort to name your tracks properly. It will save you time and possibly some embarrassment, depending on how many people are in the room watching you screw up. (As a side note, coloring the three tracks differently probably would've helped me avoid this mistake as well.) Keep your track names organized. Forming good organizational habits now will pay off in the long run.

Toolbars and Different Views

The first time you launch your software sequencer, an overwhelming number of buttons and controls bound onto the screen. There's one that looks like an arrow, and another resembles an itty-bitty hand. There's a speaker icon, a clock, scissors, multiple drop-down menus, buttons, *and* your transport controls. How many of those buttons, controllers, and options do you actually use when mixing, editing, or recording?

As you work with digital audio, you'll develop a workflow. It's important to customize your digital workspace so that it complements that workflow and contributes to your efficiency. Any functions or windows that you use frequently should be easily accessible from your primary digital workspace. Any buttons or menus that you will never use basically take up space in your toolbar. Additionally, when you're sitting in the studio with a client who isn't very familiar with digital audio programs, it is far less intimidating and daunting for the client to look at a less cluttered screen. It's a good general practice to keep your workspace as clean and as minimalist as possible (see Figures 7.2 and 7.3).

Figure 7.2 Workspace chaos.

Figure 7.3 The minimalist approach.

It is equally important that you understand what all the buttons do before you choose what will be shown in your toolbar. If you spend 10 minutes looking up what menu path will lead you to a particular function, when the button was sitting on your toolbar the entire time, that's 10 minutes that you were *not* mixing. Sometimes, just going into the setup and window controls of a program can be very revealing and quite helpful with regard to how you view and navigate your software programs. But there is a reason why there are faster and more efficient ways to access certain functionalities through buttons—it's called time. Although exploring the menus of your software program is a great way to learn what it's capable of, it's generally not the most efficient way to operate. It's in your best interest to find the fastest ways to move around your digital audio workstation. Knowing what all the buttons and shortcuts do is a good place to start.

Most sequencing software developers realize that the world of digital audio is becoming increasingly complex in the amount of different features it offers and what you can do. If you have 50 tracks of audio, it is not likely that you will be able to see all 50 tracks in your mixer view. You can also bet that trying to make your arrangement window, wave editor, MIDI editor, and mixer window all viewable at once while still being functional is a task just short of impossible. For this reason, many software programs have alternative viewing options available, so you can switch between different windows within the program for better organization.

When I am arranging, I like the arrangement window to fill the entire screen, so I have room to work and move files when necessary. When I'm mixing, I like a screen that shows my mixer on the bottom half and my arrangement window on the top half. When I need to make a quick edit to a piece of audio, I want to call up my wave editor window and have it split the screen with the arrangement window *and* the mixer. Another view I use frequently is just a set of mixer channels that make up two complete fader rows, so that I can *listen to* more than *look at* all the audio and get my head out of the visual domain for a while.

The Blind Leading the Blind   Sometimes, the absence of visual waveforms allows you to take a more innocent listen to the audio. Instead of staring at the screen and anticipating a part change, see whether you can hear all the elements that you know are going to change during playback. If some of the details disappear, then you know you have to work on them to get them to cut through the mix better. You'd be surprised at what can you hear when you take your eyes out of the equation!

Using the alternative viewing options in my software program, I can quickly switch between all these different screen setups with a few quick keystrokes. When I'm finished working in one window, a quick keystroke has me right back where I want to be. The ability to set up workspaces or alternative window views can be very useful for expanding your available workspace and keeping visual clutter at bay.

The most important thing to do here is to get into a project that you aren't worried about messing up, and try *everything* the software has to offer in those drop-down menus you don't usually dabble in. Check out all the buttons. Experiment with different window views. Everyone should spend the time to get familiar with software and its features. Sometimes, a day of messing around and getting the transports, toolbars, and views set up properly for your personal applications can make the workflow of future projects much faster. Not to mention that doing so will help make complex/multilayered studio operations easier to negotiate.

Love Me Two Times (Multiple Screens)

One of the best investments a post-audio engineer can make is a solid additional monitoring screen. Most pros have at least two monitors in their studio—one for the main sequencer window or the arrangement/editing view, and the other with only the mixer on it. This can be an alternative to setting up alternate views within your software, albeit an expensive one. With two monitors, hardly any brain power is required to figure out the organization scheme. The second screen allows you to look over to the right and do a little EQ and level mixing here and there, and then get back to the edits on the main screen. It's a bit of a timesaver over flipping through plug-in, editing, mixing, and arrangement windows, but you have to weigh how much time it'll actually save you versus how much you're willing to spend to save it.

Another idea I've seen a lot lately in major studios is hooking a larger HDTV or LCD screen above your primary monitor so everyone in the studio can see the work that's going on. This is especially helpful if you are doing voiceovers or re-tracking anything that requires everyone involved to know exactly where you are in a song or project. This way, it's really easy for the overdubbing party to look up at the screen and see where the engineer is going to stop, start, loop, or punch in and out a new performance. Additionally, while you are working on something else, clients can be listening and making valuable yet simple suggestions, such as, "You should use that second pink section every time. That's the best chorus by far." You can easily have two sets of ears going at one time with the same visual frame of reference. Unfortunately, this is both a blessing and a curse because it's an invitation for the client to bombard you with suggestions that require a great deal of patience to field and time to execute. The suggestions themselves are fine; it's the rapid firing of them that can become overwhelming.

Consistency Is Key

I'd like to wrap up this section on organization with my two cents on consistency and how valuable it is in a business setting. As post-production engineers, we should strive to keep everything as consistent as possible from project to project. That includes everything you can think of, from the names of types of files, to software, right down to the way we set up takes for voiceovers. This is as much for your own benefit as it is for your clients' benefit. Once you develop a particular way to do things (record, mix, master, and so on), you begin to develop your own sound. If you produce a stellar-sounding project, clients will come to you for that sound.

For the client, being consistent establishes a work method between you. Suppose you sent the film company some music tracks called Fusion Demo for review, and then after you took the company's advice and made some revisions, you sent them the revised file, but named as Audio 20-01. Chances are someone would be confused by what the file is. An intern at the film company might delete the email in which the file came, thinking it was a virus. Or, someone might even save the file into another folder of Audio 20-01 files, causing countless hours of listening to the wrong file, trying to find the correct one. This is just one example of why it's important to keep your naming conventions consistent—or, at the very least, consistent for each individual client.

I've had trouble when I've named a series of projects for a client as Song 1, Song 2, Song 3, and so on. Then, when I went to compile stereo versions of these projects to present to the client, in an effort to have my best work heard first, I renamed and reorganized the files (not the projects) out of order. So Song 3 became Track 1, Song 1 became Track 2, and Song 1 became Track 3. Are you confused yet? It seemed to make sense at the time, but when the client came back to me and said, "We like Track 2," I couldn't remember which original project was eventually renamed Track 2. I had to listen to each project to figure out which one it was. After much wasted time, everyone ended up happily ever after. But we could have been happier a lot sooner if I had been a little more organized.

Consistency contributes to the overall experience that a client has with your post-production services. You might end up getting more work simply because your last client spoke so highly of how easy you were to work with. People generally seem to get uncomfortable when they have to constantly adjust themselves to what you are doing. It's bad enough that they have to adjust to the way you work; throwing more confusion on top of that makes for a random and chaotic working experience.

Have you ever had a job in which the policies and procedures seem to change daily? Let's use a hypothetical example of ordering office supplies. You just started working at this new job, and you need to order office supplies. To purchase office supplies, you tell the office manager, and your supplies arrive at your desk the next day. During your second week on the job, the employer changes the ordering system. Now, in order to get supplies, you need to call the store, get a quote for the items you want, submit an authorized purchase order, and wait for it to be approved. A week or two goes by, and it seems as though the policy change isn't very efficient—too many employees are having trouble with it, plus it takes too long. So the policy is changed once more to try to correct the issues with the initial policy change. I hope you can see what I'm getting at here. If I was a new employee, I would feel as though there was no organizational structure in the way that policies were developed and enforced. Nothing about the order procedure would stick with me, and I'd probably just be confused about whether I was supposed to tell the office manager what I want or submit a form to someone.

Remember that a client is usually only with you for a few weeks at a time. If your procedures and methods change each time the client visits your studio, there is nothing familiar for the client to get comfortable with. The client may never loosen up enough to be comfortable working with you, which in turn could make you uncomfortable. And what keeps the client from taking the project to finish at another studio if they know that they're going to have to adapt to something new the next time they step foot in your studio, anyway? Often, when clients hire you, they simply are looking for someone to do the job right. Regardless of what your methods are, consistency will help establish your methods and reduce client confusion from the beginning.

The gist of this whole section is to do whatever you can to make your life easier in your post-production work. Giving yourself more screen space, learning to access and navigate your software more quickly, and keeping all your projects organized will help you stretch your skills and services further without you getting burned out too quickly.

8 Mixing Techniques

In this chapter we will discuss the mechanics, mysticism, and mojo involved in the world of post-audio mixing. To properly put this in perspective, let me say that mixing is a lifelong learning process. The best mixers in the game aren't exactly young audio gods. They're usually people who have worked for years developing the ears and learning the gear to be able to get exactly what they want from any variety of audio situations. Mixers who know and understand their job are some of the best paid people in the music business. Many artists, producers, and record labels send their mixes out to the big-name mixer guys to get these sonic elements of a recording right.

I once read an interview with a famous mix engineer who is well known for a lot of the current pop and hip-hop mixes on the radio today. He said, "I've finally discovered the secret to getting my bass bigger than life on the radio. I do it by tricking the radio station's output compressors. It only took me 15 years to figure it out!" With that being said, the long journey of mixing begins with a single step. This chapter is a collection of tips and elements that are used as a starting point for mixing. I wish I could have read a chapter as comprehensive as this when I started out in post. Keep in mind, the only real rule about a mix is that if it sounds good, it *is* good. You really do have the ability and tools within most software programs and plug-ins to create professional-quality mixes. All you need are the ears, the attention to detail, and the drive to compete in this business. So let's begin.

EQ

Equalization, or *EQ,* is the process of altering the frequency curves of an audio source. To EQ an audio signal means to correct it or to make its frequency response *equal.* EQ is to mixing as sugar is to molasses.

Without sugar, you can't make molasses. EQ is the primary ingredient in an audio mix. It allows you to unify and separate sounds by carving out unwanted frequencies or adding essential frequencies to reveal the true clarity of the audio material. If all music were performed at appropriate volume levels (and with no performance issues), a good mix *could* shine with EQ being its only post-audio treatment, in theory. Unfortunately, this is usually not the case.

The Frequency Spectrum

The hearing range of humans is measured in *Hertz*, or *Hz*. Hertz refers to the measurement of cycles or vibrations of sound. Typically, humans can perceive tones from 20 Hz to 20 kHz. This outlines the frequency spectrum within which we usually operate EQ, with 20 Hz being the lowest, slowest, biggest cycles of the spectrum and 20 kHz being the highest and fastest cycles. The slower the vibration, the lower the sound is perceived, and the faster the vibration… well, you get the idea. Figure 8.1 shows a graphical representation of the full frequency spectrum divided by the frequency ranges we'll discuss in this section.

This is the spectrum where all EQ manipulation will take place. Even if you are using a non-visual EQ, it is important to know how you are affecting the frequencies in this spectrum. I want to discuss a few of the principles of EQ that are available in most software programs and plug-ins.

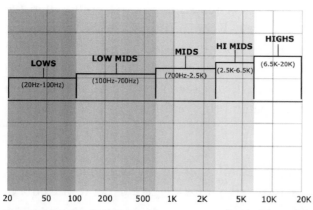

Figure 8.1 The full frequency spectrum divided into frequency bands.

Frequency Maneuvering

It amazes me to see how many people who work in audio know so little about what frequencies they are constantly affecting. It takes time and experience to fully understand what frequencies to isolate to make the instruments and parts really pop. I'm going to break down the spectrum right now with some basic guidelines for frequency in the hopes that we'll be able to accelerate the learning curve a bit. As time goes on, you will find your own magical equations for navigating the sonic spectrum. But for now, let's embark on a five-part journey that explains the characteristics of each frequency band.

The Lows (Sub-Frequency)

All the thump and thunder you hear pumping down your street at midnight are the sub-frequencies on the low end, or the far left side of the frequency spectrum on a visual EQ. I usually consider this frequency area to be from 20 Hz up to just less than 100 Hz. This is where the big bottom in a bass synth, bass guitar, and kick drum are. Unfortunately, it's the most damaging area for most mixes. Often, when mixing on studio monitors, you may be tempted to push (or use additive EQ) and mix these frequencies way up to make them more noticeable. But when you check that mix in your car, all you will hear is the sound of explosive Armageddon. Instruments that are designed to provide low end have *tons* of sub-bass frequency naturally. Many times, you actually have to remove bass on instruments such as these. The process of reducing or rolling out unwanted frequencies is called *subtractive EQ*, and instruments of this type will be the first to get it.

Low end is always a battle in mixing. When is it too much? When is it enough? Some people think new rock-music mixes have too little low end. Many people think contemporary rap music has too much. Only your ears can be the judge. Audio signals usually contain a broad range of frequencies. Though a bass guitar is a low-frequency instrument, there are also other higher frequencies present. Otherwise, there would be no note definition whatsoever.

As you layer audio tracks that have the same frequencies present, you are compounding the identical frequencies and making them ever more present. This will undoubtedly reduce the overall clarity and cause sonic confusion in a mix. So what do we do as engineers? We trim the fat by reducing or boosting the appropriate frequencies to give each individual instrument distinction. Keeping the low end tight and under control allows the rest of the elements in the mix to be heard clearly.

The Low Midrange (The Mud, the Warmth, and the Brown)

The frequencies from 100 to 700 Hz are my favorite area of the spectrum. This is the area I always refer to as the *brownness* because it reminds me of how cardboard or wood would sound. It is where a lot of the foundation and "meat" of the audio spectrum takes place. The round, warm tones of bass, keyboards, and organs live here. It's also where the perceived low frequencies of guitars and some male vocalists exist. This is the frequency range that makes audio on a vinyl record sound warmer and richer than a compact disc.

This is often another spot in mixing that can get congested pretty quickly. An album that immediately comes to mind with a lot of low mids is Smashing Pumpkins' *Mellon Collie and the Infinite Sadness*. When it was released in 1995, people were amazed by the way it sounded like an actual vinyl recording on CD. This was primarily due to the low mids being so muddy and swimmy that it sounded as if the vocals and cymbals were struggling to get through the mix.

This area of warmth was most focused on in the late '60s and throughout the '70s, when many recordings had a big, warm, vintage-sounding low end. Many engineers in the '80s and early 2000s were reducing these frequencies like crazy to get a more scooped-sounding mix. The *scoop* is where the muddy mids are reduced or eliminated with subtractive EQ and the highs, high mids, and sub bass areas are excited or pushed. This scoop provides a more transparent sound. How much of this frequency is used or reduced is really like the low end on a case-by-case basis, where you need to decide what the music is trying to say and use these frequencies to your advantage. Figure 8.2 shows what a scooped EQ looks like.

Most of the time, I find certain instruments, such as vocals, keyboards, drums, and guitars, can use a healthy reduction in this area. The world

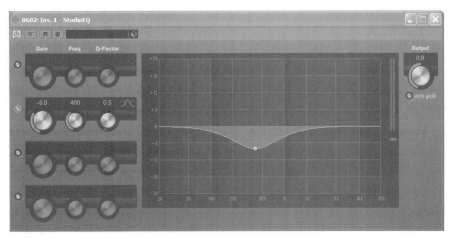

Figure 8.2   A scooped EQ in which the midrange is "ducked," or reduced, using subtractive EQ.

of "real sounds" is a very brown place. In real life, midrange like this is rampant and the most exaggerated frequency area. Any time you are trying to clean up a track or make it sound less congested, this would be the first place to start reducing frequencies. Usually the only time I find myself adding these frequencies is when snare drums need more boom, or maybe when an acoustic guitar is very bright and needs something to help fill in where it lacks warmth.

A very common way this area gets too excited in tracking is called the *proximity effect*. When a singer (or any source, for that matter) gets too close to a microphone, the first frequencies to increase are the low mids. Most of the time, the result of this closeness in proximity is muddiness. This may be a good thing for balancing out a twangy telecaster through a Marshall amplifier, but on vocals (unless they are really high and wispy), the result can be chaos.

Proximity effect on a vocal can add literally +10 dB of low midrange (or more) that will eventually have to be reduced. It is very typical for low mids to sound great during tracking to a recording engineer because fewer instruments are sounding simultaneously at that point. You will know when a vocal is suffering from proximity effect if it fights with the bass and low end of pianos and organs for sonic real estate. The good news is that with subtractive EQ, this is a quick fix in post.

The "Nasal" Midrange

Quick, grab your nose and close off your nostrils. Now try to talk or sing. The frequency you are hearing with irritating clarity right now is roughly 1,000 kHz. The middle of the frequency spectrum is a place that most often sounds like a flugelhorn in a Chuck Mangione chart. This is where most of the perceived volume or loudness lurks in a track. The area this occupies is from about 800 Hz to 2,500 kHz. It can be deceptive, though, because although you need midrange to provide definition, volume, and relative loudness, too much midrange is irritating and "honky" sounding and may be perceived as nasally by the listener.

A good example of where this frequency is often boosted is in bass guitar or bass synth. Though these instruments are good at producing lows, low mids, and midrange snaps, the main note clarity of these instruments exists in the nasal area. If a bass player is complaining that his part is lacking clarity or note definition, saying that, "You can't even tell what I'm playing," the problem is more than likely in the mids. It seems weird, but this is really where the bass fundamental notes can be found.

Another area where mids like this need to be added is in heavy-metal distorted guitars. A lot of the time, they are recorded with a "scooped" EQ and minimal midrange. Though this makes for a heavy sooled-up guitar sound, in a mix these guitars can kind of disappear or sound fizzy and passive. Sometimes just making a small EQ hump and sweeping through these nasal frequencies as you listen for the sweet spot can make a huge difference in the power and punch of guitars. In fact, strings can use a little midrange boost treatment as a general rule.

Using the wrong microphone to record the source material can cause all sorts of high midrange issues. A lot of times, people record with "the only mic they have" and ask you—the post-audio miracle worker—to clean up the fallout. Many microphones are tailored for different types of voices or instruments. As an example, a mic designed for a male vocal will probably have an EQ boost between 2 and 3k. Female vocalists naturally have more presence in the 2- to 3-kHz frequency range because women typically sing higher than men do. So if the recording engineer puts a female vocalist with lots of natural midrange in her voice already on a mic with a boost in the 2 to 3k range, you should get your bathing suit because you'll be swimming in midrange.

I've had to use a very narrow band of EQ to reduce almost -20 dB of midrange frequency before because of an issue just like this. By applying this treatment, the vocal was considerably more under control and finally listenable in the mix. But both the artist and I agreed that it should have been recorded with the right mic in the first place. There are some things in this frequency range that require an aggressive EQ treatment.

The High Mids (The Cut, Clarity, and Consonants)

The area of 3k to 6.5k is a monster. How much clarity is too much? How much is too little? Is it clear and loud, or is it just piercing? In many forms of music, this is the spot where things can get a little hairy. For example, in music laden with percussion (such as most Latin and world music formats), many different instruments fight for these frequencies. In rock and pop music, this area is the beginning of a frequency brawl as well.

Here are some examples of the typical high midrange conflict:

- **3.4k to 3.6k.** Vocal consonants, middle tom hits, traditional piano key sounds, high end note definition for horns.

- **4k to 4.5k.** Kick drum snap, some tom hits, snare crack, conga and percussion hits, pizzicato strings.

- **5k to 5.7k.** Guitar-pick attack, upper piano keys, bass clanks and slaps, hi-hat barks.

- **6k to 6.5k.** Vocal essing, beginning of lower cymbals, bottom snare, bow crispness, and chirp of violins and violas.

All of the instruments listed here have cutting and clear accented frequencies in the high midrange. As you can see, it has the potential to get messy. My best advice for applying EQ here is this: Most of the time in post, you are boosting these high mid frequencies, so you need to decide which tracks are the feature and brighten, or enhance, the upper midrange of those elements. Anything that is a secondary feature, such as a rhythm guitar or other sonic layers that exist mostly for texture, may not need quite as much additive EQ in these high mid areas. Whereas you would push a kick drum +6 dB at 4 kHz, you may not want to push the low conga hits quite as hard in the same frequency. The simple reason is that in our example, the kick is present for the duration of the tune. Driving it forward with constant repetition makes it a feature, and the congas are filler material (or background figures) because they occur far less often. If both the kick and the congas had the same amount of EQ added and subtracted and were panned in the same direction, each time they sounded in tandem, they would create a sonic conflict with each other in the track.

The most important thing to remember in this part of the spectrum is a little bit goes a long way. If there is too much additive EQ here in the high mids, the clarity and precision of an instrument may actually compromise the overall continuity of a piece by making the instruments obtrusive and obvious in a mix. This approach can be appropriate for some types of music, but completely inappropriate for others. For example, there are elements in an R&B mix that are features, such as drums, vocals, and bass—these things need to be loud and clear. You do not need guitars to cut like they do on a rock recording in this instance. Guitars would need to be more passive and fade into the background. Pushing volume or EQ on the guitars might cause conflict and take the focus away from the vocals.

In a mix, certain elements that exist in certain types of music are okay playing passive and supporting roles. Many instruments in large arrangements are felt and understood more than heard and notably perceived by the listener. In most cases a background vocal should not be pushed like the lead vocal. It's just there to add color and harmony and not conflict, so keep this in mind before you dig in and *really* start turning some knobs.

The most important questions to ask yourself are, "How does it sit in the mix? Is it uncomfortably up front? Does it drown out in the background?" You want the things that need to stand out to be accented with EQ, and you want other things in the mix taking up less space to make the song seem colorful and like it has some depth. A good way to practice this EQ treatment (in all areas, not just the high mids) is to set up a project with mono playback only and try mixing a track using EQ only. You'll be amazed at the amount of headway you can make using EQ alone to adjust the frequencies of fundamental tones within the track.

The Highs (Sizzle, Sparkle, Crispness, and Headroom)

Finally, we reach the highs. What's funny to me is how musicians and average listeners often perceive treble and highs as opposed to how audio engineers and post-audio professionals do. For a listener, high end is really more like the high mids. For a guitarist it's what the treble knob does on his amp (adds about +18 dB of 3k to 5k). For audio professionals, we're talking about "sizzle"—areas at 7k to 15k and up. The sparkle and sheen of cymbals, the "tsst" of a closed hi-hat, the air and headroom of a vocal track—all take place in the high frequency. On a visual EQ, this area is the far right side of the frequency spectrum, and in many visual EQ interfaces, it's abbreviated because most people can't hear much above 16k.

The primary difference in equalization between semi-professional and pro audio recordings is how the high end is managed. When mixing and mastering their own projects, most people find they have problems reproducing the highs found in most commercial recordings or that they can't get it "bright" enough. Commercial records are set up for those highs and clarity from the get-go. Cymbals are often recorded with particular set of cymbals and the right microphones to get the desired sound. High-frequency vocal problems are resolved before they begin with appropriate microphone selection and recording techniques upon input. Good engineers solve these problems and work out their excited frequencies during tracking. As a post-audio person, you may not be lucky enough to get properly recorded material with the right amount of highs included. In some cases, you will have to make do using additive EQ.

It seems that over time, newer commercial recordings have accumulated even more high end. The theory behind boosting all these super-high frequencies is that the low end will sound even lower, and the mids will seem more detailed because the amount of sonic space between frequencies seems greater. When a unit such as a BBE Sonic Maximizer or a Mega Bass on a stereo is used to enhance low end, it will also provide a high-end boost, operating on the same principle that the perceived space between frequencies creates the illusion of a more exciting and dynamic mix.

If you go back and listen to a CD from 1986, you will notice the tracks are quieter, "browner," and seem significantly smaller in space and frequency than those on current CDs. All the exaggerated high end in today's music is due to the additive high end and compression processing that is typically applied in the mastering phase of a recording. The difference you may notice between your old Def Leppard CD from 1987 and your new "remastered" version (besides volume) is the super-pronounced nature of the high mids and high end. Adding highs really does seem to sonically open up recordings. Now, many albums and mixes take place with these highs already attached. So be aware. Again, the world of "real" audio signals is a pretty brown place. Know that you'll have to use a fair amount of additive EQ in the high end at some point.

It is possible to go too far in adding highs. If there is too much high end in the recording, it may sound brittle, glassy, and artificial. I've heard some current rock recordings where the areas of 6k to 10k were close to unbearable. Though they seemed great and impressive the first time I heard them, over time the highs began to bother my ears, making repeated listening to the same track a little painful. This is called *ear fatigue*.

When working with high end, too much can literally be physically taxing. *Always* do side-by-side comparisons with records you know you like and you have listened to repeatedly. Emulate high frequencies you hear and develop a balance with a familiar recording as a reference point. Maybe you'd like a little more glassy sheen than Radiohead. Maybe you want it as brown as an old jazz recording and you need to reduce the highs so that it doesn't sound like a Kenny G recording. Remember, nothing is worse than a harshly recorded open hi-hat (think Stone Temple Pilots) with tons of highs rolled in. After a while, it may be too taxing for the listener to come back for a second listen.

Running the EQ: What Does This Knob Do?

We've already touched on the basic definitions of the controls found on a standard software EQ in Chapter 5, but now we're going to dig a little deeper into the functions of these controls.

The most basic control on an EQ is the frequency control, or the *freq*. This control allows you to decide on the center point for the frequencies you are about alter or affect. Usually, this is located and separated into frequency bands, or the spectrum ranges we just discussed: low range, low midrange, midrange, high midrange, and high range. Sometimes software EQ plug-ins will automatically limit the values of a frequency range so that if you're adjusting the high range, the frequency control will only affect 5k and up. Similarly, if you're adjusting the low range, you might be limited to affecting 20 Hz to 300 Hz. But don't worry; you'll have plenty of access to the full frequency range—or at least enough to be dangerous.

Next up is the Q control, an elusive little number that basically decides how much bandwidth or frequency area will be affected by any EQ adjustment. The Q setting is a sub-function of an EQ band, meaning that it can be found with the controls that affect a particular frequency. You will never find a Q control without an EQ band to govern it. Also, the value of the Q control doesn't *always* have to be adjusted. Although you usually *must* alter the value of an EQ band's frequency in order to select the range that will be altered, and you *must* use the gain control to specify the how dramatically the frequency range will be affected in order to hear the effect of the EQ at all, the EQ alteration for that frequency band will still function even if the Q setting is at its default value. If the relative frequency band in which the Q parameter resides is bypassed or if the gain is at −0 dB, the Q setting for that frequency band won't have an impact on the equalization at all. A frequency band must be active in order for any of its parameters to have any effect.

Q setting values can range from 0.01 to about 12, and sometimes more. The rule here is that the higher the number of the Q setting,

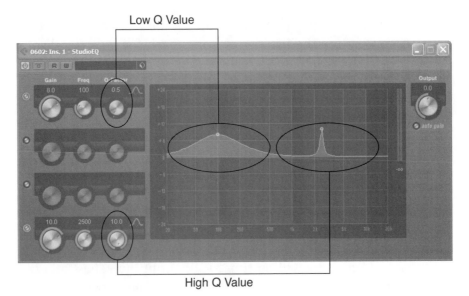

Figure 8.3   The left side of the EQ shows a wide or low (value) Q setting. The right side shows a narrow or high (value) Q setting.

the more narrow or specific the range of frequency you are affecting is. For instance, a boosted frequency at 5k with a Q control setting of 5 will make a smaller and less noticeable difference than that same 5k boost with a Q setting of 2 (which will probably affect the spectrum all the way down to 3.5k and up to 6.5k) and boost those surrounding frequencies as well. Figure 8.3 shows what the two different Q settings look like on a visual EQ. On the left is a Q with a low value setting, which will cause a blanket effect over a wider frequency range. On the right is a Q with a high value setting, which causes a more specific effect over a narrower range of frequency.

The shelf control (sometimes a Q option) is different from Q controls because shelves are a blanket effect that lifts in only the high and low frequencies. Usually these "shelves" are slow-ramping EQ boosts or cuts for which you can define a starting point. Whatever frequency value you define is where the EQ alteration will begin, and it will affect the rest of the frequency spectrum from that point. There are two primary types of shelf EQs: high shelf and low shelf. If you set a high shelf at a frequency value of 7k, then all of the frequencies from 7 kHz to 20 kHz will be affected. A low shelf at 300 Hz will affect all frequencies

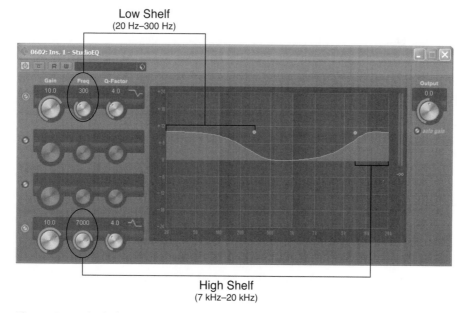

Figure 8.4   The left side of the EQ shows a low shelf that affects 20 Hz to 300 Hz. The right side shows a high shelf that affects 7 kHz to 20 kHz.

from 20 Hz to 300 Hz. Figure 8.4 shows the high shelf and low shelf used in this example.

Shelving is a very difficult thing to use properly without getting carried away, and usually the increases are much lower in gain than those made using a Q setting. In shelving, a +4-dB increase is a *lot* of EQ due to the fact that you are affecting very broad areas of the frequency spectrum. In the low shelf example I just mentioned, you would literally be adding +4 dB to every frequency below about 300 Hz. Usually this type of EQ shelf is used in already mixed and balanced elements of the mix. Suppose you have the background vocals on one bounced stereo track and they just need to be a little brighter overall—adding a touch of high shelf (+2 to +4 dB) in this application is very common.

The EQ's gain control is the amount of volume (expressed in decibels) by which you are increasing or decreasing the frequency. Most EQ alterations become apparent after only about +/−2 dB of alteration. However, it is not uncommon in mixing to alter a frequency +/−10 dB either way.

The gain control is where you can get into trouble by doing too much tampering. Usually, I tell people to raise or lower until they hear a substantial difference and then reduce the gain until what they're equalizing fits in the mix. I may take out −5 dB of highs in some bright cymbal tracks, and then slowly ease back the gain to −2.7 dB until the cymbals sit in the mix properly. The key to maximizing this control is to listen to the track with all audio signals audible as you alter the EQ's gain in real time. It's important to check the EQ of individual elements in the context of the entire mix. Just because something sounds great soloed up, that doesn't mean it will sound that way when all the other instruments and frequencies are in. Always know that a little bit of EQ gain goes a long way, and if you are altering in the areas of +/−18 dB, you may be dealing with improperly recorded source material. Either that, or inappropriate EQ decisions have been made elsewhere in the mix and will need to be corrected.

The most important thing to remember when operating an equalizer is that EQ gain is not a volume level control. Theoretically, your track should already be at the correct level before you start to EQ. The EQ should be the frosting, not the cake. Most high-end engineers believe in the process of subtractive EQ rather than additive. A properly recorded source should require little EQ enhancement to get it where it belongs. However, in a post-production project studio environment, you will be getting sources that are less than adequate on input level the majority of the time.

Know this, and make your customers realize that *input* directly affects *output*. Even though there are a great number of post-production "tricks" you can use to resolve audio-fidelity issues, the source material you receive has a *direct* effect on the outcome of the final mixes. If you are supplied with marginal to poor audio due to bad input signals, you probably won't be able to make a stellar mix with it, but you can polish it enough to make it decent. With EQ it's easy to manipulate a track into better shape and make it more listenable overall. But you can only polish a turd so much. The truth is that you can EQ forever, and some turds are gold waiting to be uncovered… but some turds are just turds. Be aware of which is which when you start, and never claim that you can make a $10 mic plugged into a cassette deck sound like a Norah Jones album.

Compression

We are about to open the biggest can of worms in audio. A discussion to end all discussions… the everlasting battle between the audio post-production engineer (good) and the listener (evil—I'm kidding, really!). Because this chapter is related to mixing, I'm going to cover only basic compression techniques here. There is another type of compression that *can* be used on some elements within a mix, but it is far more common in the mastering stage. So, multi-band compression will be discussed later, in relation to mastering. And now… welcome to the battle between dynamics and compression!

Dynamics in audio are easily defined as the relative loudness or softness of a note or frequency. So between the peaks, or *transients*, and the valleys of a waveform lies the dynamic range of your audio sources. *Compression* is the process of limiting and manipulating the dynamics of a recording. Compression, sometimes called *dynamic processing*, makes the distance between the peaks and valleys of a waveform or audio source more equal in volume. If you are using a vocal track as an example, compression will make the contrasting volumes between the breathy whisper and the sung note at full voice less apparent, while still sounding natural. With compression, the relative volumes between a whisper and a scream are closer together, more under control, and more balanced-sounding overall. And man, does it sound simple when it's spelled out like that! Unfortunately, the battle hasn't even begun yet….

In my experience, compression is one of the main components that allows most listeners to identify how professional and well-balanced a performance or recording sounds. If it sounds like there are a lot of transients or loud dynamic parts of audio fighting for space and attention rather than existing peacefully among all the other audio elements, they are doing what is referred to in post-audio as *standing out of the mix*. When one or more things is standing out of the mix, the music has a tendency to sound chaotic and out of control. Compression allows for the dynamic differences to sound less significant while simultaneously drawing attention to the finer details of signals that are quiet in comparison.

On the individual tracks of a pop mix, you could use compression to make the drummer's occasional uneven snare hits closer to the same volume as the even snare hits. The snare hits would then be relatively the same in volume and attack, allowing the listener to ignore the variances in the initial performance and focus more on the entire beat itself... or whole song, for that matter. Conversely, in a vocal track, you could use compression to draw more attention to the smaller details of the performance. With the vocal wide open and no compression applied, you would not be able to hear the breaths and quieter syllables of a vocal track.

Most of the time, compression is pretty generously applied to a vocal in order to make the nuances stand out. Before digital mixing was available, you might have had to manually resolve these types of dynamics issues by using an outboard hardware compressor, riding the fader on the console, or using automation to regulate volume throughout the performance. But now, such inconsistencies can be managed with minor manipulation of a software compressor plug-in.

What's unusual about compression is that most of the time it goes unnoticed by the listener unless it is obviously overdone or applied improperly. A vocal with too much compression can sound squashed, muffled, and lifeless. Overdone compression actually subtracts from the overall professionalism of a track. Herein lies the fine balance of the battle of the ages. Compression is far more obvious to an engineer than to a listener. Untrained ears know so little about compression that they're not even sure what it does. What a listener or client perceives as sounding better, more professional, under control, and balanced might have been you applying generous amounts of compression.

The goal here is to keep the music sounding natural, balanced, and even. The only real problem with using compressors is that there are no hard-and-fast rules for their application. There's nothing I can say that's a quick fix to use compression properly or tastefully. All you can do is play with the knobs and controls and listen closely for the desired effect. You can certainly become accustomed to what *might* work for a particular application and develop your own preset library for future use, but the first step toward the correct application of compression begins with understanding the basic controls.

Threshold

Compressors reduce the dynamic range of an audio signal. They use a user-definable threshold level to determine at what point an audio signal will be reduced. When an audio signal exceeds that threshold level, the compression begins to take effect. The numerical symbol for as loud as an audio signal can be without clipping or distorting is -0 dB. If your threshold setting is at -15 dB, then each time the audio signal is louder than -15 dB, it will start to be compressed.

As a rule of thumb, I would say for most "normal" audio signals, start with -8 dB for most threshold applications and slowly reduce the value ($-$dB) to the point where you can hear the proper balance and limiting points of the signal. With something like a poorly recorded "peaky" snare drum that has lots of large transients, I would start at a -0-dB value and begin reducing from there. The applications for levels over -0 dB are usually for analog situations with consoles, where the signal peaking and compression in the console is part of the sound. It is also possible that if you've added lots of effects and you have made multiple EQ adjustments to the audio signal already, a compressor's threshold may need to be raised to a positive value in the final stages of mixing just to help keep things under control.

Ratio

The *ratio* mathematically defines *how* the audio signal will be compressed. The compressor's ratio setting is a user-defined value that tells the compressor how much the signal will be reduced in decibels. It works hand in hand with the value of the threshold setting, as it only affects signals that exceed the threshold value. For example, a ratio of 2:1 means that for every 2 dB the input signal exceeds the set threshold level, it will only increase by 1 dB above the threshold. For example, a threshold of -4 dB, a ratio of 2:1, and an input signal of -2 dB would result in a signal level of -3 dB. The same threshold and ratio values with an input signal of 0 dB would result in a signal level of -2 dB because the input signal would have exceeded the threshold by a total of +4 dB, and thus would be reduced by −2 dB because with a 2:1 ratio, every 2 dB above the threshold gets 1 dB back. The same would be true for any compression ratio. Obviously, the higher the ratio, the more reduction takes place. A ratio of 8:1 would give you 1 dB of gain for every 8 dB above the threshold value, and 12:1 would give you 1 dB back for every 12 dB exceeded over the threshold, and so forth. You can think of it almost like a trade-in program for decibels.

If the threshold value is not overly aggressive, 2:1 is pretty light for a compression ratio setting. If an aggressive ratio of, say, 20:1 or greater is applied, you've started to destroy the couch and mess with its structural integrity, as you would with the audio signal. The most functional ratios for mixing range from 2:1 to 9:1 with varying threshold sizes. Ratios of 10:1 and over take you closer to limiting, or using compression as a distortion effect, which we will cover later in this chapter, in the "Limiting" section.

To determine where the ratio should be on a track and how it will fit in the mix, I often play a track of audio and set up a relatively loose −16 dB threshold level. As the track plays, I turn the ratio knob or controls until I hear something I like as far as balance and effect. When it feels right, I leave the ratio alone and play more with the threshold control until the compression level feels perfect.

I used to read many books in which they would say never to use high compression ratios because you will ruin your audio, but in the real world this couldn't be further from the truth. It used to be that compression was considered *strictly* a post-production treatment, which meant that the less noticeable it was, the better. Now, an obviously overcompressed signal can be accepted as an effect designed to intentionally crush musical elements, making them distort and adding texture. Different ratio levels have different uses. The use of compression in general really depends on the type of audio signal and the desired effect.

Attack and Release

Attack and release is often the most misunderstood area of the compressor's controls. Engineers who are new to using compression sometimes have a tendency to overlook the importance of these controls.

The attack and release actually have more to do with sculpting the affected signal's tonal characteristics than the actual compression/ dynamic reduction level.

Attack

The *attack* control defines up how quickly the ratio of reduction is applied to the audio signal. This control is usually measured in milliseconds and typically goes from 0.5 milliseconds up to a full second. The longer the attack time, the more of the original audio signal will be heard before the compression kicks in. You can think of attack this way: If your nephew is going to say a swear word, how fast would you need to get your hand to cover his mouth? Do you want the word completely eliminated and squashed, a muffled mess like Kenny on *South Park?* Or do you want him to get out the "shhh" sound because it would be kind of cute and funny in front of Grandma? You don't want him to get the entire word out of his mouth, but slamming your hand over his face in anticipation may be a bit too much.

Your hand covering your nephew's mouth before he even gets the word out would be an example of a fast attack. In reference to a waveform, the transient or peak would barely exist in this instance. If your nephew gets out the "shh," it's a slow attack because you aren't exactly on the ball when he starts to say it. Both types of attack are acceptable in different situations. If you were in church, you would want the attack to be as fast as possible; at a family picnic, he may nearly get the whole word out if the attack is less aggressive or slower.

That being said, the attack value is really a case-by-case basis. Sometimes it's appropriate to squash a signal completely, and sometimes it is better to let a little of the tone come out before the compressor takes effect. How you work this out or justify the attack's use is completely a matter of taste. For example, in a choir-type chamber song, you would not want a bunch of snappy words standing out from the mix. You would want these words compressed, and you would want them to be mellow and fit more into the ambience of the track. In this choir/ chamber case, a fast attack would be appropriate to eliminate the snappy, percussive nature of some words. In a rock mix in which the vocal is a little bit more rhythmic and a bit improvised, you would want those consonants to remain intact and for the clarity of the rhythmic phrases to be apparent. You would use a slower attack to maintain more of the natural tone before the compression begins to affect the signal.

You could say that by cranking down the attack for an immediate effect, you are dulling the signal's tone. When I use a quick attack, I'll often add a little EQ after the compression has been applied in order to brighten the audio back up a bit.

When dealing with percussion, if you are going for a natural sound, you will want to use a slower attack so that you can hear that initial striking hit before the attack starts. Begin with the attack control back around 100ms and move it down slowly until you hear the drum hits sound the way you want them to. It's an all-too-common mistake for an engineer to just crank the snare compressor down to 0.5 milliseconds and lose all the snap/crack from the get-go. The engineer might end up trying to roll in a bunch of high and high midrange EQ to compensate, but this only adds noise to the track. Percussion is probably the toughest thing on which to properly use compression. When applied correctly, compression should fix the problem you're trying to resolve, not create new ones for which you'll have to compensate with yet another process. Take it slowly and really listen to how you are affecting the original audio.

Release

The *release* defines how long the compression will last once the input signal drops below the threshold. So if the threshold is set at −14 dB, any parts of the signal that are above −14 dB will be compressed. When the signal drops below −14 dB, the compressor will allow the signal to return to its normal volume. Release is how quickly the signal will recover its original gain when the compressor is no longer affecting it.

The idea behind the release control is to help make a smooth transition between parts of a signal that are compressed and parts that aren't. If the release is set too slow, the compressor's effects may last longer than desired, causing it to compress the audio material that occurs after the part of the signal you *meant* to compress. If it's set too fast, the compressor will be overly sensitive to minor level changes in the signal, releasing them too quickly and causing a noticeable and highly undesirable "pumping" effect. I usually begin with about a one-second release time and then listen while reducing the value until there is some definition and I don't hear the smear of a slow release anymore.

There are times when you may need to use different attack and release times for the same audio track in one song. Suppose a section of a vocal has a lot of sixteenth notes at 140 BPM. The attack and release of the compressor will have to be a little quicker during that section to maintain the clarity and tone of the vocal part. When you're working with compression, it's a good idea to dial in a general setting to treat the entire track, then listen to the whole project and make note of any areas where you may need to adjust the compression levels to regain clarity for a given part. Rather than load another instance of my compressor plug-in on a different track, I'll often use automation to adjust the parameter values for different parts if I need to use multiple compression settings.

Makeup Gain

The *makeup gain* on a compressor is fairly self-explanatory. When you compress an audio signal, you will inadvertently reduce the volume of it. The harder you compress, the quieter the signal will get. Now you've got the ratio, threshold, attack, and release settings dialed in so that the audio sounds even and under control, but the volume has been greatly reduced as a result of all your meddling. This is where you would look to the makeup gain on your compressor's interface. Need more volume? Crank it up. I recommend adding enough makeup gain so that the volume of the signal after compression is similar to the volume before compression. This way you can easily judge the effect of compression by disabling/enabling the compressor, without being distracted by volume changes. Then use the track's level fader to make volume adjustments from there.

A fine balance of all these parameters makes compression sound professional and natural. Spend time with different compressors on different types of instruments and vocals. You will begin to develop preferences as to which one works best for a particular instrument or vocal style. Most studio pros and high-end mix engineers have their own specific compressors, plug-ins, and settings for every scenario. They arrive at those selections by experimenting to see what is appropriate, and so should you. If you worked on a killer-sounding R&B vocal with one lady two weeks ago, and a new project comes in with a vocalist who has a similar style and sound, try the same compressor setting as a starting point and tailor it from there. Reference points are important things in post-production—otherwise, we'd approach every project as if we didn't know where to begin.

Limiting

A *limiter* is basically a "hard" compressor with a very high ratio value and a fast attack. There are no rules that define at what point a compressor becomes a limiter, but the way their distinct functions are perceived is clear. Unlike a compressor that reduces the dynamic range of highly dynamic content, a limiter makes sure that the input level never exceeds a user-defined output level. In the case of a limiter, the threshold level is the absolute volume level, so whatever the threshold is set at is as loud as the output signal will ever be.

There are three very common and basic controls on a limiter: input, output, and release. The *input* allows you to adjust the level of the incoming signal. The *output* is the threshold or maximum output level. The *release* behaves exactly as it does on a standard compressor, by defining how long it takes for an effected audio signal to return to its normal gain level.

Limiters are primarily used during tracking to keep the audio from distorting as it's being recorded. They are also used in mastering to maximize overall volume. It's commonly considered hard limiting when the ratio is above 10:1. It's used a lot in post-audio and mixing for instruments (such as rock bass and bright, punchy guitars) to keep hard picking and aggressive dynamics under control.

When you get up to about a 50:1 ratio, you enter the neighborhood of something called *brick-wall limiting*. Brick-wall limiting, or *brick-walling*, with a ratio of 50:1 or higher is the only sure way to see that an input signal *never* exceeds the set output level or threshold.

However, it's more of a safety precaution used to prevent input clipping than it is a tool used for shaping sound.

Panning

I find panning to be one of the most interesting parts of mixing. *Panning* can be simply defined by how far left or right of center a musical element or a recorded track sits in a stereo mix. Panning is sometimes called *horizontal space* or *horizontal positioning*. In properly executed panning, the goal is to have each instrument and/or voice in its own spectral area on a mental sonic stage, allowing the listener to perceive each one's position naturally.

Every track in your software mixer will have a pan control. It should appear as either a knob or a slider. Pan controls default to center as a reference point, and you have the option of moving the tracks left or right from there. It sounds simple enough, but a lot happens within these pan controls. In this section, I'll be covering some of the basic concepts and misconceptions about pans and mixing. In post-audio, these special "positions" affect the balance and quality of your mixes more than you might think. I'll be using the common terminology found in most software mixing programs to discuss this topic, so here's the secret decoder ring—which isn't really a secret at all, nor is it a ring....

- C or 0 = Center.
- # = Value of the pan in the relative stereo channel. This value may be scaled differently from application to application.
- L = Left.
- R = Right.

The Soundstage Theory (The "Make It Look Like the Band" Method)

The first theory of panning is to design the mix as you would visually see music performed on a stage in front of you. This is the most common practice for rock, pop, and country music post-production mixing. In this type of mix, the vocalist and the drums are usually centered in the mix, and the other elements (guitars, bass, keyboards, horns, strings) are where they would be located on the stage in relation to the drums. So if the kick drum and the singer are in the same spot in the center of the stage, they may both be defined as being center panned. The bass may be located at 15L, just a little to the side of the kick drum, and the guitarists may be at 64L and 55R (stage left and right). Let's not forget about our keyboard player all the way over on the right at 74R. This is a simple layout for most band/performance-oriented panning. It's very visual and aurally easy for the listener to interpret.

Focal Perspective Panning

The next theory uses the audio focal point of a track as a starting reference for the mix. This is common in styles of music such as jazz combos, acoustic singer/songwriters, layered instrumental soundtracks, and so on. Suppose you have a small jazz combo. The drums are usually center-prominent in a rock or pop mix, but in this type of setting you want the sax player to be the feature and the drums to be just another organic part of the musical landscape. Because you don't want the kick drum to compete with the soloist, and there is no need to punch every beat as if it's a dance track, the kick drum or entire drum set might be shifted to the left in the mix.

In another example, suppose you have a simple singer and guitarist playing a folk song. Panning them both to center would kind of mess up the mix and create competition for the focal point. If you use the vocal as the focal point and move it a little to the left (15 to 25L), and you use the guitar as a supplement and move it harder right (40 to 55R), this is focusing the listener more on the singer and less on the guitar because of the horizontal positioning. And at the same time, it's providing what might be an accurate stereo representation of the performance.

Remember, in these cases of focal perspective, the closer you get to center, hard left, or hard right, the louder and more focused the sound will become. If you want something less emphasized and "tucked in," staying farther away from the extreme hard left, hard right, and center pans is the way to go.

Effect Panning (Artistic Statement/Canvas Panning)

In experimental electronic and dance formats, in which music is as much about technique as it is about creativity, panning is essential to the art of creating a wide musical soundscape. Just like a filter or delay would be employed as an effect, so are the panning and positioning of these mixes. It's also common for this genre of music to be based on musical loops and synthesized elements that pan themselves as part of the way the sounds are designed.

In these mixes, musical elements may suddenly shift positions and span wide pans in fractions of seconds. So an instrument's (or a sound's) individual importance and prominence takes on a less focal approach in the panning. Tracks in these styles are more about the overall ambience, vibe, and feeling. The crafting of pans is just one small element of these vast arrangements.

Effect panning mixes will do many things uncommon to other music types. Pans will often occur much faster, more frequently, and more drastically than they would in a pop song or a basic soundstage mix.

Things to Listen For (Tips)

Panning has an effect on tracks that is a bit surreal and tough to identify at first. When elements of the same frequency cross over in pans, a certain amount of phasing, modulation, and cancellation occurs. The best way to explain this is to record two distorted guitar tracks on your computer. Play the same part twice, and leave them both panned to center. On playback, you will hear tons of phasing and slight modulation. You may even start to get a headache from the surplus of layered midrange frequency after a short amount of time. Now move one of these guitar tracks to 75L and the other to 75R, and hit play. As you will hear, the level of sonic separation you can achieve with panning alone is pretty dramatic.

When I begin a mix, the first thing I do is tune the pans. I listen to the elements of a mix and position them one at a time, starting with the rhythm instruments. Then I'll move all the tracks around until all the phasing and sounds feel properly separated and balanced. I typically approximate pans before adjusting any EQ, volume levels, or compression. I've always thought that if you get the pans dialed in correctly and you keep the tracks separated in their own sectors from the very beginning, you'll have less trouble getting the appropriate volume, dynamics, and proximity into shape later.

A common mistake mixers make is to follow someone else's advice or to use a prior template for panning. All mixes are different and unique. Pans may have to be different from track to track, depending on the audio material. Sometimes the slightest panning adjustment can make a significant difference in the overall fidelity of a track. As a common example, some snare drums have the most clarity when they are panned center. Some snares can sit a few notches left or right of center until phasing and balance clean themselves up. At times I have even found myself placing a snare as far as 20L or 15R to get it to sit with the rest of the drum kit properly.

Drum kits are a whole other mess when it comes to panning. This is the area of the mix where you have the highest number of source microphones in the smallest amount of sonic space. Let's take a moment to discuss the most common configurations for panning drums.

American-Style Drum Panning

American drum panning is simply a variation on the soundstage idea with drums. This is basically, the "pan 'em like you see 'em" approach. Your pans reflect the way you perceive the positions of each individual drum as if you were watching the drummer perform onstage in front of you. In this scenario, a typical drummer has the ride on the left, the hi-hat on the right, and the toms pan right to left. In the American approach, toms are panned a bit wider than where you would imagine the toms would be on an actual drum kit. Kick drum and snare are often as dead center as can be. This method has been used on many recordings over the years and is great at getting the "live" spectator approach.

European-Style Drum Panning

European drum panning could be considered the opposite of the American style. In this method you pan the drums as if you are the drummer playing them. The hi-hat, ride, and toms are in the pan positions where you would expect them to be if you were sitting behind the drum kit. In this case the toms are usually a little closer together and panned left to right (highest to lowest). I often use this style of panning on drums because, in my opinion, it provides a more intimate perspective of the drum kit.

For the rest of the instrumentation, take the soundstage theory and reverse it. Consider that, logically, if you pan the drums as if you were sitting behind the kit, wouldn't you pan the rest of the band from the same relative perspective? Of course, there are so many different ways that a full band can stand onstage that it's more important to choose a style of panning for your drums and be consistent with it than it is to spend time trying to decide whether the bass player should stand to the left or right of the drums depending on what country you're mixing for.

Final Thoughts on Panning

Listen to all of your favorite songs. Spread the speakers wide and evenly or strap on a set of headphones to hear all the common pans in the music you know and love. You may be surprised by the space and width of the instruments panned in your favorite songs. Now that you are listening for the panning, the location of the instruments and the nuances may astound you. Have you ever noticed that the guitars in "Lightning Crashes" by Live negotiate dramatic pans to the rhythm of the guitar's strumming pattern? At the beginning of "Zero" by Smashing Pumpkins, a guitar is panned so hard left that if you turned the left speaker off, you wouldn't be able to hear the guitar at all. In the same example, you'll also notice how much attention was drawn to that guitar *because* of its panning position. Regardless of whether listeners are able to identify *why* the guitar grabbed their attention, they know that *something* was definitely different about it. Victimized by limited tracking capabilities (which, by the way, didn't make it any less great), '60s music panned all the instruments hard left and right, and often only the vocals were centered. You'd be surprised by how the little sprinkles of bells on the far right of a mix can stand out if you know what to listen for. Take notes about different mixes, and apply the new panning schemes to your own work.

Proximity standards have changed a lot over time. In the late '80s, guitars were panned left and right at around 70 to 90 percent to widen a rock mix. But these days, such hard panning isn't as acceptable in a mix, unless it's being applied for effect. Because audio recording used to be such a primitive process, music was limited in its panning options. Old Beatles records used to assign different instruments to the left or right channels, but there was no way to attenuate *how far* left or right an instrument would be in the mix without using a discrete source mic to capture the audio from a particular perspective in the stereo field. Instruments were just always either hard left or hard right, with no value in between.

Prior to the '70s, American-style drum panning was used almost exclusively in popular music. European-style drum panning didn't become popular until later. And now, with the possibility that your audio may be converted to a number of mono formats for radio, television, multimedia, or live broadcast, the panning rules have changed again. Elements that have been panned hard right or left may even have the potential to be lost completely once the audio has been converted to a single channel. In five years, you may realize that everything you've read about panning now seems mostly wrong, though at this point, with surround sound capabilities, we've pretty much exhausted the majority of possibilities in the stereo field.

Proximity and Perspective

Panning takes place on the one-dimensional X axis—or, simply, a horizontal plane. By using reverbs and other spatial effects, you also have the ability to move musical elements front to back, or along the Z axis. How far away from the listener something sits in a mix (the proximity) and how much "space" the music lives in (the perspective) are primarily affected by the reverb effects applied to the audio sources. When working with audio in which room ambience is not part of the original signal, you may have to apply reverb or delay in order to create some. Creating room ambience means that you are using virtual emulations of real environments to suggest a natural space to the listener. The same philosophy that you use with compression applies here, too: If you use reverb correctly, people won't be able to tell you've used it at all.

Before you begin adding space to a mix, you need to decide what *kind* of space will serve it best. You obviously would not use a cathedral-sized reverb on a song in which the only instrumentation is a solo acoustic guitar. Similarly, it would be difficult for a listener to comprehend an epic rock opera with the ambience of a small bathroom. Choosing the right reverb isn't rocket science. In fact, it's mostly common sense.

As a casual music listener, you might not even notice some of the spatial effects used in music to suggest proximity. This usually indicates the appropriate use of reverb in a mix. Why don't you notice it? Most likely because the reverbs seem native to the sounds they're affecting and spatially relative to the other elements of the mix. The truth is that *everything* has some kind of space to it. The laws of physics demand it. If you yell across a high-school gymnasium, do you think you will ever *not* hear the reflection of your own voice? If you were blindfolded, yelling across the very same gymnasium, would you know that you were in a large room? Whether it's the distance between a vocal mic and a singer or the overheads above a drum kit, all recorded sound has some kind of natural reflection and space to it.

A good way to learn to hear "space" accurately is to first simply heighten your auditory senses. I'm not talking about developing super hearing so you can listen through walls, but heightening your auditory senses will enhance your abilities as a post-production engineer to make you more aware of natural ambience. We rarely pay attention to everyday ambience because we accept it as being part of the way things naturally sound. But if you listen a little more closely, you can begin to understand how the parameters of reverb time, room size, dampening, and pre-delay are used to define and simulate realistic room environments.

An exercise you can use to get a better grip on the spatial aspect of mixing is to try to duplicate the amount of perceived space that exists in your favorite recordings. First try recording a cover song with all instruments as dry as possible. Then, in post, add all the reverb effects until the cover song comes close to the spatial feeling of the original. There will be all sorts of little tricks, such as a slap delay on a vocal or a particular type of reverb on a snare drum, that you may not have noticed until you tried to copy it. Or perhaps you'll find a new trick that you wouldn't have thought to try until you took a closer listen.

Recordings that sound dry or unaffected usually aren't dry at all. They're just properly mixed using appropriate reverbs. Again, this may be a case of the naked ear accepting a reverb as part of the natural sound. Until you are deliberately making listening observations, reverbs and delays can be tough to hear. But just because a reverb doesn't have a huge three-second tail that you can immediately identify and say, "Whoa! Reverb!" it doesn't mean it's not there. Without *some* sort of reverb to create space, most records would sound more like demos than finished records.

Reverb is also used to add perspective and is a reference for depth in the recording. It's common to have both dry and reverb-affected elements in the same mix. For instance, without space, drums can seem flat and really "in your face." If you're mixing for realism, such an up-front approach might make the drums, or even the overall recording, sound artificial. You don't need to place the kit 1,000 feet behind the lead singer, but you do need to give it some ambience that will help smooth it out and blend with the rest of the signals more naturally. Adding a slight reverb to only certain parts of the kit can help create this effect.

A small amount of room reverb on the snare and kick will make the entire kit seem as if it's in a space with a finite amount of real estate in which to reflect. Now, what you've essentially done is given the listener an idea about the environment in which the music is being played. Using similar-sized reverbs in varying degrees on other elements of the mix will help reinforce that idea. You've also given the affected elements a bit of texture against the rest of the mix, which creates depth by way of contrast.

Background vocals often get the "distance treatment" as well because they are not a focal point of the music. They should usually be downplayed to the lead vocal and should also be perceived as being farther away from you than the lead vocal. This will help prevent any competition between the background and the lead for attention in a mix. Supporting vocal parts are typically a background figure, especially in modern music, and should be treated as such.

When it comes to giving a mix perspective and proximity, sometimes I'd rather receive dry source material from a client and define the space myself than have to try and work with the ambiences that were captured (sometimes unintentionally and inappropriately) in the original recording. Not everyone has been trained as a professional recording engineer, and a lot of precious time can be wasted trying to fight with preexisting ambience if the client is not careful. I've received *terrible* source material in which it sounded as if the drums were recorded in a huge room, but everything else sounded like it was recorded as a direct signal or with very little ambience. In this situation, it would have simplified things quite a bit if I just had dry, "space free" tracks to work with.

Really, the only time that it's not appropriate to add space in post-production is if something is the sole focal point, such as a voiceover for a radio ad or a book/reading recitation. In these situations the distance from the voice talent's mouth to the microphone is often just enough space to do the trick. For these applications, you typically want to get that warm, upfront, and inviting presence that resembles the voice you imagine in your head when you read or think. Other than that, almost everything else will get some degree of reverb.

Now that you have a background on the functional uses of reverb, let's take a look at the parameters you'll use to create the aforementioned environments as the sonic architect.

Reverb Types

There are two primary types of reverb plug-ins: basic and convolution. There are many fine third-party basic reverbs available, but many software sequencing programs come with basic reverb effects in the box. Until you are comfortable with using reverb effectively, you may want to stick with the included reverb before you spend hundreds of dollars on a better one. Basic reverbs simulate reverberating environment types, such as plate, spring, room, chamber, church, and hall. These are great for post-production because they are the most common and effective types of spatial environments due to their organic-sounding qualities. In these types of basic reverb plug-ins, you may also find a few less common room types that are used as obvious spatial effects to intentionally bring about artificial-sounding results. Some of these more "extreme" reverb types may include gated, reversed, or other non-linear (or unnatural) reverb types.

Convolution reverbs simulate a specific space, not just a type of space. From Row F in the Ryman Auditorium at the Grand Ole Opry or the center of the Cathedral of Notre Dame, to a large room with wooden ceilings or a popular recording studio, measurements and actual recordings are made of real acoustic environments to develop impulse responses or acoustic samples on which to base the reverb type. A convolution reverb basically learns from the recordings of these physical spaces and then applies the same kind of reverb to your audio signals. Just as amp modeling models different types of gain structures, convolution reverbs model specific acoustic spaces. Convolution reverbs are mainly for applying real-world environments to a recording. If you had an *a cappella* men's choir, you'd probably want to use a convolution reverb over a basic reverb. I highly recommend having a great-sounding convolution reverb for when you need it, but because it would be impossible for me to discuss the characteristics of every impulse response available, we'll look at only the most common types of reverbs that are used in post-audio.

- **Plate reverb.** This is based on the sound of a speaker or electro-mechanical transducer sending an audio signal to a reverberating sheet-metal plate in a controlled area. As funny as this sounds to us in the digital age, many older (or vintage-conscious) studios have spaces set up for these large, wonderful-sounding plates. This was the staple of old rich reverbs used on many vintage recordings to add space in post-production and mixing. I know that sheet metal might imply that a plate is a harsh-sounding reverb, but it doesn't usually sound harsh at all. Plate-type reverbs are most commonly used on vocals and snare drum.

- **Spring reverb.** This is not the sound of the outdoors in the months between February and June, but the sound that is most fondly recognized as "guitar amp reverb." If you've ever rolled your Fender combo amp to your car and hit a bump, you know exactly what this is. A good example of spring reverb is found in old recordings of surf guitar from the late '50s and early '60s. In guitar amps, the signal is sent into a small metal tube attached to the amp, causing a long, stretched spring to vibrate. The vibrating spring is then blended into the original signal. This type of reverb is very noticeable as an effect and is recognizable to the average listener as a "tunnel-sounding echoic thing."

- **Room reverb.** This is the sound of an enclosed environment with standard reflective walls. In fact, wall reflection is usually referred to as *room reverb*. Usually room reverbs are very pleasant, warm, and natural-sounding. Most of the time, room reverb is the type that goes virtually unnoticed to the listener. Gently applied room reverb is the most commonly used reverb for instruments in a mix (other than snare drum or vocals, for which plate reverb still seems to reign supreme).

- **Chamber reverb.** This is a simulation of a real physical studio room that has been specifically designed for use as a natural echo chamber. This was typically an empty but controlled space that recording engineers would build in order to send a speaker signal into it. Then, with room or boundary microphones, they would record the "chamber voice" or the resulting signal, reverb and all. This works in a similar way to a plate reverb, less the metal surface, but it sounds similar to some types of room reverbs. Unlike your standard room reverb, though, most chambers are specifically tuned to maintain certain frequencies and acoustic characteristics.

- **Hall reverb.** This type of reverb is based upon the same values and principles as room reverb, but with the sound of a larger, more reflective, and more acoustically friendly concert hall. Usually the reverb time will reverberate longer and a little brighter in a hall reverb than in a room reverb. Concert halls are areas designed specifically for good acoustics and the proper reflection of sound. This is usually a nice reverb for things such as strings and keyboards.

Common Controls for Reverb and Their Uses

There are a few universal controls that you will run into on almost every reverb plug-in on the planet. Their functions are the same no matter what reverb you're looking at. However, some of the parameters that are available on algorithmic reverbs may not be available on convolution reverbs. Here's an overview of the common control parameters you'll find when working with spatial effect plug-ins.

- **Reverb type.** This is the kind of reverb or spatial audio environment you want to apply to the original signal. Decide what type of space will be appropriate for your application and choose it here. Do you want a small, intimate room? Or do you want a large, cavernous wall of reflections? Common reverb types that are found in almost *every* reverb plug-in available today are plate, spring, hall, chamber, and room. There are some reverb types that are used purely for effect, such as the endlessly reverberating cavern I mentioned a moment ago. Although you may find yourself using a reverb like this only once in a blue moon, it demonstrates the extreme end of the reverb spectrum. Select a ridiculously large reverb type and take a look at the values of each of the parameters we're discussing here. Then, select a small room type and compare the differences between the numerical values that define the two.

- **Pre-delay.** Pre-delay simulates the time that it takes for sound to travel to the reflecting walls and bounce back to the listener. This is usually expressed in milliseconds to seconds. Small rooms have a small amount of pre-delay, whereas large rooms have a greater amount of pre-delay. This allows you to make larger spaces sound more realistic by increasing the time it takes for first reflections to reach the listener. Also, some cool and weird-sounding effects can be achieved by turning the pre-delay way up.

- **Dampening.** Dampening is a method of controlling how quickly the high or low frequencies of the affected signal will decay or fade out. This parameter changes the character of the reverb tail by simulating different types of reflective surfaces (such as tile, hardwood, carpeting, brick, and so on) within an acoustic environment. It's basically a high-shelf or a low-shelf EQ that is continuously applied to the reverb of an audio signal.

  Here's how it works. As a reverb fades away, so do the high and low frequencies of the reverb. If the room is filled with less reflective surfaces, the high end is naturally dampened, so it will decay more quickly because there is nothing for the reverberations to bounce off. This would be relative to a high level of high-frequency dampening and will produce a warmer, smoother-sounding reverb. On the flip side, a high level of high-frequency dampening essentially increases the amount of reflective surfaces in the acoustic space. When a reverb bounces off more reflective surfaces, the reflections last longer and sound brighter because the high frequencies take longer to decay.

In a way, this is a bit like an acoustic padding treatment to your reverb area because you are using the padding to reduce the reflective surfaces in the area. Just like you put up soundproofing to reduce the number of sonic reflections that naturally exist in a studio environment, dampening keeps the frequencies of reverb tail from bouncing around too much.

Most reverbs have two separate controls to define the dampening levels—the separate high and low frequencies. The midrange frequencies are not usually affected at all. If you turn the high-frequency dampening control all the way up, the high frequencies would take longer to decay than the midrange. And as you can imagine, a high level of low-frequency dampening would cause the low frequencies to decay more slowly than the midrange as well.

Dampening is basically giving different reverb times to the high and low frequencies of the reverb signal. One way to really understand it is to apply a reverb to a dry signal and play with the dampening control so that you can relate the dampening adjustments to what you actually hear. This parameter can really affect the way your reverb sounds. Don't be afraid to dig in and really get a grip on it.

- **Diffusion.** Diffusion defines how much density a reverb has. It allows you to change the intervals of time between echoing reflections. The higher the level of diffusion, the closer together the echoes will be. This is ideal for percussive sounds because it will make the reverberating echoes tight so that the reverb tails don't overlap. As you can imagine, more diffusion creates a longer echo. High diffusion levels are ideal for sustaining elements. So, more diffusion makes the reverb smoother. Less can make it clearer.

- **Room size.** This parameter defines how large or small the selected reverb type is. If you choose a bathroom reverb setting, only expect the virtual room to sound as big as P. Diddy's bathroom or as small as a service station bathroom. A hall reverb is obviously going to have a much larger room size and ambience than a small room reverb will. In a hall reverb, if the room size is set to 50 percent, you are in theory only using 50 percent of that hall's space or reducing the size of the hall by half.

- **Reverb time.** This determines how long the actual reverb tail will sound. It can last anywhere from 0.5 seconds in a small bathroom simulation to three full seconds, depending on the size of the room or the proximity application you are going for. Reverb time is usually fixed in most audio applications, but it *can* be adjusted if it's appropriate. For instance, sometimes a chorus may need a longer reverb time to make a vocal seem bigger. Or a verse may need to have a shorter, more subtle reverb time to give it more presence. Automation is a great and efficient tool that you can use to change the value of this parameter over the course of your audio project.

- **Filter/EQ.** Many reverb plug-ins allow you to have control over the reverb's global EQ. This is not the same type of shelving equalization that is used in dampening. You're now taking time out of the equation. Adjusting the EQ characteristics of the actual reverb is a good way to get your reverb to blend into a mix more naturally. In the same way you use EQ to shape an audio element so that it plays well with others in the mix, you can use EQ to shape the way the reverb sounds.

Many reverbs can be bright and slappy-sounding out of the gate. It's possible that this sterile and impersonal characteristic might work for a particular mix, but most of the time when reverb is used as a post-production process, you'll want to try to make it sound as natural as possible. A harsh, too-bright reverb on inappropriate sources may stand out as sounding unprofessional and misplaced.

When a reverb has the controls to sculpt the EQ, take the time to carefully adjust it to suit your tracks. A piano may need subtractive EQ in the low end of the reverb and a push in the highs added, whereas a voice may require less high end while retaining the lows in order to control the sibilance in the mix.

- **Wet/dry percentage or mix control.** This parameter simply adjusts the overall amount of reverb applied to the dry input signal. If you have 100-percent wet, you are hearing only the affected signal. At 50 percent you are hearing half of the original dry track mixed with 50 percent of the reverb effect.

  A common practice in mixing is to turn the wet/dry mix up to 100 percent and export the affected audio to a separate track specifically for controlling the reverb mix. Then use the volume control of the exported track to blend as much or as little of the effect as you want into the original dry track. This can be an efficient way to have an automatable mix of reverb because you no longer must have the resource-intensive reverb plug-in loaded. The downside is that if you want to change the reverb type later, you'll have to kill the reverb mix track, insert the reverb plug-in again, and start over. Before you print a reverb mix track, I recommend that you have some level of commitment to the reverb you're going to use.

The appropriate use of a combination of these parameters will get you one step closer to a professional-sounding recording. Take the time to get acquainted with your reverb plug-ins and their parameters and uses. The better you understand them, they more useful they will be.

Delay

Delay is similar to a reverb effect in that it often deals with a spatial environment. The primary difference is that it repeats itself, adhering to user-defined parameters that define the length and timing of the repetitions. We're not talking about reflections here; we're talking about actual repetitions of the audio material. When delay is applied, you hear the original signal first, and then, depending on the settings, a copy of it is played back. With each repetition the signal decays or becomes lower in volume and, in some cases, it spreads out across the stereo field. Figure 8.5 illustrates the way the volume of a delay effect decays over time.

Before delay technologies were available, in order for music to use spatial effects at all, it had to be recorded in an environment with natural reflections. Then along came the ability to produce echoes, and after

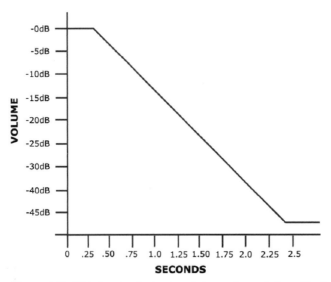

Figure 8.5 This is a typical rate of decay for a delay effect set to tap on quarter notes, or roughly 1237ms, with the feedback and mix controls set to 50 percent.

that, the ability to produce them at any volume and consecutive interval. When we talk about *analog delay,* we're talking about delays that were created using an analog recording medium. Audio signals were captured on magnetic tape and then looped over and over again. You could adjust the speed of the tape and the level of your input signal, but that was pretty much it. In these units (such as an Echoplex), the first repeated notes, or *taps,* are louder than the later taps that get significantly less defined and more out of time the longer the effect lasts.

This process of creating delay on an analog medium gave the delays a certain warmth and sonic characteristic. These days some of the early echo units are still in use, but it is more common to use digital hardware or a software plug-in to emulate the effect of slightly less than perfect analog delay. This is a great type of effect for vintage applications, and it works especially well on guitars and vocals. The delay getting more out of time and degenerated is actually part of the way that many vintage recordings sound. You'd be surprised by how much your ears may like this less-than-perfect effect because you have heard it your whole life and there is a certain comfort and familiarity to it.

Like reverb, different delays can be used to add dimension and texture to the elements in a mix. Although they're not the most natural-sounding effects, they can really help draw attention to vocals, background vocals, guitar, or almost anything, really. If you're mixing purely for effect, you can use delays more drastically on snare drums and melodic instruments. I find that a little multi-tap delay, panning from left to right with a medium decay, can really smooth out and draw focus to a lead vocal. The correct delay can do wonders for the overall contrast between instruments when used appropriately and in moderation.

Digital delay is a very precise effect. The original audio is sampled using an analog-to-digital, or A/D, converter. The signal then passes through a series of digital signal processors that store the sample in their memory and play back the stored signal according to the parameters you've defined. Digital delays are very pristine-sounding and don't typically add any color to the original signal. Also, the accuracy is unreal. If you set your digital delay to repeat in eighth-note values, it will do exactly that with no drift whatsoever. Digital delay also allows you to define a greater number of parameters than simply the volume and intervals of the repetitions.

Several modifiers classify delay effects. All delay effects are either mono or stereo. Mono delay effects, such as the one shown in Figure 8.6, are single-channel, meaning that the effect will be equal in volume and repetition in both the left and right speakers. You can specify the note value to define how quickly you want the audio to repeat, or tap, and how long you want the taps to last before fading out.

Under the category of mono delay, you have multi-tap delays, which actually give you multiple delay processors to work with. It's like having two or more delay effects affecting the same piece of audio at the

Figure 8.6 A single-channel mono delay plug-in.

same time. Suppose you're using a mono multi-tap delay with two processors. You could set one to tap on quarter notes and the other to tap in eighth-note values to create a tapping smorgasbord. Each delay processor usually has its own discrete EQ/filter section so you can customize the resonating frequencies of each delay.

Using a mono delay means that you are restricted from applying pans to the effect. You will be able to make the original audio signal seem a little wider, but you won't be able to separate the delay channels from one another. However, this doesn't mean you can't pan the original audio if you want to, but that's kind of the long way around.

A stereo delay is a bit more flexible and produces a flashier effect because you have both the left and right channels to play with. Under the category of stereo delay, there are basic single-repetition delays; multi-tap delays; and even ping-pong, or panning, delays, in which you can define and tailor the taps for each discrete delay processor and then alternate their positions across the stereo field. So if you were using a stereo version of the multi-tap delay such as the one used in our mono example, you could set the first processor to tap at quarter notes and the second processor to tap at eighth notes, and then pan one hard right and the other hard left (or somewhere in between). Now your delays seem to have movement as they scatter left and right between the two processors. Figure 8.7 shows a stereo multi-tap delay plug-in.

I love delay. I think it's one of the coolest things since sliced bread… which I guess doesn't really say much for me. But I encourage you to play with your delay plug-ins as much as possible. There have been times when I felt like I had exhausted every sound-sculpting possibility in search of the right texture and dimension, and it turned out that the answer was back in basic effects—a simple multi-tap delay was exactly what I was looking for. As you get deeper into digital audio, you'll accumulate more plug-ins that do all sorts of crazy different things, but remember that most effects that offer something seemingly unique are built on basic effects such as EQ and compression. Even reverb is derivative of a delay effect. So don't be afraid to get back to basics when processing audio.

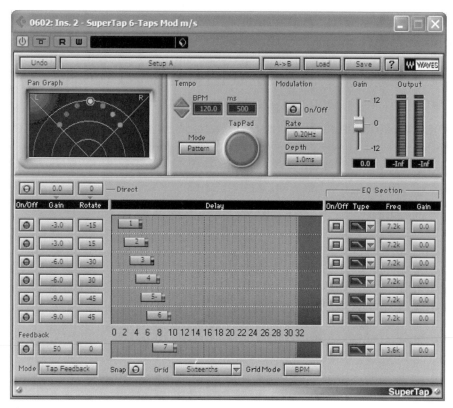

Figure 8.7   A multi-tap, stereo-panning, six-delay effect processor plug-in.

Now let's take a look at some of the common controls you'll find on a delay plug-in.

Common Controls for Delay and Their Uses

As with any other effect, there are universal controls that are the same from plug-in to plug-in. Here are the most common ones.

- **Delay time.** This parameter determines how often delay taps are triggered. The greater the value, the farther away each tap will be from the next. Delay time is usually measured in milliseconds. On a basic delay, there is a single global delay time controller that designates the interval time of each tap. That means every tap that the delay processor produces will adhere to the value set for the global delay time setting.

Multi-tap delays that use multiple delay processors have independent delay time controls for each processor. The tap interval of a single delay processor can be defined independently of the other delay processors. Setting each independent processor to a different delay time will create a complex succession of taps in the audio signal.

- **Sync.** Most delay plug-ins have the option to sync the delay taps to the tempo of the project. *Sync* is usually identified as a button relative to the delay time controller on an independent delay processor. When activated, the value field of the delay time changes from milliseconds to note values. You should now be able to select the note value at which you want the delay taps to occur. When you begin playback, the taps should sound perfectly in time with the rest of the project. This is a great feature when there is a lot going on in a mix, and you need the delay affected to sound really tight and almost percussive in rhythm.

- **Feedback (regeneration).** *Feedback* is how long the delay taps will last. The value is usually expressed as a percentage. The higher the percentage, the higher the number of repeats or playbacks the effect will generate. Feedback also has a direct effect on the decay of the effect. As the taps begin to fade out, they decrease in volume. So the higher the feedback level, the longer it takes for the effect to decay. Some taps on the tail of the effect can become so soft that they are inaudible in a mix over short periods of time. If I want to hear three taps in the mix, I'll set up the feedback so that I can hear five, then listen to it in context and adjust as needed.

- **EQ/filter.** Most delay plug-ins also have an EQ/filter section on their interface. These filters are similar to those found on the reverb plug-ins that I mentioned in the last section. On a basic delay, these are simply a high shelf and a low shelf with adjustable frequencies.

On more complicated multi-tap delay plug-ins, you can get several filter shapes, such as bell, bell with a narrowed frequency range, high shelf, low shelf, high pass, and low pass. Furthermore, you can tailor the frequency at which the filter affects the delay and adjust the gain to define how drastically it is affected.

- **Pan.** Many all-in-one stereo delays have left and right pan controls to set the horizontal positioning of the repeated delay taps. You may want to "tuck them in" or move them closer to the center position, slightly behind the vocal at about 30 percent left and right. But you should evaluate every scenario when it comes to the proper stereo placement of delay taps. You may want to use the pan control to slide the position of the taps from left to right across the stereo field so that you can find the sweet spot where the delay doesn't conflict with other elements or effects in the mix.

- **Mix level.** Just as it works for reverb plug-ins, the *mix level* is the percentage of the affected signal being mixed into the original dry signal. It's common for the mix level to be set somewhere between 10 percent and 50 percent for most applications. But, like everything else, it's a case-by-case basis. Mix level can be a tricky thing from one track to the next, and it's good to develop templates and presets for common delay uses (such as eighth notes) and their levels as reference points from application to application.

Level

A common misconception about commercial audio is that a good recording should be as loud as possible. The volume of music has gone up considerably in the last 10 years. Modern music is as loud as commercially broadcasted music has ever been. This leads novice mix engineers astray, making them believe that louder is always better. I personally do not agree with this opinion. Although you don't want the listener reaching to turn up the volume knob up on the stereo when one of your mixes comes on, I find that making everything as loud as possible in a mix has a tendency to rob a piece of its dynamic structure.

Level is pretty much the last stage of mixing for me because it's the easiest aspect of the mix to control. I'll usually make sure that all my EQ, dynamic processing, and spatial considerations are worked out before I really get into adjusting volume levels. Naturally, while trying to get signals to sound right, I will attenuate level faders to compensate for any processing that I've done that may have caused the signal to increase in volume, but when it comes time to determine the appropriate volume levels for the final mix, it's all faders down.

Starting out with all your faders at total silence will allow you to introduce the individual tracks of the mix one at a time and raise their levels in context. Begin with the sonic foundations, such as drums. Get the levels of the drum kit mixed the way you want them, and then put them in a subgroup (sometimes called a *group channel, folder track,* or *bus*). That way, if you need to reduce or increase the volume of the drums, you can affect the global volume of the kit with a single fader rather than change/re-mix the level of each individual drum mic.

When you've got your drum kit dialed in and placed in a subgroup, start bringing up the bass. Whether it is a synthetic, electric, or upright bass, this instrument will make up an important part of the foundation of your mix. This is the rhythm section, as well as where most of the fundamental low end exists in the mix. I recommend gradually bringing up the level until its volume is relative to the volume of the drum kit. They should be pretty well balanced with each other, and you shouldn't be able to hear one stand out over the other.

A Track by Any Other Name...   Don't underestimate the power of labeling your tracks correctly. I can't tell you how many times I've gone to start mixing and I can't seem to find where one of my guitar tracks went because I didn't label it correctly... or at all! If you haven't been managing your track names up to this stage, it's as good a time as any to get on top of it before you start messing with levels.

At this point, I'd start bringing in rhythm guitars, rhythmic synthesizers, or anything that is not a lead instrument or an accent. Again, raise the levels until they seem balanced relative to the rest of what is going on in the mix. If you're working with guitars, make sure that the guitar in the left speaker isn't significantly louder than the one in the right speaker. Also remember that you're creating just the initial mix here. You should get the levels pretty close to where you want them, but you'll inevitably make some minor adjustments later in the process.

The lead vocals come next. A common mistake that people make is monitoring too loudly when they are mixing vocals... or anything, for that matter. Not all studio monitors are created equal, and your ears perceive sound a bit differently at higher volumes. Vocals have a tendency to be too quiet when mixed at a loud volume, so I recommend mixing at lower volumes, especially when you're working with vocals. Bring the vocal up high enough that you can hear it clearly even at low volumes.

The last things you want to pull into your mix are the accenting elements. These are typically momentary musical figures that occur on a downbeat or for a short period of time and only during certain parts of the project. It's kind of a matter of taste when it comes to how loud or soft accenting elements should be in music. I believe they should be loud enough to be noticed. There have been times when I've made accenting elements (such as an impact sweetener or some other musical element that isn't a major focal point) so quiet in a mix that I didn't even realize they were there when I heard it back. Again, mixing at a lower volume should help you resolve this. If you can hear accenting elements when the entire piece is played quietly, then you will be able to hear them when it's played loudly.

Realize that if you can't fix an audio signal by changing its level at this stage, then the problem isn't the level of it at all. Something most likely went awry during the EQ or compression process. The beauty of digital mixing is that you *can* go back if you need to. With good planning and occasionally saving new versions of your project, you can go all the way back to before the audio snafu that's holding you up ever occurred, without having to start all over again. In addition to changing panning positions, you can apply some subtractive or additive EQ to try to work out a problematic source before going back to the mixing board. I often find myself reducing the lows and low midrange on most recorded sources, and then adding a little high range here and there to increase clarity. Once the signals are EQ-treated and panned to my satisfaction, I'll bring the fader for that track back down and try to bring it into the mix gradually again. Remember, if something is low-end heavy and muddy, increasing the overall level increases the rumble and mud in the mix. If you have to increase the level of something to +6 dB (6 decibels above 0 dB), it's probably time to go back to the EQ and compressor settings and see what more you can do to improve them.

After you've got all the levels just about where you want them, it's time to start making minor adjustments to dial in the mix. I listen to the entire mix, considering each source one at a time. Are the drums balanced? Is the snare drum cutting through the way it should? Is the bass clearly defined? Can I hear both guitars? Are the accenting elements noticeable enough? If the answer is no to any of these kinds of questions, a slight level adjustment should be made. If I'm not sure what the answer is, I'll either mute the track to see whether its absence makes an audible difference, or I'll solo it up so I know what I'm listening for, and then play it back again. When it comes to final touches, I believe in making small incremental adjustments of +/−2 dB at a time. You'd be surprised at how far 2 dB goes in a final mix.

Just as this chapter is laid out, level should be one of the last processes in a mix. Bringing down levels, adding EQ treatments, and using proper panning are how you get perceived volume and clarity in a mix. EQ should never be used to get more volume out of a signal. The way to make audio sources sound louder and clearer is more complicated than simply riding up on the fader.

Mixing Dos and Don'ts

When you're starting out with anything, you'll make your share of mistakes. Some will be small mistakes, and some will be big... sometimes REALLY BIG. Hopefully, this section on "Mixing Dos and Don'ts" will reduce the risk of big mistakes. If you see something here that I mentioned earlier in the book, it's not an editing error—it's because it's *really* important to know.

Dos

- **Know what you are going for from the very beginning.** If you are thinking, "This song needs to be mixed like *Led Zeppelin IV*," and the band is thinking it needs to be mixed like the latest digital monstrosity from Puddle of Nickelcreed, your ideas about the mix may be too different for *anyone* involved to be satisfied with a final mix. That being said, it's best to get everyone on the same page from the get-go. If you're the post-production engineer, that basically means you're going to have to talk it out with the client and make sure that you fully understand what the target is. Furthermore, make sure the client understands what it is that you understand about the project, so that any confusion or miscommunication can be clarified before there's a problem. Get an accurate grip on how the project currently sounds and what the client expects it to sound like when mixing is completed. At this point, be ready to ask all of your questions, present the options, and make any suggestions if the client is open to them. In some cases, you may have to have a conversation about how a Casio organ recorded with an SM57 will never sound like a real Hammond B3 with a Neumann U87 on it, no matter how well it is mixed! You may have to tell the client that they ought to go for a more indie lo-fi rock thing this time. Not to discredit the client, but if you're not already aware of this, you'll be surprised to find out how many musicians have little or no understanding of the recording and post-production process.

- **Compare your work to professional CDs.** There is nothing more revealing than a quick foray into pro-audio reality. Just when you thought everything was as great and massive-sounding as it could ever be, you put on the latest recording by [*insert major recording artist's name here*] back to back with your mix, and you suddenly realize that you have way too much bass, and everything in the mix is competing for the same frequencies. It's difficult during the throes of a mix to determine the outcome of what the finalized and mastered product will sound like. Often, after each major revision of a mix, I'll export a stereo track, apply a quick mastering job (as if there *is* such a thing!), and listen to it side by side with a similar commercial project. You will get closer to the goal a great deal faster if you have a constant reference for what your work *should* sound like. Don't be afraid to compare your work to that of known pros. It can be a truly eye-opening experience.

■ **Know your monitors and the room in which you monitor.** Few things are as valuable as a mix engineer who knows his speakers and room. Truth be told, no room or set of studio monitors is the "perfect" listening situation (except for maybe Ocean Way in Los Angeles), but you can learn to deal with and modify your personal listening space to be, at the very least, predictable. On different speakers and in different rooms, things will have more bass or sound brighter, walls will reflect frequencies differently, and you will go insane trying to figure out these logistics to mix in some alien area.

A daily good long listen to your favorite music in your work area is a *huge* advantage. I laugh at people who want me to come out of my studio and mix or record in their studio because my sound reference is completely different once I get there. If I move my speakers into their smaller room, the bass could sound too big, and I'd be constantly rolling more and more bass out of the mix, possibly doing it a great disservice. A large room might cause me to do the exact opposite. Commercial studios are a slightly different story; although no two are exactly the same, they've been acoustically treated, they've had the same monitors sitting in the same place since the beginning of time, and they typically employ their own mix engineer so that there *is* someone who's familiar with the room and the reference monitors.

Regardless of whether your room is perfectly treated or whether you monitor on $100 speakers or $1,000 speakers, for the most part you should just stay put. The key to working with what you've got to make a great mix is to develop reference points that will help you accurately translate the audio from your monitors to other listening environments. Mix in the same spot on the same speakers, and learn what is common for your mixing area. When you check your mixes, make note of what is different about them from when you heard them in your own studio. Then verify the differences with multiple comparisons between the different listening scenarios for consistency, and develop a reference that way. If the bass sounded fine in your studio, but on a consumer stereo system there is nothing *but* bass, you know that you'll have to mix bass to be perceptually quieter in your studio in order to get it to translate correctly.

After days, weeks, months, and years, you can be absolutely sure of your sonic reference point. I hate getting into a new room or a new set of monitors. It's kind of like getting used to driving a new car—it can sometimes takes six months to a year before I truly understand the way it responds to the road and my driving. And so it is with monitoring and understanding how studio monitors respond to the room and the mixing adjustments I make. We will discuss proper monitoring in *great* detail in Chapter 9, "Three Sides to Every Story: Monitoring in the Project Studio."

- **Start with broad strokes and then get more specific.** This statement basically means that you should make large blanket judgments first, and then tailor small adjustments to refine the mix. For instance, suppose you put on a mix, and in the first few seconds of playback you notice that the drums are dull and boomy, and they have no clarity. Let's deal with those drum tracks first, keeping the broad-strokes concept in mind. When you narrow your focus, you can get more specific about what sonic issues exist and need resolution. Is the snare present and crisp enough? Are the hi-hats too crisp and harsh? After a while, the pieces of the mix can really evolve and come together, but you have to start with broad generalizations. If everything sounds bassy and woofing one at a time, isolate the tracks that are typically bass-heavy and remove some of the lower frequencies that are known to be problematic. If that doesn't fix it, then you have to move on to the next possible solution. Listen to the mix again and get more specific.

  I would say that the average mix requires anywhere from three to five *major* adjustments, followed by several hundred minor ones. But you'll also have to draw the line somewhere. You could spend hours getting the best snare tone on earth and realize that it doesn't work at all for the song. Try to see a mix for the forest and not the trees.

- **Get listener and customer feedback.** As rough as it can be sometimes, you must have a balance between what the public likes and what the client likes. Bringing in a friend who likes music but who doesn't know the ins and outs of recording is sometimes a great idea to get some feedback. It's like having an immediate ability to hear the mix through someone else's ears, if your friend is impartial and has limited recording knowledge. The best thing to do with a first-time listener is take the music into his or her listening environment, such as in a car or a bedroom, and have the person tell you what immediate impressions he or she gets about the music and the fidelity. Usually, the first thing the person will attack is the performance or musical style... you know, the things you don't have any control over. But don't interrupt the listener's cavalcade of opinions just yet. You may get some great feedback about things you overlooked because you are too close to the mix.

The majority of third-party "civilian" listeners with fresh sets of ears have spent most of their lives listening to only commercial-quality music. Therefore, they have only professional-sounding recordings to use as reference points when they hear your mix for the first time. These commercially trained ears will pit you right up against the big boys, which is exactly where you want to be. You'll want to find some objective listeners, and you will probably want to avoid people who get hung up on criticizing performance and stylistic choices only. Girlfriends (or boyfriends, for that matter) who don't like specific styles of music might not be the best audience off of which to bounce your mix.

The client—on any project, be it the label, an investor, or a band member—must have the final say. Sometimes this means that your opinions about a mix may be overridden. A stubborn client might have to make a mistake in order to reevaluate and do what is best for the mix. If "Joe Bass" guy wants his bass cranked because he's paying for all of it, let him know that you think it might be a mistake—and why. Then let him make the call. Sometimes, you just have to wait for your phone to ring once he has come to his senses and realized that the bass level is grossly inappropriate.

If you're in this business to build a career on what you do, which most of us are, then also understand that when you release a bad mix of something, your reputation is on the line. When I hear a great-sounding record, I pick up the CD case to find out who mixed, produced, and engineered the album. Although some casual music listeners could care less about who did what, there are plenty of people who do care. If a sonic monstrosity somehow escapes your studio with your name on it, it won't matter whether or not you engineered, mixed, and mastered the entire album by yourself. You will eternally be connected to a bad-sounding product. I try to find a delicate balance in providing enough information to the client about *why* certain mixing choices are necessary and letting them do what they want. Most of the time, if a client understands why the bass can't be turned way up and what other problems doing so might cause, they will usually make the right choice without a fight. You will save time, and they will save money. Everyone wins!

Don'ts

- **Don't make decisions when your ears are burned out.** Throughout this book, I've reinforced the idea that you should always trust your ears. Now here's an addendum to that statement: Always trust your ears... *unless* they are tired. If you sit in front of a set of speakers mixing the same project for eight hours, you are bound to experience fatigue. You have to know when you need to call it a day or maybe just take a break. I'm sure we've all worked on projects until it felt as if our ears were going to fall off. In the beginning, it's often like the first day of doing manual labor. After eight hours of unloading a truck, you'd be exhausted and ready to go home or, at the very least, take a break. After eight hours of using your "ear muscles," they may become so tired that you are no longer capable of making good decisions. If you continue, you may listen to your mix the next day, after resting your ears overnight, and wonder what drugs you took. We're not machines. Over time you'll build up your listening stamina, but for now, take it easy.

If you have three songs to mix in two days, ration out the days so you have four hours on and two hours off. Take breaks to eat and drink. Most importantly, enjoy your downtime doing something that doesn't involve listening to music. When I'm mixing a project, I listen to talk radio in the car rather than music, just to give myself a little vacation from the project. Watch a movie or some TV. Go for a walk. You'd be surprised what a difference having fresh ears and taking much-needed breaks can make during mixing. Granted it may take longer, but mixing 10 songs in one day is unheard of. Make sure you have a realistic grip on how long it will take you to mix a project, and relay that information to your client. I would even say that it's better to overestimate the timeframe by a few days than it is to surprise the client by having to ask for a few more days because you're burnt out.

- **Don't over-compress or over-effect a mix.** It's easy to get carried away, thinking that more effects are more impressive. Just because you're adding 25 plug-ins doesn't mean that your mix is getting better. Unnecessary effects can damage a mix. So unless the goal of the music is to use effects in an artistic way (such as in electronic music), you really only want to apply enough effects to bring out the best in the source material. Most music does not require fast-shifting pans, crushing compression of death on acoustic guitars, or the sound of a football stadium's large ambience to sound good. If I am unsure about whether an effect is helping or hurting the mix, I'll listen to the project with all tracks active and then mute and un-mute the effects in question. By doing this, you should be able to hear exactly what the effect is contributing to your mix and determine whether you should keep it.

- **Don't try to make a mix into something it's not.** If a local funk band has recorded an album live in their living room, and they bring the tracks to you for mixing, you most likely will *not* be able to make them sound like Earth, Wind & Fire's *Live at the Greek*. There are too many variables and obstacles due to poorly recorded source material. You could spend 10,000 days mixing it, and it still wouldn't be nearly as funky. This is another important topic to discuss with your client. Remember that the input directly affects the output. If there is a lot of bleed from track to track, uncontrolled sources, and bad mic placement, is it likely that you can make it sound better? Yes. Can you make the record something to compete with a commercial-music big-budget recording? Probably not. Be realistic about what you can get out of the source material. The client should have realistic expectations of what you can do with their project, and that begins with you.

- **Don't get so creative with mix that the message of the product is lost.** Remember what I said a moment ago about over-compressing or over-effecting? It's easy to get carried away with creativity in a mix, too. I know that as musicians, we are driven by creative ideas. However, mixing a project for the client may not be the best place to express them. It's fine to try out some new ideas in a mix. Just don't get carried away by creating 10 guitar tracks, all with different effects and panned in different positions, in an attempt to "widen" the mix. Sometimes keeping things simple can help convey the correct point. Unless you are mixing electronic music or art rock, in which the mixing is an integral part of the craft, you don't need to impress people with mixing. You just need it to sound good and communicate the right things with it.

- **Don't believe everything the pros tell you.** Not everything someone says in a magazine or on the Internet is right. It may have been right for that particular situation, but it's not necessarily true for everything. Just because Rick Rubin used a certain mic and said it's great, that doesn't mean you should run right out and buy it because it's "the one." In fact, you may have a totally different experience with the same mic. Here's an example: Many times when recording electric guitars at my studio, I use a Shure SM57 microphone. My friend uses the same mic in his studio, but through the preamps on his unnamed hard disk recorder, the SM57 was piercingly harsh on a guitar cabinet.

When someone recommends a product, process, or procedure, understand that it worked best for their situation, with their pre-amps, in their rooms, on particular types of audio signals, and so forth. This also can be said for compressors, EQ, settings, and other software plug-ins. Just because it worked perfectly for someone else's situation does not mean it will work for you.

When it comes to buying equipment, do your own research and have a good idea about what you want before you walk into a store and are bombarded by 15 commission-driven 16-year-old sales people. If you hear about a new trick that a famous producer is using for compressing vocals or tweaking drum sounds, definitely try it out, but know that you might have to adapt it to your individual situation. Not all pros know your gear, ears, and techniques the way *you* should. But don't take my word for it, either. These are all just suggestions based on my experience. Some may benefit from them, and some may not. If nothing else, you've got some new ideas about how to approach mixing. So why are you still reading? *Start mixing!*

9 Three Sides to Every Story: Monitoring in the Project Studio

The phrase "three sides to every story" has always been a way of saying that every scenario has three perspectives—yours, mine, and the truth. This is really no different in audio. The "truth," or the accurate reproduction of sound, has been one of the biggest topics of debate when it comes to studio monitors. It's tough to say whether it will ever be resolved because there are so many variables to factor in. Every set of monitors is different. Every listening environment is different. Every set of ears is different. And every audio signal is different. The opinions regarding what is a professional-sounding mix are all over the map. Somewhere between your speakers (your side of the story) and my speakers (my side of the story) lies the sonic truth for which we are all searching.

As a post-production engineer, you want to do your best to make sure that what you hear coming out of your monitors *is* the truth, or at least something that you can easily translate to the truth. In this chapter we will try to eliminate common monitoring pitfalls, discuss the difference between what you might or might not be hearing, and get you on track to overall better monitoring practices in your project studio environment.

Then and Now

Project studios have changed the way we monitor audio. The days of hearing your mix blazing over the "fatties" (dual 15-inch speakers commonly found in large studios) while standing in a large control room with wooden floors, bass traps, and acoustically treated, non-reflective surfaces are nearly over. Although big studios with ideal room acoustics are still in operation, more and more professional-quality mixes are being turned out of the spare bedrooms and garages of the world.

One of the reasons that this is possible is because project studios have become much more common. They've established themselves as a big chunk of the music retail market. Studio equipment manufacturers know that their demographic is no longer limited to pro studios with deep pockets. And thus, a vortex has opened up and created a market need for low to moderately priced digital audio equipment targeted at the average project studio. But affordable digital audio equipment is pretty much useless if it can't reproduce audio accurately. If you can't reproduce audio accurately, you can't turn out a professional mix. If you can't turn out a professional mix, you can't get any work to make any money to buy professional equipment with which to create a professional mix.... It's a vicious cycle, really.

The good news is that at the rate that digital audio technology is evolving, there may soon be no reason why you can't have access to professional recording and monitoring equipment that is also easy on your wallet. But until that bright future is upon us, there are things we can do to work with what we've got.

Format standards are part of this monitoring revolution as well. It used to be that you could only get a cassette tape of your mix (added hiss and all) by enduring a lengthy bouncing process from reel-to-reel, 2-inch magnetic tape. In mixing, the audio would have to come out of the 2-inch multitracker, through the console and played back on a single set of studio monitors. From that point you could bounce down to a cassette tape to make your "real-world" comparisons on other playback devices. The trial and error in real-time bouncing took forever, and due to mixing on a foreign set of monitors in an unfamiliar acoustic environment, the tracks almost never came out right on the first try. To think that you had to go through all of this just to get a cassette tape that you could listen to on your home stereo or in the car (that didn't even sound that great) is completely ridiculous by modern standards. But it used to be the way things were done.

Today, audio is more portable than ever. The endurance trial of trying to get your recording to a common medium is a thing of the past. How easy it is to burn an audio file to a CD or transfer it to your portable music player, and then listen to it in your car or on your home stereo moments later? This is really as simple as it gets. We can now monitor our studio mixes on almost any playback device we want. You will probably do the majority of your mixing in your own studio, through your own studio monitors, but previewing your mixes on various playback devices is just one of the things you can do to help yourself produce more accurate mixes—even if your studio monitors leave something to be desired. I get into this concept in great detail later in this chapter, but right now, I want to discuss the different types of monitors and common monitoring scenarios that you might encounter.

Different Types of Monitoring

Monitors are technically anything on which you can listen to audio. In the digital audio world, monitors can be your best friend or your worst enemy, depending on the scenario and how you look at it. If you have a good set of monitors that is positioned correctly in an ideal listening room with good acoustics, there is no reason why you two can't be B.F.F. (Best Friends Forever!). But if you've been spoiled and you have gotten too comfortable in your native listening environment, when you find yourself in an inferior listening arrangement, you may shake your fist in fury, curse, and maybe even cry a little at the fact that your monitors are so awesome that you are having a tough time monitoring on anything else.

On the flipside, if you can make your mix sound good on a crappy set of monitors, it will most likely sound good on any speaker system. However, keep in mind that a cheap set of studio monitors may not reproduce sound accurately. When it's time to listen to the great mix you did on your crappy monitors in your car, the levels may seem all wrong … let the fist shaking commence! The wrong monitors can also cause you physical pain. Not from lifting them, but from the ear fatigue they may cause. Specifications are important, but it is equally important to put faith in your ears when it comes to monitoring and *choosing* monitors alike. So let's get started by familiarizing ourselves with the different types of monitoring available.

There are commonly two main categories that monitor speakers fall into—reference and consumer. *Reference monitors,* or *studio*

Figure 9.1 Reference monitors.

monitors, are loudspeakers that are specifically designed for audio production applications (see Figure 9.1). They typically have a very flat frequency response. The speaker cabinets are often tuned to react to the specifications of the speakers' internal components. This is done to offer the most accurate sound reproduction possible. Reference monitors are designed to let you hear the detail in a recording. They can usually reveal all of the ugly little things about a mix. This is great because if you can hear them, then you can't ignore them. And this ultimately serves the greater good of the mix.

Reference monitors yield the subcategories of active and passive. *Active speakers* have a matched power amp built into the speaker cabinet that produces the appropriate amount of power it takes for the speaker to operate accurately. This is in contrast to *passive speakers,* which require an external power amp to function. Active speakers are generally regarded as being more accurate because all of the components—internal amplifier included—are designed to work together.

Passive speakers, on the other hand, have power requirements, such as wattage and ohm ratings, that *must* be adhered to for optimal performance. Proper power for passive speakers is important not only for accurate listening, but because your speakers can actually be damaged by the wrong power configuration. I personally prefer to use active monitors. They are more expensive than passive monitors out of the gate. But once you take into consideration that you'll also have to supply a power amp to work with passive speakers, it's worth the extra

Figure 9.2 Consumer monitors.

money just to know that your monitors are as accurate and efficient as they can be without you having to calculate power variables.

Consumer monitors are like those that you find in homes, restaurants, vehicles, and other everyday environments (see Figure 9.2). These types of monitors are the most common type of speaker on which the finished product will be heard. They are typically connected to a consumer-type preamplifier that not only provides power to the speakers, but is also designed to sweeten the listening experience by way of preconfigured equalizer enhancements, such as BBE and MaxBASS.

When people buy stereos, their decision is usually based on the way the stereo sounds. Whichever stereo sounds the best is the one they'll take home. These types of consumer systems reproduce music the way most listeners think music *should* sound. Many people like to exaggerate the high frequencies in music to enhance the top-end clarity. Others like to boost the sub-frequencies so that everything in the room trembles with low end. As the listener makes these enhancements, very little consideration is given to whether the music was actually meant to sound that way. The end result can compromise what the mixing and mastering engineer thought was a beautiful mixing and mastering job. As engineers, it is beneficial to us to create a mix that can really take the punishment and inconsistencies of real-world listening situations. Checking your mixes on consumer-type hi-fi stereos and vehicles will help you produce a better mix by letting you hear what the translation will be between your reference monitors and common everyday monitoring systems. It will also help reduce the number of unpleasant sonic surprises *before* you commit them to a master disc.

In my studio, there is a speaker selector for several different sets of monitors. I have large far-field speakers, near-field speakers, a boom box, a home stereo system with typical consumer sound enhancement features, a set of 1–inch computer speakers (that cost me a whopping $6), and, finally, a good set of studio reference headphones. Though this may seem excessive to some, there is a good reason why I've got so many monitoring options within arm's reach—I'm lazy and I don't like to do a lot of walking for the sake of hearing my mixes through different playback devices. But seriously, I like to know how my mixes are translating from one system to the next. My ears are familiar with the way commercial audio is reproduced through these different types of speakers, so I know that if it sounds up to par through every single one of them, my mix is probably finished. It's a bit compulsive, but hey, you are who you are.

Near-Field Monitors

Near-field monitors are a type of reference monitor that is meant to be listened to from only a short distance (see Figure 9.3). They usually have 5-inch to 8-inch woofers and are capable of anywhere from 25 to 150 watts of power. The woofer is wired with a tweeter whose sole responsibility is to produce the high frequencies. Tweeter drivers are typically about half the wattage of the woofer with which they are linked.

Near-field speakers are designed for flat response, meaning that they are transparent or produce sound accurately without flattering or exaggerating any of the frequencies. Maximum recommended listening range is between two and five feet. If you are more than 10 feet away from a set of near-field speakers, you run the risk of compromising the true representation of sound. Think of the listening range of near-fields like the viewing angle of an LCD computer monitor. With LCD computer

Figure 9.3 Near-field monitors.

monitors, there is only a certain range of viewing angles within which you can accurately perceive images and color. If you move outside of that range, the colors may seem to change, they may appear inaccurate and unnatural, or whatever is being displayed on the screen may become only partially visible. This is the same with the listening range of near-field monitors. If you physically move beyond the intended listening range at which the speakers were *meant* to be used, you may not hear an accurate representation of the sound they are producing.

Near-field monitors are best for monitoring and balancing the frequencies in a mix. They are specifically designed to be sonically irritating when any one frequency is pushed too hard. If you crank a lot of midrange into a vocal, a near-field monitor will make the boosted frequency very pronounced and unpleasant, whereas with other speakers, it might just seem like an indiscernible volume increase. Near-fields are designed to be controlled listening workhorses and are really the detail detectives in the studio. Ninety percent of all your mixing will occur on your trusty near-fields.

The only downside to listening to near-fields in close proximity for long periods of time is ear fatigue. Ear fatigue occurs when a lot of midrange and highs are heard for hours on end. It's that feeling you get when you've been mixing all day, nothing sounds good, and your head is swimming. If near-field monitors are your only source of monitoring, you may want to give yourself lots of breaks from the listening environment during the workday. Often the uncolored, flat tones are unpleasant, especially at louder volumes. If you're listening to anything for extended periods of time, ear fatigue is inevitable. Some monitors will make you feel it faster than others, though.

One method I use to reduce ear fatigue is to keep the light low in the room in which I monitor. I know this sounds nuts, but give it a chance. My control room is pretty large, with a small 75-watt bulb lighting the whole room. With less light in the room, I am apt to depend on my ears more than my eyes, and thus I require less volume to hear more detail. If you don't believe me, try this out. Get up in the morning and turn on your stereo at 9:00 a.m. as you make breakfast. That night at 11:00 p.m., go and turn the radio back on. You may be surprised at how much you have to lower the volume just to make it listenable. In darker environments, less volume is needed for the details to be heard. I don't typically like to mix at high volumes anyway. It tends to make me mix vocals and midrange instruments too quietly due to the pronounced irritation of those frequencies that is inherent in near-field monitors to begin with. Mixing at high volumes also forces the room to "have its say," and with non-professionally designed monitoring environments, it will have an immediate impact on the quality of a mix. Truth be told, everyone has different ears, and every speaker is a little different due to materials, power, room, and distance. Find a set of near-fields that work for you and your room, and give all your favorite records a listen or 30.

Far-Field Monitors

Far-field monitors are for long-distance listening at higher volumes (see Figure 9.4). These are the "fatties" I mentioned earlier. These speakers usually have 10-inch to 15-inch woofers and pack a real wallop, with typical wattages of around 300 to 500 watts with a 150- or 200-watt tweeter. They are made for the "throw," or a distance of anywhere from 10 to 30 feet from the monitors themselves. This is the intended listening range where the full sonic field can be perceived accurately. Far-field speakers aren't usually known to reveal as much

Figure 9.4 Far-field monitors.

detail as near-fields. It's basically like having a PA system to check volume levels to see how a product may hold up at a club, convention center, or concert over the main PA system.

Far-field speakers are not recommended for mixing. I usually only use them to check a mix when I'm finished mixing it on my near-fields to see whether anything stands out inappropriately, or *doesn't* stand out the way it should. Hearing a mix back on far-fields *can* be an impressive way to let your client preview their mixes because larger speakers with capable power amps can handle significant frequency boosts, much like consumer component systems can. Not to mention, they're wicked loud! And who doesn't want to hear themselves rocking out loud?

But it is for these very same reasons that you can't actually obtain an accurate mix on far-fields. With high volume levels and perceived coolness factor comes the tendency to push certain frequencies inappropriately because of the way they make you *feel*. Rolling a lot of heart-thumping low end into a mix that is being monitored on a set of far-fields may translate to a speaker-destroying, barely audible sub-frequency on any other playback system. While auditioning your

Figure 9.5 Consumer speakers.

mixes on far-fields can be impressive, it is by no means the best or most accurate method of monitoring audio to get an accurate mix. You can use them to check your mixes as an additional set of monitors, but I wouldn't recommend basing your final mix on them.

Consumer Speakers

Consumer speakers are best defined as common, everyday audio systems (see Figure 9.5). These speakers can be any size, shape, or wattage. The best examples of these types of systems are home stereos, bookshelf units, car stereos, and computer/media or boom box speakers. Checking your mixes on these types of systems is the quickest way to find out how your mix is translating to listening situations out in the real world. Consumer speakers often have features such as BBE and MegaBASS enhancement, simulated surround sound and reverb settings, style-based EQ presets, and lots of automatic compression. They also generally suffer from limited bandwidth or narrowed frequency response, and the inability to truly customize their sound settings. However, these are the types of speakers on which you can expect your mixing and mastering jobs to be heard. There is probably one or more of these types of speakers in your home, or even the room you're sitting in now. Who knew that they could serve a greater purpose than simply providing hours of musical enjoyment?

Real-world reference points are an important part of monitoring audio. I believe that this is the setting where the truth reveals itself.

It can be immensely helpful to know what the final destination of all your hard work will be. And it helps you out even more to be able to preview your mixes in those supposed destinations. You want to give others the ability to hear how fantastic your mixes sound on *any* consumer audio system. If they are impressed, then it speaks well both for the project and for you. And if they are not impressed, you will have to work harder on getting the translation right just to repair your reputation.

No matter what speakers you use to mix on, the most important thing is to have a reference point. How will your mix translate to the speakers people use in everyday life? You can define a standard by making real-world comparisons. If your mix sounds fine on your near-fields but is bass heavy in your car, home stereo, or various other consumer audio playback systems, especially when compared to other similar-sounding recordings, then you will know that it's either your monitors that are lacking in bass response or your room, and that you should start mixing low-frequency instruments a little quieter. Until you are absolutely certain of how a mix that is monitored on your near-fields will translate to real-world listening environments (which could take a really long time), these comparisons will be invaluable.

Headphones

Headphones are perhaps the most difficult topic to discuss when it comes to monitoring. Although they are indeed a method of monitoring, they are not commonly used for mixing. The average headphones are basically a small set of padded, low-wattage speakers that are utilized for convenience and privacy purposes. Professional audio applications weren't really addressed in the original headphone design because headphones were never really meant for demanding pro audio monitoring applications. Now, *studio headphones* or *reference headphones* are typically defined as high-quality, flat-response, closed-back headphones (see Figure 9.6). These are more commonly used in studios to give performers an isolated listening solution that prevents microphone bleed.

Recent developments have yielded much higher quality headphones that are more transparent and have better frequency response. Some

Figure 9.6 Studio headphones.

headphones, much like consumer stereo systems, have certain frequency enhancements that are meant to improve overall audio quality. But if the goal is to monitor accurately, this is not always desirable.

Headphone monitoring is *highly* controversial, but like any other method of monitoring audio, it's really about whether you're familiar with the references and how your mixes will translate. If you listen to a *lot* of commercially recorded music on your studio headphones, it's possible that they may be your best shot at producing industry-standard mixes. But in most cases, headphones are an occasional accessory and not a permanent fixture on your head.

I personally think it's fine to check mixes on a set of "cans." There have definitely been times when I've made a deeper connection to the music I was listening to *because* I was hearing it through a nice set of headphones. I often strive to achieve that level of dynamic impact in my mixes, so using headphones to see whether I've achieved that goal is a common practice. Here's the catch; Headphones are generally subject to even more inconsistencies than speakers when it comes to monitoring. They will be positioned differently each and every time you put them on your head. Just like pretty much everything we've discussed, not all headphones are created equal. They vary in frequency response, internal driver size, sound pressure levels, and various other specifications that affect the way they reproduce sound. Because of these inconsistencies, I support the use of headphones as a reference and even for production, but unless you've been using the same pair of headphones since the beginning of your career and you have a solid grip on how they will translate, I probably wouldn't recommend them for serious mixing applications.

In the past few years, music equipment manufacturers have started producing in-ear reference monitors (IEMs) specifically for critical listening on the go. Originally designed to allow performers to hear themselves with clarity and isolation during live performances, in-ear monitors offer the unique advantage of the exact same positioning (relative to your ears) each time you use them. This is because they are designed to fit *in* your ears. They're a lot like earplugs, but with a tiny low-wattage speaker driver inside. You can even get custom molds specifically for your ears so that it's an *exact* fit every time. Other advantages include portability, flat frequency response for more accurate and detailed listening, as well as virtually total isolation from distracting outside noises.

Although I really like my in-ear reference monitors, I probably wouldn't mix with them if I didn't have to. That isn't to say that you couldn't, but most would choose traditional near-fields over in-ears no matter how accurate the in-ears were. I've actually heard some really impressive mixes that were done using only a laptop and a set of in-ears. But know that they came from people who already had a firm grasp on a broad range of different sound references and years of experience with mixing audio. Mixing on in-ear monitors exclusively won't give your mix the opportunity to be tested in a real-world environment. After all, sound is about moving air. And there is no air to move with in-ear monitors, is there? (Or at least for your sake, I hope not.)

It's not always easy to get around using headphones. Sometimes they might be all you have to work with. If you're unable to use amplified speakers because of the mixing environment you're in, headphones might be the only option you have to keep yourself from getting evicted for disturbing your neighbors. You can always check your mixes on headphones, but if you intend to mix on headphones, invest the time in really getting used to them.

Room Acoustics for Project Studios

Your monitoring environment is important. The room directly affects the accuracy of what you are hearing. Sometimes small room modifications can have a huge impact on what you are hearing and experiencing during playback. You may not be a skilled building contractor or have the ability to modify a rented home or apartment, but you would be surprised at what you can do to improve your listening experience and environment. You may be equally taken aback by how much of a real difference it will make in your performance as a post audio engineer. All you have to do is put your best ears on and get a studio monkey or a friend to help you move some stuff. This section includes some budget-conscious ways to help treat a room.

Resonant frequency is the first thing to look for in a room. Play back 10 of your favorite songs. Try to make sure they are in a variety of styles and keys. Listen for bass notes that excite the harmonics of the room. In my studio, the G on the third fret of a bass guitar's E string would flood the room with frequency and cause it to shake in a very unnatural way. I was just about to call a paranormal psychologist until I realized that G was the resonant frequency of the room I was in. The next thing I did was move my desk and monitors from the 90-degree corner I was in to the dead center of the room. This alone was enough to almost completely change the resonant frequency of the space. Then, in order to make my studio space efficient, I moved the monitors and desk closer to the wall. I was still getting a little rumble, but not nearly as much as before. Then I discovered that when I walked behind the speakers, the resonant rumble completely dissipated. So I left the monitors a few feet from the wall and turned them at a 30-degree angle (away from the corners of the room), and then hung a large, heavy curtain behind them and a few inches away from the wall. I no longer experience resonant G's.

There is a much more scientific explanation for what I did to the room than the way I actually explained it, but what I'm trying to say with my intentionally unscientific example is that the physics of sound are unchangeable. Everything has a resonant frequency. Harmonics are found everywhere. In a listening environment such as a post-production studio, you want to go for even, flat, and unexaggerated response. To treat a room correctly, you have to work with the variables. While it's not the easiest thing in the world to move a wall or remove all the reflective surfaces in a room, you do have the ability to change the physical properties of the room and the objects in it. An exception, of course, is my car, which has a resonant frequency of F... not much I can do about that.

After resonant frequency, the next thing to listen for is wall reflection. If the sound coming out of your speakers is hitting the surrounding walls too quickly or evenly, it can cause high, chirpy-sounding reflections and tin can–like noises that can really mess with your ears and interfere with your ability to hear what's really going on in a mix. Rooms that are completely square or rectangular are the worst for this type of reflection. Resolving this kind of problem is a process of literally altering the space of a room. Sometimes just adding a couch or rug can help, but most of the time there are less involved alternatives you can pursue.

I will usually sit in the captain's chair (my mixing seat) and clap my hands as loud as humanly possible. If you hear a strange, ringing slap back that sounds like a cheap reverb, chances are you have unwanted wall reflections that will need to be eliminated. Have a buddy walk around the perimeter of the room while you clap. At a certain point in your friend's walking path, the reflection should seem to cease. Have your friend stay in that spot and mark it. This is an ideal location to hang something to absorb the reflections. What is happening is that when the reflections stop, your friend's entire body is absorbing the reflections. I had someone walk around until the two walls on both sides of my listening environment stopped reflecting sound unnaturally. I hung a large piece of acoustical foam about a foot or so above my friend's head level, and it more or less eliminated any reflections. As we learned in talking about reverb, the high frequencies of a sound's reverberation travel farther. In a small room, they have a tendency to bounce around quite a bit. If you regularly experience ear fatigue after only a few hours of mixing at low levels, it's probably due to an abundance of high-frequency reflection, and it may be time for a reflection check.

Acoustically dead monitoring environments are almost as bad as extremely reflective ones. I've seen people go crazy with too much acoustical foam, egg crates, and blankets, making a real disaster area out of a room. By over-treating a room, you run the risk of ruining any trace of real-life resonance. Even the most expensive mixing and monitoring rooms are padded just enough to make them pleasant for optimal listening. They are never sonically deceased and flat. Padding a room is a lot like operating a compressor properly. Just enough padding keeps the room alive with somewhat dynamic reflections, but too much will make it sound lifeless. Try to use sound-absorbing materials to catch unwanted reflections only where necessary.

Bass frequency and bass trapping are difficult concepts to understand. Rooms with high, pointy, or A-framed ceilings are the worst for this. Additionally, things such as stairwells, bay windows, crawlspaces under houses, and other elements can totally suck up your low-end frequencies. Sometimes you need to actually control where the playback frequencies go and stay. If all of your bass sound is running up the stairs behind you, you can easily fix that by putting in a makeshift door. If you have a high, pointed ceiling, such as in a garage, maybe hanging some fabric layers or blankets above the listening area would help keep the bass from rushing upward. Also, if your speakers are in a small room and close to corners, you will get a surplus of bass bouncing off the corners that will affect the way you perceive the low frequencies that your monitors are producing. In this case, you may want to get some pre-made bass traps that are designed especially for corners.

Room acoustics can be a tricky thing. What do and don't you treat? What is the correct way to treat it? To reduce reflections, you want to use some type of absorbent material, such as foam or egg crates. If there seems to be an abundance of sound waves collecting in one area, some diffusion may be necessary. If the room seems to be abundant in low frequencies, you can usually contain and control them with a bass trap. Also, only treat a room or an area if it's really necessary. A wealth of detailed information and a range of acoustical foam productions can be found at www.auralex.com.

Check Yourself before You Wreck Yourself

The standard for what sounds good is one of the most subjective things in the world. One of the best ways to have a more solid reference point than just "he said, she said" is to compare your mixes to the standards that are accepted by the majority and to begin with the proven practices of the pros. I know that it can be really tempting to go against the grain for most of us, but when it comes to audio, doing so will only make your mixes seem less professional. Often, these comparisons can be apples to oranges because all of the commercial audio you hear on the radio, from CDs, and on the Internet has already been through the mastering process. However, once you are comfortable with the mastering process (which we'll get into later), you will begin to see just what mastering really does for a record. This will help you better understand and decipher the commercial mixes you hear because you will know which sonic characteristics come from mastering and which ones actually come from mixing. Eventually, your ears will be able to hear right through a mastering job and allow you to read a mix like a book. This will help you develop a solid baseline for what today's acceptable volume and fidelity standards really are.

During the learning process it's really nice to be able to compare your mixes to those found in professional recordings through your own monitors. Listen to your favorite music on your studio speakers often. What you hear can be a truly eye-opening experience. You'll discover crazy little sounds and tones that you never even realized were there before. Furthermore, listen to commercial recordings that are sonically similar to the project you're trying to mix. This is a great way to check the spatial and tonal characteristics of your mix with industry-standard mixes.

I listen to instrument tones a lot on my studio monitors. If I hear an instrument in a song that I think has great sonic characteristics, I'll spend some time trying to figure out how to recreate it in my own recordings. But know that if you recreate the bass tones found on a

Muse record, it doesn't mean that your mix will sound like a Muse mix. There are still a lot of variables to calculate, such as performance and recording methods. The best thing you can do is choose the tones that you want to be the focal point and create the best mix you can around them. If you attack the mix from this angle, the tones you've chosen will never seem out of place in *your* mix. You can't really expect to copy a mix tone for tone, but making these individual tonal comparisons through your studio monitors will help you identify how they will ultimately translate to common listening systems.

Loops and samples can be another useful tool to help you create a reference point for making elements within a mix sound more professional. Samples, in the context of digital audio, are pre-recorded instruments or pieces of music that are designed for royalty-free commercial use in original musical compositions. They are most commonly found on sample CDs that you can purchase either online or from a local retailer. These CDs are usually created by people who produce music professionally. Often the samples and loops found on these discs have already been compressed and equalized to commercial standards. This makes them good candidates for examples of a properly treated solo instrument to which you can compare your own sonic elements. And here is the obligatory word of caution: Sample CDs are not cheap, and while *most* of them are produced by pros, not *all* of them are. Anyone can make sample CD demos sound good, but to get an accurate gauge of the audio quality of any sample CDs you're considering, listen to actual samples before you buy them. Otherwise, you may just be throwing your money away.

Checking your mixes for reference to consumer translation may involve a few trips to the car or living room. Highs and lows are usually the problem areas when it comes to inaccurate frequency reproduction. Home and car stereos do not supply the same even-keeled frequency range that flat response studio monitors do. In the beginning, when you preview your studio mixes on other audio systems, the highs may seem considerably reduced or dull, and the bass may seem overbearing and have more "boom" to it than you remember hearing in the studio. I've even found myself visiting a home electronics store in the middle of the day to hear a mix on every consumer sound system they had available, all the while making notes about what could be fixed across multiple different speakers. Again, it's an extreme but thorough example of checking mixes on different systems.

Another way I check the accuracy of monitors and mixing is to go to an online forum of mixers, engineers, and audio people I can trust (such as www.gearslutz.com or Sound on Sounds user forums) and send some files out to folks who really know what they are doing. People have given me great feedback in the past that has helped me create better mixes overall. When dealing with forums and peers that you've never met before, prepare to be criticized. They usually mean well, but strangers can really tear a mix apart. Always take everything with a grain of salt and don't give up. There are some great audio people out there who are just like you and me. They can often give your mix a quick listen from an outside perspective and provide constructive feedback that will help you out infinitely more than pounding out a couple more hours in front of the computer. There have been times when someone has pointed out a folly that I didn't catch that was caused by something completely different than the issue I thought I was trying to resolve. It's a lot easier to fix a mix when you hear that your vocal track needs a −2-dB reduction in the 2-kHz frequency range from a pro than it is to have your significant other say, "Umm… sounds a little bit like it's in a tin can, and I don't like it."

Monitoring Dos and Don'ts

So before you exit this somewhat extensive chapter on monitoring, I want to review a few common monitoring dos and don'ts.

Dos

- **Understand the variables.** Realize audio is a completely different experience from speaker to speaker and person to person. You are making generalizations that work across the board in many different formats, not just ones that sound great in the studio to you on your particular set of speakers.

- **Use multiple speakers and reference points.** My opinion is that you *must* do this in the beginning because it will drastically accelerate your mixing education. Find a few different sets of speakers that sound good and that you have access to on a regular basis. Listen to a lot of commercially recorded music and check your mixes on them.

- **Optimize your listening environment.** Set up your listening room for the best possible and most accurate monitoring situation. The optimal position for near-field monitors is to create an equilateral triangle between you and the left and right speakers. The speakers should be set at a height that puts your ears right at tweeter level. You should be able to hear both speakers at equal volumes if they are set up correctly. If you can hear the speaker levels become unbalanced when you move your head from side to side, keep moving them slightly until you achieve balance when you're in the center position.

- **Listen at recommended distances.** If you have near-fields, ideally you shouldn't be more than six feet away from them. If you have far-fields, you should be no less than 10 feet away from them. Your common sense will come into play very much here. Your ears will know when you are too far outside an accurate listen range.

- **Dare to compare.** At the start, be sure to check your mix against professionally recorded mixes on the same speakers. This will help you develop an auditory reference for modern level and fidelity standards.

Don'ts

- **Don't just take *anyone's* word for it.** Try to filter out marketing campaigns and "pseudo-professional" advice about choosing a set of studio monitors. Do your research, of course, but just because something is regarded as an "industry standard," that doesn't mean it is the best choice. If the monitors sound good and deliver results, they are the right setup. The keys to using monitors effectively are simply getting used to them and understanding how they translate.

- **Don't buy monitors because they're inexpensive.** As a modifier to my previous statement, buying the least expensive monitors isn't a good thing either. As previously mentioned, low to moderately priced monitors have entered the market, and you kind of have to wonder what makes them affordable. If it's not cabinet materials and aesthetics, it's the internal components. Cutting corners on monitors can lead to a speaker that isn't as accurate as it should be. When considering a decent set of monitor speakers, visit a lot of forums, read user reviews, and actually listen to several different sets of speakers before making a purchase.

- **Don't underpower or overpower.** Make sure that you understand the specifications and power requirements of your monitors before you hook them up. Underpowering or overpowering passive monitors can drastically affect their performance. This is much less of a concern with active monitors because the built-in power is designed to operate with the speakers' components in an optimal way.

- **Don't over-treat a room.** You can seriously compromise the accuracy of your monitoring environment with acoustical foam if you're not careful. Just treat it enough to keep the playback under control, pleasant-sounding, and free of any abnormal reflections.

So concludes our section on monitoring. I bet you didn't realize there was so much involved in just listening to audio playback on a set of speakers. Every decision you make about your room and equipment will directly affect the accuracy of your mixes. Hopefully, I've provided enough information here to help you make better choices and give you somewhere to start with monitoring your mixes like a pro. See you in Chapter 10!

Effects for Digital Audio Post-Production

10 Rack in a Box

When most people think of effects, they think of chorus, delay, distortion, and other drastic-sounding effects that produce dramatic results. Although the level of creativity you can achieve through the use of effects is nearly limitless, in post-production, subtlety is the key with very few exceptions. These same effects used with a light touch can help shape a mix in various ways. The use of mild distortion on overheads can help add a little warmth and overall unity to your drums. A bit of delay with a stereo spread and a touch of chorus can help fill out a lead vocal when used appropriately. If the client wants a huge delay on a particular guitar part, that is for them to decide. Often, as the post-production engineer, you can make suggestions, but unless the client *wants* to use a dramatic effect, you probably won't employ one often.

This section is dedicated to introducing different types of effects and effect plug-ins. We'll explore what they do, how they do it, and how they are most effectively used in post. I'll also give you some ideas on how to make using effects and plug-ins easier and more efficient. Understanding what effects to use and how to use them appropriately is an integral part of being a good post-production engineer. So where do we begin? How about at the beginning.

What Are Effects?

By now you should know that when we are talking about effects, we're not talking about the "BOING!" you hear when a cartoon cat steps on a rake. Although you may end up creating a sound effect like a "BOING!" in your audio post-production endeavors, an *effect,* for our purposes, is anything that manipulates or enhances a sound.

207

Effects are tools that help modify the original sound to get it closer to the way you want it to sound.

Consider that raw audio material is like a huge stone block and you are a sculptor. The stone block is rough around the edges, but you know that there is a work of art in there just waiting for you to remove the unnecessary stone layers and give it some detail to bring it to life. You'll use effects like a chisel to achieve the exact same thing with audio. You'll carve away unwanted sonic material and bring out the details to sculpt a piece of rough audio into a refined, natural, and globally unified sound.

If an effect is anything that modifies a sound, then technically, a minor change in volume could be considered an effect. However, compression, EQ filters, reverb, delay, distortion, and modulation are more commonly linked with the term; these are the types of effects that will be discussed in this section. These are the foundation on which more complex effects are built. If you understand how to use a basic EQ and compressor, you should be able to understand multi-band compression without much effort. Similarly, if you can operate a basic reverb, you can work a convolution reverb. By the end of the section, you will have consumed enough information to get a good, solid understanding of different effects. The next step will be to experiment with your own plug-ins and see them in action for yourself.

Past, Present, and Future

If you started into pure digital audio production with software sequencers and plug-ins without ever having used analog recording equipment, chances are you've never had to use a patch cable or a patchbay before. When recording audio was a completely analog process, a collection of outboard effect processing units were routed in and out of an analog recording console by way of sends and returns, using a patchbay and patch cables to introduce the effects into the signal chain.

Many studios employed multiple patchbays to grant access to all of their different effect processors. The backs of the patchbays were generally configured and hardwired to these effects, but you could change the routing of the sends (outs) and returns (ins) by physically changing the position of the color-coded patch cables on the fronts of the patchbays. You could also route one effect processor, such as a distortion effect, into another, such as a delay, to apply the effect of both to the original audio signal.

The inputs and outputs on the front panel of a patchbay often were marked with a sticker or masking tape with writing on it that indicated which effect a particular input or output was for. (For example, Reverb 1, Reverb 2, Reverb 3, Delay 1, Chorus 1, and so forth.) It didn't take a rocket scientist to operate a patchbay, but it did take an engineer who was knowledgeable about the different effect units themselves. If you wanted to change the parameters on Reverb 2, you had to know which reverb unit in the rack was considered Reverb 2 and then manually tweak the knobs on the front of the appropriate reverb effect unit to change the settings. The act of applying effects was not terribly complicated, but it took more than patching cables to be good at using them in post.

Integrating outboard effect hardware into a digital audio environment still requires routing of some sort. Usually, this is done using the inputs and outputs of your digital audio device. These days, most digital audio device manufacturers are doing their best to produce more products that offer multiple inputs and outputs to serve the modern project studio's connectivity needs. Patchbays are still used in project studios if the post-production engineer has a *lot* of outboard hardware to connect and not enough native inputs on his or her interface to connect them all.

In a completely digital project studio environment, computers have made the act of applying effects even easier. Now, with a few mouse clicks or keystrokes, you can load up your favorite software sequencing program and add a software effect plug-in as an insert. The way that inserts allow you to introduce an effect into the signal chain is in some ways similar to the way sends and returns grant access to the use of an outboard effect. Or at least it's the same general idea. We'll discuss inserts, as well as other effect routing methods, later in this section.

Something else about using effects that has been made easier (and arguably better) through technology is the ability to adjust parameters and get the effect sounding just the way you like it. Need a little more space from your reverb? How about a faster delay interval with more feedback? No problem! Just open up the plug-in's user interface, and your perfect effect is nearly at your fingertips. Furthermore, once you get the effect just right, you can save it as a preset so that when you want to use the same settings again, rather than writing down the controller values in a notebook to be dialed in later by hand, you just have to load a preset and you're done.

The use of effects in digital audio isn't limited to *only* audio, either. Audio+MIDI sequencing programs allow the use of MIDI effects as well. But as a post-production engineer, you usually won't use these on a client's project.

Outboard effect units are still in production, though the market has narrowed due to the advent of software effects. Some engineers prefer hardware over plug-ins because some specific outboard effect units have their own *sound*. These units typically fall in the price range of $2,000 to $5,000 and up. These are most common in big studios with big budgets. We are talking about hardware effects that have survived in the market decades after their initial release because they are so sonically unique or fantastic that all the major studios must employ them. There is another category of more affordable hardware effects available for project studios; these fall between $100 and roughly $500 per unit. Although a $500 reverb unit will produce reverb and do the job, there might not be anything that defines it as a sonically unique "must-have" effect processor.

Software plug-ins tend to be priced to fill in the middle ground from $200 up to $1,000 for a single plug-in. You can also get multiple plug-ins that have been bundled together for particular production needs; these run between $1,000 and $2,500. The popularity of software plug-ins has increased significantly in the last five to seven years. A wide variety of effect plug-ins is available in today's digital audio market. You can have your own "rack in a box" with literally hundreds of high-quality effects in your virtual rack for a fraction of the cost of outboard gear. You can even buy plug-ins that emulate popular outboard effect units.

One of the benefits of software is that there is always someone out there familiar enough with code to design their own plug-ins and offer them for free. I'm not talking about pirated software, because we all know that stealing is *bad*, right? However, there are great number of websites that offer free effect plug-ins to the public. Many plug-in developers who normally sell their products usually have at least *one* plug-in that you can download and use for free. You might have to register with them to get it, but in most cases, I've found it to be a worthwhile expenditure of my time to use a really cool plug-in.

I don't believe that outboard hardware effects will ever be completely dismissed by the digital audio world, but the digital age is upon us and has changed the way we work with effects and audio in general. Not only have effects become easier to apply, but our minds are pretty open to finding new and innovative ways of using them. Even if you only ever use effects in a subtle way for post-production, I highly recommend that you spend a good amount of time learning all different kinds of effects. You never know what is going to do the trick and be the right tool (or combination of tools) to work out a rough spot in a mix. Being able to understand and navigate the parameters of your software and plug-ins will give you more options to work with in post audio. And that will make you a better (and more marketable) post-production engineer.

11 Software Tools for Effects

Software tools for effects are essentially effect plug-ins. Composers, sound designers, and engineers in studios large and small use them daily to create, mix, and master audio on their digital audio workstations. From Pro Tools to GarageBand, most digital audio programs ship with a handful of plug-ins to help you get working with effects immediately, without you having to go out and spend more money on third-party plug-ins just to get out of the gate. The plug-ins included with your software sequencer are great for a lot of situations, but they are not the only options you have.

I have sprinkled general information about plug-ins throughout this book. If you need a quick refresher course, Chapter 5 briefly discussed the different plug-in formats (RTAS, TDM, VST, AU, and DirectX), as well as basic control functions. But now I'm going to focus in a little and discuss some of the available options, as well as provide information that will help you develop and use a plug-in library to suit your needs.

What Are Effect Plug-Ins?
Simply put, effect plug-ins are auxiliary software programs that run inside your software sequencer. They cannot be used as stand-alone applications, which means they can only be launched from inside your main software application. For this reason, your software sequencer of choice is considered to be the *host* program, and your plug-ins are like little add-on software modules that have specific purposes. It's a bit like the average media player software available today. Upon installation, a basic media player probably won't be able to play back high-definition video. But you can usually purchase (or find a download that will install) a codec (or a plug-in) that will provide this functionality within the

media player. A basic software sequencer would not be capable of applying compression, reverb, delay, and so on to an audio signal without a plug-in designed for that purpose.

There is a wide variety of third-party plug-ins available for the modern digital audiophile. The advent of digital audio has spawned an entire industry around the development of different types of software effects and virtual instruments. So, why do you need third-party plug-ins if your sequencer already has some? Third-party plug-ins can typically produce better results than the factory set of plug-ins. I would say that eight times out of ten, a third-party plug-in will sound better and have more customizable options than a stock plug-in.

There are always exceptions to this, of course. The factory sets of plug-ins included with some of the major sequencers out there are pretty darn good. Pro Tools, for example, ships with a great set of tools for treating audio. So does Logic. Steinberg has made great strides in the quality of their stock plug-ins as well. In fact, many software sequencer developers are focusing more on creating better factory-included plugs. Will they *always* be the best tool for the job? The answer is no. No plug-in will *always* be the best for everything. That is why it's good to have a variety of different plug-ins from different manufacturers that you can try when your normal go-to plug-in isn't doing the trick.

Another reason why third-party plug-ins thrive in the music industry marketplace is because it is becoming more obvious that not just *any* plug-in will do (or sell, for that matter). The manufacturers of popular high-end hardware effect processors got smart and partnered with software developers to produce signature plug-ins that model popular hardware units. Specific hardware units from the days of analog were famous for the coloration they introduced to an audio signal. The problem is that these sought-after outboard effects will cost you an arm, a leg, your kidneys, and your firstborn male child. Now, if you've always wanted a Teletronix LA-2A Leveling Amplifier, but you can't part with $3,000 to buy the hardware version, you can get a Teletronix LA-2A Leveling Amplifier plug-in that does a pretty decent job of emulating the real thing for a fraction of the cost.

There is some debate over whether these software emulators are comparable to the real hardware units. Some say yes, and some say, "No, but they still sound amazing!" This debate has gone on for decades and will probably continue for quite a few more. The important thing for you to decide is whether *you* think it sounds good. If you're just starting out with digital audio, the specific brand names of these popular hardware units and plug-ins may not mean very much right now. But know that plug-ins have been around long enough that the standard for excellence has been set. Be aware of the bar so that you have a reference point for when you're trying to determine what sounds good and what doesn't.

Effect Plug-In Formats

The vast majority of plug-ins are developed first for the major formats (RTAS and TDM for Pro Tools only, VST, Audio Units (AU) for Mac only, and DirectX for PC only). Because Pro Tools is considered the industry standard in digital audio recording, it is common for high-end software effects developers to release RTAS and TDM versions of their plug-ins before they release any other format. It's also common for certain plug-ins to be developed as Pro Tools–*only* exclusives, meaning that the developer *never* releases a VST, AU, or DirectX version of it. These exclusives typically hold strong reputations for impeccable sound quality. As you can imagine, this would be an incentive for a lot of people to go with Pro Tools as their primary sequencer. Many audio professionals I know have a Pro Tools system in their studio, regardless of whether it's their main digital audio program. I used to occasionally kick myself when I saw a plug-in that I *really* wanted, but that was only offered in RTAS and TDM formats. But before you go out and buy yourself a Pro Tools system, be aware of the other options as well.

There are literally hundreds of great-sounding, high-quality plug-ins for the other popular formats too. I'm a PC user. I typically run Nuendo with Ableton Live as a ReWire slave. I *do* own a Pro Tools rig, but I do most of my work in Nuendo, using mostly VST-format plug-ins.

VST, AU, and DirectX plug-ins are generally less expensive than RTAS or TDM plug-ins. Why? Because they *can* be. If you own a Pro Tools system, you can *only* use RTAS- or TDM-formatted plug-ins, so you really don't have a choice but to pay what is asked for them. VST, AU, and DirectX plug-ins don't normally rely on a specific audio program. Furthermore, they are designed to use your computer's internal CPU and RAM for processing. This is both good and bad. It's good because it means you don't have to own expensive DSP cards to use these plug-ins, but it's bad because they *do* use RAM and tax your CPU. Let me put CPU usage into perspective. My primary studio machine is an Intel 3.2 GHz on an Asus P4P800E-Deluxe motherboard with 4 GB of RAM that I built nearly two years ago. I've run it every day, taxing it heavily with audio projects containing sometimes 100 audio tracks and up to 100 plug-ins simultaneously. I have yet to experience a problem or any kind of noticeable decline in performance. And seeing that in the space of only two years my current motherboard isn't even available anymore, I'll probably build a new machine before that ever happens. So while the taxation of your CPU may be a consideration when choosing plug-in formats, it shouldn't be the deciding factor.

Another option for effect plug-ins is to use DSP cards or interfaces. DSP cards usually come in the form of a PCI or PCI-E card that is installed in an appropriate slot on your motherboard. And DSP interfaces are usually an external box with FireWire or Ethernet connectivity. They are sold with specifically formatted plug-ins that use the DSP hardware itself for processing effects. This means that like a Pro Tools|HD system, the load is taken off your CPU, and most of the work is done by the DSP chips on the DSP card. The plug-ins that are offered in most DSP packages are of a very high quality. If you're looking to go with a DSP card, be sure to check out user reviews and forums to get a better idea about what might work for you.

Here's a quick breakdown of the different major plug-in formats and the major applications with which they're compatible:

- **AU.** Audio Units is a Mac-only, system-level plug-in architecture provided by Core Audio in the OS X operating environment. Because the architecture exists at the system level, it allows for correctly formatted plug-ins to be used in *any* OS X application that is capable of using Audio Unit plug-ins. This means that the format is dependent on the operating system and not the specific program that you're using.

AU is compatible with Apple Logic, GarageBand, Soundtrack, Final Cut Pro, Bias Peak and Bias Deck, MOTU Digital Performer, and Ableton Live.

- **DirectX.** DirectX, or DX, plug-ins rely on your computer's internal CPU to process audio, but CPU taxation is really a concern of the past because computers have become much faster and more powerful since the DirectX plug-in format was introduced. Compared to VST plug-ins, the CPU usage for DirectX plug-ins is a bit higher, but I honestly doubt the difference will be noticeable in practice. Created by Microsoft, DirectX-formatted plug-ins can only be used in a Microsoft Windows–based operating environment.

  DirectX plug-ins are compatible with Cakewalk SONAR, Steinberg Nuendo, Cubase SX3 (or older) and Wavelab, and Sony Creative Software Sound Forge, ACID, and Vegas.

- **RTAS.** RTAS is a proprietary plug-in format that was developed by Digidesign. It also uses the CPU for audio processing, and it's only available for use on Pro Tools systems.

  RTAS is compatible with all Pro Tools systems, including HD, LE, and M-Powered for both Mac and PC.

- **TDM.** TDM is another Pro Tools–specific plug-in format for HD systems that is designed to communicate with external I/O devices and DSP cards to ease the workload on your computer's internal PCI bus and CPU. In theory, this helps lengthen the lifetime of your CPU because the CPU is not doing nearly as much work as it would be using plug-ins that are CPU-dependent.

  TDM is compatible with Pro Tools|HD systems only, for both Mac and PC.

- **VST.** VST is the most widely supported format for digital audio. Nearly every major DAW software program is compatible with VST (except Apple Logic and Pro Tools, of course). The VST format was developed by Steinberg Technologies, the makers of

Nuendo, Cubase, and Wavelab. It's considered to be the most efficient of the CPU-dependent plug-in formats.

VST is compatible with Ableton Live; Steinberg Nuendo; Cubase 4 and Wavelab; Sony Creative Software Sound Forge, ACID, and Vegas; Cakewalk SONAR; and Bias Peak and Bias Deck.

■ **Other.** There are a few other plug-in formats that are worth mentioning here. MAS, or MOTU Audio System, is a CPU-reliant, proprietary plug-in format for MOTU's Digital Performer. Audio-Suite is a secondary plug-in format for Pro Tools.

Bundles versus Individual Plug-Ins

Building the right plug-in suite can be an arduous task. Some just try *everything*. Others begin with peer recommendations. Some really take the time to research what the industry is using and arrive at a logical conclusion as to what will suit their needs the best. But until you have had some time to work with plug-ins and really get a feel for what they do, it's tough to know what to look for. To help make the initial selection process easier, third-party plug-in developers offer a wide range of plug-in bundles for every studio environment.

These plug-in bundles range from pretty basic to extremely comprehensive. Basic bundles may include only three to five essential effects on which you can begin building your plug-in library. These are on the low end of the investment scale, ranging from around $400 to $1,000. More advanced bundles, ranging in price from around $1,000 to $3,000 or higher, can offer extensive plug-in libraries that include 200 effects or more. These larger plug-in bundles are typically designed to be the bulk of your effect library. They generally leave you wanting for very little else. Inevitably, there will always be an individual plug-in here and there that you'll buy to supplement your collection, but for the most part, any effect processor you'd ever need for general audio production will probably be included. The quality of the plug-ins themselves obviously matters as well. I can't really offer an opinion about who I think makes a pro plug-in and who doesn't, but there is more than enough information on the Internet to help you make that determination. The higher the quality or the more plug-ins that are included, the more expensive the bundles are.

Try not to be deceived by price. (As if $400 is pocket change, right?) Some of these basic bundles are composed of great-sounding plug-ins that may prove themselves invaluable in your studio. Every once in a while, I'll be surprised by a plug-in gem that has amazing sound quality and functionality but was developed by an independent software company or an individual who coded it in his spare time from home. One of my favorite plug-ins for providing texture to an audio track is something I downloaded years ago that was being offered for *free*. Realize that the cost of manufacturing software for retail sale is very low. When you see plug-ins and bundles that cost a small fortune, what you're paying for is mostly the research and development and labor involved in bringing those products to market. So just because it's cheap, that doesn't necessarily mean it's not good.

Here's a rundown of popular third-party effect plug-in bundles.

- **Waves.** Waves offers many different high-quality multi-format plug-in bundles that have been assembled for specific audio purposes (see Figure 11.1). They've got bundles for audio mixing, mastering, restoration, working with surround sound, vocal tuning, guitar recording and processing, vintage hardware emulation, and more. See www.waves.com for more information.

- **McDSP.** McDSP (McDowell Signal Processing) produces plug-ins in RTAS, TDM, and AudioSuite formats for Pro Tools systems (see Figure 11.2). They've quickly become a favorite among digital audio professionals the world over for their efficient processing power, ease of use, and impressive sound quality. Check out www. mcdsp.com for the full scoop.

- **Sonnox Oxford Plugins.** Sonnox Oxford Plugins offers flexible bundles that allow you to choose which plug-ins you want to be included (see Figure 11.3). Pick and choose from professional top-quality plug-ins for mixing and mastering. The more plug-ins you buy, the deeper the discount. Oxford plugs are available in TDM,

Figure 11.1   Waves plug-ins.

Figure 11.2   McDSP plug-ins.

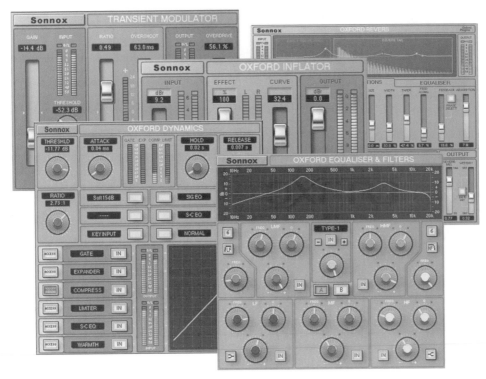

Figure 11.3 Sonnox Oxford plug-ins.

RTAS, AU, and VSTTC Powercore system formats. Visit www.sonnoxplugins.com for complete details.

- **Universal Audio.** Universal Audio is behind the world-renowned UAD-1. All UAD-1 bundles come with a UAD-1 DSP card and a select number of Universal Audio's professional-quality plug-ins, depending on which version of the bundle you purchase. The advanced bundles also offer a voucher that can be used to purchase additional Universal Audio plug-ins of your choice, offering a semi-flexible DSP hardware-based bundle solution. Visit www.uaudio.com to see for yourself (see Figure 11.4).

- **TC Electronic.** The TC PowerCore is a high-end hardware DSP system by TC Electronic. PowerCore bundles include an array of exclusive TC Electronic–designed plug-ins that utilize the full processing power of the DSP card (see Figure 11.5). There are also quite a few third-party plug-ins for the PowerCore system that are sold separately to give you even more options for building the

Figure 11.4 Universal Audio plug-ins.

Figure 11.5 TC Electronic plug-ins.

Figure 11.6   URS plug-ins.

perfect plug-in library. Check out www.tcelectronic.com for more info.

- **URS.** Regarded for their efficiency and sound quality, Unique Recording Software offers professional-grade vintage-style plug-ins in TDM, RTAS, AU, and VST formats (see Figure 11.6). They group their bundles by device type—compressor bundles, EQ bundles, channel strip bundles, and so forth. You can even get an Everything bundle, which, as the name suggests, gets you pretty much everything URS makes. Preconfigured bundles are available, but they have flexible bundles as well. Visit www.ursplugins.com to see what they have to offer.

- **Sonalksis.** Sonalksis offers high-quality digital audio plug-ins for mixing, mastering, and creativity that deliver a lot of bang for the buck (see Figure 11.7). These analog modeling processors have great sound quality, are CPU-efficient, and have a feature set that

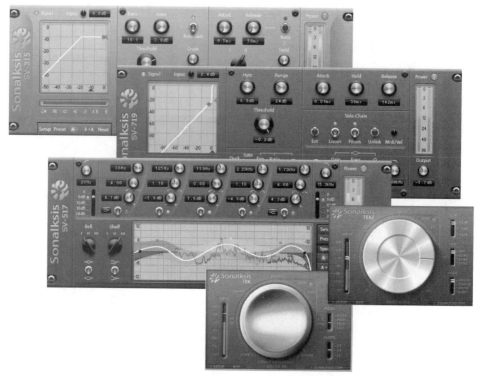

Figure 11.7 Sonalksis plug-ins.

you'd be hard-pressed to find in higher-priced plug-ins. Bundles are available in VST, DirectX, RTAS, and AU formats. See www.sonalksis.com for details.

Apart from bundles, you can purchase plug-ins individually. Suppose you've purchased a bundle already, but it didn't come with a compressor plug-in. Or maybe you're just looking to have some different options to choose from when one reverb isn't quite what you want for your current project. There are also specialty plug-ins available for pitch correction, noise reduction, all-in-one mastering solutions, convolution reverbs, boutique hardware emulation, amp modelers, creative sound design solutions, and much more, but they aren't typically included in the average plug-in bundle.

It's pretty easy to drop $300 on a specialty plug-in because what it does is so unique that you can't seem to live without it. But, it can be difficult to commit to individual plug-ins in the beginning because you kind of have to *know* what you want before you buy. I'd recommend finding a good starter plug-in bundle and then supplementing it with individual plug-ins or a complementary bundle from there. You can also take advantage of the plug-ins that are available as free (not pirated) downloads on the Internet. The downside to using free plug-ins in lieu of purchased ones is that you are limited to what's available. I'll give you some ideas on where to find free plug-ins a bit later in this chapter, in the upcoming "Where to Find Plug-Ins" section.

My best advice for trying to choose the right plug-ins to start with is, "Research! Research! Research!" Just because a bundle is expensive or includes a lot of plug-ins, that doesn't mean it's the best your money can buy. If you don't do your homework, purchasing plug-ins can be a real shot in the dark. If you're not sure about something and you *know* it can't be returned to the retailer, then $400 to $3,000 is a lot of money to spend. Be sure that you know what you're getting into before you commit to an expensive plug-in purchase.

Where to Find Plug-Ins

You can find effect plug-ins everywhere. The most obvious place to look is in your software. As I mentioned, most sequencing programs include a basic set of plug-ins for processing audio. The next most common place is the Internet, which is home to informative websites where you can learn about all sorts of different plug-ins, third-party-developer web portals where you might be able to download some demos and try the product for free, as well as flat-out *free* plug-ins that are available to the public for download. As for retailers, although some may have a vast selection of tangible products that you can physically inspect, retailers typically are not the best place to get accurate and honest information about software and plug-ins. I've certainly been proven wrong on this before, but not often. If you plan to purchase from a local retailer, my advice is to do your own research first, so that when you walk into the store, you know exactly what you want.

With the amount of malicious software lingering about the Internet, remember that before you download *anything*, you should try to verify the legitimacy of the manufacturer. Search for reviews from people who have used the application before. Visit the developer's website. Ask around. Also stay away from "cracked" or illegal software. You don't want your crusade for the perfect plug-ins—and your DAW, for that matter—to be taken down by some computer virus. Having said that, you should know that there are hundreds of websites out there that offer information and free software for the purposes of digital audio. Some are legitimate, and some are not. It would be impossible for me to list every single one, let alone use all of them to verify their integrity, but here are a few websites that I have actually used before. These will, at the very least, help you get started.

- **KVR (www.kvraudio.com).** This is a fantastic resource that has the 411 on pretty much every available plug-in and software program in existence. Here, you can find information on every application that I've mentioned, or will mention, in this book.

- **Tweakbench (www.tweakbench.com).** This site has a host of free creative effects and virtual instruments for Windows only.

- **Smartelectronix (www.smartelectronix.com).** This site contains various effects and virtual instruments from many different independent developers.

- **Voxengo (www.voxengo.com/group/freevst).** On this site, many free effect plug-ins are grouped by device type and use Windows only.

- **Free Plugin List (www.free-plugin-list.com).** This site offers a list of free plug-ins, ratings, and downloads.

Honorable Mentions

It's pretty easy to get addicted to plug-ins, especially if you're not exactly sure where to start. When I started out, I downloaded every plug-in that I had ever heard of. It wasn't long before my plug-in library was so massive that there were a good number of them that I hadn't even looked at. Since then, I've streamlined a bit. Although I've still got a *lot* of plug-ins installed on my primary DAW, I've narrowed it down to what I actually use.

In this section, I've taken all of my plug-in trial and error and compiled a list of various plug-ins that are my personal favorites. Not all effect categories are represented here, nor have I gotten around to trying *every* plug-in known to man, but I've listed certain plug-ins that have great sound quality and are easy to use. They are listed in no particular order.

EQ

- Waves SSL EQ
- Waves REQ
- Digidesign EQIII
- Sonnox Oxford EQ
- Universal Audio Neve 1073
- URS A Series

Filters

- Antares Filter
- Steinberg Q
- McDSP FilterBank

Compression and dynamics

- Waves C1 Compressor
- Waves SSL Comp
- Sonitus:fx Compressor
- Sonnox Oxford Transient Modulator
- Universal Audio LA-2A
- Universal Audio 1176

Reverb

- Audio Ease Altiverb
- IK Multimedia CSR Reverb
- Voxengo Pristine Space

Delay

- Waves SuperTap
- Steinberg Stereo Delay
- Big Tick Dual Delay

Distortion

- Antares Tube
- PSP Vintage Warmer
- IK Multimedia Ampeg SVX
- iZotope Vinyl

Channel strip

- McDSP Channel G
- Waves SSL Channel

Using Plug-Ins Efficiently

Software tools for effects encompass the tools found in your software sequencer that interact with your effect plug-ins. Inserts, auxiliaries, sends, busses, and signal flow all play important parts in the way that your DAW communicates with your plug-ins. Taking advantage of what they can do is a good habit to develop for audio production in general because they can make your digital audio environment more efficient and easier to work with. I'm going to take a stab at demystifying the functionality behind these tools so that you can begin using them immediately.

Inserts, Sends, and Busses

Let's disconnect effect plug-ins from the way they sound for a moment. Let's forget about the use of effects and focus on *how* they are used. I'm not talking about the controls or the application of effects anymore. I'm talking about program-level functionality, which has to do more with your sequencer than with the effects themselves. Effects can be used and routed many ways and have varying degrees of intensity and effectiveness, depending on their location within the application. The effects used as channel inserts are quite a bit different than the ones that are applied using a send or those that are sub-grouped in a bus assignment. Where you put it matters a lot for some effects and not as much as for others, so let's discuss the basic routing and principles of what goes where and why.

Inserts

Effects used as inserts, or *insert effects*, are like post-signal, pre-channel strips. Insert effects affect only the audio on the track on which they are inserted. The signal then passes out of the insert effects, through to the track's channel strip, where you can typically change the equalization, panning, and level of the affected signal. Still with me?

If you have a vocal track, for instance, and you apply a compressor and a de-esser as insert effects, you are putting the effects as if they were inline after the microphone and preamp themselves. (Mic > preamp > compressor > de-esser > track channel strip.) You usually need to first compress and then EQ as a typical rule of thumb. If you were to EQ first, then send the vocal to a compressor, you might actually ruin the EQ job you just completed.

Always keep in mind that insert effects enter the signal chain *first*, before anything else, and they remain in the order in which they were inserted. Realize that as you add multiple insert effects to a track, you are creating a signal chain on the track itself. Each new effect will be applied to the one that came before it. If you have one effect, such as a compressor, then you add a distortion plug-in, you are distorting the already compressed signal, not the original signal. If you go a step further and add a delay, you're creating a delay on the sum of a signal that is first compressed and then distorted. The resulting signal would sound totally different if you inserted the effects in a different order.

Typical effects for inserts are things such as pitch correction, compressors, de-essers, gain, distortion, tube preamps, and any microphone or amp emulators. These are the plug-ins that are most commonly applied as insert effects. You can certainly try other effects as inserts to see how they work. Just know that for every effect that is added, you are altering the level and changing the EQ of the resulting audio material. Feel free to experiment. You can always remove an insert effect from a track if you don't like it. One of the great things about inserts is that they only affect the one track on which they're placed, and none of the other elements in the mix. This allows you to add and remove effects as you please without any real consequences.

Sends or Auxiliaries

One of the more efficient ways to use effects in post-audio production is to create an *auxiliary*, or *send*, effects track. (To simplify things a bit, I'm just going to call them *sends*.) This is when you set up a channel for the sole purpose of housing a single effect that can be applied to multiple tracks simultaneously. Let's use a reverb as a send effect to cite an example. Suppose you create a send with a reverb effect on it. You'll first want to define the parameters of the reverb to make it sound just the way you like. When you're finished adjusting the effect, you can pretty much leave it alone. You would then go to a reverb-less track of your choice and activate the send channel. Adjust the mix level, or how much of the reverb effect you would like to be added to the dry signal, and you're finished! The reverb from your send effect track is supplying the specified amount of reverb to your audio track.

Why use a send over an insert? Sends are practical for several reasons. You can apply a single effect to several different tracks simultaneously using only one instance of the plug-in. As you can imagine, it is far more efficient to apply the same effect in varying degrees to multiple tracks using just one plug-in than it is to apply the same effect to each track individually using multiple instances of the same plug-in. You can also control the balance between the dry (unaffected) and wet (processed) mix for each individual channel. In most cases, the ability to use the same reverb from our last example in varying degrees on multiple tracks will result in a more unified sound than using different types of reverb on different tracks.

Send effects come after insert effects in the signal chain. If you're worried about messing up the time and effort you put into equalizing a track by adding a send effect, try not to lose any sleep over it. Most sends allow pre-fader and post-fader assignment.

A drawback to using send effects is that you have to commit to the same set of effect parameters for each track that accesses the effect. If you change the parameters for the send effect, it affects all the audio tracks that have the send effect enabled. Also, if you decide that you don't like the send effect on a particular track, you can disable the send on the track, but you can't remove the send effect track completely. If you remove a send effect track, it will be removed for all the tracks that are affected by it. This is why it is more common for effects that can be blanketed over multiple signals, such as reverb and compression, to be used as sends than it is for those that must be tailored for each individual audio signal, such as auto-tune or EQ. So, if you have developed effect presets that really seem to work for everything, you can try running them as send effects. Overall, it will make your sequencer run a bit more efficiently and prevent you from having to sort through multiple instances of the same plug-in from track to track.

To help save time, I set up track templates in my audio+MIDI sequencer with preconfigured send channels for effects that I commonly use, such as compressors and reverbs. When I launch one of these templates, my sends are already set up and good to go. All I have to do is define the wet/dry mix for the channel that I'm working with. I know it doesn't seem like setting up send effects would be time-consuming, but you'd be surprised. Some software sequencers make it more difficult than others. And because you're a busy post-production engineer, you want to save as much time as possible.

Busses, Group Channels, and Subgroups

Busses, or *group channels,* also known as *subgroups,* are used when you need multiple tracks to be treated like a single sonic element. An example is with discrete drum tracks, in which the kick, snare, hi-hats, toms, and overheads have all been recorded as separate tracks. Once you're finished mixing the levels of the drum kit together, you can create a bus track (for the purpose of this example, we'll call it Drum Bus) and assign each of the discrete drum tracks to it.

Now, Drum Bus acts as a master channel strip. Anything you do to the bus track will affect everything that is assigned to it. On the Drum Bus track, you can control volume, panning, and EQ, or even assign insert and send effects that will be applied to the sum of the drum tracks within the bus. If you want to get crazy, you can define automation for it as well. So what we've done here is combine multiple tracks without ditching the originals, and we've optimized our resources by effecting the tracks as a group rather than individually. I'll often create a bus for drums that I've already EQ'd and tailored, and then apply an equal treatment of compression, reverb, and EQ again on the bus track if necessary. Busses are also useful for multiple tracks of guitar, background vocals, and pretty much anything else that fits the profile.

Hardware Considerations

As you probably already know, the more effects you have, the more resources it takes to run them. We've all seen the CPU resource meter in our digital audio program cross over into the red as we hold our breath and try to restrict our mouse movement. Most plug-ins are pretty consistent in the resources they use. With some plug-ins, such as delays, it depends on what you're doing with them. An infinite feedback loop that keeps repeating itself over and over again will eventually catch up with you and choke your system. Some plug-ins are *so* resource-intensive that you can't even use them… and this will make you very sad.

One of the most important hardware considerations is system memory. It used to be that you could get away with having only 512 MB of RAM. Older software programs were much less complicated and therefore much less resource-intensive. As software programs become more complicated, more processing power and memory are required to run them efficiently. It's a vicious cycle. This acceleration applies to plug-ins too. Some developers assume that you will upgrade your computer technology to keep up with the rest of the world. Although this is true for many hardcore digital audiophiles, it isn't *always* the case. Digital audio software is often developed to run optimally on enhanced high-performance machines. So, if you are running the latest version of Nuendo on a machine that is more than five years old with 512 MB of RAM, you probably won't get very far with it. The current standard is more like 1 GB of RAM or better. There are very few things that are absolute in the world, but this one thing will always be true: The more RAM you have, the better off you'll be.

When a new version of your favorite audio software is released, it is extremely tempting to just jump right on it. Before you know it, you'll be scouring the couch cushions to come up with enough money to march right down to your local retailer to pick it up. Because of the aforementioned speed of technology, I have trained myself to resist the urge. I prefer to run slightly older software on newer computers (with lots of RAM). That way, I'm not stuck in an endless cycle of having to upgrade my hardware just to keep up and accommodate newer, faster software. I can actually run the software I *already* have more efficiently because my computer is already optimally spec'd out.

Something else that has an impact on the use of effects is your sound-card. Built-in consumer-level soundcards typically aren't designed to handle digital audio. Chances are that at some point, you'll experience garbled audio or what sounds like crackling and popping during play-back. To remedy this, I recommend you upgrade your factory-installed audio card to one that was designed for digital audio. I personally pre-fer PCI- or PCI-E–based soundcards over those with more modern con-nectivity interfaces, such as FireWire or USB 2.0. Each has its advantages and disadvantages, and it really depends on your baseline hardware configuration and needs. This is something else that will require a lot of user research to determine. I've always had good luck with PCI cards. I like the fact that my soundcard is hardwired to my system. At the same time, the potential for IRQ conflicts, which in some cases are irresolvable, is more common with PCI/PCI-E interfaces. PCI/PCI-E also has the advantage of speed over FireWire or USB. However, mobility is on the side of FireWire and USB 2.0 interfaces, though they are susceptible to port burnout (especially Fire-Wire) if not handled carefully. All of the above can suffer from manufacturer-level software and hardware issues, such as poorly written drivers or faulty circuitry, among other things.

Regardless of which interface you choose, your professional digital audio card will allow you to change its buffer settings for better audio performance. This can really be useful when you are dealing with resource-intensive plug-ins and programs. If you are experiencing garbled audio because of the plug-in you just inserted, you can raise the buffer size to free up some resources to get the audio to play back smoothly.

DSP cards are always an option as well. But although they handle the processing of certain CPU-heavy effects, DSP cards won't handle *every* plug-in you use. In fact, they will only handle the plug-ins that are written for them. They won't have any effect on the resources that your main sequencer program is using, either. As you can see, optimizing your hardware to deal with effects more efficiently is another problem for you to solve. It is often a combination of these different variables that will bring you to a reliable digital audio workstation.

This concludes Chapter 11. There are *tons* of effects available to the modern project studio. It can be overwhelming, but the good news is that digital audio has been around long enough that if there is ever a piece of software you want to try, chances are that someone out there has already tried it and can offer some helpful feedback before you take the plunge and spend part of next month's rent on the newest, hottest plug-in, only to find that it barely runs on your system. But, seriously, I hope that the information in this chapter will lead you to new and exciting effect options that move you closer to completing your ultimate plug-in library, as well as help you make the most out of them in your digital audio endeavors. In Chapter 12, "Software Effect Techniques for Post-Production," we'll explore software effect techniques. It's a long one, so get ready!

12 Software Effect Techniques for Post-Production

When you're striving for creativity, there's no *correct* way to apply effects to elements within a mix. Actually, even when creativity isn't the goal, there really aren't any hard-and-fast rules that govern effects. There are no official standards that say, "You can do this, but you can't do this." When you're the engineer, you are a slave to no laws... other than the unchangeable physics of sound, of course. Having said that, know that there *are* a number of different techniques and methods for the application of effects that have been proven effective by countless engineers over the years. Over time and through experimentation, you'll find that some methods work better than others in different scenarios. You may even discover some new ones that will be commonly practiced by others five years from now. Although there are no rules with effects, when you're just starting out, it's nice to be able to use these proven methods as a guideline or reference point for where to begin.

Your ears are an essential component to applying effects, just like all other sonic aspects of post-production. They're just as important as understanding the parameters of an effect so that you can bend it to your will. I've said this before and I'll say it again: If it sounds good, it *is* good. But if you don't know what you're listening for or you can't hear it accurately, then what sounds good might not *really* be good. Critical listening skills and an accurate perception of the sonic landscape are of the utmost importance for *everyone* in an audio-related field, including engineers, sound designers, audio editors, and musicians alike. Although some individuals, such as Beethoven, could write symphonies without the use of their ears, I don't think *anyone* could mix and master a recording without being able to hear it. And no one could do it *well* without hearing it accurately.

Remember that no one magical thing will get your signals to sound right. A combination of different treatments will result in a great-sounding recording. All the plug-in settings I offer in this chapter are suggestions for how to sculpt a mix from the ground level. They're just building blocks. Once you EQ an instrument, you'll have to decide what the right compression settings are, what type of reverb to use, and so on.

In this chapter, we'll discuss *proven* methods of applying different software effects. We'll discuss common settings for common scenarios, as well as some ideas on how to tailor the effect to suit your needs. You can use this section as a reference by jumping directly to the type of effect you are using right now, or you can read the entire chapter as a primer for making overall improvements to your mixes. Either way, I hope the information in this chapter will have a positive impact on your mixes.

Compression

Compression has been a frequently discussed topic in this book. Because most raw recorded audio signals are so dynamic, you end up using compression a lot in post. Whether it's to get more consistency in dynamic range, to reduce the sibilance on a vocal, or to just get a little more volume, punch, and prominence out of an audio signal, compression is one of the most commonly used effects in audio post-production.

Application

There are different ways to effectively apply compression. To apply compression directly to an audio signal, you can run a compression plug-in as a send effect to allow one set of parameters to be applied to multiple audio tracks, or you can use it as an insert effect that will affect only one audio track.

Another method used to apply compression is something called *parallel compression*. This is sometimes referred to as *New York–style compression*. Parallel compression is a method in which a dry, or slightly compressed, signal is mixed with an identical signal that has been heavily compressed. It is believed that you can maintain the detail, subtleties,

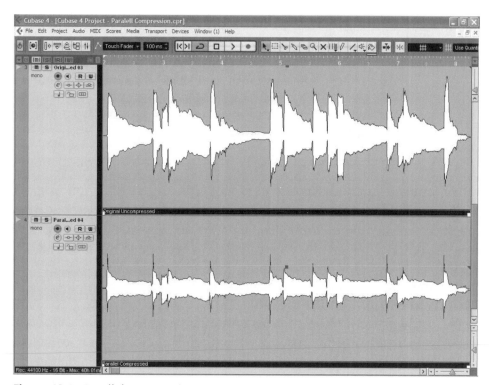

Figure 12.1   Parallel compression.

and nuances of the original audio signal while simultaneously equalizing its dynamics, keeping it under control in the mix. Figure 12.1 shows what parallel compression looks like on a guitar track in Cubase 4.

Parallel compression can be achieved in any multitrack audio sequencing program. When I use parallel compression, I like to duplicate the original audio track and apply a generous amount of compression to it using my favorite compressor plug-in as a real-time insert effect. Then I'll export that track to a new track that has the heavy compression "printed" to it as part of the new audio signal. I'll bring the fader of the newly compressed track down to −0 dB, then listen carefully as I slowly raise the fader, blending its volume level with the original signal to achieve the desired effect.

Printing Effects   When you "print" an effect to a track, you are exporting the original audio file with the effect applied to it. The result is the original audio plus the effect rolled into a single signal. Before you "print" or export your affected tracks, you want to be sure that the effect is exactly the way you want it to sound. Once printed, the effect parameters cannot be modified from the newly exported track. The only way to make adjustments to the effect parameters at that point is to go back to the original audio track, reapply the real-time effect, and export it all over again.

Either of these methods can be used to apply any effect to an original audio signal. If you are running low on resources, a parallel application might be the way to go. Some people prefer the way one method sounds over the other. This is really your call. Try to become familiar with both, regardless of whether you end up using one more than the other.

Sound Advice for Compression

There are *many* common misconceptions about the use of compression. In fact, when you first get into digital audio, it can seem like the least important, yet most daunting, effect plug-in you'll use. As you've probably gathered, that couldn't be further from the truth. I believe that compression is often misunderstood, which is why we've spent so much time trying to make it less of a mystery. In this section, I'd like to clear the air of a few of the most common misunderstandings that people have about compression. So, the following statements about compression are *false!*

- **Professional recordings use minimal amounts of compression.** This is totally untrue. In fact, the most common limiters and compressors in pro studios usually start at 8:1 ratios with thresholds of −20 to −25 dB. Vocals, bass, acoustic guitar, percussion, and drum kits often have a *lot* of this type of compression on them. The only sources on which you may not be too concerned about compression are signals such as electric distorted guitar or synthetic bass. The reason is that these types of audio signals are typically heavily compressed already. You can actually *see* that there are no dynamics when you look at the waveform.

  Vocals are often compressed with an optical limiter on input at about a 10:1 ratio. Then, they are compressed *again* in post-production.

If you listen to pretty much any Kelly Clarkson single, there are almost *no* dynamics between the loud notes and the soft, whispered parts. She sounds so consistent that it's unreal. That's what 14:1 compression on an already compressed mono input signal sounds like once all is said and done. My recent rule of thumb is to turn down the threshold of the compressor until the audio starts to sound like it sits in the mix where you want it. Don't look at the numbers on the plug-in interface. You may make yourself sick or feel bad for breaking a rule. I've certainly felt guilty about applying massive amounts of compression to an audio signal before. But eventually, you stop fighting yourself over it and get back to doing whatever it takes to make the recording sound good.

■ **Compressors should always have a quick attack and a slow release.** This is definitely a case-by-case basis. If the attack is too fast, you can literally kill the definition in the dynamic transients of your audio source. I'd start at around 15ms and slowly increase the time until you feel as if the compressor is doing its job without ruining the tonal quality of the audio. Though a fast attack and a slow release may work well on a drum bus, the same attack and release settings may totally ruin a perfectly good bass track.

■ **Pumping audio or destroying a track with compression is a bad thing.** Much of the color in recordings comes from artifacts and distress caused by a compressor. Sometimes applying compression until it really starts to affect the audio signal can be a good thing for a mix. Cymbals on a drum kit are often treated with what I call *smear compression*—where the overheads are so compressed that the cymbals seem to become dirtier, smearing together while simultaneously becoming more unified and smooth-sounding.

Some instruments even pump slightly throughout an entire mix, but in context you'd never be able to tell because it contributes to the overall unity of the entire track. In a bass track, for example, it's common to hear a compressor working on the transients when played back alone. But it wouldn't be noticeable in a mix in which other parts of the arrangement have transients that are only hitting semi-simultaneously. If the kick drum is present in the mix with a lot of snap or kick "beater," it would mask the lacking bass transients, and the whole mix would sound fine despite the pumping of the compressor.

Another scenario using heavy compression is on drum-room mics. You can create a distressor-type effect by totally destroying the mics with 20:1 compression or better. This creates a gritty harmonic layer out of your room mics that will make acoustic drums sound less sterile.

- **Two compressors on a single source can only lead to peril and an over-compressed product.** Sure, if you are living in 1985 and listening to vinyl, this may be the case. However, we live in the age of the MP3. These days, audio is LOUDER and more compressed than ever. It is common to bus out multiple background vocals with compression already applied to them and compress them *again* as a single track. Though the second compressor is usually set to a lighter or "over easy" setting that doesn't apply nearly as much compression as the first compressor, it will help catch the peaks and any harshness that the first compressor didn't get under control. Don't fear compression. Learn enough about it to know when to break the rules regarding what is considered an acceptable amount of compression.

Exceptions

The exception to the use of compression is a situation in which the instruments are meant to be very dynamic, such as orchestral or symphonic music. Typically, these types of instruments will lose their detail if they are compressed. You might be able to get away with a little parallel compression, but often you won't end up using it all. You're going to have to put your ears back to work in order to decide for sure. Listen carefully to what makes the instrument sound rich and detailed. Try to do your best to retain these qualities if you choose to compress them at all.

A further exception is in situations where you want to give a certain musical element the feeling of being over-compressed for a dramatic effect. Sometimes vocals, kick drums, or entire drum parts are over-compressed to create a distortion-like effect that gives the element more perceived texture in a mix. This is great for electronic drums, accents, or background vocal parts.

Compression can become a destructive thing when overdone, but this is especially true in the mastering process. It is a modern practice to over-compress a mix to make it louder. You can hear seriously over-compressed tracks played all over the radio these days, particularly in hip-hop and hard rock genres. I personally do not advocate this type of over-compression because I feel it hurts the finished product more than it helps it. Think for a moment how music would sound without dynamics at all. Louder is not always better. Learn to hear the difference between an appropriately compressed signal and an over-compressed one.

Reverb

Reverb is another effect with which you will want to become well acquainted. It's probably the second most used effect in post-production. As I've mentioned before, reverb can help provide realism by defining an environment in which a recording exists by simulating real room reverberations. Chances are that your clients will not know what type of room they'll want you to use on their recording. Most of the time, they may only be able to tell you how they want it to *feel*, at best.

Often vocals are perceived to be smoother with a good deal of reverb, but too much can make vocals sound washed out. These days, a small to moderate amount of reverb is acceptable for snare drums, but too much can take you right back to the 1980s. Reverb walks a fine line between being helpful and hurtful to a mix. It's up to you as the post-production engineer to decide what kind of space and how much of it is appropriate for the project.

Sound Advice for Reverb

Here are a few ideas that will help you use reverb more effectively:

- **Vary reverb levels within a track.** In a mix, it's all right to use different reverb levels for different parts of a project. This is especially true for vocals. A big reverb might work in a chorus where the vocal has to have more space in order to fit the energy of a track and play nicely with dense instrumentation, but the same reverb on an instrumentally sparse verse section would probably seem very out of place.

The most effective way to manage varying reverb levels is through automation. Most software sequencers give you the option of defining effect automation by either drawing it in or using a fader to control a given parameter (in this case, the reverb level) as you listen to the song play back in real time. Using a fader in your software mixer to define automation is often referred to as *riding the fader*. This is a great way to get a good general idea about how much reverb you want to use for each part of the project because you will be able to get a better feel for different levels of reverb within the context of the entire project, not just a small section of it. Then, you can go in and tweak the automation by hand to make the values more precise.

- **Space, the final frontier.** All organic audio sources by nature have some degree of space, whether it's natural reverb caused by the distance the source was from the mic to sing a part, or artificial reverb from a spatial plug-in preset. Although all recordings utilize reverb, not all audio sources need it. Drums and vocals may require reverb, but keyboards and bass often don't. However, the recording will still have space because *some* of the elements within it have reverb applied to them.

    Do some entire mixes have reverb? Absolutely! Years ago, there was no choice. The only option for reverb was to use one large plate to record an entire band to only one or two tracks. The effect blanketed the entire recording because the ability to apply reverb to the individual instruments was nonexistent. These days we *do* have the option to apply reverb to individual instruments, so it isn't common for reverb to blanket a final mix. However, the exception is when that final mix goes to mastering. Some mastering engineers like to apply a light amount of reverb as a master effect over an entire track to help unify the overall sound.

Are some things in a mix dry? Usually guitars, bass, and pianos require less reverb in post because the instruments have inherent space from the rooms and the method in which they were recorded. Even something seemingly bone dry and aggressive (think Metallica's ...*And Justice for All*) has some reverb present on some instruments. The only mixes I've ever heard devoid of any spatial effects were jazz or classical recordings in which the reverb was captured with 30 strategically placed microphones in the actual acoustic environment in which the performance took place. For as in-your-face as *Toxicity* sounds, even System of a Down has space in the recording. You may have to listen closely for it. The space applied may only be the size of a small bathroom, but it's there.

The bottom line is that the devil is in the details. Don't be afraid to use reverb, but be mindful of overusing it. Dial in a nice reverb for whatever source you're working with, and then listen to it in the context of the mix for the way that it balances with other reverb-affected sources and the track as a whole. As you can imagine, compounding many different sources that all have varying degrees of reverb can create a real problem in a mix. If things start to sound too washed out, go back and reevaluate to decide which sources *really* need space and which ones don't.

- **I can't believe it's not reverb!** Again, reverb is one of those things that the average listener will probably never notice... that is, until you take it away. In most modern recordings, reverb is used all the time, but it's often only to enhance a mix, so you may not even notice it. There are many reverb sizes and types to choose from, ranging from itty bitty to monstrously huge. Many small room reverbs can add just enough space to provide a bit of ambience without being too obvious.

At this point, you might be asking yourself, "Why would I want to use reverb at all if the goal is to make it unnoticeable?" The answer is perception. Even subtle amounts of reverb contribute to the overall sound of a recording. Reverb naturally exists all around us, but we rarely pay attention to it. In post-production, reverb is meant to simulate auditory environments that are native to the audio material—environments that often go unnoticed in our day-to-day lives.

To further illustrate the way that even subtle amounts of reverb are perceived, you could do another taste test. Between a signal that has a bit of reverb applied to it and an identical signal that is dry, the listener would definitely be able to tell that the two signals are different, but probably not *why* they are different. In mixing, you want reverb to be perceived, but not necessarily heard. On the other end, having *some* reverb is more natural-sounding than having no reverb at all. Remember that fine line we were talking about?

- **Be in control.** Take the time to really understand what role each parameter of a reverb plug-in plays. They all affect the reverb that is produced in some way. If you need your reverb to sound bigger, brighter, or more natural, the most obvious solution may not always be the best solution. It's okay to use a larger amount of space or a hotter reverb mix, but make decisions about the amount of decay and tail length on a case-by-case basis. Do you want to make it bigger with a larger room or more time? The snare does not need four seconds of reverb trailing behind every hit to sound big.

- **Command decisions.** Make decisions about reverb based on how congested you feel the mix is to begin with and what the focal point of the style of music is. Use it sparingly and where it is necessary.

- **Everything is connected.** Realize that the way a reverb *sounds* will affect the mix as well. If one reverb is smacking around a whole bunch of high-end whisks and is long to decay, and another one is dark and short-decaying, is this the same sonic space? Experiment with the available frequency controls as well and determine which frequencies are pleasant reflections and do well for the entire mix.

EQ

EQ is a tool more than an effect. That is, until it is used in conjunction with a filter shape that will drastically change the way an audio signal sounds. If you use your EQ plug-in to reproduce the two different equalizer settings shown in Figure 12.2 and apply them to an audio

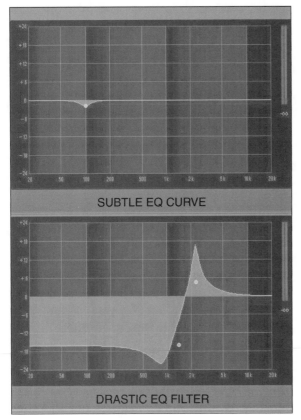

SUBTLE EQ CURVE

DRASTIC EQ FILTER

Figure 12.2   A subtle EQ curve versus a drastic EQ filter.

signal, you'll be able to hear what I mean. Because EQ can be used as both a drastic effect and a tool, I will take the time to discuss both—as a tool now and as a drastic effect later (in the "Filters" section later in this chapter).

In post-production, EQ is typically used on every bit of incoming source material. Whether it's a mild boost of high mids to sharpen up a vocal, or a large 200-Hz reductive scoop in the low mids to make drums less muddy, you can count on using *some* EQ on pretty much every track. Unless it was recorded by a big-time professional engineer who has years of experience getting the best sounds to tape or disk, there will always be little frequency discrepancies that will have to be altered before you can have a professional-sounding mix. Most people these days stick a mic in front of a person or amplifier as the entire recording technique. So it's important that we, as post-production engineers, know how to compensate for their lack of effort.

When EQ is used as a tool, there are a great number of common EQ curves that can be used to get instrument signals into shape for your mixes. There are inherent tonal characteristics to certain instruments that almost always have to be boosted or reduced in order for them to sit correctly in a mix. No two vocalists are the same, just as no guitar player uses the exact same tone as the guitar player in your last project. There are always some exceptions to what we think will work, but you should at the very least be able to get a good starting pointing for customizing EQ to whatever audio material you're working with.

The following sections discuss some ways to fix common problems with different types of source material.

Drums

Great drummers and drum engineers always say the same thing about recorded percussion: "Low mids are the devil or death of good drum sound." This may or may not be true, but the truth for me is that nine out of 10 times, we are reducing 100 Hz to 900 Hz in the toms, kick, and snare. And then we accent the sticks and hit transients with frequencies between 1 kHz and 5 kHz. This makes drums punchier overall and better defined.

The low mids can make toms and kicks a little too big and boomy in the average mix. And that is my guess about where the aforementioned quote comes from—because typically on these types of sources, there would be no way to remove the inherent amount of boom and resonance without a little bit of low-mid reduction. The added high mids accentuate the hits themselves, and you might be surprised, depending on the recorded material, by how much high mid you have to add to get the definition across.

With drums, I suggest that you always start with a narrow Q and move to a wider one. I usually will begin with a Q of 5 or 3 and widen it up to a 1.5 or 1 depending on the drum sounds. It is always good to find the most accurate frequency that needs to be reduced or expanded first, and then slowly bring the neighboring frequencies back into the picture.

Vocals

Most of the "big vocal" sound people usually go for comes again from an abundance of low mids. Usually you have to reduce vocal sources by about −2.5 dB to −4 dB at around 200 Hz to clean up the surplus of vocal warmth. This is usually accomplished with a Q factor of 1 or so, moving it across the frequency spectrum until you feel the boom is gone. Adding a sharp Q of 2 or 3 at 3.6 kHz to a vocal will usually brighten it up and help provide more clarity. In some cases adding a bit of gain with a high shelf at 7 kHz can provide a little more air, space, and crispness. Women's voices are often recorded poorly, with the incorrect microphones, and they often need additional mid and high-mid reductions. This should be done in the same manner as mentioned for drums. Start with a narrow Q factor to find the sweet spot of the affected area.

Guitar

Guitars often require a good deal of equalization. The distorted guitars in modern recordings are often too muddy and require a low-mid reduction at about 200 Hz to 500 Hz. Big, heavy, guitar-loving Korn listeners are all about this frequency being exaggerated, but 90 percent of the time, you don't need a frequency boost like this in guitars because the bass occupies this frequency. Guitar clarity exists between 2 kHz and 5 kHz. This area usually requires a boost of some sort to enhance its clarity, much like the vocal boost we just discussed.

Many times I hear guitars that haven't been EQ'd correctly—there is either too much or not enough of the right *and* wrong frequencies. This can make a recording sound *much* less than professional. I typically look at the guitar in relation to the vocal. Where the vocal is pushed at 3.6 kHz, I might boost the guitars at 2.5 kHz or 5 kHz just to reduce the competition between the two instruments. Clean guitars are usually recorded with a somewhat scooped EQ. There is lots of low and high end, but nothing in the midrange. These may require some thickening in the midrange and can usually benefit from some warmth. This will make them less snappy and will make them sit in the mix more comfortably.

With clean guitar, you should play with the 700-Hz to 2-kHz area and see where you can add a little bit of "nasal" so that sparkly Stratocaster or acoustic guitar comes through with a little more midrange and a little less in the high end, where the ride cymbal typically lives.

Bass

Bass sources are almost always too heavy in the 98-Hz to 130-Hz area. I usually start by pulling out 3 to 4 dB between these frequencies and then listen to see how much more might need to come out. The definition of bass notes, however, is typically more in the 1-kHz range. Bass instruments and bass guitar are often misunderstood in mixing because of their names. Bass is, in fact, *not* a big, subby, low frequency–heavy instrument. Its frequencies reside primarily with the lower midrange frequencies of guitars. Once you understand that bass is actually a midrange instrument, your recordings become infinitely easier to affect and manipulate in this area.

Most of the time, when there is perceived low end in guitars, it's actually the bass supporting the guitars with the right frequencies. The reason we remove so much of the low mids in the *other* instruments is to make room for the bass. In recordings where people cannot hear or point out the bass part, there are probably too many sources occupying the same low midrange frequencies as the bass, which are thereby masking it.

Keyboards

Common EQ settings for keyboards are a bit difficult to define. The sounds that keyboards produce are often very full-range instruments already. With sounds such as piano, harp, and organ, feel free to add a little bit of a high shelf and boost the midrange a bit, but don't go crazy. Exaggerated midrange can make a synth track *abnormally* synthetic. The most common EQ with keyboards is, again, a low-mid reduction. Most of the sources coming at you from a keyboard can, like everything else, be a little too brown or low-end heavy.

Delay

Delay effects can be a lot like an untrained 110-pound dog—difficult to control. But if you have a good grip on the leash, you can keep the dog from running away. The same goes for delay: If you've got your head wrapped around the different parameters, you can rein in the chaos to keep the delay under control. What may sound like an instantly cool effect for a guitar can easily turn into a sonic massacre if the feedback is set too high and the affected signal begins to create a never-ending delay loop. I don't even want to think about that mess in the context of a mix. Not to mention the strain on your computer as it tries to keep up with the calculations it takes to play back that infinite loop. In most cases this ends in a system hang or even a complete system crash. You can help avoid such disasters by letting your plug-ins know who's the boss. (I'll give you a hint: It's not Tony Danza.)

In post-production, we strive to keep the audio signals as controlled as possible so that the final product is well balanced and sonically pleasing. You first work with the raw audio material to bring it up to mix-ready standards, and *then* you work with the effects. What's the point of working so hard to keep the original audio signals under control if you are just going to let chaos reign free once the effects are applied? So not only does the original audio have to be controlled, but the effects need to be controlled as well. One directly affects the other, and they both affect the final mix.

This effect has two sides, just like the others. Delay is often used as an obvious effect for guitars in rock music (think U2's The Edge). As far as post-production effects are concerned, delay is perceived as a pretty dramatic one. You can almost always hear when delay has been applied to an audio signal within a mix. I'll often use a delay over a reverb when it comes to adding dimension to an audio element or while creating sound effects. You can afford to be a bit more experimental with delay on things like the lead vocals in a dense pop or rock mix, instrument solos, long sustaining notes, background vocals, and when you are using instruments to create a polyrhythmic effect for texture.

Many great mixers these days will use a stereo delay with rhythmic repetitions that pan from left to right to thicken a vocal. You can usually set your delay taps to sixteenth, eighth, quarter, or half notes, or variations thereof. The most common is the panning eighth note that repeats three or four times after the original audio has sounded. This creates the illusion of space. The most important thing about delay is to keep an eye on the volume of the repeats. You don't want the repeats to distract the listener from the performance; you just want the effect to add to the ambience of the entire track. In mixing, you will typically only use about 20 percent of the mix level on a delay effect. If you use more than that, the effect may end up being too noticeable and somewhat unnatural to the listener.

Modulation

Modulation effects fall under the category of more dramatic signal processors. They are by no means considered natural-sounding audio treatments and are typically pretty obvious in a mix. To *modulate* means to change or vary the pitch, intensity, or tone. Modulation effect plug-ins can usually do one or more of these things at a time. The most common types of modulation effects used in post-production are chorus, phasing (or phase shifting), and flange. Ready?

Chorus

In a way, chorus is akin to delay because it produces short *pitch-modulated* delays. The pitch modulation of a chorus effect works much like a section of choir singers. If you have a group of tenors, each individual's voice will have a unique timbre to it. And although they are all singing the exact same notes, the pitch from singer to singer will vary ever so slightly. If you were listening to them sing with your eyes closed, you would definitely be able to identify that it's not just one tenor, but a group of tenors. Even though they are unified, you can hear that they are many because of these subtle differences. So, this slight pitch modulation is applied to a series of short delays to create a doubling effect, or a simulation of the same audio signal being produced by multiple sources.

Chorus effects are good for thickening background vocals. You may find that they're a bit too dramatic for a lead vocal, but that isn't to say you couldn't roll back the wet/dry mix level so that effect is perceived more than heard. Sometimes chorus can be useful in making guitars seem less harsh. And of course, as with all effects, you can crank up the chorus effect for a really dramatic effect on almost anything when it's appropriate. Bear in mind, the more chorus effect you use on an audio signal, the further it will be pushed back into the mix. In some cases, this can be remedied by applying some additive EQ to brighten the affected signal.

Phasing

Phasing is an effect that is created by taking a copy of an audio signal and running it through an *all-pass* filter. The all-pass filter leaves the signal's amplitude untouched, but alters or shifts its phase response. When you combine the original signal with the altered signal, the frequencies that are out of phase will cancel each other out. This cancellation creates the notches in the frequency response that are responsible for the amplitude modulation in the resulting signal. (See the "Filters" section in this chapter for an explanation of a notch filter.) The existence of these notches creates the phasing effect. Figure 12.3 shows an example

In Phase

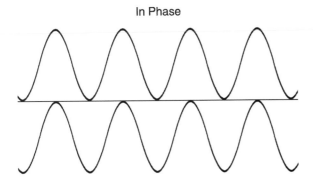

180 Degrees Out of Phase

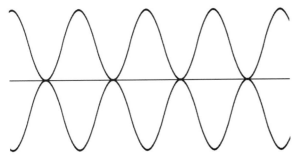

Figure 12.3 Top: Two sine waves that are in phase with each other. Bottom: A sine wave combined with an identical sine wave that is out of phase.

of a basic sine wave combined with its out-of-phase counterpart in contrast to two sine waves that are *in* phase with each other.

The mix ratio is the parameter that controls the depth of the notches. Fifty percent is when the notches are most noticeable. The level of phase shifting is measured in degrees, so a 90-degree shift would be a quarter-cycle phase shift. A 180-degree shift would be the exact opposite phase position from the original signal. You'd basically be reversing the phase, in which case the two signals would cancel each other out completely, and nothing would be heard.

Okay, now that we've discussed phasing as an effect, it's time to *really* confuse you by discussing phase shifting as a separate, yet related, tool. Phase shifting is useful for cleaning up a mix. In a mix, you often are dealing with copied tracks, copies of copied tracks, multiple mics on the same source, and other variables that can cause a lot of phasing issues. In drum mixes, there is a common misconception that each mic you add to a drum or cymbal adds another phasing issue to remedy. A quick fix is to invert the phase on the outer kick drum mic track and hear how it jives with the internal mic after the phase has been shifted.

Many times when you are mixing and hearing midrange weirdness in a multi-mic or multitracked source, it's not the inherent frequency; it's a phasing issue. A good rule of thumb is whenever you are mixing a drum kit or multiple tracks of transients that occur on the same beat but at different times (think guitars and keyboards), invert the phase of just one of the conflicting tracks. Listen for when the audio seems to clean up and what frequencies become lost or enhanced. When the phase issue sounds as if it has been worked out, take a step back and assess whether you have to EQ some of the frequency back into the signal.

Phase can be a useful tool, and a lot of people have a tendency to overlook its importance. It doesn't really take a lot of effort to activate the invert phase button and just listen to what is affected in the track. You may be surprised at how much of a difference it makes.

Flange

Flange is a specific type of phasing that is also related to delay. It is created by mixing an audio signal with a copy of itself that is affected by a slight time-modulated delay, in which the delay time is constantly changing. The delay time itself is typically less than 15ms. In fact, it's so short that our ears don't even perceive it as an echo. What we hear sounds like a type of sweeping filter effect that almost resembles the sound you hear when an airplane flies overhead.

Like phasing, the combination of the dry signal and the affected copy creates a series of notches in the signal's summed frequency response. But *unlike* phasing, the notches are evenly spaced. This effect on the frequency response is sometimes called a *comb filter* because, visually, it looks like the teeth of a comb. Figure 12.4 illustrates this concept.

Like a phaser, a flanger plug-in allows you to define how deep the notches are with the ratio mix. Even if the notches are shallow or low in amplitude modulation, you will still be able to identify that they're there. But it's the movement of these notches across the frequency spectrum that produces the characteristic sweeping sound of a flanger. The parameter used to define the timing of the sweep is called the *rate*.

Some flangers even allow you to send the output signal back into the input of the effect, which produces feedback and resonance, but keep in mind that doing so basically creates an endless loop, and your flanger plug-in will be using precious CPU resources as long as it's

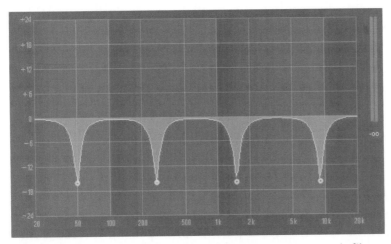

Figure 12.4 A series of evenly spaced notches create a comb filter.

active. One way to resolve this is once you have the effect dialed in just the way you want it, bounce the track out with the effect printed on it. If you think you may need to make changes to the effect, keep the original track, but deactivate the plug-in to lighten the workload on your CPU.

Flange is a pretty dramatic effect. It can be used to give a little dimension to drum overheads and guitars. Flanging drum overheads are created by lightly affecting the cymbals and high frequencies of the kit with a slow flange. By doing this you can give a creepy, slow, almost science-fiction feel to the percussion on the track. This may not be useful for everything, but it happens in a lot of Zeppelin and '70s tracks that are not crash-cymbal heavy and are more groove-oriented. Listen to some of these groove tracks, such as "Fool in the Rain," and you will hear the top-end flange. It makes the cymbal crashes really stand out. This effect was employed often in the '70s and is still employed in projects reminiscent of that 1970s sound (think Lenny Kravitz).

Other types of effects that produce modulation, such as vibrato (pitch) and tremolo (amplitude), aren't as common in the post-production process. They are more likely to be used as creative elements than as sound-shaping tools. However, occasionally you may be called on to use them by your client, so we'll discuss them briefly.

Vibrato

Vibrato is a modulation of pitch. It is created by oscillating between a natural pitch and a pitch slightly below natural. Most plug-ins that offer vibrato-style effects allow you to tempo sync the oscillations by adjusting the rate at which they occur. You can also generally tailor the pitch oscillation to suit your needs by adjusting the pitch depth.

The most common instrument associated with vibrato is the human voice. In fact, when it's used on instruments, it's usually to give them a more vocal-like characteristic. Vibrato is commonly used as a natural playing technique for stringed instruments, such as violin, viola, cello, and guitar. When produced by a voice or an instrument, it almost sounds as if the note is wavering or pulsing. Natural vibrato is typically captured as part of the performance during the recording process. The player or vocalist will usually apply it to single sustaining notes rather than to an entire musical phrase. The main difference between natural vibrato and artificial vibrato lies in the amount of vibrato used.

Artificial vibrato that is produced by a software plug-in is a blanketed effect. If you apply it to a guitar part, it will be applied to the entire part, not just a single note. It is unlikely that you will ever apply vibrato to a vocal or orchestral string part in post—unless, of course, your client requests it. But even then, the goal would not be realism; it would be for effect. Like any modulation effect, vibrato is not a mix-dependent effect. Unlike EQ, compression, and reverb that are usually mandatory for any mix, you could produce a perfectly professional mix without ever using a single modulation effect. I like to throw one in on occasion for texture, but by no means do I make a habit out of using them in every mix.

Tremolo

If you've never heard a tremolo effect, think about surf guitar. Tremolo effects produce amplitude, or volume modulation. They create almost a type of gated fluttering effect by oscillating the volume of an audio signal. This effect can be produced manually by using automation to create a comb-like shape with evenly spaced drops in volume...but with any luck, your software sequencer includes a tremolo-style effect plug-in that will take the guesswork out of it.

The speed of the amplitude oscillation is controlled by the tremolo's rate. This can typically be tempo-synced to your sequencer's master tempo to offer unity between the effect oscillation and the rest of the audio in the project. The depth will determine how dramatic the drops in volume are. The greater the depth, the more "gated" the effect will sound.

Tremolo is definitely a cool-sounding effect that can be manipulated to provide a little creative color to an audio signal. Combined with things such as panning and filter sweeps, you can create sonic textures that even the most sober person will find trippy. But as another blanket/anti-realism effect, in post-production its use is, again, the client's call.

Distortion

There are two kinds of distortion of which you need to be aware. There is intentional distortion that is induced with a software plug-in specifically designed to distort your audio signal, and then there's distortion that is the result of your audio signals being too loud. Obviously, you should try to avoid the latter distortion at all costs. But when distortion is used as an intentional effect in post-production, it is often just to provide some texture to an otherwise pristine audio signal. I'll often use a parallel method so that I can get just a little dirtiness out of a vocal, bass, or drums.

There are basically two types of software plug-ins you can use to apply distortion. Tube emulators provide what is called *tube warmth* to an audio signal. Tube warmth plug-ins basically emulate the tonal characteristics of vintage preamps by exciting the midrange frequencies in an audio signal with mild harmonic distortion while attenuating high frequencies to keep them from sounding harsh. Take a moment to consider the way that tube distortion works in a guitar amp. The louder the input gain, the more the audible signal will distort. These types of distortion plug-ins work the same way, but the results may vary. It is common that by the time you have the input gain loud enough to produce the desired level of harmonic distortion in a realistic way, the output of the tube plug-in is in full clip, so it's important to keep your eye on the output level of the plug-in itself. You can use tube warmth to make a thin vocal part seem thicker and fuller, as well as to give some harmonic excitement to guitars and bass.

Next up is basic overdrive distortion. The more drastic of the two plug-ins, these simulate the sound of guitar amplifier distortion. Varying degrees of distortion, from a low-gain mild fuzz to an eardrum-destroying high gain distortion, can be applied to your original audio signal. Basic overdrive can be good for drum overheads, as a texture layer for lead vocals, and it is a lot of fun with synthesizers.

Overdrive distortion can sometimes be disguised as an *amp modeler*. These days, it can be difficult to tell whether the guitars and bass on a recording are "real." Have they been recorded using mics and real amplifiers, or were they all recorded direct, using an amp-modeling plug-in or program?

Amp modelers produce customized tones that are specific to popular guitar and bass amplifiers. Because they aim to model a real guitar rig, they often include different guitar-style multi-effects that allow you to create a signal chain consisting of the amp distortion and various effects that can be applied to the original audio signal. Amp-modeling plug-ins were originally marketed as a recording software solution for digital audio–savvy guitar players; the plug-ins would allow the musicians to record a direct, clean guitar into a computer and then apply any type of amp distortion to it in post. But amp-modeling plug-ins aren't just for guitar anymore. You can use them on anything you wish to distort.

Lightly applied distortion usually translates to warmth and smoothness in an audio signal. Many of the vocals that we have enjoyed over the years are actually pretty distorted. To our ears, they may sound vintage, with thickness and warmth. But the reality is that there is some distortion going on. The history of this begins with channel clipping. Back in the day, people would set up a mic for the singer, and of course the singer would sing quietly to test it. Then, as soon as the singer got into the recording booth to sing, he or she would blast at full volume into the mic, much louder than anticipated. This caused distortion by clipping the analog input channel. This was music to some, but just noise to others. Either way, over the years it translated into how we think certain dynamic sources, such as vocals, *should* sound. If you are trying to distort a vocal and deliver this smooth, vintage vibe, look to plug-ins and sounds described as mild overdrive, saturation, or tube warmth. Apply them in small amounts with the gain usually no greater than about 60 percent. This should excite the midrange and harmonics of a vocal quite nicely.

An instrument that is often overlooked for distortion use is the bass guitar. Bass guitar amps are often very clean and don't have much pronunciation in the midrange. "Fuzzing it out" with some overdrive can do amazing things for the compression and clarity of a bass tone. Just don't overdo it. If you listen to old Green Day albums, you'll see what I mean. The bass is distorted in what is considered to be a good way. If you are in a situation where you have a direct or very clean-sounding bass amp track, a bit of gnarl might help make it less punchy or glassy and more pronounced.

It's important that bass tones stay out of the way of the kick drum. Some people say, "Let the kick handle the sub-frequencies"; some say, "Let the bass do it while the kick remains passive in the lows." Either way, I find that distortion and amp emulators are great ways to keep the bass out of the kick drum's way. A little EQ to reinforce your sub-frequency intentions, and you're off to the races!

Distortion can also be used to totally decimate a vocal or destroy any source for that matter. In the mid '90s, it became popular for bands such as Nirvana and Smashing Pumpkins to crank lots of pedal-type crunch distortion into a vocal for some superb, albeit gnarly, distortion effects. In this same era, we also had bands severely altering the sonic character-istics of any source, such as drums or even entire mixes. Next, industrial rockers went crazy with the concept of the big, ballsy, fuzz type of dis-tortion that became a staple in the '90s. You can hear it on tracks made famous by Aphex Twin, Marilyn Manson, and Gravity Kills.

There are so many different types of distortion that it may be hard to keep them all straight. Much can be defined by the names of the plug-ins or the presets themselves. Here is list of what to expect:

- **Smooth distortions that enchant:** Saturators, overdrive, tube emu-lators, vintage channels, and classic analog.

- **Moderate, more noticeable distortions:** Fuzz, amp simulators, and anything usually labeled as "hard driving" or "hot" are effects from which you can expect to get anything from a Vox to Marshall amplifier type of distortion.

- **Out-of-this-world decimating distortions:** Anything labeled "black," "grunge," "extreme," or "crushing."

Filters

Now it's time to talk about EQ as a dramatic effect by combining it with a filter shape. We already know that there are four basic types of filter shapes: high-pass, low-pass, band-pass, and notch. Some EQ plug-ins have an entirely separate section to define high- and low-shelf parameters, but regardless of the placement of the controls, these too are filters and will be discussed here. When you use these filter shapes over a range of frequencies, you can drastically alter the way an audio signal sounds. We briefly touched on these different filter shapes in Chapter 5, but now I want to take a closer look.

High Shelf

Shelves are for more of a blanket EQ filter effect that will change the general tonal quality of an audio signal. A high-shelf filter basically allows all frequencies to be heard, or "passed," but will boost or reduce frequencies above the specified cutoff point. If you have a high-shelf filter with the cutoff frequency set to 7 kHz, then only frequencies between 7 kHz and 20 kHz will be affected when you increase or decrease the gain of the filter. As one of the more subtle EQ filter shapes, high shelves can be extremely useful for brightening an overall muddy signal. Conversely, they can help remove nasty high end from signals so bright that you have to squint your eyes to listen to them. A high-shelf filter shape looks like the one in Figure 12.5.

Low Shelf

A low-shelf filter again allows all frequencies to pass, but will boost or reduce frequencies *below* the specified cutoff point. In a similar

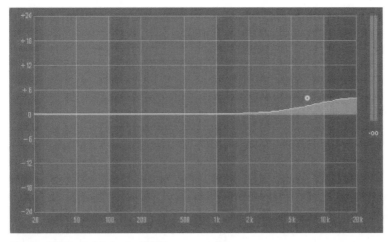

Figure 12.5 A high-shelf filter.

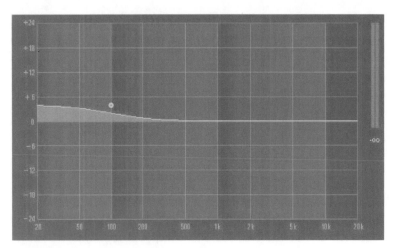

Figure 12.6 A low-shelf filter.

example, if a low shelf was applied at 100 Hz, then the frequencies from 100 Hz down to 20 Hz would be affected by the filter's gain. Low shelves are great for reducing unwanted low end. Also you can make a thin audio signal that is lacking in low frequencies sound a little thicker and more filled out. Check out Figure 12.6 to see what a low shelf looks like.

The Q setting, as it applies to an EQ shelf, determines the range of frequency over which the gain is increased or reduced, above the specified cutoff frequency. So if you have a high shelf set at 2 kHz with a +6-dB gain increase and wide Q setting of, say, 0.75, then the gain of the EQ curve will gradually increase up to +6 dB over a range of frequencies prior to 2 kHz. Once at 2 kHz, the gain will remain at +6 dB all the way up to 20 kHz. As you can imagine, a narrow Q causes a more immediate gain alteration up to the specified cutoff point by narrowing the range of frequencies over which the gain increases.

A good way to get a better understanding of the Q control in relation to a shelf filter is to open up your sequencing program, load an EQ plug-in with a graphic representation of the frequency spectrum, and recreate the settings we just discussed. Apply a high shelf at 2 kHz with a fairly drastic +6-dB gain increase to an audio file of your choice. I've chosen these dramatic settings so that you can hear the difference and get the most out of the demonstration. Also, it'll help to pick an audio file that utilizes a broad frequency spectrum. Guitars, piano, or a stereo track of drums or a complete song will work well. Try to avoid using a file that is abundant in low frequencies, such as a solo bass, because you may not be able to hear what the EQ is actually doing. As you listen to the file play back, raise and lower the Q setting while watching and listening to the way your adjustments are affecting the sound. The effect of Q controls when using an EQ shelf is subtle, but it's definitely there.

High Pass

The name of this filter can be deceiving because it actually affects the low end, not the high end, of the frequency spectrum, as the name might suggest. It's more closely related to a low shelf than a high shelf. While a low shelf can boost or reduce frequencies, a high-pass filter can only reduce them. A high-pass filter essentially allows high frequencies to pass (hence the name "high pass"), leaving them completely unaffected, and blocks the low frequencies from the user-defined cutoff point down to 20 Hz entirely. High-pass filters are good for reducing low-end rumble that might not be entirely audible, but that make the woofers in your studio monitors jiggle like gelatin. Figure 12.7 shows a high-pass filter.

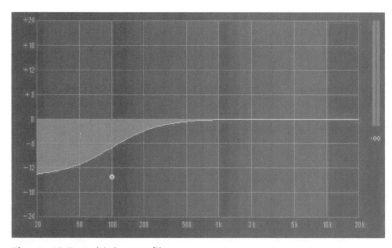

Figure 12.7 A high-pass filter.

Low Pass

A low-pass filter lets the unaltered low frequencies of a signal be heard while reducing those that exist above a user-defined cutoff frequency. It's pretty much the exact opposite of a high-pass filter. If you have the cutoff frequency set to 10 kHz, then the frequencies below 10 kHz will remain untouched, and those from 10 kHz to 20 kHz will be reduced. You can use this type of filter to reduce irritating high-frequency over-tones from drum overheads. If you're just looking to reduce overall high-end brightness, it's probably a better idea to use a high shelf with a gain reduction than a low-pass filter so you can actually atten-uate the high frequencies you're affecting. A low-pass filter would sim-ply reject any high frequencies above the cutoff point.

Gain control settings mean very little to a pass-type filter. The two effective parameters are frequency and Q, in that order. The frequency control defines at what frequency you want the low-pass filter to take effect. And Q again determines how wide or narrow the frequency range over which the gain reduction occurs is. A higher Q means a narrow range of frequency and a more immediate reduction at the cut-off frequency. A lower Q is a wider frequency range with a more grad-ual, beat-around-the-bush reduction that allows some of the frequencies that occur just after the cutoff point to pass. Figure 12.8 shows an example of a low-pass filter.

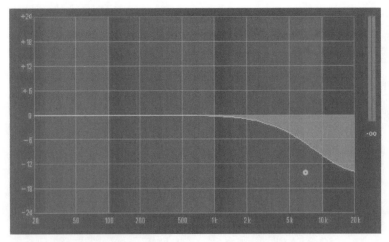

Figure 12.8 A low-pass filter.

Band Pass

A band-pass filter allows only a certain range of frequencies to pass and rejects all others. The shape of a band-pass filter is similar to that of an EQ bell. The difference is that an EQ bell boosts or reduces the specified frequency range, leaving all others unaltered. A band-pass filter allows only a specified frequency range to be heard and rejects all others. Many EQs have an automatic preset that you can use to call up a band-pass filter shape, but in the event that a band-pass preset isn't available, you can create one by combining a low-pass and a high-pass filter. This would cause frequency rejection on both the high end and the low end of the frequency spectrum, allowing only a specific range of frequencies in between the cutoff frequencies to pass. Take a look at Figure 12.9, and you'll see what I mean.

Notch Filter

Notch filters are pretty much the opposite of band-pass filters. Characterized by a narrow Q setting, a notch filter passes most frequencies and rejects only a small specified range of frequencies. These types of filters are applied in live sound situations to reduce the risk of acoustic feedback through PA systems. Notch filters are also useful in audio restoration for reducing unwanted noise, hum, or presence in certain areas of the frequency spectrum without drastically affecting the original audio signal. Figure 12.10 shows an example of a notch filter.

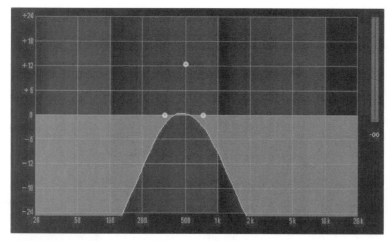

Figure 12.9 A band-pass filter.

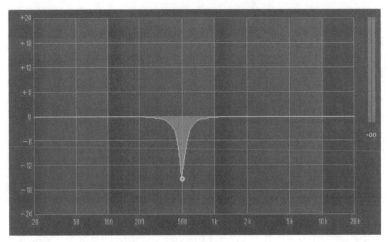

Figure 12.10   A notch filter.

Again, the best way to wrap your head around all these EQ filter shapes is to try them out for yourself. So crack open your sequencer, import an audio file, load up an EQ plug-in, and recreate the different filter shapes discussed in this section one at a time. Give your filter shape a little gain and roll the frequency control around across the frequency spectrum to hear how it affects the audio. I'm sure that the way each shape changes the tonal characteristics of your audio material will be as clear as day when you can relate what you hear to the value of the frequency, gain, and Q parameters.

Pitch Effects

When it comes to pitch correction, it really depends on the material you're working with. By no means do I think it's a good idea to auto-tune an entire vocal track or guitar solo. This goes back to the idea of tweaking a performance so much in post-production that it isn't an accurate representation of what the performer is actually capable of. However, there are times when parts of a performance will need it.

I prefer to use pitch correction as a spot treatment, just to keep things in line for the greater good of the mix. Remember when we talked about stacking identical frequencies on top of one another, and how it creates a real sonic mess by compounding the volumes of those frequencies? The same principle applies in a piece of music when multiple notes sound simultaneously. Every note that sounds at any given moment should exist peacefully (for the most part) with the other notes being played at the same time. If four different notes are being played simultaneously, and one of those notes is out of tune, that out-of-tune note will draw negative attention to itself. If you correct the pitch of that one note, it may not make or break the song. It may not even be noticed. But it certainly won't be identified as a *bad* thing.

And then, there are dramatic pitch effects that can be extremely useful in sound design and some forms of music. Again, in cases of creativity, you can use effects in any way you see fit. So if you want to gradually "bend" a solo violin or a synth lead-up a few semitones, go right ahead. Need to create a surreal vocal effect? Maybe turn a dog growl into that of a monstrous beast for a video game? With some care and perhaps a few supplemental audio processes, pitch effects can be an extremely versatile tool in your post.

Pitch correction is often overused and can make a vocal sound completely unnatural; most pitch-correction-experienced listeners can immediately identify it on the radio in the lead vocals of pop mixes. In such cases it seems that the pitch correction is applied to the entire vocal, and that every note has a "blanket" effect that pushes and pulls the vocal "in tune" for the duration of the track. I personally do not support applying pitch-correction effects over an entire track of *anything*. The reason is because the plug-in is basically a predictive machine that has no way of compensating for incorrect pitch corrections. The best way to treat a pitchy performance is highly focused spot treatment.

First, duplicate the vocal or solo instrument track you want to treat. Then mute the original track and work with the copied track. That way, you can always revert to the original if needed. Next, listen to the copied track play back carefully in the mix and identify the pitchy areas. Then, take the Cut tool and separate the problematic areas from the rest of the audio track. Don't move them; just separate them and leave them where they are.

To affect the parts of the track that you've separated, some sequencers require that you bounce the target part to a new file so it will truly be isolated from the original audio. When you're finished, you want to apply a pitch-correction plug-in to just the problematic areas, one at a time. Make sure your plug-in has the correct key, retune, and tracking parameters before actually processing the audio. Also, if your software allows, preview the effect before committing to its application. Make sure your transitions between tuned and non-tuned tracks are pop- and click-free by adjusting the fades, and play back the track and make sure all the transitions and pitch corrections are correct.

There is an alternative method of performing a spot pitch correction. First, duplicate the vocal or solo instrument track you want to treat. Then, delete the audio on the newly created track. Apply a pitch-tuning plug-in as the first insert on the copied track's channel strip. Define the correct key and typical retune and tracking speeds for this copied track, and then hit Play and listen to the original with the mix. Where the initial track sounds as if it needs pitch correction, cut the pitchy sections from the original track, and then paste or move them into the exact same position in the timeline, but on the copied track where the pitch plug-in is active. Make sure your transitions between tuned and non tracks are pop- and click-free by adjusting the fades, and play back the track and make sure all the transitions and pitch corrections are correct. Hopefully, you won't have to do this very often.

Some things to watch out for when you are spot pitch-correcting are as follows:

- Make sure you correct the right note. Tuning sometimes can be unpredictable, especially if you are not intimate with every note of the song. Stay true to the closest note or one desired by the artist.

- At times, the part may be so far out of tune that you'll need to export the file or part into a third program, such as Celemony Melodyne or Serato Pitch 'n Time, and fix the actual waveforms of the performance. Know what you can clean up in editing, and know what you may need to enlist a different specialized application for.

- If the tuning treatment doesn't seem to help, makes it worse, or makes the performance less natural-sounding, you may need to just forget it. Some "vocalists" use more style than musical substance, and you may just be experiencing something that can't be tuned. I'm sure post-audio people have done battle with Shakira, Mick Jagger, and David Lee Roth over style versus pitch. Some battles you lose in order to win the war.

Audio Restoration and Cleanup

In my opinion, the restoration of audio files falls into the same category as audio cleanup. They both have a common goal—to make an existing audio file as clean and pristine as it can be. It seems a bit silly that we would want to clean up our audio files and then later use distortion and other effects to make them "dirty" again, doesn't it? The idea behind cleaning up your audio files is to give you a clean slate to work with. If you have an audio file with a huge pop in the middle of it, when you go to enhance frequencies or dirty it up a bit, you're affecting that loud pop too. That loud pop, combined with other loud pops that get left behind, will eventually become something that you'll have to go back and fix anyway. So start resolving the problem before it begins, and get rid of the pop.

DC Offset

In cleaning up an audio file, the first thing I do is remove the DC offset. *DC offset* is essentially the overabundance of direct current (DC) or electrical noise in an audio signal. This is usually caused by inaccuracies in A/D, or analog-to-digital converters of the recording equipment. The presence of a DC offset actually reduces the amount of headroom that an audio file has. Visually speaking, an offset would make the center of the waveform appear to sit above the zero-crossing line. This is because a DC offset is taking up headroom, and the file's natural amplitude is higher than it should be. Figure 12.11 shows an example of what a severe DC offset looks like.

Removing the DC offset in an audio file is to cleaning an audio file as cleaning an audio file is to mixing. It basically brings you to ground zero so you can begin editing, processing, and utilizing the file from a clean slate, without having to fight against any preexisting problems. If it is not removed, the audio file may not be able to be normalized or it may not react correctly to effect processors. In addition, the file may display

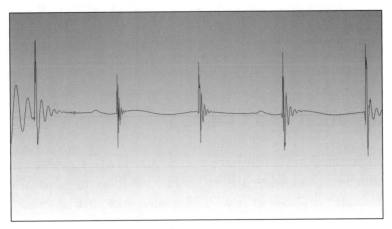

Figure 12.11 A severe DC offset.

artifacts when transitioning to and from another audio file. Once you begin adding effects to a signal with an uncorrected DC offset, what may not have been a noticeable problem before will only get worse.

DC offsets may not always be visible in a waveform, but that doesn't mean they're not there. Most sequencers and wave editors have an option that allows you to remove an offset with a single click of your mouse... three clicks at best. When you remove a DC offset, you're centering the waveform on top of the zero-crossing line and getting rid of the direct current voltage noise. The process of removing a DC offset is pretty much automatic, so there's really no excuse not to do it. Removing a DC offset is a good start to getting a cleaner audio file and making your life slightly easier in the long run.

Artifact Removal

After the DC offset has been removed, I take a close listen to the audio file. I'll let it loop three or four times (or sometimes more, depending on how fresh my ears are) to see whether any obvious artifacts jump out. I'm listening for any pops, low-frequency hum, hiss, or anything that I would consider to be undesirable noise. There are a variety of little digital audio gremlins that can cause problems in an audio file. Upon listening, depending on what you hear, there are a number of actions you can take.

Pops and Clicks

If you hear pops and clicks in the middle of the audio material, first determine whether they are consistent. If an artifact doesn't occur consistently and in the same specific spot every time, such as an artifact that was inadvertently recorded with the original audio file, then it's possible that it's a system-generated noise and not a *true* artifact. These "just kidding" artifacts are loosely referred to as *compression artifacts*. Sometimes compression artifacts can be caused by a poorly written audio driver or a system hiccup. These types of artifacts are not a permanent part of the audio file; therefore, they can't really be removed. The good news is that if they don't occur every time you play the audio file back, it's probably only a temporary issue that can be resolved by raising the buffer settings on your audio interface or following another recommendation from the audio card's manufacturer. Be sure that the artifact occurs each and every time you play back the file before you begin to take corrective measures.

True or False?   A true artifact is part of the audio file itself, which means that it will most likely appear in the graphical representation of the waveform. Because a pop or a click is usually a result of a brief amplitude spike, when magnified (at a 1:1 ratio) these types of artifacts appear as abnormal peaks in the waveform. Figure 12.12 shows what this type of artifact looks like when magnified.

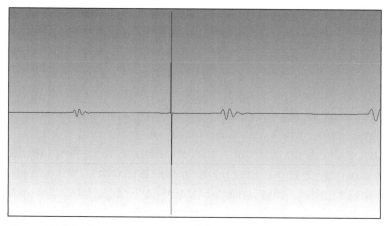

Figure 12.12   A common pop or click.

Next, you'll want to pinpoint where exactly the artifact occurs. I like to create a loop in my sequencer or wave editor over the problematic area so that after I've made some adjustments to eliminate the artifact, I can focus on what I hear in just that section of audio. After isolating the problem area, I'll cut it from the rest of the audio material and call up an EQ plug-in that I can use to process just the problem area in place for a spot treatment. For artifact removal, I prefer to use an EQ that has a visual interface and is capable of a narrow Q value. When removing an artifact, you're trying to get rid of the unwanted noise without affecting the rest of the audio in a noticeable way, so a narrow Q is desirable for isolating a specific range of frequency in which the artifact exists. I will then create a notch filter shape with a negative gain value of around -10 dB. If I'm not sure where in the frequency spectrum the artifact lives, I'll start with a wider Q value and slowly roll the frequency value up and down the spectrum while I listen for when the artifact is least noticeable. When I've isolated a more specific range, I'll make the Q even narrower to really pinpoint the little bugger and try to find where the artifact seems to be reduced the most in that smaller range of frequency.

Over time, you'll start to memorize at what frequency range certain types of artifacts exist, and this whole process won't be nearly as much of a guessing game, but for now, using this method to isolate the problem will produce the desired results just the same.

Now that you've isolated the artifact, increase the amount of gain reduction until you can't hear the artifact anymore. If the artifact is no longer audible, I suggest that you do an A-to-B comparison by listening to the audio file with your EQ plug-in activated, and then bypassed. This will help determine whether your EQ adjustment has affected the overall audio in a negative or a positive way. In many cases, an EQ like this is enough to remove most artifacts. You can eliminate anything from clicks to the sound of a turning page that was accidentally picked up through the condenser mic—or, at the very least, you can make these less noticeable. But if the EQ adjustments you've made affect the overall tonal characteristics of the treated audio material in an obvious way, you may have to take a step back and see what other solutions you can come up with to resolve the problem.

Additive EQ. One of these alternative solutions would be to export the EQ'd file to a new track that has your adjustments printed on it, and then use some additive EQ to try to brighten the signal to compensate for any dull tonal changes that might have occurred during the initial EQ treatment. The inherent problem with this is that you run the risk of boosting the frequencies that the pop was in, possibly making the artifact audible again. However, the second EQ adjustment you make should be a blanket adjustment using a bell curve that will affect a broader range of frequencies equally, so the problematic frequencies that were originally reduced are still at a much lower volume than when you started.

Reshaping Sound. Another means of scrubbing out an artifact is to use your wave editor to reshape the waveform. Most wave editors or software sequencers capable of deep level edits allow you to alter a waveform by redrawing or manipulating the shape of it in some way. Once you pinpoint the artifact, magnify it until the waveform looks like a single line that weaves above and below the zero-crossing line (commonly magnified at a 32:1 zoom ratio), as shown in Figure 12.13.

You can use the Draw tool (usually a Pencil icon in the program toolbar) to reshape the waveform and reduce the spike to eliminate the

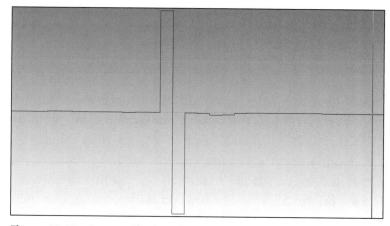

Figure 12.13   A magnified artifact.

Figure 12.14 Redrawn waveform.

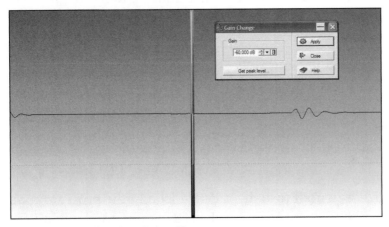

Figure 12.15 Silencing the artifact.

artifact. Figure 12.14 shows the waveform after the artifact has been removed using the Draw tool.

If your software program *doesn't* have a Draw tool, there is still hope. Wave editors and sequencers offer many different methods of editing your waveforms. Maybe you can't draw in your changes, but you can use gain-type effects, such as silence and fades, to manipulate the waveform just the same. You can highlight the artifact and choose to use the silence function, or simply reduce the gain until the artifact cannot be heard (see Figure 12.15). The artifact will be gone, but there is still a bit of cleanup that you can do to smooth the transition between the original audio and the silence.

Figure 12.16   Fade out of silence.

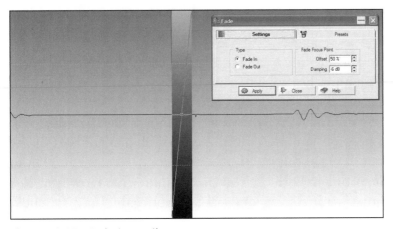

Figure 12.17   Fade in to silence.

You'll want to highlight the transition point where the original audio turns into silence and apply a fade-out, as shown in Figure 12.16. This will make the transition from the audible audio material to silence much less abrupt.

Next, highlight the transition point from silence to the original signal and use a fade-in, as shown in Figure 12.17. This will create a smooth transition from the silence back into the audio material. If the transitions between the silence and the rest of the audio are not cleaned up, the edit may only generate more artifacts because of uncorrected zero-crossings.

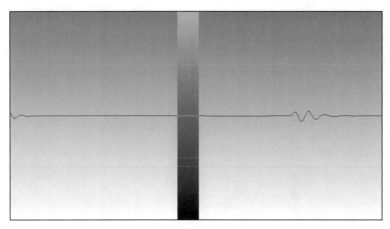

Figure 12.18 Where did the artifact go?

Figure 12.18 shows that the artifact has now been *completely* eliminated.

You might be wondering how you can alter an audio file like this without causing other audible problems. After all, you *are* messing with the physical properties of the sound, and you already know that the more you process an audio file, the more likely it is that artifacts will be created. But because you are working with such a small part of the audio file (we're talking about fractions of a second), it's not enough to cause an audible problem with the rest of the audio file. However, it *is* enough to remove an irritating and all-too-noticeable pop or click. When all is said and done, a listener will never be able to tell that an artifact existed at all.

Zero-Crossing Artifacts

While we're on the topic of removing artifacts, I'd like to take a moment to have a detailed discussion about resolving zero-crossing artifacts. To remove these types of artifacts, you'll typically use the Fade function in your sequencing software, rather than an EQ or other type of plug-in. This editing technique must often be performed as a finishing touch to the application of any effects on the original audio file in order to keep the transitions between different parts of the audio material smooth. This goes back to the idea that the more you process a file, the more likely you are to encounter/create artifacts.

Zero-crossing artifacts are another type of artifact characterized by a pop or a click. The difference between these and the artifacts we just discussed is that zero-crossing artifacts more commonly occur at the beginning and end of an audio file. They are also much easier to fix. Zero-crossing artifacts *can* occur anywhere that an audio signal turns to silence or vice versa. They are the result of an immediate and abrupt drop in amplitude that does not transition gradually to silence. Basically, the sound just cuts off. If the audio signal was a flat piece of land, a zero-crossing would be an unexpected cliff with a steep drop-off. Figure 12.19 shows an example of a typical zero-crossing artifact at the end of an audio file.

Now all you have to do is create a gradual transition between the audible signal and silence by smoothing the drop-off point, making it more of a big hill than a steep cliff. Perhaps "gradual" might not be the *best* word to describe the transition you will create to remove the artifact because, again, we're working with milliseconds. In reality, it's an extremely quick transition, but on a magnified level, we're still making the transition more gradual than it was.

To do this, you'll want to apply a "mini-fade" at the very end of the file. It will take that truncated audio signal and fade it to silence, thus removing the abrupt amplitude cutoff and leaving the rest of the audio file untouched. The mini-fade is dubbed so because it's a small-scale fade that occurs over only a millisecond or so. Unlike a regular large-scale

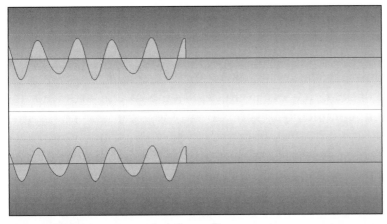

Figure 12.19 A zero-crossing drop-off.

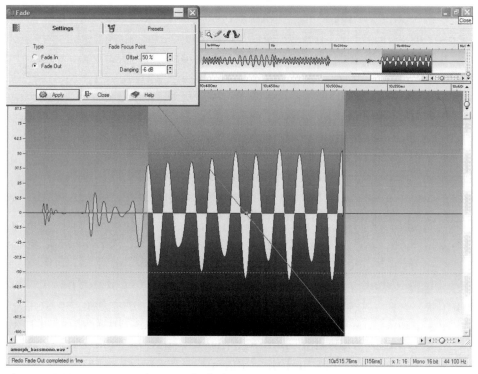

Figure 12.20   A common large-scale fade.

fade that would sound like an obvious transition from the signal at full amplitude to silence, like the one shown in Figure 12.20, a mini-fade creates an itty-bitty little fade at the very end or very beginning of the file, as shown in Figure 12.21. Other than removing the artifact, it doesn't affect the original audio file at all.

There are, of course, a handful of plug-ins available that will do a fair job of scrubbing the clicks and pops out of an audio file. If you take the time to learn how to use them, they can usually be pretty effective. Even so, plug-ins that claim to remove artifacts might not always do the trick. Some of them may even only *reduce* the volume artifact without removing it completely, especially if they are not configured correctly. It's also kind of embarrassing when you can't remove an artifact with a client sitting right next to you. I'd recommend getting comfortable with removing artifacts using plug-ins *and* by hand.

With some experimentation and practice, removing artifacts will be as easy as forgetting to save a project. It takes some time, patience, and

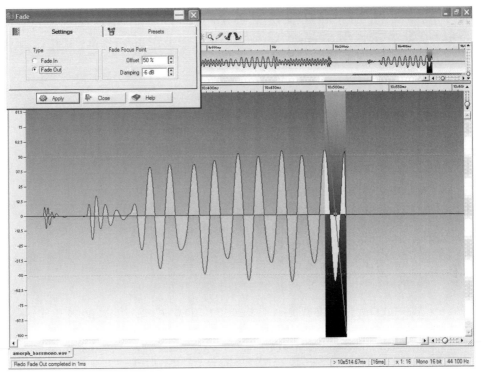

Figure 12.21 A mini-fade.

attention to detail, but your audio files will be much cleaner and easier to work with in the long run. Not all artifacts are audible in the context of your mix and, therefore, some won't necessarily *have* to be removed. But there will be occasions, such as sound effects, sample content, and transitions between audio files, that demand it. If you spend some time getting good at removing artifacts now, you won't end up wasting precious time trying to figure it out in the heat of a project. So don't wait. Begin a search for the crappiest artifact-infested audio files you can find, and get to work!

Removing Hiss

When we talk about *hiss*, we're usually referring to what is commonly called *tape hiss*. Hiss is a high-frequency noise that is caused by the recording medium. The term "tape hiss" was used at the time because, in the days of analog, the prevalent recording medium was magnetic tape. Sound recordings that are made on modern digital audio workstations usually don't suffer from this type of noise because of the obvious absence of magnetic tape. Now we just use "hiss" as a blanket term for any high-frequency white noise that exists on a recording and contributes to raising the noise floor.

White Noise   When you combine the sound of all audible frequencies together, it produces an indiscernible hissing sound known as *white noise*.

Let's look at this from another angle. Think about the concept behind white light for a moment. When you combine every visible color in the color spectrum, the result is white light. Now, relate those visible colors to audible frequencies. It's because of this similar connection between the way that white light and white noise are created that we use the adjective "white" to describe the noise that the combination of all audible frequencies makes.

When it comes to getting a nice, clean audio signal, white noise is typically *not* your friend. However, it can be used in *some* scenarios (such as dithering) to mask or make other sounds less noticeable.

Hiss can be caused by a number of things. The most common, of course, is magnetic tape, but you will often encounter recordings where hiss was caused by excessively high trim levels on a microphone preamp, vinyl records, or corrupted source material.

Another culprit for hiss is a factory-installed soundcard. The soundcards that are installed in most preconfigured computers are not designed for the rigors of recording professional digital audio. They can sometimes have a high noise floor that is well beyond acceptable for digital recording. If you are also the recording engineer, I *strongly* recommend that you upgrade your factory-installed soundcard to a professional-grade digital audio card to help avoid unwanted noise issues, among other things. And if you're *not* the recording engineer... well, you *should* still upgrade, but aside from that, there is only one thing you can do with hiss—get rid of it.

There are many third-party plug-ins on the market today that can help you deal with hiss. They basically automate the process by allowing you to define what type of hiss you have, and then they respond with what they think will work best to reduce the noise, all the while using specific noise-reduction algorithms to keep the original signal from degrading during reduction. They are often composed of a combination of controls that are common to effect processors we've already discussed, such as compressors and equalizers.

Because hiss lives in the higher frequencies of a sound, a high shelf with a user-defined frequency and value is often used to help suppress or accentuate the high end. Most noise-reduction plug-ins also offer a threshold-like control to allow you to define what decibel level the signal must reach before it is reduced. Another basic control parameter you might find on a noise-reduction plug-in is one that allows you to define by how many decibels the noise is reduced once it reaches the threshold level.

I'd recommend beginning with a preset. Head to the trusty preset library of your noise-reduction plug-in and poke around a bit. There may even be a preset for the specific type of noise you are trying to reduce. Use these settings as a reference point for where to begin.

The threshold on a noise-reduction plug-in usually defaults to −0 dB. I'd recommend starting at about −6 dB just to make sure that you catch all the unwanted noise present. Next, start increasing the value of control that determines the amount of reduction that is applied to the audio signal. Listen carefully as the value changes so that you can relate what you are hearing to what you are seeing. When a high shelf is used as part of a noise-reduction plug-in (and it's not *always* used), it's more likely that it defines how the reduction plug-in operates at higher frequencies, rather than acting as an equalization filter. The high shelf essentially takes the reduced signal and compensates for the loss of brightness as part of an effort to preserve the quality of the audio.

Because the noise you're trying to remove exists in the higher frequencies, the more you boost the high shelf, the more reduction may be required. Finally, I always recommend ABing the audio signal with the reduction plug-in active, and then bypassed. You want to be sure that your reduction attempts make the audio signal sound better, not worse. Sometimes, after all that reduction has taken place, it's hard to tell whether the audio signal sounds better unless you compare it to the original signal.

And now, the road less traveled...

The first step in manually removing hiss is equalization (EQ). Big surprise, right? Start with a bell that covers a broad range of high frequencies with about a −6-dB reduction. Adjust the frequency until the hiss seems to be less noticeable. Remember that hiss lives in the high end, so don't waste too much time listening attentively to whether the hiss is less audible with a gain reduction at 100 Hz.

You can also use a high shelf to make this first broad stroke. When you've isolated the frequency, narrow it down to affect the most specific range of high-end frequency possible while keeping the noise suppressed. Then adjust the gain control that affects the problematic frequencies. Reduce it slowly until you have as little noise as possible without compromising the quality of the original audio signal. Don't be afraid to make a small adjustment at first. You can always make another small adjustment until you get it to sound just right. But bear in mind, the more you process the file, the more you bounce and export the audio, the greater the chance of artifacts and signal degradation.

Most engineers turn to a somewhat foolproof plug-in before taking the long way around to resolve an audio problem. There is truly nothing wrong with that as long as it gets the job done. As I've mentioned before, the names and available controls vary from plug-in to plug-in. So be sure to check the manual of the particular plug-in you'll be using to see what parameters are referred to as what.

Dos and Don'ts

Woo! Time for dos and don'ts! This means we're nearing the end of the chapter! Effects are an important part of post-production and can really be a lot of fun to work with. In the case of mixing, it's better to be more conservative and keep the effects subtly under the radar. On the other hand, the sky is the limit when it comes to using effects creatively. The application of effects can be a very free-spirited experience, but just like anything else, there are some things that you just shouldn't do. Let's chat about some ideas that will help make your post-production life a bit easier.

Dos

- **Experiment with different plug-ins.** There is always more than one way to get from point A to point B. Try using different combinations of different plug-ins to bring about a specific result. You might want to take a raw vocal track and spend a few hours trying out different ways to get it more even and under control. Or take all the drum tracks from a project and try new ideas for making them more balanced, giving them different kinds of space, or getting them to really cut through a mix. Try to use different effects to solve all types of audio problems on all different types of audio sources. You really never know about the audio material you'll be working with, or even the tools you'll have available, if you go from studio to studio, so it's good to have an idea about the different options you have to get a mix in shape.

- **Compare your affected audio to the original audio.** It *is* possible to be too close to a project, especially if you've been neck deep in it for an extended period of time. Try to hold onto your objectivity so that you can make the right decisions for the mix. Once you've tweaked an effect and are ready to apply it to the audio source, be sure that you do an AB comparison between the original signal and the affected one. After you have spent some time crafting an effect to do exactly what you think you want it to do, you have to be sure that what you've done is what is best for the entire mix. This is especially important for the elements of a mix that are meant to be a focal point in the overall production. That perfect reverb or delay may not sound the same in context. If it doesn't sound right in context, save your tweaked settings as a preset and try something different.

- **Try to keep your original, unaffected files *somewhere*.** I highly advise that you keep your original audio material backed up somewhere on your hard drive. In the event that a vigorous effect session goes horribly wrong, it's really nice to be able to start again at zero. This becomes especially important when you are printing effects to tracks in order to save CPU resources. Also, as we all know, digital audio is basically data. At some point in a lifetime of experience with personal computers, we will all encounter files that have been corrupted. It's true that personal computers are getting more advanced by the day, but data loss and file corruption are still somewhat of an unpredictable anomaly. Whether it's a dormant track with inactive insert effects or just the raw original audio file neatly tucked away in a folder on your hard drive, you'll be surprised by how comforting it is just knowing that it's there if you need it.

When I receive a client's original source material, I usually create a new folder, copy the files into it, and work off the duplicates rather than the original material. There is almost nothing more unprofessional—or embarrassing, for that matter—than having to ask your client for his or her files *again*. You might as well just tell them that you've made a mistake and you need to start over. Backing up the original files will save you from having to do damage control due to shaken faith in your ability to complete the project.

■ **Become familiar with automatic *and* stick shift.** I personally believe that it is worth the time and effort to be well-versed in both the shortcuts *and* the long way around the bend. Sure, you can pick a preset and go to town, but what happens if you're working on a DAW that doesn't have the same plug-ins? Additionally, presets are developed for common scenarios, but they weren't developed with your specific source material in mind. Even when you use a preset, there is always *some* level of parameter tweaking that must be done. Knowing the intricacies of your plug-ins is an important part of working with effects and audio production in general. If you're riding in a car but you have your eyes closed, how will you know the way back to your destination? The idea is to know the way so well that, if necessary, you *could* still get there with your eyes closed. Knowing both ways will give you a good balance of efficiency and effectiveness. And you'll be a far better post-production engineer for it.

- **Use presets as a reference point.** When you first start using plug-ins for digital audio, all of the different control settings and their meanings can be rather daunting. If you're not sure what to do or how a parameter control will change the effect, then there are two things you should do. First, look for the definition of the parameter (most of these can be found in this book) so that you can better understand what you're working with. Second, start by selecting a preset so that you can see which parameter values do what. This is also a good way to get started using an effect quickly if you're in a rush. Presets can often offer a great reference point for what pro engineers think will work for a specific purpose. Start there and adjust as needed. Remember to save your settings to a preset when you arrive at a set of parameters you like. Before long, you'll be customizing your own presets from the ground up.

- **Effect efficiently.** These days you can build computers that are fast enough to melt your face off. But even the fastest digital audio computer can benefit from optimization. Run your effects as efficiently as possible. Utilize sends and group effect tracks. When it's available, use the Freeze function to help lighten the load on your CPU. Many plug-in developers already know what kind of strain their products can put on a DAW, so they typically offer suggestions in their manuals or on their websites for ways to optimize RAM usage for their plug-ins.

  Furthermore, there are many ways that you can tweak the root-level performance settings of a computer's operating system to lend more resources to audio applications. The Internet is full of digital audio forums in which users discuss performance tweaks specifically for computer recording. Consider this with a word of caution: If you are not familiar or comfortable with making alterations to your operating system, don't do it. It's a lot easier to mess up a computer than most people think. A single-digit entry in the wrong registry value can cause a universe of headaches and wasted time over what should have been a relatively easy procedure. If your DAW is working fine without the performance tweaks, then remember: If it ain't broke....

Don'ts

- **Don't snap to zero-crossing when cleaning up audio files.** Most wave editors and digital audio sequencers have a setting called Snap to Zero-Crossing. You should be able to turn it on and off as needed. Here's how it works: When you place the mouse cursor over an audio file, Snap to Zero-Crossing automatically moves the cursor to the nearest zero-crossing. This might be useful when you're truncating, cutting, or changing the duration of an audio file. It ensures that the edit occurs exactly on top of a zero-crossing to minimize the occurrence of artifacts from an abrupt drop in amplitude. But then there are times when Snap to Zero-Crossing will just get in the way. Sometimes you need to make precise edits, use mini-fades, or make a piece of audio a specific length for sample accuracy. For these types of edits, you need to have complete control over the placement of your cursor. You can't make precise edits when the cursor jumps around everywhere but where you need it to be. I usually leave Snap to Zero-Crossing active when I arrange and record, but I turn it off when I'm editing. So, if you're deep editing and you can't seem to get the cursor to sit right where you want it, try turning off the Snap to Zero-Crossing setting.

- **Don't rely on graphic interfaces.** Your eyes do not determine what sounds good. And your ears will never fully be acclimated to *hearing* what is going on in a mix if you rely on your eyes to provide feedback for the changes you make to the audio. For this reason, try not to become dependent on visual plug-in interfaces. If you can believe it, there was a time when "seeing" audio wasn't even possible! So we *know* that a competent engineer can do his or her job without the benefit of sight. Good ears are something that will make the difference between a good audio engineer and a great one.

  I'm sure you don't need me to tell you that our senses are constantly at work. We are bombarded by an array of simultaneous sensory input messages from moment to moment. The more input messages we receive, the more difficult it is for us to focus on any one thing. It's bad enough that we have to work around all of the normal distractions that occur when you work from home. If you're lucky, at any given time, you're only trying to block out the sound of a loud fan, the neighbor's dog barking, and intervallic requests from your significant other, trying to find out what you want to do for dinner. With all this distraction, it can be really easy to let your eyes do some of the work to help your ears focus a little better. There's nothing wrong with this in the beginning, but in the long term, you definitely don't want to become reliant on visual aids.

- **Don't over-process audio.** Each time you apply an effect, edit, normalize, or do any other kind of audio processing, you are changing the properties of your audio material ever so slightly. If you process audio excessively, you run the risk of completely wiping out any identifiable trace of the original signal. If you're processing creatively, then please, go about your business. But if you are processing audio for a mix, over-processing audio is something about which you need to be careful.

  This is another reason why it's important to have a good grip on what your effects will do to the audio once they have been applied. Knowing what the result will be helps to minimize the number of applications you have to make to a given audio file. The audio material you'll work with most likely has a specific sound with its own unique tonality and identifiable characteristics. You don't want to process an audio file so much that you lose what makes the sound what it is. If you think you've processed something off the deep end, it might be time to go back to the original audio file and start again.

- **Don't underestimate the power of EQ.** EQ is literally the first thing I reach for when I'm preparing audio material for mixing. It can make opposing audio signals work together, remove artifacts and harshness, add texture, provide perceived fundamental frequency, and, in some cases, even overcome electrical issues. Almost any audio problem I encounter can benefit from EQ somewhere in the signal chain.

  Most mixing problems are solved by using EQ alone. And all the things typically complained about when it comes to a bad mix are usually EQ-related. If you have been mixing a track for a while and still can't seem to get the separation, unity, and clarity required to get your mix to professional standards, it may be time to dig back in and EQ again. The fundamental frequencies involved in the individual tracks are really the defining variables for professional mixing. You may need to really work an EQ hard to get what you want out of it—depending on the source material, of course.

At times I've found myself adding +15 dB of highs to get "that kick sound," and I think to myself, "This is ridiculous! I shouldn't have to add that much!" But lo and behold, it was the answer! And what's more, my ears knew the right answer regardless of what some guy in a book wrote about adding too much EQ. In some cases I've actually stacked multiple EQ plug-ins to get the results I needed. Other times, something that seemed so insignificant and simple as reducing an additional −2 dB of low mids from the bass track did miracles for the entire mix. So work those parametric knobs, shelves, and faders to find the right combination. I mean, they named that mix magazine *EQ* for some reason, right? EQ is the very definition of mixing—"to equalize." Most of the power of post-production is right in front of your ears—you just have to be able to hear it.

- **Don't get caught with your pants down.** Make sure you know the tools you use inside and out. Part of running a successful post-production studio is improving the perception that your client has of you. If it's clear to your client that you know exactly what you are doing, in their mind you'll be filed as a pro. The word of mouth alone will get you more work through referrals. I'd say that after the first year on my own, nearly 80 percent of my business came from referrals or clients I had worked with before.

Word of mouth doesn't *have* to be positive, though. If you appear to be perplexed and fumbling through your software and plug-ins while trying 10 different things that aren't producing any results, chances are that *if* the client finishes the project with you, you won't be seeing them again. And you certainly won't be seeing any of their friends. I've been at gatherings where I've heard someone recount a negative experience they've had with an audio production person, and part of me thinks, "Wow, that's totally unprofessional. I hope you got your money back." But another part of me just feels bad for the engineer because such client experiences really smear an engineer's reputation and keep that person from getting more work down the line. So what is the best way to make it look like you know what you are doing? It's to *actually* know what you are doing!

Let's Wrap This Up

If it sounds good, it is good, right? But if it doesn't sound good, it doesn't necessarily mean that it's bad. It just means that there may be a better solution than the one you're using. Don't be afraid to experiment. Just don't spend so much time experimenting that you start to compromise your project timeline. Often, when I've got some downtime, I'll sit down in my project studio and try out new techniques that I've heard about or download trial versions of different new effects and take them for a test drive. That way, no one's project timeline is at risk. We're not machines and we can't work *all* the time. But know that those who take the initiative to improve their skill set and continually educate themselves will be the ones who excel in this business. If you're reading this book, chances are you're *already* one of those people.

Mastering in the Project Studio

13 Mastering Audio in the Digital Age

astering is an art form. Its mysteries can only truly be revealed through years and years of hands-on experience. As with many other aspects of audio production, mastering requires strong problem-solving skills. What might work for one mix probably won't work for the next. A well-developed set of ears, as well as a very firm grasp on the intricacies of audio engineering and the physical properties of sound, are skills that will aid you in troubleshooting and enhancing a mix more effectively. Many professional audio engineers will draw the line when it comes to mastering. More often than not, they will send their mixes to another facility to be mastered by a professional mastering engineer. It's true that you can go to school or read a book to learn the ins and outs of the mastering process, but a true mastering engineer is part of an elite class of audio professional that has been forged on the front lines of recording studios and post-production facilities focusing specifically on this area of their craft. Mastering engineers are everywhere, but *great* mastering engineers (or mastering artists—however you choose to see it) are tough to find.

Is mastering really necessary? I've been asked that very question by a great number of clients. It's often difficult for them to justify the cost because they don't exactly understand how their recording can benefit from it. I've actually had some clients decide against it, try to release their unmastered material, and then call me a month later saying that they've changed their mind. The only way I know to answer that question is to let clients hear the difference for themselves. I'll call up both the mastered and unmastered versions of a project that I've worked on and let them decide. Do you *have* to master your audio? Well, you don't really *have* to do anything, do you? But if you want your recordings to sound professional, the answer is yes.

There are entire volumes dedicated to the subject of mastering because it is a very important aspect of audio post-production. The process is so complex and subjective that you could read several different books on the topic, all written by different authors, and still be completely confused. And if, after all that, you *aren't* confused, you can at least be sure that you've barely scratched the surface. Lucky for you, this is not a book about mastering. The next few chapters will lay down the basics. You'll get enough core information to begin using common mastering techniques in your own studio. We'll also take a look at software tools for mastering, and I'll reveal some of my own personal mastering techniques. When this section is all said and done, you won't be Bob Ludwig, but you'll be on the right path to better mastering practices, and you'll have an understanding of the basic principles and perhaps even a heightened curiosity about the art and specialization of mastering audio.

If you'd like to get a truly in-depth look at the art and science of mastering audio, check out *Mastering Music at Home* (Thomson Course Technology PTR, 2007) or *The Mastering Engineer's Handbook, Second Edition* (Thomson Course Technology PTR, 2007).

What Is Mastering?

Mastering is the final stage in the post-production process. It's commonly regarded as the most crucial step and the key to obtaining that "professional sound." Mastering is widely misunderstood and often underappreciated because most music listeners don't even realize that mastering occurs, let alone what it actually does for a recording. The truth is, almost every song that has ever been publicly broadcast has been mastered. If an average music listener heard the same track, both mastered and unmastered, one after the other, he would immediately be able to tell the difference. However, because unmastered versions of commercial recordings are *never* released, the problem with that statement is being able prove it.

Although I can't offer an auditory example of the difference that mastering makes, I can *show* you an example. Figure 13.1 shows the waveform of an unmastered stereo track that is relatively quiet and highly dynamic. Figure 13.2 shows the same track *after* mastering processes

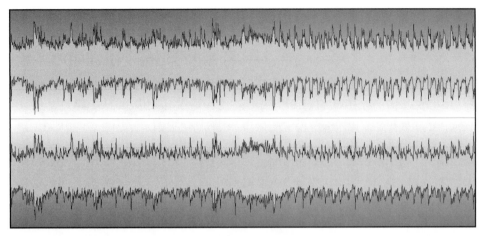

Figure 13.1 The waveform of an unmastered audio track.

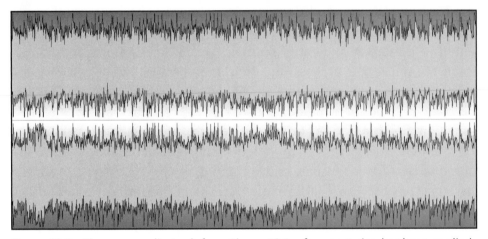

Figure 13.2 The same audio track from Figure 13.1, after mastering has been applied.

such as equalization, compression, and volume maximization have been applied to it. At a glance you can immediately see that the waveform in Figure 13.2 has transients that are more even (due to controlled dynamics and frequency attenuation) and bigger overall (due to an increase in volume) than the waveform shown in Figure 13.1. Even from this graphic representation of an audio file, you can see evidence of the dramatic difference that mastering can make.

It is difficult to explain what mastering *sounds* like. It's the cherry on top, the shine and sheen that makes a recording sound big and open. Have you ever completed a mix, bounced it out to a stereo track, and then burned it to a CD, only to find during playback that it doesn't measure up to the commercial albums you own? The sonic difference you hear between a commercially recorded CD and a final mix hot off the hard drive *is* the difference that mastering makes. The most common observations that you might make about an unmastered track are that it's not loud enough; it sounds muddy, dull, or lifeless; and it has either too much or not enough bass definition. If this describes the final mix that you've been slaving over a hot keyboard all day for, it doesn't necessarily mean that you didn't do a good job—you're just not finished yet. And if it still sounds that way after being thoughtfully mastered, please review Chapter 8 to brush up on mixing techniques.

Mastering your audio serves three primary purposes: It gives a recording that professional, polished sound; it creates continuity between multiple audio tracks; and it prepares the audio material to be duplicated or presented to the target audience. To make this a little simpler, let's break down the mastering process into two main phases. We'll call Phase 1 *sonic enhancement,* and Phase 2 will be *media preparation.* Phase 1, the sonic enhancement phase, consists of five primary tasks: equalization, compression, noise reduction, reverb, and loudness. Secondary sonic enhancement tasks may include stereo image enhancement, harmonic excitation, de-essing, and dithering. We've discussed several of these tasks as they apply to mixing, but the mastering process modifies the functionality of each task a bit. Chapter 15, "Mastering Techniques for the Project Studio," will discuss each task's specific function in relation to mastering. I should mention that not every mastering job will undergo *all* of the aforementioned processes. It will be up to you to determine which ones are necessary and which ones you can do without based on what the project calls for.

Phase 1 is where you polish a final mix to bring out its commercial luster, volume, and punch. This is where you will spend the majority of your mastering efforts. Phase 1 is normally performed on a two-channel stereo sum of a final mix. When a project mix has been completed, it's bounced down to a single stereo-interleaved track that contains the left and right channels, or two mono tracks that represent the left and right channels, respectively. (Generally, only in instances of multi-channel surround will you ever deal with more than two tracks in mastering.) You then use noise-reduction processes to remove unwanted noise; equalization to see that all the frequencies are represented appropriately; compression, limiting, and expansion to control the overall dynamics; reverb to provide ambience and perceived space; and various other tools to help enhance the overall sound quality of the recording. It seems pretty cut and dried when I lay it out like that, but it's not quite so black and white. Effective sonic enhancement is not about the processes themselves, but using the *right* combination of them.

The recording of audio material and/or mixing audio rarely take place in one day. These processes are usually spread out over several days, and sometimes a single project can take place in different studios from one stage of production to the next. It is ideal to have a multipart project recorded in the same studio with the same equipment, but this can't always be accomplished. Unfortunately, a multi-studio project can lead to sonic variances between the final mixes.

Other contributors to discontinuity are different producers, or mix and audio engineers working on different parts of the project, vastly different instrumentation from track to track, and the use of varying equipment throughout a recording, such as changing a microphone on a singer midway through the project. Hopefully, you won't run into these incongruent circumstances often—most audio professionals know better. But it's not unheard of to receive audio material from a client that is sonically inconsistent from one track to the next.

Having said all that, Phase 1 is also where you give the tracks continuity with one another. Often albums or projects that contain multiple tracks have their own *sound*. It's almost as if every project or album has its own individual style. (Remember that we're talking about the sonic quality of the audio only, not the music itself.) Depending on who produced, mixed, and/or mastered the albums, it's possible for two different records from the exact same band to have different sonic characteristics—but, even so, there will be unity between the songs on each album individually. Part of preparing final mixes for manufacturing (or other general consumption) is balancing out the levels and equalization from track to track. The idea is to make each track as consistent as possible from one to the next, unifying the overall sound of the project. In mastering, you are striving to make each individual track sound better, but you are also trying to make each track sound good in relation to the others.

The second phase of mastering is preparing the tracks for production or presentation. If you're working with bands or artists that will require mass production of the final product, this will include creating a track layout, determining track spacing and transitions, and creating a final master disc that can be sent to the manufacturing facility. If a master disc is not required—perhaps in the case of web or multimedia projects—then Phase 2 simply entails making sure that the audio is converted to its final delivery format.

Red Book Audio Standard   The Red Book audio standard is a set of specifications that an audio CD must meet in order to be manufactured. The specifications are as follows:

- Maximum playing time is 78 minutes (including pauses).

- Minimum track length is no less than 4 seconds.

- Maximum number of tracks allowed is 99.

- Maximum number of index points (subdivisions of a track) is 99, with no minimum time limit for the gaps between songs.

- International Standard Recording Codes (ISRCs) should be recorded on CD-Rs to appear on the replicated discs.

Any manufacturing facility will be able to mass-replicate an audio CD that meets these standards. Although these are the most common guidelines, not every facility will *require* that they be met.

As with any audio process, you can't just jump in and start making changes without understanding how they are going to affect the entire track. Improperly mastered recordings have repercussions. If they have too much of any one frequency (particularly in the lows and the high midrange), it can lead to ear fatigue in the same way that listening to inappropriately boosted frequencies through lousy studio monitors can. If the volume levels are overdone, it can cause distortion on the track. Too much reverb can rob the recording of definition and make it sound washed out. Too much compression may suck the life right out of a song. Over the better part of a century, audio evolution has developed standards for what is considered to be sonically acceptable for a finished recording. Through careful everyday listening, you can identify these standards... you're already on the path to understanding how to reach them.

A Brief History

Mastering wasn't always so complicated... but then again, the sound quality of a lot of old recordings wasn't very good. In the 1920s, the mastering process was completely automatic. A performer would do his thing into an acoustic horn, and through a series of mechanical processes, his performance would immediately be transferred, or "cut," to a vinyl record with a lathe. Up until the late 1940s, when magnetic tape came along, the mastering and manufacturing of vinyl master discs almost always occurred in an immediate "direct-to-disc" process. The creation of the master disc was considered the most primitive form of mastering audio, even though it barely has anything in common with the modern definition of the term.

The 1950s marked the beginning of a 30-year evolution that would transform mastering into the multistep process that we are familiar with today. At the time, mastering only entailed manipulating the sonic characteristics of the audio enough to conform to the physical limitations of vinyl records. As an example, an excess of low-end frequency would cause the record grooves to be cut too wide, resulting in reduced playing time. Too much high end would cause audible distortion and lead to the accelerated degradation of a record's grooves. And phasing issues might cause the grooves to be too shallow for a record needle to follow, which would then lead to skipping. Although magnetic tape allowed pre-recorded audio to be mastered at a later time and place, the audio quality was still slave to the vinyl format.

In the 1960s, cassette tapes were introduced, offering improved audio quality over vinyl. By this time, we were already making reasonably high-quality recordings using reel-to-reel tape machines, and mastering was being done using all-analog equipment and processing. But no matter how good the final recording sounded, it would eventually lose fidelity when it was transferred to cassette. Even though the cassette format was a more advanced technology than vinyl, it still had limitations.

In the 1980s, compact discs became a prominent playback format as the first consumer medium capable of digital-quality audio resolution. We were no longer restricted to the fidelity limitations of vinyl records and cassette tapes. As sound quality became more important, the audio production process, mastering included, became more involved. It was commonly thought that a great mastering job could make or break a commercial recording. Mastering was now considered a highly skilled trade, and a good mastering engineer's stock went *way* up.

By the time the '90s rolled around, audio recording and post-production had joined the digital revolution. Digital audio workstations gave us the means to process audio using a visual interface. Digital formats made it easier than ever to transfer, manage, and alter recorded audio. And digital processing put the tools of a mastering engineer inside a computer tower. For the first time, it was possible to create and manufacture high-resolution audio without major fidelity loss somewhere along the way.

These technological strides, both in media format and in production techniques, have delivered us to an age in which audio fidelity *can* be the best it has ever been. The "seven-layer dip" that is mastering seeks to make a recording sound the best that it possibly can within the confines of the current media format… just as it always has. We've already begun producing consumable audio that is greater than CD quality (though it's getting off to a very slow start, and compact disc is currently still the primary format) and can even exceed the fidelity threshold of what the human ear can perceive on the production end. However, we lack the means (format) or the need to truthfully reproduce it for mass consumption. Our little walk through the development of audio formats over the past 50+ years has led up to this: As audio quality and formats evolve, we'll have to adapt in order to maintain an acceptable fidelity standard. This means that if the future holds a higher-resolution playback medium, post-production techniques will have to change and possibly become more complicated than they are now. And that goes for all aspects of audio production, not just mastering.

If you can believe it, the eternal question still remains—analog or digital? After everything that I've said, it seems logical to assume that mastering digitally would yield better results than mastering with analog equipment. But in the audio world, when it comes to the raging debate over which is really better, it's important not to assume *anything*. Some of the best-sounding records I've ever heard were mastered with a great deal of analog processing. Then again, I've heard amazing results from mostly digital processing. It is very common to use a combination of both, and it could lean one way or the other depending on what the project calls for. Both have their strengths and weaknesses, and in my humble opinion, it is more about the ability of the mastering engineer to make a good call on what type of processing to use and when to use it. Analog or digital makes no difference in the hands of someone who doesn't know what he is doing. A great mastering engineer can make a final mix sound good no matter what tools he's using.

First Impressions   Have you ever heard that saying, "You never get a second chance to make a first impression?" The same is true here—you can never hear something for the first time twice. Letting a client hear your work in an unfinished state can be a real gamble. The majority of your clients won't be the creative visionaries you might be, and if your work sounds less professional than the current standard right out of the gate, it might be difficult for the client to get past the sonic quality to hear how brilliant it really is. These days, a recording isn't considered finished until it has been mastered. So although you may not choose to specialize in the mastering aspect of audio production, it's good to know the basic principles behind it so that you can put your best foot forward with your clients.

There are many people who claim to be mastering engineers these days, especially in the project studio category. It seems to be more of a marketing strategy than an actual skill to be revered and respected. I've even seen the availability of sight-unseen online mastering—you send in your tracks, and some anonymous person "masters" them and sends them back to you in a couple of days. Each person that *claims* to be a mastering engineer or offers it as some kind of gimmick to sell other products and services actually damages the credibility of *real* mastering engineers.

A great mastering engineer is someone with great ears who can hear like a safe cracker and tell you the frequency at which nearly any sound occurs. A great mastering engineer also performs a thorough assessment of the audio to decide which course of action should be taken to improve its sound quality. And a great mastering engineer knows how to get the desired results of out the equipment he works with. Maybe we can't all be great mastering engineers, but we can at least be good ones. In truth, there is no absolutely *right* way to master a recording. As with everything else in audio production, it's subjective. You can only use the information you have to make the best decisions about how to proceed. Knowing what you have to work with, what the target is, and what the standards are is a great place to start.

14 Software Tools for Mastering

Every mastering engineer has a specific set of software and plug-ins that he or she will use on the job time and time again. These tools vary a bit from engineer to engineer depending on what works best for that particular person. Which ones sound the best? Which are the easiest to use? Which ones have the best feature set for the engineer's needs? And which ones will encourage an effective and efficient workflow? The software you use is very much a personal preference, but the options are vast. There are a lot of user-specific questions to address when considering the right software for your studio. Hopefully, I'll be able to help you navigate through the selection process and shed some light on the answers.

Digital audio software for a functioning project studio is an investment. The right software will pay for itself after a few projects. The wrong software could end up costing you valuable time and money (which apparently has some value as well). But before you go out and spend a small fortune on a software suite, it's important for you to know what you're getting into and what you're going to get out of it. This chapter is designed to present the different available options and provide you with enough information to help you make a more educated decision about your studio software. Would you blindly invest your money in something you knew little or nothing about? I didn't think so.

In mastering, you'll use a wave/sample editor, or a mastering suite, a handful of effect plug-ins, some audio analysis utilities, and a CD burning program to transform a final mix into a finished master. We'll take a closer look at these tools as they relate to mastering, exploring common parameters and discussing features. I'll make some recommendations on software solutions for mastering in your project studio. Ultimately, it's up to you to determine which programs and effects will suit your needs and earn a spot in your mastering toolbox.

Programs for Mastering

If you remember, we discussed software applications as they related to mixing back in Chapter 2. Many of the same programs that are used for mixing can also be used for mastering. It is common to use a two-track wave editor over a software sequencer for the specific functions of mastering. But isn't unheard of for mastering to be performed in your multitrack sequencer. Most sequencers are well equipped to handle mastering functions, though I find it a bit easier to focus on a mastering job in a two-track wave/sample editor that isn't cluttered with multitrack functions that will never be put to use in mastering. Additionally, wave/sample editing suites tend to have feature sets that have been developed specifically around mastering. We are going to chat about some of the same software programs mentioned in Chapter 2, but focus more on their mastering features and functionality.

Sony Creative Software Sound Forge

Sony Creative Software's Sound Forge is a PC-based, industry-standard sample editor that is used in studios around the world for editing and mastering. Known for its ease of use, speed, and stability, it's capable of supporting bit rates of up to a 64-bit float and sample rates up to 192 kHz. Of course, it's capable of basic processes, such as trimming, fading, and removing DC offsets, but one of the features that I frequently use for mastering is the Plug-In Chainer, which allows you to create an effects chain by simply selecting the plug-ins you wish to have in the chain (see Figure 14.1). Once you've selected your plug-ins, you can easily change signal flow by dragging and dropping effects in the desired order. You can also edit each plug-in's parameters individually, save individual plug-in presets, and then, after you've slaved over creating the perfect signal flow, save the entire effects chain as a preset, allowing for the instant recall of complicated effects chains and parameters.

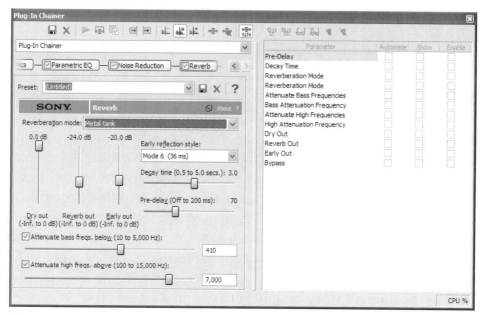

Figure 14.1 The Plug-In Chainer in Sound Forge 9.

The Bit Depth Converter allows for program-level bit-rate reduction without the use of a third-party plug-in, although it's always your option to employ one because Sound Forge supports both VST and DirectX plug-in formats. The latest version of Sound Forge can even handle multi-channel file editing and processing for up to 7.1 surround sound.

On top of an already extensive plug-in library, the latest version of Sound Forge (version 9) ships with a mastering effects bundle powered by iZotope, which includes a mastering EQ, a mastering reverb, a multi-band compressor, and a mastering limiter. You also get the Noise Reduction 2.0 plug-in collection, consisting of four DirectX sound restoration plug-ins, Vinyl Restoration, Noise Reduction, Clipped Peak Restoration, and Click and Crackle Removal. Finally, to sweeten the deal, version 9 now also includes CD Architect, a professional CD sequencing, mastering, and burning program.

Sound Forge has a street price of around $300. If you're looking to get a complete package without breaking the bank, Sound Forge may be the right solution for you. For more information or to download a trial version of Sound Forge, please visit www.sonycreativesoftware.com.

Steinberg WaveLab

WaveLab is a comprehensive, PC-only wave editor and mastering suite developed by Steinberg. It can perform basic editing and effects processing with support for bit rates up to a 64-bit float and sample rates up to 384 kHz. (Of course, in order to achieve such high sampling and bit rates, your hardware must be up to this high-performance task.) The Audio Montage feature allows simultaneous editing and processing across several tracks, with multi-channel support for up to 7.1 surround sound. You can save, reroute, and recall effects parameters and signal chains with ease. You can even sequence and burn Red Book audio CDs with the option for error checking and repair, as well as create CD reports and export track sheets. With support for other more common CD information features—such as copy protection; CD-Text; and UPC/ EAN, PQ, and ISRC codes—WaveLab has everything you need to master your final mixes from beginning to end in a single program.

CD Information   There is certain information that an audio CD should contain in order to be considered replication-ready, especially if the project is destined for the retail market. There is also some information that *can* be added, but that is entirely optional. Most Red Book–compatible burning programs are capable of adding this information as metadata or data tags. These tags are often identified by acronyms such as CD-Text, UPC, EAN, PQ, and ISRC. Here's a quick rundown of what these acronyms mean:

- **CD-Text.** This allows the storage of additional information on a master disc, such as album name, song name, artist, genre, and more. When the master disc is played in a compatible CD player, the information can be shown on the CD player's display.

- **UPC/EAN/JAN.** These acronyms are barcode standards used to identify a product. If the master disc is intended for replication and sale, it will need one or more of these codes, depending on the country in which it will be sold. UPC stands for *Universal Product Code,* EAN stands for *European Article Number,* and JAN stands for *Japanese Article Number.*

  Although you can add the metadata to include these codes on the master CD, they really don't mean anything until the barcode has been registered to identify its association with your disc and has been printed on the outside of the retail package. *You* do not assign the barcode. Typically, this is a job for the replication facility. If your client wants you to add it to the CD as metadata, they must provide you with the barcode number.

- **ISRC.** The International Standard Recording Code, or ISRC, is an international identification system used to uniquely identify sound and music video recordings. Think of it as a digital fingerprint for CDs that are intended for commercial distribution. ISRCs are used to automatically identify recordings so that royalty payments can be made to the appropriate parties. Again, you can add ISRC metadata to individual tracks, but it won't be of much use until the ISRC has been made active.

- **PQ.** PQ codes communicate information about track starts, subindexes, and pauses. These can be user-defined if you or your client wishes them to be. Otherwise, this information is generated automatically as you sequence your audio tracks into a final master.

The WaveLab mastering suite also includes a host of mastering, audio restoration, and analysis tools, including Crystal Resampler, Loudness Normalizer, and the UV22 and UV22HR dithering algorithms (originally developed by Apogee—see www.apogeedigital. com for more information), in addition to VST and DirectX third-party plug-in support. The latest version of WaveLab (version 6) also includes the new Spectrum Editor, a restoration tool that allows for the precise editing of an audio file's frequency information, giving you the ability to execute procedures such as the complete removal of unwanted noise and/or frequency ranges (see Figure 14.2).

WaveLab goes for about $550. If that seems a little steep, the WaveLab family also offers streamlined versions of this mastering suite in WaveLab Studio (with a moderate feature set) and WaveLab Essential (with a basic feature set). More detailed information about WaveLab, WaveLab Studio, and WaveLab Essential can be found at www.steinberg.net.

BIAS Peak Pro

BIAS Peak Pro is a professional-quality sample editing and CD mastering suite for Mac OS X (see Figure 14.3). Peak goes well above and

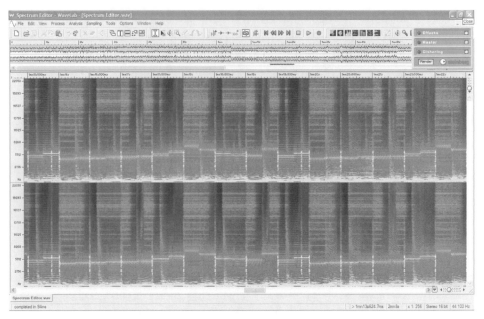

Figure 14.2 The Spectrum Editor in WaveLab 6.

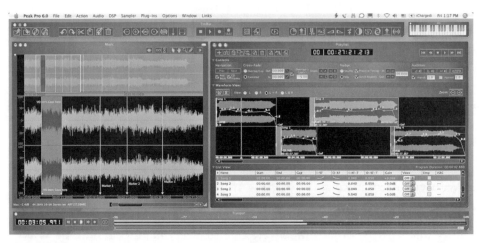

Figure 14.3 CD mastering in Bias Peak Pro 6.

beyond basic editing and effect processing with Red Book audio CD burning; POW-r dithering algorithms; VST and Audio Unit plug-in support; up to 32-bit, 10-MHz audio resolution (if your hardware can handle it); and built-in high-quality effects, including BIAS' Sqweez compressor/limiter, Bias' Freq four-band paragraphic equalizer, and an

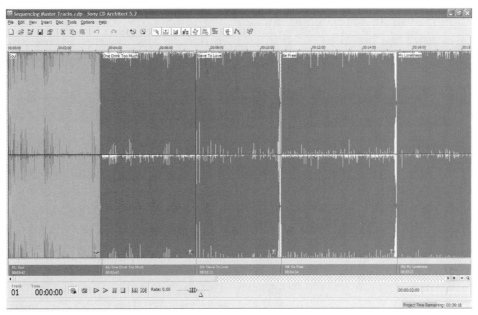

Figure 14.4 Sequencing master tracks in CD Architect.

SFX machine LT with 21 real-time effects for all your audio-processing needs.

Peak Pro weighs in at about $600, but if you're running on a Mac, you'd be hard-pressed to find a better mastering suite for the money. BIAS also offers Peak LE for entry-level users at around $130 and Peak Pro XT, an extended technology bundle that includes SoundSoap and SoundSoap Pro for noise reduction and the new Master Perfection Suite plug-ins—all for the low, low price of $1,199.

For more information about Peak Pro, please visit www.bias-inc.com.

Sony Creative Software CD Architect

CD Architect is a program designed for professional Red Book audio CD mastering (see Figure 14.4). I mentioned this Windows-based application earlier as part of the Sound Forge software package, but I feel as though it deserves some dedicated page space as its own entity. CD Architect basically picks up where Sound Forge leaves off. It will allow you to sequence, edit, effect, and process multiple audio files with audio resolutions of up to 32-bit and supporting sample rates of up to 192 kHz. It includes more than 20 real-time DirectX effects, supports audio layering to manage complex cross-fades, and burns CDs with audio clip detection, automatic paused time indication, and buffer under-run protection.

Sound Forge and CD Architect were designed to work together. Sound Forge cannot burn Red Book audio CDs, and CD Architect is capable of only basic wave editing. In the event that you already have a preferred wave editor, you can purchase CD Architect separately for around $100. However, if you're looking for a good wave editor anyway, the Sound Forge bundle that includes CD Architect *and* the Noise Reduction 2.0 suite may be the way to go. The combination of Sound Forge and CD Architect includes everything you need to get your final master disc.

More detailed information about CD Architect can be found at www.sonycreativesoftware.com.

Roxio Toast

Roxio Toast is a multifunction CD/DVD burning and authoring program that sits a little closer to the consumer end of burning software (see Figure 14.5). But don't be deceived. Toast is capable of far more than your average CD burning software, with features such as Blu-ray disc support for audio and data, the Audio Conversion Assistant for converting your vinyl records and cassette tapes to compact disc, the ability to burn audio DVDs, and the ability to make 9 GB of data from a dual-layer DVD fit onto a standard 4.7-GB DVD. This not an extensive two-track wave editor; it's more of a tool for sequencing your masters, attenuating individual track volumes, adjusting track spacing, and burning a master disc. All the basic editing functions, such as effect processing, trimming, and cross-fades are covered. It also includes 16 different Audio Unit mastering plug-ins for equalization, reverb, limiting, and multi-band compression.

On the burning end, Toast might be a bit more than you'll ever really need for digital audio, but the latest version, Roxio Toast 8, goes for about $80, which is significantly less than the other solutions we've discussed so far. Keep in mind that you will still probably want to have a full-featured sample editor at your disposal, but if you've already got a good wave editor and you just need something to help

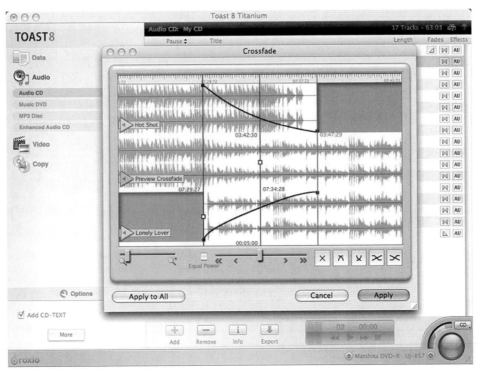

Figure 14.5 Roxio Toast.

you sequence tracks, apply some light mastering, and burn your Red Book audio CDs, then Toast might be right up your alley.

For more information on Roxio Toast, visit www.roxio.com.

Apple WaveBurner

WaveBurner is a Mac OS X application for assembling, mastering, and burning Red Book audio CDs (see Figure 14.6). Like most other burning applications out there, it supports copy protection, UPC/EAN codes, and CD-Text. You can also reorder tracks, copy, trim, split, adjust gain, apply cross-fades, apply built-in or third-party Audio Unit effects to your heart's content, and even dither down your high-resolution audio files using POW-r dithering technology. WaveBurner also has a handy little feature called Mastering Notes that allows you to enter information about the mastering session, such as the session date, the session engineer, the studio it was in, the client, and any comments about the session itself. This can be useful for when you're working on a project with

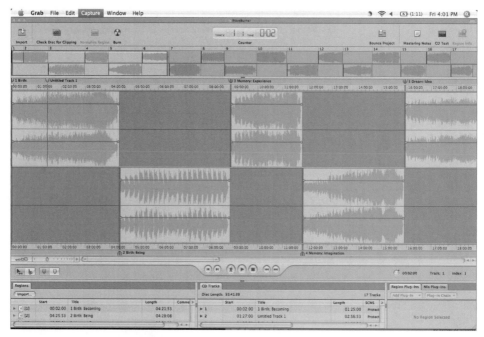

Figure 14.6 Apple WaveBurner.

several different people in many different studios, or just to help keep your mastering sessions more organized in general.

WaveBurner is a very simple yet powerful application for burning demo and master discs alike. However, there is a catch. Beyond being Mac OS X–exclusive, as of the writing of this book, it ships only with Apple Logic Studio (which costs about $500). However, if you're on a Mac and you have been looking at Logic as your primary sequencer and/or mixing environment, WaveBurner could be just the right solution for your disc authoring and mastering needs.

You'll find more information on Logic Studio and WaveBurner at www.apple.com/logicstudio.

Plug-Ins for Mastering

Under the broad category of software tools for mastering falls mastering plug-ins. Other than the method in which they are used, the effects plug-ins for mastering really aren't that different from the plug-ins you use for mixing. You need a good set of analysis tools to help you make the right decisions about level and frequency, a good compressor, a multi-band compressor and a limiter to give the tracks some energy and volume, a parametric EQ to shape the frequencies, reverb for space and unification, and maybe a few other miscellaneous effects and utilities to help get the job done.

When selecting a plug-in set, it's always best to do your homework. Choose plug-ins based on your specific needs first. Make a decision about the primary function of your studio and go from there. Next, pay close attention to sound quality. The way a type of plug-in sounds may vary from developer to developer. Two plug-ins that *supposedly* do exactly the same thing can sound very different from each other.

I know that it's difficult to really preview sound quality without just buying a plug-in and trying it (especially since most retailers don't allow returns on software), but make your best attempt at getting feedback from others about the sound quality of prospective plug-ins. Visit forums, read reviews, listen to samples, and download lots of demos until you can get a feel for the way that different plug-ins sound in comparison to one another. Then narrow the choices down by which ones sound best to you. A handful of good plug-ins is no small expense, and it's important to feel confident that you've made good decisions and are getting the most bang for your buck. There are hundreds—possibly thousands—of plug-ins from different software developers available, and it will be to your benefit to try out a lot of different options to see which plug-ins will work best for your needs.

Have you ever walked into a music store and noticed a guy staring blankly at the software wall? Well, that's the guy who didn't do any research and who doesn't really know what he's looking for. Chances are that he'll end up going with whatever the sales clerk tells him to buy, regardless of whether it's the right choice. My hope is that by the time you finish reading this chapter, you'll have a pretty good idea about what you need and how to find it, so that when *you* walk into a music store, you're not that guy. In this section, we'll explore different types of plug-ins that are commonly used in mastering. We'll chat about their specific uses, and I'll make a few suggestions to help jumpstart the selection process. So, without further ado...

Analysis

One of the benefits of digital audio is, of course, having a visual reference for working with audio. This ability has made digital audio analysis tools easier to interpret and use. (And it looks pretty, too!) Analysis plug-ins are diagnostic tools that allow you to look at the fine details of an audio file in many different ways. A comprehensive analysis plug-in will "listen" to the audio being fed into it and output visual information about the current stereo positioning, frequency spread, and Peak/RMS levels of your stereo track. You can use this information to establish a baseline for your mix prior to making any changes. The feedback from the analysis will give you a starting point for where to begin making changes so that you're not just shooting in the dark. For example, if the analyzer says that there is an excess of bass in the frequency spectrum, you will know that at some point, you will need to address the amount of bass in the mix. You can even export the analysis information to a text file or take a "snapshot" of the analysis so that you can reference it later.

Yes, mastering *can* be done without the use of visual aids, but if you're just starting out, analysis plug-ins can be an extremely helpful tool for troubleshooting a stereo mix during mastering. When selecting an analyzer suite, go with the one that makes the most sense to you. These tools will mean nothing if they are loaded with windows and parameters that you don't understand. Most mastering suites, such as Steinberg WaveLab, BIAS Peak, and Sony Creative Software Sound Forge, have a full complement of factory analysis plug-ins. Logic Pro even has a built-in analyzer on every audio track. However, if the need should arise for a third-party analysis plug-in, some of my favorites are Waves PAZ Analyzer (shown in Figure 14.7), iZotope Ozone, and Metric Halo SpectraFoo.

Equalization

We've talked about several different types of EQ throughout this book. The most common type that is used in mastering is fully parametric EQ. If you recall, fully parametric equalizers are the most flexible types of equalizers because they allow you to reduce or enhance specific ranges of frequency all across the full-frequency spectrum. In mastering, your stereo track may undergo several different EQ treatments,

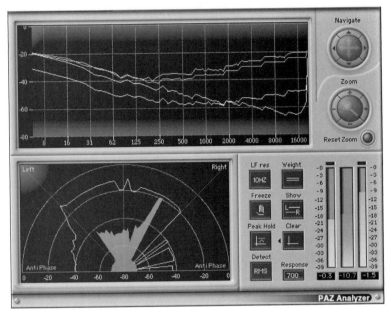

Figure 14.7 Waves PAZ Analyzer.

depending on what the track calls for. You might apply an intial EQ treatment over the entire track to remove some of the rumble that isn't contributing to the audio in a positive way, and then apply a secondary EQ later to reduce a more specific range of annoying frequency in the high end. You may then apply yet another EQ after that, just to bring out the brightness in the upper frequencies without over-accentuating the annoying frequency you just reduced.

Always remember that when you are using EQ in mastering, every adjustment you make will affect the entire track, not just elements within the mix. If your vocals aren't bright enough, before you go cranking in some high midrange, remember that your guitars might exist in the same frequency range and will be affected by the adjustment. When choosing equalizer plug-ins, try everything, but stick with the ones that are easy to use and get good results. Some of my favorite third-party equalizers for mastering are Waves SSL G-Equalizer (see Figure 14.8), Nyquist EQ, Steinberg Q, and Sonnox Oxford EQ.

Compression

There are two primary types of compression used in digital audio. First, there is your standard, full-band compression that can be applied

Figure 14.8 Waves SSL G-Equalizer plug-in.

to a track as sort of a blanket effect. This is the type that is commonly used in mixing. With full-range compression, you get one set of parameters to govern the behavior of the effect on the entire frequency spectrum. Standard compression views the full range of frequency as a single entity and treats it as such so that the entire signal is affected equally. However, a common problem with full-band compression is that abnormally loud or low-frequency transient spikes can set the compressor off, not only compressing the spiked transient, but everything else in the passing signal as well. Full-range compression is more commonly applied on solo instruments during the mixing stage than it is on full mixes in the mastering stage.

Multi-band compression, on the other hand, is used primarily in mastering. This type of compression divides the frequency spectrum into different frequency ranges, or "bands," and affects each one separately. These user-defined frequency bands let the effect know which *parts* of the audio to compress. Then, you can set up different ratio, attack, gain, and threshold settings for each band individually. As an example, if you needed to equal out the dynamics in just the low end, you could compress the low-frequency range between 20 Hz and 120 Hz, leaving all other frequencies in the mix uncompressed, treating the different frequency ranges as separate entities. This allows the use of varying levels of compression on different frequency bands to actually reshape a mix, giving weaker elements within certain frequency ranges more presence. Between the two compression types, multi-band is the more flexible, but it also requires a bit more finesse and familiarity with the entire frequency spectrum to use it.

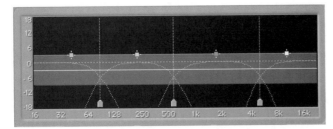

Figure 14.9 Different frequency bands and their crossover points.

When working with multi-band compression, you'll want to define the separate frequency bands for maximum effectiveness. Naturally, the actual frequency crossover points, or the frequency at which one band ends and another one begins, will vary depending on the audio material being processed. A compressor with three to four frequency bands is a good balance between versatility and ease of use. Much more than that will make the task of multi-band compression increasingly complex at this point.

A three-band compressor is typically divided into high-range, mid-range, and low-range frequencies. A four-band compressor commonly has separate bands for high range, high midrange, low midrange, and low range. Please note that while you can affect a single band of frequency without affecting the others, you cannot exclude or skip any frequencies in the frequency spectrum. If your low-range band is set up to cover from 20 Hz to 120 Hz, the midrange (or low midrange) band will begin at around 120 Hz and will go up to whatever frequency the next band begins at. In truth, this isn't an exact science. There aren't any *absolute* crossover filter points. The different frequency bands actually kind of overlap as one transitions into the next, as shown in Figure 14.9. But the range of frequency in which this transition occurs can always be adjusted for your specific needs.

In choosing a compressor plug-in, again sound quality is king. Also, at least in the beginning, you'll want to find a compressor that adds little or no coloration. It's all too tempting to succumb to hype and move toward plug-ins that emulate vintage compressors, but I recommend that you find a transparent compressor to work with so you can accurately focus on getting the results you want. You're going to have to try out a lot of compressor plug-ins on a lot of different types of audio material before committing to just one (or just several). I generally keep three to five different compressors handy because you never know what a track will call for. Some of my favorite full-range compression plug-ins are Waves C1 Compressor, Waves SSL G-Master Bus Compressor, Sonitus:fx fx:compressor, and Digidesign Dynamics III. My top picks for multi-band compressors are Waves C4 Compressor, Waves Linear Phase Multiband, iZotope Ozone, and Wave Arts MultiDynamics.

Noise Reduction

Noise reduction is a common process in mastering. The more you equalize and excite certain frequencies or reduce the dynamic range with compression, making all the elements of a mix more equal in volume, the more you will increase the amount of unwanted noise in the stereo track overall. If this happens, it doesn't mean that you've done something wrong somewhere along the line, but you may want to address any noise issues prior to applying reverb or increasing the volume.

Realize that if you apply reverb to a signal with noise in it, the noise will be affected by the reverb as well. The same goes for increasing the loudness of the mix. If there is noise on the track prior to increasing the volume, the noise will be increased too. After your mix has been EQ'd and compressed, listen carefully to determine whether noise reduction is necessary. If you do need to reduce the amount of noise on a track, there is a wide variety of tools at your disposal. Many sample editors have built-in features for reducing noise and artifacts, and there are many plug-ins designed specifically for this purpose. Check out the Waves Restoration Bundle, Wave Arts Master Restoration (see Figure 14.10), Sony Creative Software Noise Reduction 2.0, and BIAS SoundSoap Pro.

Reverb

In mastering, you can use reverb as a subtle effect to unify a stereo mix. In mixing, there are times when different types of space are applied to different signals. An acoustic guitar may get a small, intimate reverb; a

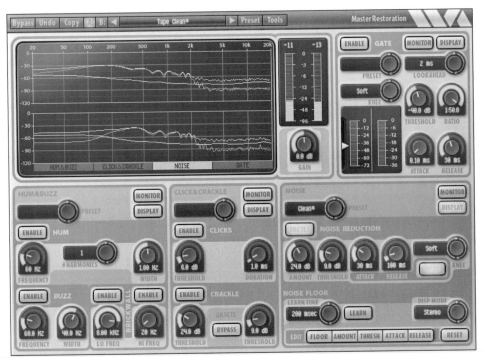

Figure 14.10 Wave Arts Master Restoration.

piano may get a medium-sized room; and a background vocal may get a large room with its fair share of reflections bouncing around. You can use a little bit of reverb on a final mix to help "gel" all these different artificial spatial environments together and give them unity, making them feel as if they all belong to the same space, while at the same time preserving their individual acoustic environments. Reverb is also sometimes used to make a mix seem fuller, using reflections to fill in the negative space in a recording. However, reverb is not an *essential* part of mastering. Some mastering engineers choose not to use reverb at all. Whether *you* decide to use reverb is entirely your call.

I tend to shy away from convolution reverbs in mastering because they are typically based on real existing spaces somewhere out there in the world and they may be too specific to produce the desired effect for simply "polishing" a mix. I suggest a good, customizable room reverb. Again, try a lot of different reverb plug-ins to decide which ones will help finish off your mastering projects. Some of my favorite reverb

Figure 14.11   IK Multimedia's Classik Studio Reverb (CSR Room Reverb).

plug-ins are IK Multimedia Classik Studio Reverb (see Figure 14.11), Waves Renaissance Reverb, and Sonnox Oxford Reverb.

Stereo Imaging

Stereo-imaging issues are problems that you should tackle in mixing, not mastering. Although you do have the ability to enhance the stereo image, nothing can take the place of a well-balanced mix with an appropriate sense of space, panning, and proximity. However, in the event that you encounter a mix that leaves something to be desired in the stereo imaging, there are plug-ins available that can do a pretty decent job of masking a poor stereo image. These plug-ins achieve stereo widening by subtracting the left and right channels of a stereo file away from one another, while reducing the center elements of the mix to ensure mono compatibility or the preservation of clarity and separation even after the file has been converted to mono. The best part is that they do so with minimal side effects (if any).

In a good stereo image, you should be able to close your eyes and decipher the placement of each instrument across the stereo plane within the mix. The mix should also sound well balanced, as opposed to "leaning" to the left or right due to heavy instrumentation or panning positions, and all the instrumentation should still be audible and clear even after you convert it to a mono signal. Above all, if you choose to use stereo enhancement on a final mix, you need to make sure that you keep the audio sounding natural.

In addition to a stereo image–enhancing plug-in, you may also want to look into a stereo analyzer. Stereo analyzers listen to the stereo audio

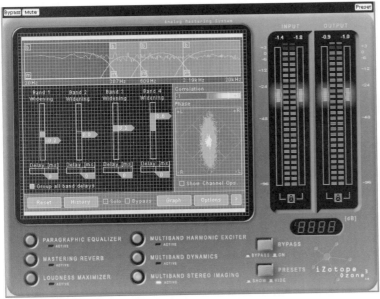

Figure 14.12   The Multiband Stereo Imaging module in iZotope Ozone.

file and estimate the correctness of the stereo image. You can use this to diagnose your audio file so that when you go to make modifications to the image, you're not just shooting in the dark. Again, when choosing a plug-in for stereo imaging, you'll have to try them out. Compare them to determine which most effectively enhances the stereo image with the least number of unwanted artifacts. Some of the stereo imaging plug-ins I like are Waves S1 Stereo Imager, iZotope Ozone (see Figure 14.12), and the PSPaudioware Stereo Pack.

Harmonic Exciters

One way to get that sought-after shimmer or sparkle that you hear in commercial recordings is to use a harmonic or an aural exciter. These exciters will help you get more presence and brightness out of a master track by using low-level distortion to create additional harmonics within selected frequency bands. These harmonics are then mixed back into the original signal, and *bam*—sparkly happy fun time! I know that throughout the mastering section of this book, I've stressed avoiding distortion at all costs. But distortion isn't *always* a bad thing— only when it's excessive and unwanted. In small, controlled doses, however, it can actually be quite useful. Harmonics created by light tube or

Figure 14.13 Elogoxa X-cita.

tape saturation can bring out a track's inner shimmer in a way that you can't necessarily achieve with a simple EQ boost. An EQ boost will only raise the existing harmonics, whereas a harmonic exciter actually creates *new* harmonics to be blended with the original audio material.

Harmonic excitation is again not an essential process in mastering. But should you need it, there are two general options for plug-ins that can help make your mixes shine—low-frequency exciters and high-frequency exciters. If you find your mix to be lacking brightness, try using a harmonic exciter in the upper midrange. If the low end is dull and lifeless, try using a bass enhancement plug-in to excite the lower frequencies in the mix. For high-frequency excitation, I dig the Aphex Aural Exciter, the Arboretum Harmonic Exciter, the Elogoxa X-cita (see Figure 14.13), and the iZotope Ozone Harmonic Exciter. For low-frequency excitation, I like Waves Renaissance Bass, Aphex Big Bottom, Apple Logic Exciter, and yet another vote for the iZotope Ozone Harmonic Exciter. Some harmonic exciters have a tendency to be noisy. A noisy plug-in can usually be identified the moment you load it, so be sure to listen cautiously when you are auditioning different plug-ins and choose one that is quiet, yet effective.

Loudness Maximization

An essential part of mastering a stereo track is making sure that the final volume of the audio is loud enough to compete with other professional recordings. This is usually the final stage of the mastering process. Chances are that after mixing, exporting, equalization, compression, and whatever else a stereo track undergoes in mastering, it won't be at its maximum volume potential.

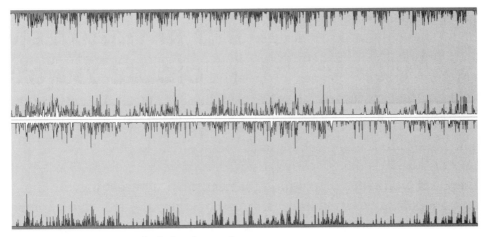

Figure 14.14   An excessively loud waveform.

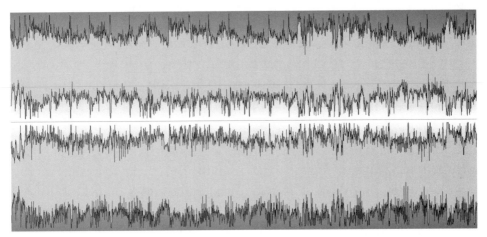

Figure 14.15   A waveform with good overall volume and dynamics.

The volume of commercially mixed and mastered recordings is getting louder by the day. New recordings are much louder than those made 30 years ago due to the "miracle" of compression/limiting. But louder isn't always better. Sometimes the overuse of compression can lead to lost dynamics. You might be able to squeeze a few more dB out of the track, but it may sound less dramatic, squished, or even distorted. The idea *is* to get the audio to be as loud as possible, but you also want to maintain dynamics and fall just short of audible distortion.

Figure 14.14 shows the waveform of a track that is too big (loud) for its britches. Figure 14.15 shows a waveform that is at a good volume, with good dynamics. The waveform in Figure 14.14 looks as though it may have *no* dynamics, and there are many peak transients that have been drastically truncated. Now, notice how the transients of the waveform shown in Figure 14.15 are still fairly dynamic from peak to peak, and very few of the peak transients are cut off. Even someone who knows nothing about digital audio or what they are looking at could examine these two side by side and identify that the waveform shown in Figure 14.15 is the healthier of the two.

There are two types of plug-ins that can help with getting the most volume out of your master. Ultimately, they do the same thing. There are limiters that you can use in conjunction with compressors to get more perceived volume out of a track, and there are loudness maximizers that are typically a peak limiter and a level maximizer rolled into one. A loudness-maximizing plug-in is a bit of a shortcut over traditional limiting for the sake of volume. And while most maximizing plug-ins work great, occasionally there may be situations in which they just aren't the right tools for the job. In such cases, you may want to try some old-fashioned limiting.

First, allow me to draw the distinction between normalization and limiting. With normalization, the entire waveform is analyzed by your software application. It finds the loudest peak and raises it to the verge of clipping or 0 dB. The rest of the audio file is raised in volume by the same amount. Although this technically raises the overall volume, it's a relative increase. And due to the highly dynamic nature of a final mix, normalization alone probably won't get your final mix up to the volume level of a commercial record that has been properly treated for loudness.

What a lot of people don't realize is that the peaks of an audio file actually *could* stand to clip a bit, and no one would ever notice. So what if we could "limit" or reshape the peaks that exceed a set threshold level so they didn't distort, and then bring up the rest of the mix? In theory, you would be able to get more overall volume out of the track because the loudest peak would no longer determine the maximum amplitude, right? Well, you're in luck because that's exactly what limiting does. Loudness plug-ins work very much the same way, except they use specifically designed algorithms to effectively minimize artifacts that may result from the limiting and reshaping of transient peaks.

Limiters are essentially compressors with a high ratio setting, a fast attack, and a quick release. Common parameters for limiters (and compressors alike) were outlined back in Chapter 5. You can also check out the glossary in Chapter 17 for a quick refresher. What's important for you to know about the parameters of a loudness maximizing plug-in is that, like a compressor/limiter, the threshold determines at what decibel level limiting begins. The output level, sometimes called the *margin,* sets the maximum level that the audio can reach. If the output level is set to 0 dB and the threshold is set at −6 dB, it means that the peaks that exceed −6 dB are being limited to prevent them from clipping when the rest of the audio is being brought up +6 dB to reach the output level of 0 dB. If you tried to get an overall volume increase like this without the use of limiting, each time a transient peak exceeded 0 dB, the signal would clip and most likely distort.

Loudness maximizers differ a bit from one to the next as far as parameters are concerned. Two loudness plug-ins from different developers may call the same parameter different names. They may have different visual feedback displays, modes, features, and so on. Be sure to check your software manual for the appropriate nomenclatures.

In choosing a loudness-maximizing plug-in, all you have to do is choose one that you understand and that sounds good. Some have more bells and whistles than others, but they all pretty much do the same thing. As I mentioned before, what makes the difference are the algorithms they use to limit and reshape the peaks. I think at this point, it's pretty safe to say that an essential part of choosing *any* plug-in is to try out as many as you can. It's the only way to see how they stack up against each other and find which ones will work best for you. Some of my personal favorites are Waves L1 Ultramaximizer (see Figure 14.16), iZotope Ozone, Wave Arts FinalPlug, Sonnox Oxford Inflator, and Steinberg Mastering Edition Loudness Maximizer.

Figure 14.16 Waves L1 Ultramaximizer.

Dithering

Dithering is a process used to help control quantization errors that can occur during re-quantization, or when you convert an audio file with a high bit rate to a lower bit rate. A certain type of low-level noise is introduced to the signal to make these quantization errors less noticeable. It's a bit like adding noise for the sake of clarity.

Let's try a little experiment. As you are reading this text, open your fingers wide and spread them across the page. If you try to read through your fingers, you can see the sections of text between your fingers with great clarity, but your fingers are masking some parts of the copy, making it difficult to read or interpret the text in its entirety. This is like a 24-bit file that has been converted to 16-bit without dithering, with the parts of the copy that you cannot read representing the quantization errors in an audio file. Now, keep your fingers in the same position and rapidly move your hand back and forth over the page. The text that was once obscured by your fingers now seems visible, and nothing on the page is completely obscured. Granted, everything is not perfectly clear and pronounced, but you can see more of the page overall, and it's easier to read and interpret as a whole. This is like a 24-bit file reduced down to 16-bit. The noise (the movement of your hand) added to the signal (the page) has masked the quantization errors (obscured copy) to allow us to see (hear) and thereby better interpret the text (the audio information). The added noise basically improves the perceived resolution of the audio file.

Dithering typically is applied to the audio file as the final mastering process prior to sequencing your mastered tracks or preparing them for their final delivery format. Because loudness is also considered a final mastering process, some loudness-maximizing plug-ins offer a dithering feature that can be applied at the same time as an increase in volume. There are a few common parameters you will encounter when using a dithering plug-in, although the options for each will vary from plug-in to plug-in. Basic dithering within a program may only offer you one or two options for customizing the way dithering is applied. Plug-ins that are specifically designed for dithering may offer three or four options. Overall, the general settings are pretty simple.

- **Quantization/bit depth.** Quantization, or bit depth, is the final bit rate to which you want the audio file to be converted. Dithering is only really effective when you are converting a file to a lower bit rate than it currently is. The options are commonly 8-, 16-, and 24-bit.

- **Dither/type.** Dither type is the mode or algorithm used to smooth over the aforementioned quantization errors. The options for this setting will vary, depending on the dithering technology that is specific to your plug-in.

- **Noise shaping.** Noise shaping is a means of making the low-level noise that is introduced to the signal even *less* noticeable. The options for this setting determine what level of noise shaping will occur. The higher the level, the less noticeable the low-level noise will be.

More often than not, a dithering utility will be included with your mastering application. In the event that you want to try a different dithering algorithm, there are several plug-ins available that have built-in dithering features to choose from. The Waves L series L1 and L2 Ultramaximizer and the L3 Multimaximizer use the IDR (*Increased Digital*

Figure 14.17 UV22HR dithering plug-in.

Resolution) dithering algorithm developed by Michael Gerzon. iZotope Ozone uses a proprietary dithering technology called MBIT. And the UV22 and UV22HR plug-ins by Steinberg are based on an advanced algorithm developed by Apogee (see Figure 14.17). If you intend to do a lot of mastering, it is worth your time and effort to try many different dithering algorithms to see which ones produce the best results.

All-in-One and Bundled Software

In the event that you don't want to assemble your perfect mastering plug-in suite just yet, there are several all-in-one mastering plug-ins and bundles available that can help you get the job done. If you're looking to get started mastering right away and you don't want to spend your kids' inheritance outfitting your studio with expensive plug-ins, I recommend starting with a good all-in-one solution and going from there. The all-in-one plug-ins incorporate several effects into a single plug-in with different effect modules. In theory, this means you should be able to do most of your mastering with just one plug-in.

I recommend using an all-in-one in conjunction with various other individual mastering effects. Just because a plug-in seems to have all the bases covered—such as EQ, compressors, reverb, and so on—that doesn't mean they're necessarily covered very well. Some features of a multi-effect mastering plug-in may work better than others. So once again, download demos to determine what *you* think is best prior to shelling out the cash. Two very popular all-in-one mastering plug-ins are iZotope Ozone (see Figure 14.18) and IK Multimedia's T-RackS.

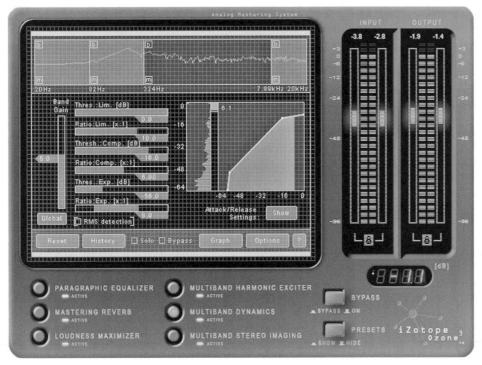

Figure 14.18   iZotope Ozone.

Multiple-effect bundles are the way to go overall, in my opinion. There is nothing wrong with all-in-ones, but bundles often come with effects that can be used for much more than just mastering. Throughout this book, I've been talking about Waves, McDSP, Sonnox Oxford, and software developers of the like. I've already recommended them for mixing and editing, and now I'm recommending them for mastering. The point I'm trying to make is that investing in a more comprehensive bundle will get you almost everything you need for *all* aspects of digital audio production. So in the end, it may be worthwhile to get a bundle and then add plug-ins individually as needed. Some of my favorite bundles that offer tools for mastering and more are Waves Diamond Bundle (see Figure 14.19), BIAS Master Perfection Suite, Wave Arts Power Suite, Sonnox Oxford plug-ins, and the McDSP Project Studio Bundle.

That about wraps up our discussion of software tools for mastering. Hopefully, you've got an idea of what to start looking at as far as

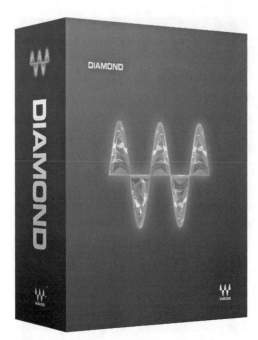

Figure 14.19   Waves Diamond Bundle.

mastering suites and effects are concerned. Remember, download lots of demos, visit forums, read reviews, get expert opinions, and, above all, *listen!* If you do these things during the plug-in/software selection process, you will never know the meaning of the term "buyer's remorse."

15 Mastering Techniques for the Project Studio

So the big question now is simply, "How do I get my final mix to a fully mastered, professional-sounding, radio-ready stereo track?" Well, the answers are as about as vague as the answers to the question, "What makes a mix sound professional?" Truly, there are a number of processes involved and a series of techniques that can be either employed or eliminated altogether, depending on what the desired result is. In some cases mastering can make or break a recording's fidelity, and in other cases it's used as just that last little bit of frosting on the audio cake to polish a mix and make it presentable. What it really comes down to is how much involvement you'll have in this final stage of production and for what purpose.

You'll encounter two primary scenarios when mastering audio for a client. The first is when you have access to the multitrack files so that you can make mix adjustments as needed. Every two-track stereo mix you receive will not be 100-percent perfect, and as you master, you may encounter issues with the stereo mix that could have been resolved during the mixing stage. There are times when I've received stereo mixes from clients, and before I've even touched the mix, the volume levels of all the instruments sound reasonably even and well balanced with one another. But as soon as I start to equalize and excite certain frequencies—BAM! Suddenly the vocal sounds *way* too loud, but the instruments that share the same frequency range sound fine.

In such cases, having access to the multitrack would allow me to go back to the mix, reduce the volume on the vocal, and bounce out a new stereo track to work with. Now, when the same frequencies are excited, the volume levels of the elements in the same frequency range still sound even and balanced with one another. If you have access to the multitrack files, such as when the mixing was performed in your studio and not someone else's, then you can make small adjustments to the mix when necessary to quickly squash any mixing inconsistencies that may interfere with the mastering process.

The second scenario—and the somewhat more likely one—is when you receive only a two-track stereo mix of the audio to be mastered. Suppose you land a mastering job from a client who did all their recording and mixing at another studio. This means that you have to work with what you've got, and you can't make any slight adjustments to elements within the mix if you encounter a mix problem while mastering.

Many mastering engineers today request the final stereo mix as well as other mix elements, such as vocals and drums, bass, and the remaining instruments, sub-grouped or bounced into solo stereo tracks. This can be a good approach when you consider that most of the time, after mastering techniques are employed, some basic remixing may need to take place. Typically, this technique is referred to as *separation mastering,* which is really just another euphemism for remixing the basic tracks during mastering.

Remixing in separation mastering is subtle. It involves only minor additive adjustments. The separate solo instrument tracks, or *separations,* are used to enhance a mix without compromising the original mixing job. When compressors and limiters are applied to a two-track stereo mix, the balance of the overall mix will inevitably be affected. Often you can restore the balance, as well as get more clarity and detail out of a final master, even at more aggressive volume levels, by using separation mastering.

Finally, in this chapter we will discuss the mysterious road from final mix to final master and address some common pitfalls. I will provide example techniques to help guide you along to the end of your journey. The order of the processes and plug-ins here is based on suggestions garnered from my own personal experience. However, don't be afraid to mess with the signal chain a bit. Different engineers have slightly different opinions about the order in which different processing effects should be applied during the mastering stage. I should also mention that few things are more helpful in learning how to master audio than sitting in on a pro mastering session (be it your own project or a friend's or client's project), even if it's just for a song or two, to see how a professional mastering engineer employs the techniques discussed in this chapter. It's difficult to top the valuable one-on-one time spent with a pro engineer and the ability to listen, look, and learn from the session at hand. So let's get started with mastering techniques!

Preparations

There are certain ways that a final mix can be prepared for mastering that will make your job a bit easier. If you are also the mixing engineer, you can see to these details yourself. But if the mix came from another studio, you want to be sure that certain criteria are met.

It is preferable to have clean mixes with the appropriate amount of headroom available. When I say *clean,* I mean that a client's final mix should not be normalized, faded, or processed in any way between the time the mixed project has been bounced out to a final stereo mix and when it reaches your hands for mastering. I've had clients hand me their final mixes, only to find that it seems as though someone *tried* to do a quick and questionable mastering job on them already. In the last decade, a type of device was marketed to musicians as a do-it-yourself multiprocessing mastering unit. The devices sold like hotcakes because no one wanted to shell out the cash to a good mastering engineer when they could pay a one-time fee and do their own mastering for life. It sounded good in theory. However, although these units were capable of a lot of cool things, ultimately they proved to be inferior to real mastering engineers. And now, you can't even give one away on eBay. The reality was that many people used these units improperly and ended up stripping all the headroom out of their mixes, which leaves nothing for a mastering engineer to work with.

Often clients will think that it's helpful or impressive to further enhance a final mix prior to mastering, but it really does more harm than good. Multiprocessing mastering devices weren't designed to help mastering engineers; they were designed to impersonate them…and they do so poorly. This is why it's important to make sure that you receive the final mixes in their purest form. Your client should be aware that final mixes rarely, if ever, sound like (or even closely resemble) final mastered mixes. This may help discourage them from trying to "enhance" the final mix in some way prior to handing it over to you for mastering. It will save you and your client valuable time if the final mixes can be delivered in the correct format from the beginning. It will also save you from getting into a mastering job in which you're expected to perform miracles.

Headroom *Headroom* is essentially the margin (measured in decibels) between the highest peak of the incoming signal and the absolute maximum level it *can* be without distorting. Figure 15.1 illustrates the peak volume of an incoming signal in relation to available headroom.

When effects are applied and adjustments are made in mastering, it is inevitable that the volume will increase. You need some room to enhance dynamics, equalization, overall volume, and so forth. If a

Figure 15.1 Level meter showing a signal's peak volume at −6 dB with available headroom.

final mix is normalized, or maxed out in volume before we begin, there will be limitations to how much you can actually improve the sound quality of the final mix.

Most mastering engineers request that a final mix be delivered with a peak volume of anywhere between −3 dB and −6 dB. If your client hands you final mixes that don't meet the headroom criteria, it might a good idea to request new ones that do, if possible.

Beyond getting a correctly formatted final mix from your client, there is a bit of groundwork to be done prior to the application of effects. These suggestions are optional, but highly recommended.

- **Back it up.** First and foremost, I'd recommend making a copy of the files you intend to master on your hard drive. That way, in the event of a freak mastering accident requiring you to return to the original, you've got a backup. No problem!

- **Listen and learn.** Take some time before you begin mastering to become well acquainted with commercial music that resembles the final result you want to achieve. Grab a couple of audio CDs that are similar to the audio material you're working with and listen to them through your studio monitors a few times so you can get comfortable with your target sound. This will give you a "big picture" to aspire to.

- **Do your homework.** Many analyzer plug-ins (iZotope Ozone and Waves PAZ Analyzer come to mind) can take EQ "snapshots" or capture a quick impression of the EQ curves from any audio source. Use this feature to analyze the EQ curves of similar audio material and compare them to the EQ curves of your masters. This will be helpful in establishing a starting point for when you begin EQing the track, as well as comparing your mastered track to a commercial piece of audio. I often take several separate snapshots for a verse, a chorus, and an instrumental part so that I have plenty of points of reference to which to compare my equalization job. Some of the newer EQ plug-ins (Waves' Q-Clone, Elemental Audio's Firium, and Logic's Match EQ) can even *learn* an EQ curve from a reference track and apply it directly to your audio track. This can be another great place to start with equalization.

- **Get centered.** Before you begin applying effects to the audio material, you should remove the DC offset in the file. Because it consumes headroom, the presence of a DC offset can interfere with an increase in volume or even cause artifacts. Removing the DC offset will ensure that you are truly starting from a clean sonic slate.

- **The bigger picture.** If you're going to be mastering multiple tracks for a single project, it's important to make sure that there is unity from track to track. Listen to each track, making general notes about dynamics and EQ. You'll want to treat all the tracks with these general considerations in mind, and *then* make specific adjustments for each track. This will help maintain consistency in dynamics and equalization from track to track.

Now we should be ready to get down to the nitty gritty. Let's begin with compression.

Compression

Though there are no hard-and-fast rules about the order in which mastering treatments should occur, I'd say that 80 percent of the time you begin with compression to even out the overall dynamics and give the track some punch. It's a good idea to compress first—or, at the very least, prior to equalization. Here's why: If you compress an equalized track, the EQ adjustments that were made would be altered by the compression.

Remember that signal flow makes a difference in the way effects are applied to the audio material. For example, if you applied reverb to a track and *then* compressed it, the reverb effect would get compressed too, and would probably sound unnatural. But if you compressed the audio first, the reverb would be the last effect in the chain and would be allowed to reverberate freely, affecting every effect that came before it in the signal chain. I wouldn't expect reverb to come immediately after compression in the average mastering session, but the use of these two effects in this example is only to better demonstrate a point about signal flow. So try to compress first…and ask questions later.

A pre-mastered stereo track will typically be very dynamic. The loud parts may be as loud as they can be without distorting, but the soft parts may seem too soft by comparison. Compressing the entire stereo track will keep the loud parts loud and will give more clarity and perceived volume to the soft parts by reducing the dynamic range between the two. Compressing a track may reveal some small sonic inconsistencies that weren't audible prior to compression. If you suddenly hear a pop that you didn't hear before, don't panic. Chances are that you didn't do anything wrong. The pop was there all along; the compression just made it more obvious. In such a case, if the two-track stereo file that you're mastering came from a multitrack project that was developed in your studio, you can go back to the multitrack session, find the pop, get rid of it, and bounce out a new two-track stereo file to master.

If the track you're mastering was mixed in a different studio, you may want to have the client get a new stereo track from the mixing facility for you to master. If you don't have access to the original project's multitrack files, it is a bit difficult to scrub out an artifact that is sitting in the middle of the audio file at this stage. The stereo track will be the sum of multiple signals that sound at the same time. Trying to remove the artifact would affect all the instruments that are playing during the pop, and it may be too obvious to get away with.

Be aware that when you use compression, it actually changes the way the audio will sound, more so than limiting does. Compression brings out the "beefiness" in a track and should be used when you want to deliver a greater impact with some in-your-face punch. If you're just looking to increase volume without affecting the sound too drastically, you might want to consider limiting the track.

As previously mentioned, limiting is similar to compression in action, but has a more aggressive ratio setting and a fast attack time. Limiting is a more transparent treatment than compression because it doesn't dramatically affect the dynamic range of a signal. Instead, limiting makes sure that the overall signal doesn't exceed the set volume threshold in order to prevent the audio from clipping and distorting. The majority of the track's original dynamics will, for the most part, be maintained after limiting has been applied.

Compression Techniques

As far as techniques for compressors go, all I can say is run them loosely and loud. You do not want to totally crush a mix the way you would a bass guitar or even a vocal. A mix needs that little space to breathe, and if you use a high compression ratio of 10:1 or greater, you are only crushing the mix and making it less loud and less professional-sounding. If you must use a higher ratio, try using a higher threshold value to avoid crushing the mix. When using compression in mastering, it's important to keep it sounding natural. The time for using compression as a drastic effect is long gone when you get to this final stage of a production.

Listen carefully for pumping. You don't want to be able to hear the sound of your brain being sucked out by an inappropriately slow attack, obviously clamping down on each syllabic transient of the audio. In most cases, you'll want to use a relatively fast attack. The attack time may even depend on the tempo or style of the song. Adjust the attack until you can hear a good balance in dynamics. I would say that the attack and release settings are the keys to good mastering compression. If the attack is too fast, you will ruin the hits and transients that make your music dynamic and powerful. If the attack is too slow, the mix won't recover to its original volume fast enough, which may create sub-accents or cause it to sound "swimmy."

Mastering is a series of *small* adjustments. When working the compressor, start loose with a low ratio value between 2:1 and 5:1, with a quick attack of around 250ms, and approximate the ratio. Then start with a fast release and fine-tune it until it sounds like the transient hits (or syllables) of the audio file recover their original volume in a natural way. If you're having trouble hearing the effect that the release has on the audio, crank it up so you can hear what it sounds like if the release is excessively long, and then roll it back until it sounds right. Adjust the attack time as needed.

You really need to rely on your ears here. The value ranges I've suggested are just starting points. Every signal will require a different set of parameter adjustments—even if they are only slight adjustments. Be sure to listen to the entire track as it plays with the compressor applied to it. Songs or audio projects may have a dynamic shift somewhere along the way that will send the compressor into a tailspin because you didn't account for the change when you dialed in your compressor settings. So in most cases, listen to the entire track to be sure that your compressor settings will work for the duration of it.

Multi-band compressors are especially useful in mastering. This type of compressor allows you to tailor different compression settings for different ranges of frequency. If you want to compress the low end to bring out the punch of the bass guitar, you can compress the low-range frequencies more aggressively while maintaining the high-end energy of the track using light compression in the top end of the spectrum. When used correctly, you can almost reshape a mix and bring "weaker" elements up front by simply applying varying degrees of compression to the appropriate frequencies.

Understanding mastering compression can be tricky. The proper use of mastering compression will make your master less dull or flat, more energetic, and more professional-sounding overall. In the beginning, what sounds right is a delicate balance of knowing what you're hearing and knowing what you're doing. The more you use compression, the easier it will be to identify how your attack, release, ratio, and threshold values are affecting the audio you're working with. So, keep at it. And now that you're on your way to being neatly compressed, let's talk about mastering equalization.

Equalization

To the untrained ear, EQ is grossly undervalued. In truth, it is a crucial part of the production process. In mixing, we equalize individual audio signals to achieve clarity and separation. Often, we use more aggressive EQ adjustments to get the desired effect. Mastering EQ is somewhat less complicated than mixing EQ because you're affecting a summed stereo signal instead of working with multiple tracks of audio, trying to carve a sonic position for each individual instrument just to make a mix "work." Mastering EQ typically uses more conservative adjustments to equalize the frequencies of the final stereo mixdown. You can think of mastering EQ a bit like adjusting the Bass, Mid, and Treble knobs on your home stereo. If you took your final pre-mastered stereo mix down, burned it to a CD, and played it on your home stereo, turning these knobs would affect the overall sound of the audio playing. Naturally, mastering EQ is more frequency-specific than simply using the Bass, Mid, and Treble knobs, but it is the same general idea.

The question that needs to be addressed in mastering equalization is: "What frequencies are lacking or excessive in the mix as a whole?" In the end, too much high frequency in a master track can wear a listener out. Too much low frequency can cause muddiness and compromise the clarity of the overall track (or even make you think your woofers are going to explode!). Too much midrange can make vocals and other midrange instruments sound nasally and irritating. Mastering equalization aims to balance out the frequencies of the final mix by attenuating specific ranges of frequency that exist in the audio material. This is where the aforementioned EQ snapshots can really be useful. You can use them to compare the EQ curves of your pre-equalized audio to a commercial audio track that is similar to what you are working toward, and then use the snapshot as a starting point to begin to understand which frequencies may need to be supplemented or reduced in order to get closer to your equalization goal.

Equalization Techniques

I typically start with three different sonic reference points for EQ for every mastering job. If it is a rock band, I will take a WAV file example of a rock recording that is bright, a recording that is darker/warmer, and finally the band/artist's example of what they think their master should sound like, and then listen to all three on the mastering monitors. I will bounce back and forth, toggling between speakers of different models and sizes, and find out where to begin. These are my points of reference. If the mix is brighter than the across-the-board "bright" example, I know I have to reduce or recheck the high-end EQ.

Often people will work on a mastering project for a few hours at a time, and this technique of having three example files readily available keeps you centered as to the reality of the project. After a few hours things can suddenly get dull because your ears are getting tired, and then you're peeling out highs simply because of the fatigue. But with your examples readily available for comparison, it's easy to cross-reference and realize whether you are within the realm of real-life highs with just a quick A/B listen.

When it comes to selecting a plug-in suitable for equalizing a final mix, there are a few things to keep in mind. First, you will probably need to select a transparent-sounding stereo (because most final mixdowns are delivered as stereo left and right channels) parametric EQ that provides as little coloration as possible. Some EQ plug-ins are designed to mimic signature analog equalizers that color, or warm, a track from the get-go.

Because you're just getting started with mastering, I would try to avoid these types of analog emulator EQ plug-ins. Often these emulations use compression or saturation of some kind to color the signal, and though they may be useful for individual instruments in a mix, they may not be appropriate for most mastering situations. Although it's true that mastering houses often use analog equipment that has its say over the audio signal, during the learning process you need to be able to hear what you're working with accurately, so a transparent EQ is ideal. If you're not sure how transparent an EQ plug-in is, add it to your signal chain as the first and only effect. Reset all the parameters so that no actual EQ is being applied, then turn it on and off in real time while auditioning the final mixdown track. If the EQ makes any audible difference in the sonic characteristics of the audio material, you may want to check out a different plug-in. Your best shot at a transparent equalizer plug-in is one that is described as being a *linear phase* EQ. Linear phase EQs eliminate phase distortion that can cause coloration in your audio signal. These types of EQs are ideal for mastering because they offer clean, colorless performance. As you learn more about EQ and equalization plug-ins, you'll be able to make better decisions about what EQs you *want* to use on your mastering jobs.

With equalization, it is especially important to remember that everything is connected. Any change you make to any area of frequency will have an effect somewhere else in the frequency spectrum. If you pull out a small amount of low midrange, it may reflect as an over-presence of high midrange. If you remove low-frequency bass, the rest of the track might sound too bright and thin. Just be aware of how each EQ adjustment is affecting the other frequencies as you go. If an adjustment you've made has a negative effect on the track, undo it and reevaluate your approach. Again, EQ is a process that requires subtlety. If you have to add or subtract excessive amounts of EQ, chances are that the audio was not properly mixed before it got to you. And if you're the one who mixed it, then you are *so* fired.... All joking aside, if you find that you have to add or subtract an excess of 6 dB or more, it might be time to go back and address some frequency issues within the mix.

Mastering equalization can be tricky, especially at first, when you're not quite sure what to adjust and by how much. I would suggest using broad strokes to begin. That is, start by adjusting wider ranges of frequency. If you know there is too much low end in the track, start where the low end lives (approximately 20 Hz to 120 Hz) and begin subtracting −2 dB at a time. If it sounds as if you're losing too much low end, narrow the frequency range and then sweep the EQ filter up and down the low end of the frequency spectrum until reduction sounds most effective. The perceived bass, or low-end "boom" that we experience in music, is right around 90 Hz to 100 Hz. A lot of low sub-frequency overtones that cause speakers to "woof" hard ring at around 60 Hz. I will commonly apply a slight boost at 90 Hz to 100 Hz and a low shelf reduction from 20 Hz to 60 Hz to get a nice, round low end, but without the low-frequency rumble. Of course, the EQ adjustment you make will vary from project to project, depending on the mix.

The recording industry seems to use a fair amount of additive EQ in the upper midrange between 2 kHz and 4 kHz on commercial recordings. This is the frequency range that I call "the honk." The over-presence of this frequency range can be a bit irritating to the human ear when you are exposed to it for extended periods of time. It's easy to see why mix engineers often have a tendency to shy away from the honk when they're mixing a project. In mastering, you have to be sure that you address this frequency range appropriately. Most consumer reproduction systems

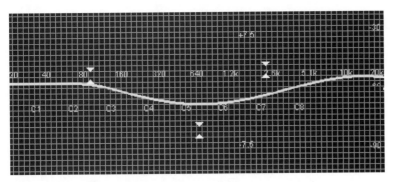

Figure 15.2 An example of a scooped EQ curve.

utilize a little thing called *Mega Bass*. When activated, it applies a "scooped" EQ curve through which the music passes. A scooped EQ curve is one that excites the high and low frequencies, but ducks the midrange. See Figure 15.2.

If you don't address these lacking frequencies at the mastering stage, they will most likely be understated when played back on a regular stereo system. Be sure that when you are checking your masters, you audition them through multiple playback devices, such as on your studio monitors, in the car, and on a consumer stereo system with any equalization enhancers switched both on and off. If a listener has the option to use sound enhancement on his stereo system, it is likely that he will use it. So it's a good idea to account for it, but don't base your final master on consumer systems. The idea is to have your mastered tracks sound good on any system through which they're played.

Noise Reduction

When you raise gain levels, add compression, and equalize audio, it's not unheard of to find some small sonic inconsistencies that didn't seem to be present during mixdown. Noise reduction in mastering can be as simple as eliminating some small pops or crackles, de-essing a sibilant vocal section, or removing audio hiss from the beginning and end of a track. There are times when I've felt 100-percent satisfied with a mix, only to find that after adding high end to the final mixdown, the vocal then needed to be de-essed. In this section I will discuss different ways to address these issues (short of remixing the track itself) and perhaps give you a few ideas about how to keep noise to a minimum. Nothing makes your recording sound less professional than audible hisses, pops, and distortion. So let's look into removing these babies as they occur.

Sibilance

After compression and EQ are applied, you may find that they really bring out the sibilance in the track, and suddenly every *S* sound in the vocal is extremely exaggerated and harsh. At this point, the track might benefit from de-essing. You may want to experiment with de-essing the sibilant parts individually and trying to get the large annoying pops under control. Because anything you do to a track will affect the track as a whole, it's a good idea to see whether spot-treating will do the trick, though it is possible that doing so will compromise the consistency of the overall audio.

If the program you're mastering in will allow you to automate a de-esser plug-in, you can try using it to make the transition between when the de-esser is active and when it's bypassed a bit subtler. Another way to handle sibilance is to use a narrowband compressor (which is pretty much what a de-esser is) that targets the frequency area where sibilance usually exists (somewhere between 2.5 kHz and 9 kHz) to reduce the number of "SSSssserpents" standing out in the track. There is always a danger that applying any type of compressor or de-esser plug-in to an entire track will make the audio seem dull and lifeless. I try to avoid this at all costs. In the event that you *do* have to use one of these types of plug-ins for the entirety of the audio material, you can always put another equalizer in the signal chain to brighten the track back up a bit. Just be careful not to add so much EQ that you defeat the purpose of de-essing in the first place.

The End Is the Beginning Is the End

The first and last things that listeners hear in your tracks are the beginning and ending of the audio file. So let's start by making sure that these sections are clean and silent. Many clients have handed me final mixdowns that have preamp hiss, excessive finger scrapes from fretted instruments, even eight bars of click track at the beginning and end of tracks. Sure, sometimes fret noise can be a desired sound as an effect, but unless the client tells you they want to keep it, get rid of it.

They assumed it would be fixed at the mastering stage, they didn't know how to remove it, or maybe they simply didn't notice it.

I like to use quick fades to transition from silence to an audible signal or vice versa. It's a bit less abrupt than digital black to a wall of sound. Mind you, it's a *quick* small-scale fade that won't even be noticeable to the listener. It's more likely that they would notice if you *didn't* fade it. Keep your fades tight to the music. Make sure there's no audible volume upsweep and apply the fade directly to the mastered file prior to rendering or bouncing out. I like to take the sections before the audio and after it ends and completely lower the gain down to zero or erase any and all audio. This way I know that nothing is happening before the first note sounds. Leave a little space, though, so CD players do not immediately snap into audio harshly. Beginning and end fades should be the very *last* process you apply to a mastered track.

Artifacts

The bad news is that not all noises can be completely eliminated from a final mixdown. There may always be something you can hear (some small pop or crackle) buried in the mix that there may be no way to fix without re-tracking, remixing, and doing a lot of other "re" things. It's very difficult to remove an artifact, such as a pop or a crackle, in the mastering phase. Because you know that the final mixdown is the sum of many different signals, you know that to remove a pop would be to affect all audio that sits underneath the pop—when, in actuality, there is nothing sitting underneath the pop. If you get rid of the pop, there will just be momentary silence. Chances are that *you* will be the only one who notices. And unless you point it out, a pop might not be audible in the context of the track, but a fraction of a second of silence might be. Pick your battles with this one. Don't slave tirelessly over remixing, re-bouncing, and remastering over a tiny little pop that 19 out of 20 people will say they can't even hear.

Reverb

Reverb is an optional part of mastering. Some engineers use it on every mastering job; others rarely use it. Since the mid-1990s, commercial recordings have sounded as though a lot of engineers are allergic to reverb or any type of space in a track…or at least, so it seems. Truth be told, music takes place in space, and there is always some kind of room or reflection going on, even in the deadest of recording situations. There is reverb on everything.

In mastering, reverb is applied in a way that is hardly noticeable while still doing its job as a unifying veneer to the overall space of the track. The idea is not to make the reverb audible, as you might do in a mixing application, but to use it minimally to enhance the overall sound of the audio. You can use reverb in moderate amounts to help fill in the sound of a track, as well as smooth out spatial imperfections that may have existed in the original instrument recordings. Understand that the creation of perceivable space *should* occur during the mixing stage. Mastering reverb should only be used as a finishing touch on a final mix, and not to compensate for lack of space within the mix itself.

Reverb Techniques

Transparency is key. You want to find the most transparent and natural-sounding reverb possible for mastering. Here again, you can audition the transparency of different reverb plug-ins by inserting them, one at a time, as the sole effect on your audio track. As you listen to the playback, turn the plug-in on and off and listen carefully. Choose the one that allows the original signal to be heard accurately while providing the necessary amount of reverb.

You'll usually want to begin with a small to medium room reverb with short reflections. The presence of the short reflections thickens and fills out a final mix. Once you find your reverb plug-in and room settings, it's simply a matter of tailoring the mix level. You will find that it requires a lot less reverb than you think to do the trick. Some mastering plug-ins (such as iZotope Ozone) will allow you to solo the reverb-affected signal so that you can hear only the effect the reverb has on the signal and not the original signal itself. This feature is nice in the beginning because it can give you a real sense of exactly how much reverb is enough for mastering.

The order in which a reverb plug-in should be inserted in the signal chain is somewhat a matter of opinion. As I mentioned earlier, some mastering engineers don't even use reverb most of the time. There is the opinion that you should add a mastering reverb before *anything* else is brought into the equation because everything that comes after a reverb plug-in in the signal chain would affect the reverb from that point on. Brightening the EQ may make a reverb stand out, and compressing it may actually make the reverb sound louder and more prevalent in the mix.

There is also the opinion that if you EQ before applying reverb, you can enhance, deemphasize, and even remove certain frequency ranges that will allow you to have greater control over the character of the reverb. Also remember that there are reverbs available that have their own EQ parameters for customizing the sound of the effect. So, as far as a reverb's place in the signal chain, my suggestion is to try both and see which one sounds better and works best for you.

An alternative to using a reverb plug-in applied directly to the final mixdown is to run a reverb-affected track in parallel and blend it in with the original. Sometimes I'll print a separate track of just 100-percent room or plate reverb with a low decay time and blend it into the main mix until I get some semblance of space. Then I will re-bounce, making a new master mix with a little overall reverb supplied. Prior to bouncing the original track and the reverb-affected track together, you have a great deal of control over the reverb-affected track. Also, it won't be subject to the effects that are applied to the final mixdown track, so you can blend it with the original audio and EQ to your heart's content without necessarily worrying about its position in the signal path.

Stereo Imaging

The concept of stereo imaging can best be described as a balance achieved by the two sides of the stereo field feeling equal and balanced with each other. In addition to balancing levels between the left and right channels, you want to create a sense of natural space and air that will give the listener a feeling of sonic equality and auditory comfort. The act of enhancing the stereo image on a final mix is called *stereo widening* or *stereo expansion*. If the stereo image of a final mix is good, you should be able to pinpoint the individual instruments and their general locations in the mix. You should be able to listen and point or motion toward where a certain instrument exists in the mix when you hear it.

Some engineers may choose to pan their guitars hard left and hard right to give an extreme sense of the position of each guitarist on the sound-stage. Although this can make a dramatic impact in the final mix, it is not an ideal panning practice if you are trying to create a mix with a good stereo image. If the final mix was converted to mono (mono being the sum of both the left and right channels), say for the purpose of broadcast on TV or multimedia, chances are that the guitars might disappear or become unidentifiable in the mix. This is an indication of a poor stereo image. Now, if the individual instruments can be clearly heard and identified even after a conversion to mono, the stereo image of the final mix is probably pretty good. Truthfully, the initial responsibility of getting a good stereo image should fall on the recording and mixing engineers. If the recording and mixing of the instruments is done well from the beginning of the production, adjustments to the stereo image in mastering should be minimal, if necessary at all.

Not all mixes can be perfectly balanced between the left and right channels due to variables such as pan positioning, the density of instrumentation between channels, and the use of simulated spatial effects, to name a few. Mixes that are especially effects-heavy tend to struggle in obtaining good stereo imaging. In the event that you do get a mix with a poor stereo image, there are various plug-ins and effects available that are designed to help correct imbalances and stereo field problems without compromising the sound quality overall. Basically, a stereo image enhancement plug-in, such as Waves S1 (see Figure 15.3) or the multi-band stereo imager found in iZotope's Ozone (see Figure 15.4), expands the stereo image of a stereo audio file by subtracting the left and right channels from one another and reducing any elements of the mix that exist in both channels, or that are "centered" in position. The result is perceived as a wider or more open and balanced sound.

It's difficult to explain in writing what it sounds like when a mix sounds wide or open, but you can definitely *hear* the difference. The

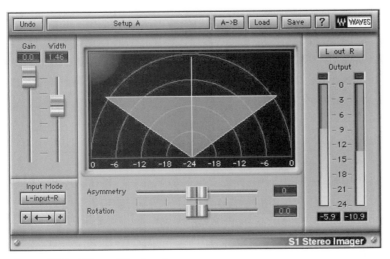

Figure 15.3 Waves S1 plug-in.

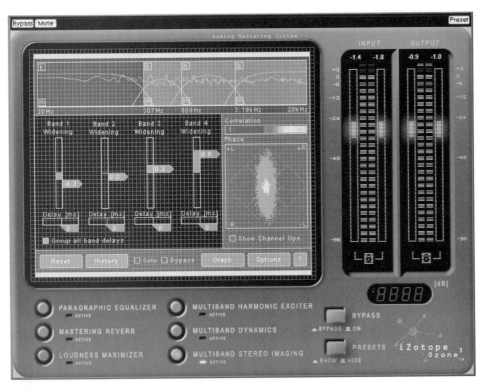

Figure 15.4 iZotope Ozone's multi-band stereo imager.

best way for you to understand stereo imaging enhancement is to work with it. I've chosen to forego a specific section on stereo imaging techniques because it really boils down to whether you know your way around your stereo imaging plug-ins. I can tell you this: As with all things in mastering, moderation is essential. The overuse of such an effect can really mess with a mix, causing phasing issues, the cancellation of frequencies, or loss of bearing in regard to where the center elements truly live. It's important to remember that if you choose to apply stereo imaging enhancements to your final mixdown, they should produce a natural-sounding result. It's a good practice to check your stereo-widened mix by listening to it in mono as well. When you decide on a stereo imaging plug-in, apply it to an unmastered stereo track and familiarize yourself with what effect each control has on the mix. As with reverb, stereo imaging enhancement is optional. Only use it if it has a positive effect on the audio.

Loudness

What is loudness? It is the magnitude of sound. In mastering, we seek to increase the perceived magnitude of the audio with which we're working. Digital audio files are typically very dynamic, containing a series of quick, high-intensity peaks. The loudest peak in an audio file will determine how much overall headroom is available to increase the gain. In theory, you can only raise the relative volume of an audio file until the highest peak reaches 0 dB. Much beyond that, and you'll start to experience clipping and/or digital distortion.

If you took a highly dynamic audio file and raised the fader level until the signal started to clip, its perceived volume would still be less than that of a commercial recording because using the fader increases only the relative volume of the audio. Although the audio file would undoubtedly be louder than before the increase, it would still be limited to the maximum level determined by that loudest peak.

So how do you get more volume out of a highly dynamic audio file without distortion? You can do certain things in mastering to increase the overall intensity and perceived volume of the track. You don't want to crush the life out of the mix, but the goal is more volume, and the best way to achieve that at this stage is to reshape the peaks and reduce the dynamic range of the file.

When discussing the subject of loudness, I feel it is my duty to first discuss something called the *loudness wars*. The term "loudness wars" essentially describes the tendency of the music industry to create progressively louder records that supposedly draw more attention, making them stand out from the crowd sonically, in order to be competitive with other albums and artists. The volume of professional recordings has been steadily increasing since the mid-1990s. If you put a pre-1990s album and a post-2000 album in your CD changer and play them consecutively, chances are that you will have to reach for the volume knob to compensate for the dramatic volume difference between the two (see Figures 15.5 and 15.6). That boost in volume is the aftermath of the loudness wars.

It has been argued that the increasing volume of commercial records is partly encouraged by factors such as preexisting noise in common, busy listening environments; the ability to utilize the full bandwidth of a compact disc; and the assumption that consumers want louder CDs. But make no mistake—it's about competition. Louder is better, right? Not necessarily. Loudness is often mistaken for or confused with intensity and impact. If your record has more intensity than another one or makes a greater impact, then, logically, it should be able to

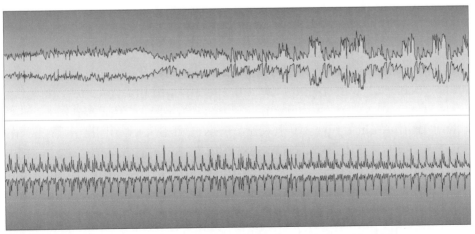

Figure 15.5 The waveform of a stereo track that was mastered in 199x.

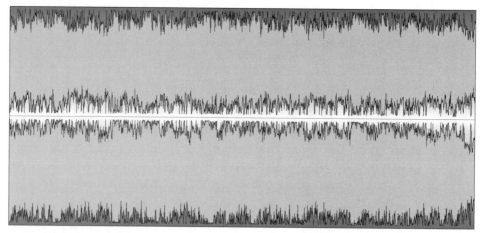

Figure 15.6 The waveform of a stereo track that was mastered in 200x.

stand out among its competitors. However, in my opinion, it takes a lot more than simply volume to make a record stand out. Elements such as composition, songwriting, and performance, in combination with sound quality, are what make a record memorable or make it have more impact than another.

And how about some dynamics once in a while? The loudest record doesn't always win. In fact, the loudest record sometimes isn't even listenable. Some albums have even fielded complaints because they were so loud that there was audible clipping! Maximizing volume to make your album more competitive with others on the market is one thing, but allowing the quest for *more* volume to compromise sound quality—well, that's just poor judgment.

There is nothing wrong with a good loud recording, but at what cost? The most significant casualty in this war has been good dynamic audio. Naturally, in trying to squeeze maximum volume out of a recording, you sacrifice dynamics. Those from the "louder is better" school of thought aggressively compress and brickwall-limit audio to squeeze every last drop of volume out of it. Sure, the recording will be *loud,* but unfortunately, this robs the audio of dynamic range, and suddenly a recording that was once very detailed and dynamically rich is now devoid of dynamic variance and is pummeling your ears at full volume until the two seconds of silence between the end of one song and the beginning of the next come to release you from an ear-fatiguing purgatory. Sadly, it's only the discriminating ear that is irritated by the overwhelming loudness of modern music. Most consumers won't care that a record is brickwalled or that it's lacking dynamics. Chances are that they will just accept that it's the way it's supposed to sound and listen to it anyway.

These days, nearly all mastered audio is pretty much "acceptably" in clip (clipping just short of distorting) all the time, especially in less dynamic forms of music (pop, rock, rap, hip-hop, and so on). Much of the punch and crispness of music has been forgone for the sake of volume. If you don't believe me, go buy a funk recording from the '70s that was released on CD in the '80s and turn it up. It will sound great. It'll be punchy, clear, and dynamically rich. Then put in "Gold Digger" by Kanye West, Gwen Stefani's "Hollaback Girl," or Justin Timberlake's "SexyBack" without adjusting the volume, and be amazed at the difference.

The next time you listen to the radio in your car, take note of how up-front, dynamically void, and consistently *loud* all of the internal elements of the music and arrangements seem. When Kelly Clarkson is whispering a part with a solo acoustic guitar, the overall volume is still pretty close to the same decibel levels that occur in the chorus, which *should* be the biggest part of the song... shouldn't it? I suppose that it *can* be said that today's music is designed to sound louder and more intense at lower volume levels. But is the tradeoff for lost dynamics really worth it? As we enter the next section on techniques for loudness, be aware that by increasing volume excessively, we could be compromising the fidelity of our recording. Make your masters loud, but within the confines of still sounding good.

Techniques for Loudness

There's a little more involved in getting the maximum loudness out of a project than simply "turning it up, dude." First and foremost, you must trust your ears. After you've started applying effects to your final mix, it is common that the level meter for the main output of your digital audio software will indicate that a signal is "in the red" or that it's in "clip." But try not to rely solely on the color of the level

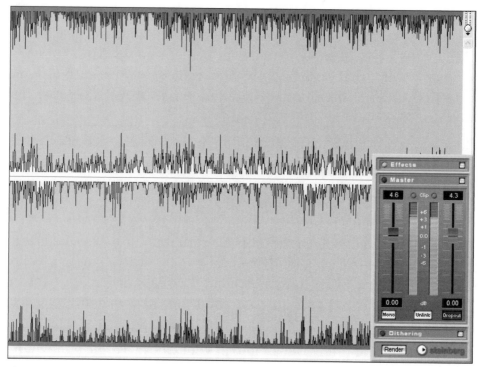

Figure 15.7 Waveform and level meter of an audio file for which I've increased the volume.

meter to let you know when it's too loud. Although you would think that decibel measurement should be constant no matter *which* software you use, some digital audio programs handle level-meter feedback a bit differently than others with regard to clip indication, so it's important to let your ears decide. When your eyes see red but your ears don't hear red, your brain should take over and realize that if you can't hear distortion or audible clipping, then there isn't any. Figure 15.7 shows the waveform and level meter of an audio file for which I've increased the volume. Just from looking at the waveform and the level indicator, without hearing the audio, you might assume that the signal is clipping. In reality, though, this signal never audibly clipped, and the volume increase did not cause it to distort.

The very first thing I'd like to say about maximizing volume is that you should try to avoid normalization. Normalizing is a semiautomatic process that searches for the loudest peak in a piece of audio and raises it to 0 dB. The rest of the audio is brought up in relative volume as well. If the loudest peak had to be brought up by +2 dB to reach 0 dB, then the rest of the audio file was brought up by +2 dB as well (including any noise that may have gone unnoticed −2 dB ago). Normalizing does not change the dynamic range of an audio file. It doesn't do anything but raise the relative volume. But, as mentioned earlier, if an audio file is already at its maximum volume by the time you begin mastering it, there will be limitations to how much you can actually improve the sound quality. Normalizing leaves no headroom for the necessary adjustments that will be made during the mastering process.

Loudness maximization is typically one of the last stages in the mastering process. After you've compressed, EQ'd, added reverb, and so on, maximizing loudness comes right before formatting the audio for its final medium. It begins with figuring out where the level currently stands. You can approximate the maximum peak level of your audio file by keeping a close watch on your main level meters for the duration of the audio's playback, or you can get the peak level more precise by using a psychoacoustic analyzer, such as a Waves PAZ analyzer. Once you know what decibel level your audio peaks at, you can load up an audio limiter plug-in.

Don't Break the Chain?   Different mastering engineers have different workflow methods. Even the software you choose can have an impact on the way you work. Should you chain all of your mastering effects together so that you can hear the signal chain in real time, or should you take baby steps and save a new version of the audio file each time you make a major change?

Though it occupies slightly more space on your hard drive, I typically prefer the latter option, especially for someone just starting out. Being able to revert to the previous version allows you to easily A/B the before and after of the audio file you're working on. Also, if you decide that you've made a change for the worse, you can start from the last version you were satisfied with. It's kind of like permanently backing up your undos. Another reason I do this is because there are certain effect processors, such as limiters, that I don't want to just throw on the end of the signal chain. I like to know how my effects are directly affecting the audio, and often I don't want to concern myself with the possibility of variable plug-in performance somewhere in the effects chain.

When I am satisfied with a mastering process, I prefer to render a file with the effect applied, save it as a new version, and then move on to the next process using the newly rendered file. I don't typically unload the effects after they've been rendered. I usually just leave them bypassed while I work with a new effect. When I'm finished mastering, I save the entire effects chain as a preset within my software (Steinberg WaveLab) so that after numerous listens and real-world testing, I can recall each effect and my saved presets should I decide to go back to the drawing board.

Keep in mind that rendering a 32-bit float file to a 24- or 16-bit file multiple times may cause unnecessary quantization errors. Unless you can render to the same resolution as the original audio file, rendering effects separately may not be the best choice. If you are working with 32-bit float files, it is best to render all the effects at once in order to keep quantization errors to a minimum.

Again, there aren't really any rigid rules that govern workflow logistics. Do what works and sounds best to you.

In this example, suppose the feedback from the psychoacoustic analyzer tells you that the peak volume of the audio file is at −5 dB, or 5 dB below its peak volume of 0 dB. To get the same peak volume increase as normalization would, simply set the threshold of the limiter to the same decibel value of −5 dB. Remember that in limiting, a threshold of −5 dB means that the overall gain will be *increased* by 5 dB. This should have the same effect as normalization, but will yield better sound quality. If you want even more level, you can push up the threshold value to get a little more overall gain.

Under no circumstances should you try raising the gain using the level fader or the gain increase feature in your software. This will only cause clipping and possibly distortion. A limiter is one of the safest ways to maximize volume without clipping or coloration. Even though you can change the dynamic range and boost the volume of a track, the fact remains that a signal cannot exceed 0 dB without distorting. If you want more perceived volume, you first have to reduce the dynamic range with standard compression, and then apply a limiter to raise the volume of the already compressed track.

Another way to increase the volume of your track is to simply use a loudness-maximizing plug-in. These types of plug-ins are specifically designed to make your audio as loud as humanly possible…short of clipping, of course. A loudness maximizer is essentially a peak limiter with a fast response time and a level maximizer rolled into one. When using these plug-ins for mastering, you want to set the peak level, or the maximum output level, to 0 dB or just shy of 0 dB. This tells the plug-in that you don't want the signal to exceed that decibel level. And because 0 dB is as loud as you can get without distorting, 0 dB is the logical choice. Then it's only a matter of tailoring the threshold and release values.

Again, determining threshold level can begin with a psychoacoustic analyzer for a starting point. Start pushing up the volume until you are getting all the volume you want. If you're trying to make the track as loud as possible, keep upping the threshold until you hear a little distortion, and then roll it back until the distortion stops. The release determines how quickly the signal will return to its original level once it crosses the set threshold. The release should, above all, sound natural. If it sounds as if the volume is recovering too slowly, reduce the release time. If it's recovering too quickly, raise it.

Refer to some of the presets in your maximizing plug-in if you're not sure where to start. Exploring presets is a great way to better understand the effect a parameter has on the audio. Remember that even something as simple as level can be overdone. Listen carefully to your audio as you maximize it. If it starts to get crispy and fuzzy in the high end or boomy and farty in the lows, it's too loud and you should crank it back a bit.

Dithering

One of the final steps in mastering is to reduce the bit rate of your audio files. Please note that dithering is only truly effective when you are converting a file from a higher resolution to a lower one in order to conform to the given media. The given media is commonly a compact disc with a maximum audio resolution of 16 bit, 44.1 kHz. Recording audio at a higher bit rate initially helps maximize the amount of headroom that an audio file has available for further processing (EQ, compression, reverb, loudness, and so on). Unfortunately, a compact disc can only handle so much audio information. If a project has been recorded at a resolution greater than 16 bit, the bit rate will eventually have to be reduced in order to create a master CD. Converting an audio file from 24 bit to 16 bit would be an appropriate occasion for dithering. The process of reducing bit depth from a higher-resolution file is called *re-quantization*. Dithering is applied in order to help smooth over any errors that may occur during the re-quantization process.

Dithering is pretty much an automatic process. Different software and plug-ins use different dithering algorithms, so it's possible that dithering with one plug-in will sound a little different than dithering with another. Most dithering software allows you to select a few different settings and then apply it to the audio file with the click of a button. It is helpful for you to know what these settings do so that you can aim for the best results no matter what dithering algorithm you use. Then it's only a matter of deciding which algorithms you think sound the best for your mastering applications. I covered the basic dithering parameters in Chapter 14, but many developers have designed proprietary algorithms for dithering that have their own cute little names and feature sets, so it's important to refer to your software manual for specific notes on your plug-in's or program's dithering features.

When it comes time to reduce the bit rate of the final mix, try out a few different dithering algorithms and listen carefully to see whether you can hear a difference between them in your audio file. Choose whichever one you think produces the best result. Once the dithering process is complete, your final mix will be a final master.

So Now What?

We're into the final stage of mastering now. This is where we prepare the client's files for replication or whatever purposes the client has in mind. Dithering should have delivered us to our final format resolution for the client's needs. If it's a CD, this is commonly 16 bit, 44.1 kHz unless otherwise specified. Now all that's left is to clean up the slop or dead air at the beginnings and ends of the tracks, sequence them for the final project, and burn the master disc.

Chances are that when you first receive the final mixes for mastering, there will be an excess of silence at the beginnings and ends of the tracks. Final mixes are often intentionally bounced out to a stereo file with this dead air before and after the audible signal to see that the audio is bounced out in its entirety. If you don't give the audio enough before and after quiet time, you run the risk of truncating the audio. This is more of a concern at the end of the file, where reverb or delay tails tend to linger at the end of a song.

Removing the silence at the beginnings and ends of the master tracks is a pretty simple process. All you have to do is open the mastered track in your wave editor, highlight the silence you want to remove, and hit the Delete key. But be careful not to trim the audio too closely, because you still need *some* silence to help multiple tracks transition together more smoothly. I usually don't like to leave more than 100 milliseconds of silence before and after the audible signal begins and ends (see Figure 15.8). I know it doesn't seem like much, but two seconds of silence is usually inserted between tracks during sequencing. So there will be plenty of silence present in the final master disc.

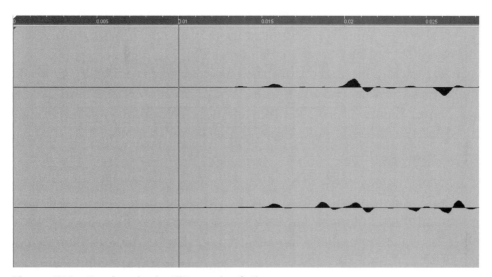

Figure 15.8   One hundred milliseconds of silence.

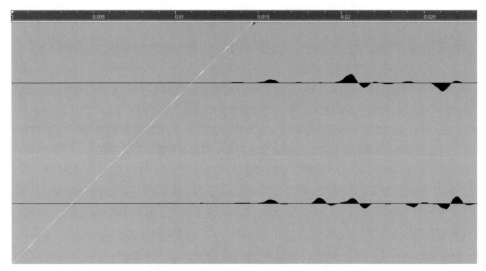

Figure 15.9 Small-scale fade-in at the beginning of a track.

At this point, it's a good idea to apply a quick little fade to help the audio transition to silence. We're not trying to make a fade obvious here. We previously discussed the use of a mini-fade to correct zero-crossing artifacts at the beginning and end of a looped piece of audio. This is really very similar, except that the scale of the fade may vary, depending on the audio material. At the beginning, I tend to keep the fade extremely short. You don't want to mess up the attack of the first sound you hear. I magnify the waveform to a close zoom ratio (1:1 should do it), until the waveform looks like a single thin line. I then apply a very small-scale fade-in to ease the quick transition from silence to the audible signal (see Figure 15.9). On the end of the waveform, I typically highlight from the last peak in the audible signal all the way to the very end of the file, and apply a standard fade-out to silence (see Figure 15.10). When your fades are complete and you've saved the file, we can move on to sequencing the master disc.

Your client may want you to sequence the final project for them. Sequencing a master disc involves renaming the tracks, organizing the track layout, possibly adjusting the track spacing, and attenuating individual track volumes. The client will most likely provide you with a list of track names and an order that they've thought long and hard about. You'll use this list to rename and organize the tracks in a CD-burning software program that is capable of creating a Red Book

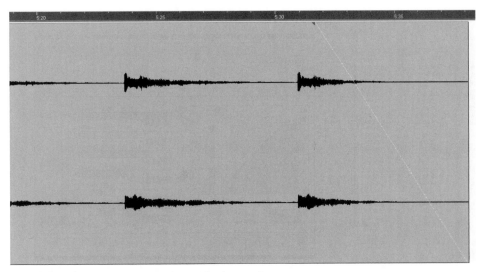

Figure 15.10   A fade-out at the end of a track.

standard audio CD. The details pertaining to track order, track spacing, and track names should be discussed and clarified with the client prior to any sequencing.

And now, a word on track spacing: The silence between two tracks is referred to as the *gap*. Most burning programs automatically insert a two-second gap as each track is added to the CD layout. This is a nice feature for traditional audio CDs, in which the songs need a bit of silence between them to get the listener ready for the next track. On some occasions, such as when the end of one song sonically introduces the next, the client may want you to reduce or remove the gap entirely, in order for the two songs to play back to back continuously. This "gapless" playback is actually a recent trend that occurs on a lot of concept albums, such as Tool's *Lateralus* and Nine Inch Nails' *The Fragile*. While gapless playback is effective for immersing a listener in the overall experience of the record, it may not be right for every project. The whole point of mentioning it now is to simply inform you that it *can* be done. It is up to the client to instruct you on any special alterations in the track spacing; otherwise, stick to the two-second standard (see Figure 15.11).

When it comes time to compile multiple mastered tracks into a cohesive project such as an album (see Figure 15.12), it's important to

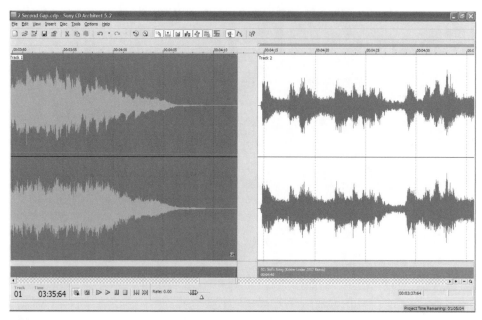

Figure 15.11   A standard two-second gap between audio tracks.

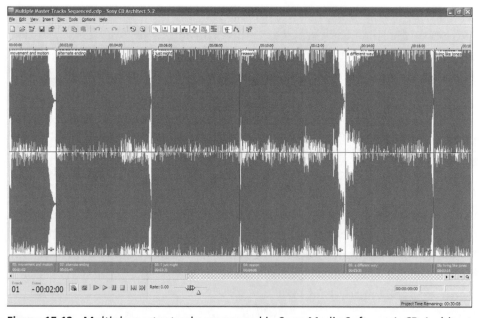

Figure 15.12   Multiple master tracks sequenced in Sony Media Software's CD Architect.

understand that most listeners judge loudness based on the average volume, not whether each track pins 0 dB on the level meter. Each track's volume will have to be attenuated for continuity. A drastic volume difference between two tracks will be most noticeable during the transition from one song to the next, so this is a good place to focus your continuity efforts. Listen to the end of each track as it transitions to the next, and make sure the volume levels of the beginning and end of each song are comfortable to listen to as they flow together. Be aware that reducing the volume of a rendered 16-bit track will actually reduce the resolution of the audio file. So, at this point, if any drastic volume changes are necessary in order for one track to flow comfortably to the next, you may want to go back to the pre-rendered master track to make the adjustment there.

When the layout is complete, the track spacing and names are in order, and the volume seems consistent overall, it's time to burn the master discs! There is really no trick to this. The disc must be burned and finalized in disc-at-once mode to ensure continuous burning. I recommend using a slower burn speed than your CD burner is capable of. Although a higher speed will save time and generally put out a good-quality disc, reducing the burn speed to 4x, 2x, or 1x will up your chances of getting a higher-quality disc and offer a lower error rate during the burn. I like to provide the client with three copies of their disc—two for the replication facility and one for the client to keep. I then archive the CD sequencing session, just in case I need to burn another copy for some reason.

Track-at-Once versus Disc-at-Once   When creating a master audio disc, there are two modes with which you can burn a CD: track-at-once and disc-at-once. In digital audio, it is recommended that you use disc-at-once mode.

When CDs are burned using track-at-once mode, the laser in your CD burner burns one track, then stops. When it stops, two blocks of miscellaneous data are written. After that, one link block and four run-in blocks are written when the laser begins writing the next track. These blocks may actually cause a click at the beginning of each track when played back in certain CD players.

With disc-at-once mode, the laser never stops, and there are no blocks of data written between tracks. If there is no extra data, then there are no extra clicks in the audio.

Track-at-once mode is fine if you're burning a CD for personal enjoyment, but disc-at-once is really the only option for professional CDs that will be sent to a replication facility.

There may be occasions when your client *doesn't* want you to sequence their project. In such a case, I will usually provide them with two copies of a data disc that contain both the 16-bit, 44.1-kHz versions of their masters, as well as high-quality MP3s, so they can do what they want with the tracks. After the master tracks have been delivered in their final format, I recommend archiving the final mixes, masters, and any project-related multitrack files on an external hard drive and in a dedicated project folder. More than once I've given master tracks to a client, only to have them call me a few weeks later asking for another copy of their files for one reason or another.

And that, ladies and gentlemen, concludes the mastering primer portion of this book. You're well on your way to understanding the finer details of the prestigious craft of mastering audio. Now let's wrap it up with a quick look at some mastering dos and don'ts.

Mastering Dos and Don'ts

Welcome to "Mastering Dos and Don'ts"! Now that we've covered the basic processes and discussed different ideas regarding how to go about accomplishing each one, I'll point out a couple of blanket rules to follow and some pitfalls to avoid. The so-called standards of the digital audio world are constantly fluctuating, so it's difficult to say that anything I've said here is a digital audio commandment. Everything in this chapter is a suggestion derived from the principles of working with digital audio and my own experience. So take a look at some of these suggestions and consider them as you begin mastering projects yourself.

Dos

- **Compress with the best of them.** Compression will always be an important part of mastering audio. You need to make sure you use it correctly. You want to make sure the mix sounds balanced and pump-free while maintaining the proper amount of volume, punch, unity, and power needed to get the point across. When applying compression, be sure that it's appropriate for the source. Certain styles and tempos require more or less compression than others.

- **Apply EQ conservatively.** If you are adding or subtracting an excess of +6 dB of any frequency to a mastering job, chances are that the recording or mix itself is flawed. Typically, you should be adding a decibel or two over very small areas of the frequency spectrum in order to make the master as rich as possible. Aggressive equalization is for the input and mixing stages of recording. Mastering EQ is just the frosting on the cake. A little bit of EQ goes a long way and can change an entire mix if you aren't careful. Yes, there will be the occasional project from "Joe's Talent-Free Garage" that may require +4 dB of low end because you are the first glimpse of a professional that the audio has seen so far. Hopefully, those situations will be few and far between.

- **Dare to compare.** Always compare your mastered projects to those of finished commercial recordings. There's no way you will know how the audio will stack up unless you take the time to gain a realistic perspective. Take your master to the car, multi-disc CD changer, iPod, *and* computer, and pit it against a comparable commercial record. After a few A/B comparisons, it should be obvious what might be lacking. And if you don't hear anything obvious, you might be onto something!

- **Take breaks.** Taking breaks is also an important element in mastering. If you've been at a project for hours and your eyes are getting a little fuzzy or you can't hear the change you just made, take a break. Get something to eat and come back to it later. People who aren't into audio production don't understand that carefully listening to the same track over and over and *over* again, trying to make subtle adjustments that will improve the sound, is an endurance trial. Ear fatigue, sitting for long periods of time, and staring at a computer screen for hours on end are actually pretty exhausting activities. If you're starting to wear out and you aren't sure whether you're making the best decisions anymore, walk away from the project and do something unrelated for a while. Then you can come back with fresh ears and make better decisions that aren't clouded by your physical condition. I often take breaks from both mastering and mixing (or even writing this book!) by taking a walk, going to the beach, seeing a movie, or even taking a nap. Sometimes I won't even come back to it until the next day if my deadline permits it. With this in mind, make sure you budget yourself enough time for each mastering job and don't get in a rush. Clients (and referrals, for that matter) respond best to good work even if it takes a day or two longer than they'd like. Take care of the client *and* yourself.

Don'ts

- **Don't over-compress audio.** Compression is a great thing. It's a primary component of mastering and essential in getting your audio to sound more professional, but it *can* be overdone. In mastering, if you start to hear a mix being crushed, seemingly overdriven, or pumped, stop right where you are. This may be a good time to either evaluate exactly what you're doing or revert back to the last good change you made. In mixing, you can over-compress for effect, but in mastering that is never the case. The moment compression starts to make the mix sound unnatural or weird, take a step back and figure out how to make it sound natural again. Remember, you're trying to enhance the sound of the audio, not make it worse. There is a world of difference between a good application of compression and a crappy one. And there really are no excuses for letting a bad master slip through your fingers and into your client's hands.

- **Don't go crazy with reverb and stereo imaging effects.** Stereo image and space have more to do with mixing than mastering. So be aware that if you choose to use spatial widening and stereo image enhancement effects, use them sparingly. There is really only so much that they can mask, let alone completely fix, in a mix. Just like any other effect, the overuse of stereo image enhancement can seriously damage the audio if you're not careful. A good mix shouldn't require stereo image enhancement at all. If you find that your mixes are not up to par in the stereo imaging department, it's in your best interest to heal the wound rather than simply putting a Band-Aid on it. Work on your mixing first, and then master stereo image enhancement just in case you need it.

- **Don't clip audio so hard that it stays crunchy in milk.** Don't turn up the master fader for the sake of getting more volume. If you find that you are clipping when you try to match the volume of other commercial recordings, leave the fader alone and look to the compressor, the equalization job, and the mix itself. There is no reason why you can't obtain a good *loud* master from a good mix using primarily compression and limiting. Also, realize that just because records are getting louder and louder by release, that doesn't mean you have jump on the bandwagon and make your mixes so loud that they actually hurt a little. Try to find a good balance between volume, clarity, and dynamics.

That does it for dos and don'ts. If you're reading this book from cover to cover, you're now in the home stretch. In the next chapter, we'll be discussing the business side of running a post-production project studio. It'll be a short one, so hang in there.

Project Studio Business

16 Operating Your Project Studio

All right, so now that you've been honing your post-production skills, it's time to put them to work for you. Sure, the reward of a great-sounding recording is enough...but why not make some money while you're at it? Now, I know that you gotta do what you gotta do to keep food on the table and the bills paid. In the beginning, we all do. But, in order to make your project studio a go, you must be dedicated to it. When someone asks what you do, you no longer answer with your day job...even if you have to have one. Your time and effort must be focused on bringing in business, improving and keeping your audio-production skills sharp, and making your clients happy. Anything you do outside of that is your second job.

There are many things to consider when running a project studio. Know that not all your time will be spent mixing, editing, and mastering. In a regular business with several employees, you have a marketing department to handle advertising, a sales department to bring in new clients, an accounting department to manage business finances, a project management team to oversee project schedules and planning, as well as a customer service department to help support and maintain client relationships. In the beginning, you'll probably spend 40 to 50 percent of your time finding new business and doing administrative work. After you have some projects under your belt, you will most likely start to get more projects from referrals, and the amount of time you spend harvesting work and doing administrative stuff will decrease Then you can focus more on the production end of your business. Which is the real reason we're here in the first place, right?

There are several different types of projects you could take on with your finely tuned skills and your new project studio. You could do anything from multistage processes, such as editing samples or mixing and mastering multitrack projects, to more simple tasks, such as audio enhancement, restoration, format conversions, and much more. The important thing to remember is this: *Don't limit yourself*! You and your studio may be capable of things you haven't even thought of yet. When you're out there looking for projects to work on, go for anything you think you might be able to do. You should know by the end of the initial consultation whether you can *really* handle the job. If you can't, don't try to fake it. But if you can, then WOO HOO!!! More experience for you…and I guess the money is cool, too.

In this chapter, we'll discuss the "shop" end of a project studio. We'll talk about getting your studio ready for business, putting yourself out there, advertising, finding clients, developing your sales pitch, structuring your pricing, and more. Starting your own revenue-generating project studio is not easy, but with hard work and dedication, it *is* possible. So hang in there. Your studio will be successful if that's what you really want.

Getting Started

There are a few preparations you should make before opening your doors for business. Your studio must be ready to receive clients. And when they get there, you should have something you can show them as you discuss their project. Your first meeting with a client will be very much like an interview. The client will want to know whether you can handle the work professionally. If a client leaves your studio after the initial meeting and feels uncomfortable or uneasy in any way, you probably won't get the job, regardless of how capable you are.

We'll discuss a few things you can do to prepare your studio to make a good impression on anyone who visits it. Granted, there may be occasions when you are simply outbid or limited by the hardware or software in your studio, but with a professional attitude, expertise, and good presentation, there shouldn't be any project, within reason, that you can't get.

The Presentation

The presentation of a project studio is often overlooked. After all, we're musicians and engineers, not interior designers. However, it's important that your studio conveys a certain level of professionalism to a client or a potential client.

It is very common for a project studio to exist in a second bedroom, a guesthouse, or a garage. This is totally fine, but realize that you may occasionally have a client visit your studio during the courtship period, or when you're initially trying to land a project, and during the course of a project. It's important to maintain a professional atmosphere in your studio. For the client, it will only reinforce your ability to do the work in a professional manner. And for you, it identifies your studio as a working environment, a temple of creativity where you turn out the best-sounding productions in the world! Besides, it will make you look cool in front of your friends.

I know that what your studio looks like should have zero bearing on your actual ability or the quality of your work, but first impressions really *do* matter. If a potential client walks into a studio where your dirty socks are lying on the floor, your empty soda cans line the window sills, and you're using old milk crates as a keyboard stand, chances are they will mentally move on to the next studio, regardless of what you say you can do.

Do your best to make your studio presentable. See that it is always clean (well, at least most of the time) and well organized. Create a comfortable space, especially for your clients, such as a sitting area (if the square footage permits) or a special "client chair" that clients will always use when they visit you. Try to arrange your workstation so that if your client needs to be present for their project, they can easily see the computer display and follow what's going on. You want visitors to feel comfortable in your studio—not like they are at the DMV, where it's cold, impersonal, and makes them feel like they are only waiting to be ushered in and out. The more comfortable your clients feel, the more likely it is that they will want to return or will tell others what it's like to work in your studio. In the end, that means more business for you.

I like my studio to look different than the rest of the dwelling it's part of. If your situation permits, cosmetic enhancements, such as painting the walls a different color, implementing different lighting solutions, using window treatments, and so on, can be effective ways to remove your studio space from the rest of the house. It also removes *you* from your day to day. This can have the same psychological effect (for both you *and* your client) as watching a movie in a movie theatre. When the movie is onscreen and the rest of the room is pitch-black, you know that it's time to watch the movie. No one should be talking on the phone, text-messaging, or doing anything else that distracts from the reason you are there. While watching, you can become so engaged in the movie that you may even forget you're in a theatre at all. (Until, of course, the lights come up and everyone files out into a blast of day-light that snaps you back to reality.)

Aesthetically separating your studio can suggest that you've crossed over into a professional and productive space that is different than where you live your everyday life. In the studio, it's time to focus on your work without distraction. You may even increase your produc-tivity by making the distinction between your home and your office. It's true that upping the swankiness factor of your studio is mostly psychological, but it will also make a good first impression on your client and suggest that you're both there to work.

More Visuals

I think it's safe to say that most people these days respond well to dif-ferent or multiple types of sensory input. So aside from making your studio look pretty, it's a good idea to have some sort of presentation ready for a potential client. This is in preparation for the pitch, which will be discussed later in this chapter, in the "Getting Clients" section.

After your first discussion about a project, you should have an idea of what the client will come to your studio for. I like to prepare some kind of visual presentation that I can walk through with the client. This can make a greater impact than simply discussing the project without any visuals. If they want me to mix a project, I typically call up a project that I've mixed before and show them the sequencer win-dows, effects, and mixer section of the software I use. And if you don't have a project that you've already mixed handy, just make one that you can use over and over again. It's worth a little bit of extra time to do so.

If the client wants me to master a project, I'll call up my wave editor or CD-sequencing software and click around to different effects, zoom in and out, and maybe apply a quick fade or two with very *brief* explanations, just to give the client an idea of what will occur with their project. Don't provide so little information that it seems as if you have no idea what you're doing, but don't provide so much detail that it confuses the client. Just say enough to let them know that their project will be in good hands with you. Offering this kind of visual presentation to go along with what you say can be a very powerful combination when you are trying to cement a project with a client.

What's in a Name?

Choosing a name can be one of the most difficult parts of having a studio. Your name is a key element of your studio's identity that will influence your logo; go on your business cards, invoices, and webpage; and, in some cases, even determine how you answer the phone. Most people want to name their new studio something that has significant personal meaning. You may spend weeks trying to come up with a name that you feel conveys the right message about what you do, but then when you go to reserve the web address or register your business name, it's taken! It may be a disappointment, but we must persevere. Sit down and make a long list of potential names. Get feedback from people whose opinions your respect.

Continue brainstorming until you find a name that inspires and is suitable for its given purpose. Sure, "Fuzzy Bunny Productions" sounds good at first, but then you realize that the name and a logo will be printed and will appear on *everything* related to your studio. Be sure that you can live with the name you choose. In the end, having a business name for your studio will make your potential clients feel a little more comfortable about what they are getting into with you. Knowing that you are some sort of business entity carries a bit more weight than simply being Joe Engineer. This will greatly enhance the professional presence of your studio.

1-800-Contact

Your studio is almost ready to open its doors, but there are still a couple more optional preparations you can make. First, you may want to consider having a dedicated phone number. It's nice to be able to separate your studio phone from your home phone, especially if you don't live alone. These days, it's very easy and inexpensive to maintain a second landline, although I don't necessarily advocate keeping a ringing handset within the studio walls for obvious reasons. If you *do* keep a handset in your studio, turn the ringer and the volume off when you're in session. You could also get a cellular phone or a second line added to your current cellular service for a small additional fee, in most cases. However, if you get poor reception where your studio is located, this may not be the best solution for you.

Another option for a dedicated phone number for your studio is VoIP, or *Voice over Internet Protocol*. These are Internet telephony services, such as Skype or Vonage, that allow you to make calls to anywhere in the world over a broadband connection. Internet telephony is fairly inexpensive, but rates vary from provider to provider, so be sure to do some research. VoIP services typically offer a full range of features, such as voicemail, personalized greetings, and optional handsets that can function without being connected to a computer. Client-to-client (computer-to-computer) calls may even allow video conferencing so that you can look right in the eyes of the person to whom you're talking. The downside is that VoIP requires and relies on a broadband Internet connection, which means that if your Internet is down, so is your phone. You may want to consider that in your calculations when deciding on the best option for a dedicated studio phone.

Another optional preparation you can make is to separate your studio address from your home address. I'm not talking about tearing down walls or renting studio space. I'm talking about mailing addresses. Often, it's easier to filter all your studio business–related mail to a P.O. box. This serves a dual purpose because it also helps protect your privacy. P.O. boxes are fairly inexpensive and can be useful in maintaining your studio's "location," even if you decide to physically move your studio somewhere else. Try to find a P.O. box service that has a *real* street address rather than a P.O. box number. Having a real street address can provide a more professional image for your studio business.

Now that you've got a name, number, and address, your studio is ready to show, and you're ready to show it. Now it's time to find some clients.

Getting Clients

Potential clients are everywhere. You never know where you might find someone who may be in need of your services. I've gotten work from everyone from my chiropractor to those I've stood in line with at the bank. By no means do I consider myself to be a saleswoman. In fact, I loathe the idea of schmoozing with strangers for the sake of networking my way into a paycheck. However, I do believe that your next client *could* be sitting right next to you. They just don't know it yet.

Making what you do known is the single most important factor in generating business. I call it putting yourself on the radar. Who will enlist your services if they don't know what you do or even that you exist? When someone asks you what you're up to these days, tell them! If the person you're talking to doesn't need your services, someone they know might.

It doesn't have to be a well-rehearsed sales pitch, either. In fact, it may happen more naturally than you think. When I made the decision to open a project studio, the first thing I did was have some business cards made up. Then, I let *everyone* know that my plans were to open a project studio doing audio post-production work. First I told my cow-orkers, friends, and family. Then I started to see the opportunity to discuss it when I met new people who asked what I did for a living. Each discussion would end with a business card. Pretty soon, I was getting calls here and there from people with whom I was acquainted, then more calls from people they'd referred, and then even more people who were referred by *those* people!

So how do you give yourself visibility that will bring potential clients right to your doorstep? Advertising is helpful. A good website is invaluable. And a demonstration of your work will communicate more to a future prospect than anything you can say. Let's take a look at different ways to help put you on the radar.

Advertising

Advertising is a major preliminary step in bringing new business to your studio. Without it, no one will ever hear about you or what you do. Promoting your studio is no small task. It will take a great amount of effort to possibly gain only a marginal return. But the return *could* be the key to forming an initial client base, which will lead to referrals, which means more business for you. The larger your client base, the better off you will be. Advertising is one of the most effective ways to get the word out about you and what you have to offer.

Before you do anything else, get yourself some business cards. Even if you don't have any of your other marketing materials ready yet, a business card is a great way to give someone your contact information. Your business card will typically include your studio's name and logo, as well as your name, position, address, phone number, email, and website address. Every good conversation you have with someone about you, your studio, or what you do should end with a business card. I realize that getting used to handing out business cards might feel a little awkward at first if you've never done it before, but again, this is something that often occurs more naturally than you might think. Don't be afraid to leave something people can remember you by.

Flyers are another method of advertising. When you're first starting out, you can make yourself some 8.5×11″ (or some other size) flyers that have information such as your studio name, your logo, the services you provide, and your contact information. Most music stores have a bulletin board of some kind where musicians can post ads for band members, instrument sales, and music services. This is the perfect place to put a flyer.

Local music publications often have a section where you submit ads for music services. You'll usually get a very limited number of words to explain what you have to offer and how people can contact you. However, although this occasionally proves to be effective, I've gotten some *really* strange calls from some *really* strange people this way. Then again, I've gotten some really good work from some relatively normal people this way. I placed quite a few ads when I started my first project studio. I would say that 70 percent of the calls I got were from people who had innocent inquiries, 10 percent were total kooks, and about 20 percent ended up leading to paying work. From all that, I gained four regular clients who are still with me today. I kind of sit on the fence about *placing* ads because the ratio of paying work to dead-end leads is low. However, this is something you may want to try and make up your own mind about.

So far, the methods we've discussed are ways of getting the work to come to you. Now it's time to go out and find the work. *Cold calling* is a term that is used often in sales departments around the world for tracking down leads and making the first contact with a potential client. You can find leads pretty much anywhere. If someone makes a passing comment about an audio-related project they'd like to do in the future, you can give them a business card, get their contact info, and call them in a few weeks to see whether they've given any more thought to it. You can use websites, such as Craigslist, or music publications to find people and companies that may be in need of your specific services. Answering an ad usually pans out a little better than placing an ad, but try to treat it as if you're applying for any other job. Put your best foot forward and proceed cautiously.

Another way to creatively solicit clients is to find businesses that specialize in sound, video, or gaming projects and reach out to them. Find out what their audio production needs might be and let them know that your services are available. If they don't need anything now, they may need something later. But again, they'll never know or think to call you unless you give yourself some visibility with them. Cold calling is where a great demo and website *really* come into play, so let's discuss those next.

Demo

Few things have a greater impact than a fantastic demo. Ever heard the saying that "the proof is in the pudding?" Well, your demo is the "pudding." For the client, it's tangible evidence of your capabilities. For you, it's a paperless resume.

Your demo should be organized based on the type of work you want to do. For example, a film composer would probably have a fairly cinematic demo with dramatic orchestral pieces. A video game composer would have examples of everything from high-energy to playful selections. As a post-production engineer, you will most likely want examples of projects that you've mixed and mastered on your demo. Only your best work should make the cut. Limit the track count to four or five pieces that really shine. That should be enough material to give a future client an idea about your work. Most people won't take the time to carefully listen to 20 tracks of audio, so try to consolidate everything they need to hear into a handful of great examples.

The presentation of your demo is something that you should consider carefully. A clean, professional-looking package will say something very different about you and your work than a CD-R labeled in your own handwriting and wrapped in a cocktail napkin. Although the packaging of your demo disc isn't as important as what is on it, it never hurts to make the "pudding" look nice.

The most common format for a demo CD is a regular audio CD that can be played back in any standard CD player. Label it…and not with a permanent marker. Get yourself some printable CDs—or, at the very least, printable CD labels that you can customize. Put your logo and contact information directly on the disc face. Print the track list for the CD insert with the name of the project, the date of the project, and your role in it. Create a nice front cover for the disc jacket or case that bears your logo and says what's inside. If you want to go that extra mile, you can have demo CDs professionally designed, replicated, and packaged to make a really good impression on your potential client. Remember that your demo is an important component in the marketing materials you'll use to promote your studio. Do your best to make it sound *and* look good.

The Internet is a crazy thing. The potential audience for any information you want to provide is, in a word, vast. People on the other side of the globe, where toilets flush backward, can access your website in an instant. With such a powerful marketing tool at your disposal, it's a good idea to incorporate your demo into your website. That way, your work can easily be heard by anyone who visits your page. Each time you hand out a business card, put up a flyer, make a cold call, or reach out to a potential client, there is a good chance that the client will end up visiting your website. They may even share the link with someone they know, giving you even more exposure. It makes sense to have examples of your work available for them to hear. Speaking of websites, let's move on to our next topic.

Website

Your web presence is an important part of your studio's identity. With the way the world is today, nearly everyone has access to the Internet. Your webpage will provide an endless sea of potential clients the ability to effortlessly find information about you and your services. Your webpage should be attractive and informative, providing enough information to get clients interested so they ultimately want to contact you about their project. The presentation and information on your site can often be the first impression that a potential client has of you, so you want to be sure that you're getting the right message across.

Before putting up your website, you may want visit other audio-production sites. Take a look at the kind of information they provide and how they structure it. This will help you get a better idea about what you want your site to look like. If you don't already have some web-design experience, it may be best to enlist a friend who does. If you don't know any web designers, you can buy inexpensive, easy-to-use webpage kits or website templates that you can modify yourself.

Your webpage should contain information such as your background experience, the background of your studio, the services you offer, media examples of your work, and a way to contact you for more information. Try to choose color schemes that are pleasant to look at. Avoid using links that direct the viewer away from your page. Be wary of using pop-up windows as a means to access more information on your site. Most people employ a utility to block pop-up advertisements, and it won't know the difference between your information and an ad. Remember that someone who visits your site wants to quickly get the information they came for. Try to avoid using design elements that take a long time to load or excessive copy that takes a long time to read. Your website will be an advertisement that works for you 24 hours a day, so the sooner you get one, the better.

A quick way to create a web portal for self-promotion is to use networking community sites such as MySpace, Tribe, or Facebook. If your website seems like it might be a ways off from being launched, this is a great way to gain exposure right *now*. These communities allow you to connect with a large network of people who are in need of your specific talents. You can typically post information about your studio and the services you offer, audio examples, photos, contact information, and much more. Additionally, potential clients can send you messages through the site itself while keeping your actual email address private. A community page takes little or no web design experience and is easy to maintain. Many studios have a MySpace page to supplement their existing site. Some studios *only* maintain a community page, as it can be a great alternative to having a traditional website. Whether or not you choose to have a "proper" website, I highly recommend starting a page in one or all of the aforementioned web communities to help increase the amount of exposure your studio gets.

In many scenarios, your web presence may be the *only* thing a client has to go on. Although a good webpage is definitely a strong marketing tool, it can't do the talking for you. Which brings us to our next topic—the pitch.

The Pitch

As I mentioned previously, the first time you meet a prospective client in your studio or talk to them on the phone, it'll be a lot like a job interview. It's basically a consultation that occurs after you make the first contact and before you have the actual job. During this consultation, you'll discuss the details and parameters of the work. You need to find out what the project entails and what it's for. What is the timeline? How does it need to be delivered? The more information you can gather about the project, the better off you'll be. Take notes. Ask the right questions and pay close attention to the answers. If you listen twice as much as you speak, there should rarely be any misunderstandings between you and your client.

Aside from discussing the project, a client may also want information about you. Be prepared to give a background on your studio and experience. It's important for your potential client to know that you're not just some crackhead who is going to run off with their money. Musicians or other people in the entertainment industry in general have kind of a bad reputation for being flaky and unreliable. Whether or not this is true, you need the client to understand that *you* are not like that. Any indication you can give them about your long-term commitment to your studio, your profession, and developing a working relationship with them will help them feel more comfortable about entering into a business arrangement with you.

While it's not unheard of to use your words creatively when pitching to clients, don't make stuff up. It will serve you best to be straightforward and honest with them about all things related to their project. They should never feel as if you're dodging a question, *especially* during the initial consultation. The idea is to let clients know that you are capable of handling their project in a professional manner and that they can trust you as an individual.

If the client is in your studio, you can use your prepared presentation project as a visual aid. If the initial consultation takes place over the phone, you will want to direct the client to your website so they can do a bit more research on their own if they don't decide to hire you immediately. In such a case, follow up. Give them a week or so and call them back to see whether they've made a decision. They'll either tell you they want to hire you or that they went with someone else. Either way, the initial consultation will gain closure, and you can move forward accordingly.

At the end of the pitching process, give your potential clients the opportunity to ask any unanswered questions. If they can't think of any, you've probably done a pretty good job. If they bombard you with questions, write them down and answer them. Then return to your notes later to see whether you need to change the information that you cover in your pitch. Your potential client may ask common questions that you didn't even think of or that you just overlooked. Use this feedback to improve your consultation pitch. Regardless of whether additional questions are asked, let clients know that they can always contact you if they think of anything else. The consultation should end with a business card if they don't already have one.

Pricing

The conversation about monetary compensation for a project is part of the initial consultation. The conversation cannot end without defining what you want to be paid to do the work. In the beginning, pricing can be a very difficult topic to discuss because you may have no idea about how to charge for your services. One way to alleviate this problem is to do some undercover groundwork by calling around to other post-production studios and getting quotes on what the average rate is for the specific services you plan to offer. That way, when you propose your rate to the client, you will know that you aren't far from the industry mark. Once you know where the standard is, you can adjust your rates however you wish.

In determining your pricing, there is far more to consider than simply what the other guys are doing. You'll want to come up with a figure that covers your studio's operating expenses (electricity, heat, drive time for off-site consultations, and so on), compensates you adequately for your time (your desired hourly rate), and allows you to earn at least *some* profit for the business as a whole. Remember that when you are working for yourself, you have to manage your own taxes. This is why independent contractors are typically more costly by the hour than onsite employees. It's a good idea to consult a tax advisor to find out what approximate tax percentage you will have to pay as a contractor in your state. You can't really base your compensation on this information, but you can keep it in mind to calculate what you'll *actually* be making after taxes.

In negotiating your price, you can start above what you hope to get. But realize that it's a competitive market. If your starting price is higher than the next studio, your negotiation tactic may not even be put to the test. See whether you can find out what the client's budget is and try to work with that. If it seems like your initial price is too high, let the client know that you'd like to do what you can to make it affordable for them and start to negotiate down.

In the beginning, it may seem as if taking any and every job, regardless of what it pays, would be a good idea for the sake of building credibility, but the reality of it is that if you take a job that pays less than you need to make in order to cover your costs and turn at least a *small* profit, you're actually losing money. Also, having a reputation for being the cheapest studio around town isn't necessarily a good thing. Something else that you can negotiate is a production credit. If you feel as if a project is going to be stellar and it is worth taking the financial hit to be associated with it, you can try to strike a deal with the client to work for slightly less money, but to be given a production credit on the project. It's also not unheard of to work on a project for free if the name credit will be worthwhile, but only you can be the judge of whether it's truly worth it.

Finally, you'll want to define a payment schedule. Sometimes clients want to write one big check instead of writing several checks for smaller amounts. The problem is that they never want to write a big check up front. For the sake of motivating you to work on their project and keeping yourself alive, I'd suggest negotiating a payment schedule. Payment schedules are great when you're doing a project for a flat rate or a predetermined dollar amount that isn't dependent on the number of hours you put into the project. Once you've decided on the total amount you will be paid, divide that number by four. This will be the payment that must be submitted each time you complete 25 percent of the project, or each time that 25 percent of the total project timeline has passed.

Requesting a payment schedule instead of a one-time lump sum helps keep the money rolling in so it doesn't feel as if you're working for free *forever*, until the project is finished and you can finally get paid. And some clients prefer to pay smaller amounts of money out of their budgets, especially if the project is expected to span more than a month's time. Some independent contractors *like* to get one big check at the end of a project. Me? I like to eat…. If you like to eat too, then you may want to consider establishing a payment schedule with your clients.

An alternative to a payment schedule is to bill the client hourly. Once you've both agreed on an hourly rate, you will most likely send the client an invoice for the hours you've worked on their project weekly or biweekly. However, the chance that comes with any billing situation in which you have to submit an invoice, wait for it to get processed, and wait for a check to be cut and then "snail-mailed" out to you is something we call *slow pay*. It's pretty much the downside to being an independent contractor. You never know exactly when that next check is going to show up. Some client organizations can take up to 30 days or more just to *cut* your check. On the other hand, there are some clients that can have you paid within a week.

This situation poses an obvious challenge in that you have to keep extremely tight tabs on your finances and who owes you what. It's a little more difficult to try to collect from an individual client, but with client corporations, you can contact their accounting departments or your internal project contact and inquire as to the status of your payments. They pretty much expect you to do it, so don't be afraid to go after your money when it's due. Also, as a safety precaution, you can make a note somewhere on your invoice stating that if the invoice isn't paid within X number of days, a service fee will be charged for each day that the payment is late. Fifteen or thirty days is a typical grace period for payment, and the average service charge is around 1.5 percent. If the idea that paying late will cost more money doesn't encourage the client to pay your invoice in a timely manner, then I don't know what will.

Now that we've got money out of the way, it's time to move on to a bunch of little pieces of paper that turn all this talk into a binding legal agreement. Oh, scary…not really.

Paperwork

Your potential client has now become your client. As far as they're concerned, you are the right man or woman for the job. They loved your pitch. You've even agreed on monetary compensation. So now what?

Contracts

The first thing that needs to be established is a contract. When you're working for an individual (meaning a person who is not part of a business entity), you may have to generate a work-for-hire contract to cement the agreement. When you're working for an established company that has their own lawyers and such, they will often draw up their own contract and present it to you to be signed.

Work-for-Hire Agreements

A work-for-hire agreement states that you are being hired to work on a specific project for a specific amount of time and a specific amount of money. For the post-production engineer, these types of agreements are typically pretty safe and straightforward, even though all that legal jargon can make them look a bit intimidating. If you have any doubts about the terms of a work-for-hire agreement that your client has provided you with, you may want to do some additional research or even enlist some legal advice until you are comfortable with understanding this type of contract.

Nondisclosure Agreements (NDAs)

Another piece of paper that you may run into is a nondisclosure agreement, or *NDA*. An NDA, also called a *confidentiality agreement,* is a legal agreement in which the signing party agrees not to disclose or improperly use any confidential materials or information that may be relayed by the organization that sets it forth. These are more common when you're doing work for an established business. You usually won't run into these when you're working for an individual person; however, it's not entirely unheard of. An NDA is usually no big deal, as long as you don't go blabbing information about a project and the company to everyone and their dog. Even if you don't speak legalese, you're probably pretty safe with a standard NDA. However, you should make sure that you thoroughly read all legal documents and that you understand the terms prior to signing.

Billing

After a contract (and, in some cases, an NDA) has been signed, you'll proceed with the project as discussed between you and the client. The next step is billing. Typically, an invoice must be submitted for you to get paid, especially if you're doing work for a business entity. You'll want to prepare an invoice according to the payment schedule that has been outlined in your contract. The invoice you submit should include the following information:

- Your contact information
  - Your business name
  - Your full name as the contact
  - Your business address
  - Your business phone number
  - Your business email address (optional)
- Your client's contact information
  - The client's business name
  - The client's contact name
  - The client's address
  - The client's phone number
  - The client's e-mail address (optional)
- Invoice information
  - The invoice number
  - The invoice date
  - A description of the work
  - The payment amount

Taxes

If you are generating revenue with your project studio, there are a couple of things that you will need to consider. First, taxes. You're an independent contractor now, which means that you are responsible for paying income tax on any monies generated by your project studio. This is even the case if you still maintain a full-time day job. The reason is that as an independent contractor, taxes are not automatically deducted from the checks you receive. You are basically being paid the net amount agreed upon, and you will be expected to report it at the end of the year. This is pretty much unavoidable. I can't stress enough the importance of knowing what you're getting yourself into with self-employment. I highly recommend consulting a tax advisor to learn about self-employment taxes to avoid any unpleasant surprises down the road.

Incorporation

A second consideration is incorporation. *Incorporation* refers to the forming of a new corporation or an official business entity. If business is booming, it may be in your best interest to become incorporated. Some people choose to become legally incorporated from the get-go. The primary benefits of becoming incorporated for a project studio owner are protection of personal assets, tax benefits, and business credibility.

Protection of personal assets means that whatever debt is accumulated by the corporation is the sole responsibility of the corporation. In this scenario, if for some reason the business were to get into debt and then fail, a creditor could not seize your personal assets for repayment. The tax benefits come in the form of write-offs. You can write off everything from the space in your home in which the studio is operated to meals for entertaining clients. Corporations are also typically taxed at a lower rate than individuals.

Finally, business credibility, or the words "Inc." or "Corp." in your business name, will help convey the positive idea of long-term stability for your business. There are a few other positive benefits to incorporation as well, such as a dedicated credit rating for your corporation and the ability to set up retirement and health-insurance benefit plans.

Keep in mind that becoming incorporated has disadvantages, too. There is the burden of statutory and accounting compliances, the fees involved in becoming incorporated, and double taxation. A corporation with a single proprietor is also considered a high-risk business. This means that it may be a bit more difficult to get business loans or claim high capital losses. You should definitely do your homework when it comes to making the decision to become incorporated. It might not be the best avenue for every project studio, so I encourage you to carefully consider the pros and cons.

Keeping Clients and Being Successful

The reasons for maintaining good client relationships are obvious. You want your client not only to come back to you with more work, but also to say nice things about you to everyone they know. Good communication, customer service, diligence, and professionalism will contribute to the client's overall experience and ultimately result in more business for you. In this section, I'll discuss a few simple things you can do to help keep the clients you bring in and find new ones.

Customer Service

Customer service is an enormous part of maintaining good client relationships. I think we've probably all experienced our share of poor customer-service moments. Consider how those moments made you feel. Did you complain? Did you want to return to the establishment after all was said and done? The bottom line is that there is no excuse for poor customer service. Even if you've had the worst day of your life, you can't take it out on your clients. They *won't* understand. I'm not saying you should be a soulless robot with a permanent smile, but your actions represent your studio, and it's important to maintain a certain level of professionalism at all times.

The basic concept of good customer service is simple: Treat your clients the way that you would want to be treated. Always give them the courtesy and respect they deserve. Always answer your phone. Establish good communication. This will not only keep you well informed, but it will also build rapport. Really listen to what your client wants and has to say about the project. Again, listen twice as much as you speak. Be helpful in answering questions, even if they don't immediately lead somewhere. Return calls and respond to emails with a sense of urgency. Provide the occasional unsolicited status update. Avoid long periods of silence between you and the client during the course of a project. Never leave them hanging. If any issues arise, do you best to squash them ASAP. And, this may seem obvious, but try to avoid arguing with a client at all costs.

Good customer service doesn't have to be a chore. It may come more naturally than you realize. You may not even really have to think about it after a while. Just do your best to keep your clients happy so that when they leave your studio, they look forward to coming back.

Follow Up

Following up with your clients is an incredibly simple task that will greatly enhance your client relations. There are quite a few applications. Each time you have an involved conversation with your client, it's a good idea to provide a recap in an email so that your client can be clear about your understanding of what was discussed, and so that your client has in writing how you will proceed based on the conversation. This gives the client the ability to clarify in the event of any misunderstanding and shows the client that you are diligent and on top of their project. If a client asks a question that you don't know the answer to, see whether you can find the answer and get back to them. This shows the client that you're willing to put in a little extra effort.

If you are waiting on feedback or information from the client in order to proceed, give them time to respond, but if they don't get back to you within a reasonable timeframe, follow up with a friendly reminder. Clients get busy too. Sometimes they can let a callback slip their minds. But it doesn't mean that it's okay for you to do it, too.

Finally, when a project is over, don't be afraid to call the client back in a month or so to see whether there is anything you can help them with. Following up is a great professional practice that will help bolster your client's confidence in you, as well as earn you a reputation for excellence.

Time Management

Time management is also a big part of keeping your clients happy. It's easy—don't promise anything that you can't deliver. You *must* be realistic about the time you need to complete a project. When making this determination, you have to factor in the estimation of how many hours you can do the work in, then divide it by the number of hours you intend to work per day. That will give you the number of days the project will take. Then, from the project start date, count the number of actual working days, excluding weekends (unless of course you *want* to work weekends).

Excluding weekends serves multiple purposes. First, we've already established that no one is a machine and can work 24/7. Scheduling around weekends gives you a much-needed break on the weekends. Second, in the event that the project is running a bit behind, you can use the weekend days to catch up if necessary. However, if you provide a realistic timeframe to begin with and you stick to a daily work schedule, this shouldn't be a problem. But, we're not quite finished yet. I also like to consider that I may need to give my ears a rest once in a while. For every five days I work, I schedule one extra day (or at least a half of one extra day) in there. So, if I estimate that a project will take me 40 hours to complete, and I plan to work on it 8 hours a day, then the total project will take me 6 business days to complete. That gives me a five-day workweek, a weekend, and one more day to wrap it up.

Every engineer works a bit differently. In the beginning, timeframe estimation is a bit of a shot in the dark because you may not be sure how long it will take you complete certain types of projects, but try not to overextend yourself so that your schedule is rushed. It can be difficult to overlap projects. In the beginning, you should try to schedule new projects to start a few days *after* the previous project. You never know whether a project will run long for one reason or another. If a project runs short, you can move the schedule for the next project up if you wish.

Most clients will understand if a starting date needs to be rescheduled or you need a one- or two-day extension…*if* you ask for it. Most people understand that sometimes there are factors beyond your control that can affect the timeline. There are, of course, always exceptions. Suppose a client is trying to meet his or her own deadline based on when *you* say you can complete the project—in that case, you had better make good on it. Two days before the deadline is *not* a good time to ask for an extension. Although the client needs to understand that quality work takes time, they are putting faith in you to know what kind of schedule you can really handle. I've actually had to turn down projects because I *knew* that I would never be able to hit the target. Pay close attention to the duration of the initial projects you accept. It will help tune your barometer for gauging project timelines more accurately.

The last thing I'll say about time management is that operating a project studio takes discipline. You have to manage your schedule like a regular job. If it's your only job, you should make sure that you put in at *least* a full eight-hour day. If you still maintain a day job, you should allot yourself a realistic number of hours per week that you will dedicate to studio projects, and then spread them out over the days you intend to spend in the studio. Don't kill yourself. Try to give yourself a couple days off in a week. But persevere. If you treat your studio as if it's a job and not just a hobby, it will become your job…not just a hobby.

Progressive Education

Never stop learning. That sounds like a public service announcement, but almost nothing can benefit you or your studio more than staying ahead of the curve. Schedule some time in your week to do research on audio production techniques, learn about new software and hardware, and find new and creative ways to market and promote your business. Read lots of publications and books on the subject of audio production. Visit audio forums. Spend time sharpening your current skill set and developing more efficient ways to operate your studio. The extra effort and invaluable knowledge will make you an audio production guru and that much more employable.

That closes our chapter on the business end of operating a project studio, or, as I like to call it, "the dark side of the moon." In the end, I think you'll find that audio post-production is a gratifying skilled craft that you'll really enjoy. Every day is different and holds a new opportunity to solve complex problems with creativity, nerdy little discoveries around every corner, and the satisfaction of turning out projects that you can really be proud of. The next chapter will provide you with a plethora of resources to aid in the *many* post-production endeavors that lie ahead for you. I hope that I've provided enough useful information to help you develop a solid post-production foundation on which you can grow. Thanks for reading, and good luck!

17 Resources

Welcome to the resource section of *Audio Post-Production in Your Project Studio*. Herein lies a collection of websites, charts, diagrams, suggested reading and a glossary of terms that are mentioned and discussed throughout this book. I don't expect that you'll read this section from beginning to end, but give it a good look so that you know what it contains. Then, in the event that you need to quickly reference some of the information, you'll know exactly where to find it.

Diagrams

This section contains a few useful diagrams (Figures 17.1 through 17.5) that you can use as a quick reference in your studio. Some of them appeared earlier in the book. Their presence here is simply for convenience, so that you're not thumbing through trying to remember which page they were on.

Documents

In Chapter 16, I mentioned that there are a few legal documents that you will run into as you turn your post-production studio into a red-hot moneymaking machine. As you get more and more clients, you will find that these documents differ slightly from one client/employer to the next. In this section, I've provided examples of both an NDA and a work-for-hire agreement so that you can become familiar with what each entails. This may help in making all this wordy legal jib-jab a little less intimidating when you're presented with the real thing.

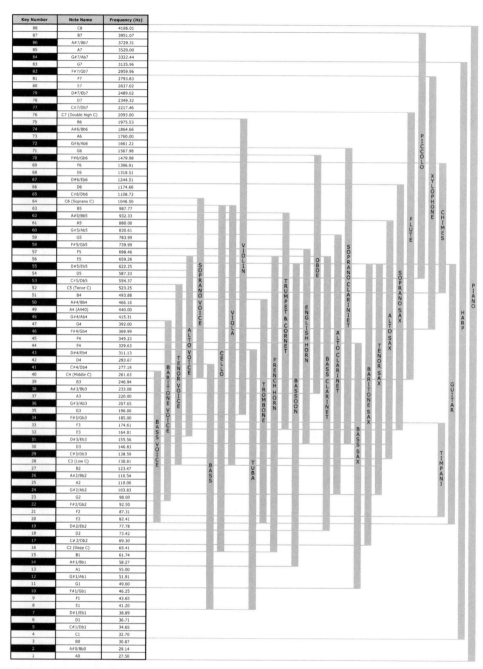

Figure 17.1 Note frequencies and instrument frequency ranges.

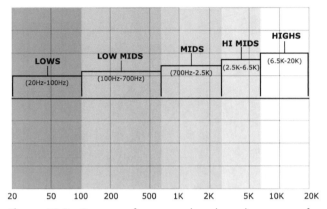

Figure 17.2 Common frequency bands and crossover frequencies.

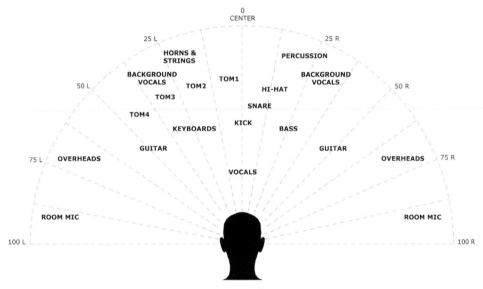

Figure 17.3 Common instrument placement for a stereo mix.

Non-Disclosure Agreement

First up is the non-disclosure agreement, or NDA. You'll encounter two primary types of NDAs—the unilateral and the bilateral. The unilateral NDA is a one-way agreement. It basically states that you will not disclose any information about the company or the individual you're working for, but they don't have to do the same. These are the far more common of the two agreements. Not to say your projects aren't important and don't deserve to be kept confidential, but before you shrug off a unilateral NDA, consider the chances of your client

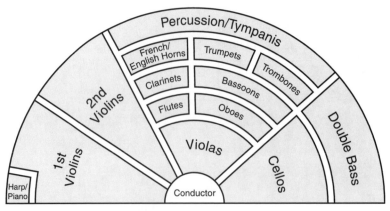

Figure 17.4 Common orchestra layout.

Sound Source	Approximate Decibel Level
Jet engine @ approx. 30m	150dB
Rifle shot @ approx. 1m	140dB
Threshold of pain	130dB
Hearing damage (due to short term exposure)	120dB
Jet plane @ 100m	110-140dB
Jackhammer @ 1m	100dB
Hearing damage (due to long term exposure)	85dB
Major street @ 10m	80-90dB
Passenger car @ 10m	60-80dB
TV set (average volume) @ 1m	60dB
Normal speech @ 1m	40-60dB
A very calm room or quiet computer fan	20-30dB
Leaves rustling or calm breathing	10dB

Figure 17.5 Decibel levels in the real world.

sharing information about your business and practices that could ultimately have a negative effect. Is it *absolutely* necessary to keep your other projects hush-hush? When you are an independent contractor running a post-production studio, this isn't typically a major concern. However, it's your call. You can either proceed with a unilateral NDA and get to work, or demand a bilateral NDA and see what happens. Personally, I'd probably go with the first option. In my experience, I've found that when dealing with a corporation or an established business entity, you will be presented with the unilateral NDA.

The second type of NDA is the bilateral NDA. This type of non-disclosure agreement basically states that neither signing party is allowed to disclose information that is deemed confidential. This is obviously the fairer of the two agreements. A bilateral NDA is more common when dealing with an individual, if they even ask for an NDA to be signed at all. Figure 17.6 provides an example of a bilateral NDA.

[COMPANY]

BILATERAL CONFIDENTIALITY AGREEMENT

This agreement is a BILATERAL CONFIDENTIALITY AGREEMENT by and between COMPANY, a [Company Name] ("COMPANY") with its principal place of business at [Address] and the corporation identified on the signature page hereto. The party disclosing confidential or proprietary information will be referred to as the "DISCLOSING PARTY" and the party receiving the confidential or proprietary information will be referred to as the "RECEIVING PARTY".

1. The parties anticipate that it may be necessary for the DISCLOSING PARTY to transfer to the RECEIVING PARTY information of a proprietary nature, including, but not limited to processes, trade secrets, customer lists, computer programs, hardware configurations and other business and technical practices and information of a confidential nature ("Proprietary Information"). The Proprietary Information relates to the following products/services of each DISCLOSING PARTY:

    COMPANY as DISCLOSING PARTY:

    [Description of information to be disclosed]

    [OTHER PARTY NAME] as DISCLOSING PARTY:

    [Description of information to be disclosed]

    The Proprietary Information will be used by the RECEIVING PARTY solely for evaluation of the DISCLOSING PARTY's products or for furthering the business relationship between the parties unless previously agreed to in writing by the DIS-CLOSING PARTY.

2. The RECEIVING PARTY agrees that it will not disclose any Proprietary Information to any other party (other than its employees who are directly participating in work involving the DISCLOSING PARTY's products and who are contractually bound to protect the confidentiality of such Proprietary Information), and that it will use its best efforts to prevent any such disclosure of Proprietary Information.

3. The limitations on disclosure or use of Proprietary Information shall not apply to, and the RECEIVING PARTY shall not be liable for disclosure or use of Proprietary

Information with respect to which the RECEIVING PARTY proves using tangible evidence that any of the following conditions exist: (a) If, prior to receipt thereof, it is lawfully known by the RECEIVING PARTY; (b) If, subsequent to the receipt thereof (i) it is published by the DISCLOSING PARTY or is disclosed by the DISCLOSING PARTY to others, without restriction, or (ii) it has been lawfully obtained by the RECEIVING PARTY from other sources, provided such other source did not receive it due to a breach of this Agreement or (iii) it otherwise comes within the public knowledge or becomes generally known to the public; (c) If, at any time, it has been developed independently by the RECEIVING PARTY without reference to Proprietary Information of the DISCLOSING PARTY.

4. The terms of confidentiality under this Agreement shall not be construed to limit either party's right to develop independently or acquire products without use of the other party's Proprietary Information. The parties acknowledge that the other may currently or in the future be developing information internally, or receiving information from other parties, that is similar to the Proprietary Information. Accordingly, nothing in this Agreement will prohibit either party from developing or having developed products, concepts, systems or techniques that are similar to or compete with the products, concepts, systems or techniques contemplated by or embodied in the Proprietary Information, provided that neither party uses any Proprietary Information of the other or otherwise violates any of its obligations under this Agreement in connection with such development.

5. All Proprietary Information shall be and remain the property of the DISCLOSING PARTY, and all embodiments and copies thereof, upon the written request of the DISCLOSING PARTY, shall be promptly returned to the DISCLOSING PARTY or destroyed (in which case the RECEIVING PARTY shall certify to the DISCLOSING PARTY as to its destruction), at the DISCLOSING PARTY's option.

6. Neither the execution and delivery of this Agreement, nor the furnishing of any Proprietary Information by the DISCLOSING PARTY shall be construed as granting to the RECEIVING PARTY either expressly, by implication, estoppel or otherwise, any license under any invention, patent, trademark, or copyright now or hereafter owned or controlled by the DISCLOSING PARTY.

7. The RECEIVING PARTY acknowledges that the DISCLOSING PARTY's products and technical data must be licensed for export under the regulations of the United States Department of Commerce. Regardless of any disclosure made by the RECEIVING PARTY to the DISCLOSING PARTY or its Authorized Distributor, of an ultimate destination of the products, the RECEIVING PARTY will not export or re-export, either directly or indirectly, any products or systems

incorporating such product without first obtaining all required licenses from the United States Government.

8. The RECEIVING PARTY acknowledges and agrees that the restrictions contained in this Agreement are necessary for the protection of the business and property of the DISCLOSING PARTY, and considers them to be reasonable for such purpose. The RECEIVING PARTY agrees that any breach of this Agreement may cause the DISCLOSING PARTY substantial and irreparable damage and therefore, in the event of any such breach, the RECEIVING PARTY agrees that the DISCLOSING PARTY shall be entitled to specific performance and other injunctive relief, in addition to such other remedies as may be afforded by applicable law, without being required to post a bond.

9. This Agreement shall be governed in all respects by the laws of the United States of America and the State of California as such laws are applied to agreements entered into and to be performed entirely within California between California residents.

10. This Agreement shall govern all communications between the parties that are made during the period regarding this subject matter from the effective date of this Agreement to the date on which the either party receives from the other written notice that subsequent communications shall not be so governed; provided, however, that each party's obligations under Paragraph 2 with respect to Proprietary Information of the Disclosing Party which it has previously received shall continue for a period of two (2) years after receipt thereof unless terminated pursuant to Paragraph 3.

11. In an action to enforce any rights under this Agreement, the prevailing party shall be entitled to recover reasonable costs and attorneys' fees.

AGREED	**AGREED**
[Your Name]	[Company Name]
ADDRESS:	ADDRESS:
BY:_____	BY:_____
NAME:_____	NAME:_____
TITLE:_____	TITLE:_____
DATED:_____	DATED:_____

Figure 17.6 Example of a bilateral NDA.

Work for Hire

A work-for-hire contract can be as simple as a single page or as complicated and specific as a dozen pages. I've tried to provide a lengthier
example that pretty much covers all the bases for what you might
encounter. The example I've provided here in Figure 17.7 has been
drafted by lawyers, but remember that I am not a lawyer and I am
not qualified to offer legal advice. If there is something you don't understand, or if you feel uneasy about a contract, don't be afraid to ask questions and get clarification from the client and/or your own legal counsel.

INDEPENDENT CONTRACTOR

WORK FOR HIRE

SERVICES AGREEMENT

Effective Date: [date]

This Agreement is made by and between [company name], (referred to herein as "**Company**"), having a principal place of business at [address] ("**Company**) and [name], an
individual, residing or having a principal place of business at [address] ("**Contractor**").

1. <u>Engagement of Services</u>. Contractor agrees to provide sound design services to
   create sound recordings (the "**Sound Recordings**"), as further described in
   <u>Exhibit A</u> attached hereto and incorporated herein by this reference ("**Project
   Assignment**"). Subject to the terms of this Agreement, Contractor will render
   the services set forth in the Project Assignment(s) accepted by Contractor by
   the completion dates set forth therein.

2. <u>Compensation</u>. Company will pay Contractor the fee(s) set forth in <u>Exhibit A</u> for
   the Project Assignment for services rendered pursuant to this Agreement. Contractor will be reimbursed only for expenses which have been approved in
   advance in writing by an Company manager, within thirty (30) days of receipt
   of Contractor's invoice, provided Contractor has furnished such documentation
   for authorized expenses as Company may reasonably request. Upon termination
   of this Agreement for any reason, Contractor will be paid fees on the basis stated
   in the Project Assignment(s) for work which has been completed.

3. <u>Independent Contractor Relationship</u>. Contractor's relationship with Company
   is that of an independent contractor, and nothing in this Agreement is intended
   to, or should be construed to, create a partnership, agency, joint venture or
   employment relationship. Contractor will not be entitled to any of the benefits
   which Company may make available to its employees, including, but not limited
   to, group health or life insurance, profit-sharing or retirement benefits. Contractor is not authorized to make any representation, contract or commitment on

behalf of Company unless specifically requested or authorized in writing to do so by an Company manager. Contractor is solely responsible for, and will file, on a timely basis, all tax returns and payments required to be filed with, or made to, any federal, state or local tax authority with respect to the performance of services and receipt of fees under this Agreement. Contractor is solely responsible for, and must maintain adequate records of, expenses incurred in the course of performing services under this Agreement. No part of Contractor's compensation will be subject to withholding by Company for the payment of any social security, federal, state or any other employee payroll taxes. Company will regularly report amounts paid to Contractor by filing Form 1099-MISC with the Internal Revenue Service as required by law.

4. <u>Work Made for Hire</u>. The Sound Recordings and any resulting musical composition(s) (the "**Compositions**") are prepared within the scope of Company's engagement of Contractor's services as a musician and shall constitute a work specially ordered by Company for use as a contribution to a collective work. Contractor agrees to perform the services and performances rendered in connection with creating the Sound Recordings, Compositions and such other services described in the Project Assignment as a work made for hire for Company, and acknowledges and agrees that the Sound Recordings and any resulting Composition(s), and all work and proceeds and results therefrom associated therewith, (collectively, the "**Work**") (and all rights therein, including without limitation, copyright) belong to and shall be the sole and exclusive property of Company.

    (a) Without limiting the foregoing, Contractor acknowledges and agrees that Company is and shall be the sole and exclusive owner throughout the universe of all right, title and interest of any nature and description in and to the Work, including without limitation the Sound Recordings and Compositions, and all derivatives and reproductions made therefrom, and all databases and other physical materials embodying the same and/or created in connection therewith, as well as all music, effects and other elements contained therein, during and from their creation, including, without limitation, the worldwide copyrights therein and thereto and the exclusive right to register the copyrights in the same in the name of Company, to renew and extend such copyrights, and to exercise throughout the world all rights of the copyright owner thereunder.

    (b) Without limiting the foregoing, the Work, including without limitation the Sound Recordings and Compositions, and all rights therein, are deemed to be works made for hire which are created exclusively for Company and shall be from the inception of their creation entirely Company's sole property in perpetuity throughout the universe, and free of any claim by Contractor. Contractor further acknowledges and agrees that the Work, including the Sound Recordings and Compositions, and results and proceeds of such Work, or any part thereof, may be assigned, transferred or licensed by Company and its successors and assigns, without restriction whatsoever.

(c) Without limiting any of the foregoing, Company will have the exclusive worldwide right in perpetuity to exploit the Sound Recordings and Compositions in any manner whatsoever without any further payment to Contractor. Contractor agrees that, to the best of his/her knowledge, all of his/her contributions to the Sound Recordings and the Compositions are original and do not infringe or violate the right of any other party. Contractor hereby represents and warrants that Company's use of the Sound Recordings will not breach the rights of any party including, without limitation, any record company with which Contractor may be affiliated.

5.   Copyright Assignment. If for any reason the Work, including without limitation the Sound Recordings and Compositions, in whole or in part, are not considered a work made for hire under applicable law, or if Contractor is deemed an "author" of any part of the Work, Contractor does hereby sell, assign, and transfer to Company, its successors and assigns, the entire right, title and interest in and to the copyright in the Work, including without limitation the Sound Recordings and Compositions, and all neighboring, and allied rights, and any registrations and copyright applications relating thereto and any renewals and extensions thereof, and in and to all work based upon, derived from, or incorporating the Work, including without limitation the Sound Recordings and Compositions, and in and to all income, royalties, damages, claims and payments now or hereafter due or payable with respect thereto, and in and to all causes of action, either in law or in equity for past, present, or future infringement based on the copyrights, and in and to all rights corresponding to the foregoing throughout the world. Contractor agrees to execute all papers and to perform such other proper acts as Company may deem necessary to secure for Company or its designee the rights herein assigned, and Contractor hereby grants to Company a power of attorney, irrevocable and coupled with an interest, for Contractor and in Contractor's name, to apply for and obtain, and on obtaining the same, to assign to Company, all such copyrights and renewals and extensions thereof, which power of attorney may only be exercised if Contractor fails to execute and deliver to Company any document which Company may deem necessary to secure for Company or its designee the rights herein assigned.

6.   Moral Rights. If the Work (including without limitation the Recordings and Compositions) is one to which the provisions of 17 U.S.C. Section 106A, or similar statute, apply, Contractor hereby waives and appoints Company to assert on Contractor's behalf Contractor's moral rights or any equivalent rights regarding the form or extent of any alteration to the Work (including, without limitation, removal or destruction) or the making of any derivative work based on the Work for any and all purposes.

7.   Disclosure and Assignment of Inventions.

7.1   Inventions. "Inventions" includes any and all new or useful art, discovery, improvement, technical development, or invention, whether or not patentable and all related know-how, designs, mask works, trademarks, formulae, processes, manufacturing techniques, trade secrets, ideas, artworks, software or other copyrightable or patentable work, that Contractor, solely or jointly with others, makes, conceives or reduces to practice within the scope of Contractor's work for Company under this Agreement.

7.2   Disclosure and Ownership of Inventions. Contractor agrees to promptly disclose every Invention. Contractor hereby assigns and agrees to assign to Company or its designee its entire right, title and interest worldwide in all such Inventions and any associated intellectual property rights.

7.3   Assistance. Contractor agrees to execute upon Company's request a signed transfer of copyright to Company in the form included in each Project Assignment for all Inventions subject to copyright protection, including computer programs, notes, sketches, drawings and reports. Contractor agrees to assist Company in any reasonable manner to obtain and enforce for Company's benefit patents, copyrights, mask works, and other property rights in any and all countries, and Contractor agrees to execute, when requested, patent, copyright or similar applications and assignments to Company and any other lawful documents deemed necessary by Company to carry out the purpose of this Agreement. If called upon to render assistance under this paragraph, Contractor will be entitled to a fair and reasonable fee in addition to reimbursement of authorized expenses incurred at the prior written request of Company. In the event that Company is unable for any reason to secure Contractor's signature to any document required to apply for or execute any patent, copyright or other applications with respect to any Inventions (including improvements, renewals, extensions, continuations, divisions or continuations in part thereof), Contractor hereby irrevocably designates and appoints Company and its duly authorized officers and agents as its agents and attorneys-in-fact to act for and in its behalf and instead of Contractor, to execute and file any such application and to do all other lawfully permitted acts to further the prosecution and issuance of patents, copyrights, mask works or other rights thereon with the same legal force and effect as if executed by Contractor.

8.   Confidential Information

8.1   Definition of Confidential Information. "Confidential Information" as used in this Agreement shall mean any and all technical and non-technical information disclosed by Company to Contractor including patent, copyright, trade secret, and proprietary information, techniques, sketches, drawings, models, inventions, know-how, processes, apparatus, equipment, algorithms, software programs, software source documents, and formulae related to the current, future and proposed products and services of Company, its suppliers and customers, and includes, without limitation, its respective information concerning research, experimental work, development, design details and specifications, engineering, financial information, procurement requirements, purchasing manufacturing, customer lists, business forecasts, sales and merchandising and marketing plans and information. "Confidential Information" also includes proprietary or confidential information of any third party who may disclose such information to Company or Contractor in the course of Company's business.

8.2   <u>Nondisclosure and Nonuse Obligations</u>. Contractor will use the Confidential Information solely to perform Project Assignment(s) for the benefit of Company. Contractor agrees that it shall treat all Confidential Information of Company with the same degree of care as it accords to its own Confidential Information, and Contractor represents that it exercises reasonable care to protects its own Confidential Information. If Contractor is not an individual, Contractor agrees that it shall disclose Confidential Information of another party only to those of its employees who need to know such information and certifies that such employees have previously agreed, either as a condition of employment or in order to obtain the Confidential Information, to be bound by terms and conditions substantially similar to those of this Agreement. Contractor will immediately give notice to Company of any unauthorized use or disclosure of the Confidential Information. Contractor agrees to assist Company in remedying any such unauthorized use or disclosure of the Confidential Information. Contractor acknowledges that any Confidential Information provided to Contractor prior to the effective date of this Agreement will be covered under the terms of this Agreement. Contractor further acknowledges that, as to any Confidential Information it may have received prior to the effective date of this Agreement, such information has been used only as authorized under this Section 8.2.

8.3   <u>Exclusions from Nondisclosure and Nonuse Obligations</u>. Contractor's obligations under Section 8.2 ("Nondisclosure and Nonuse Obligations") with respect to any portion of Confidential Information shall terminate when Contractor can document that: (a) it was in the public domain at or subsequent to the time it was communicated to Contractor by the disclosing party through no fault of Contractor; (b) it was rightfully in Contractor's possession free of any obligation of confidence at or subsequent to the time it was communicated to Contractor by the disclosing party; (c) it was developed by employees or agents of Contractor independently of and without reference to any information communicated to Contractor by the disclosing party; or (d) the communication was in response to a valid order by a court or other governmental body, was otherwise required by law, or was necessary to establish the rights of either party under this Agreement.

8.4   <u>Disclosure of Third Party Information</u>. Neither party shall communicate any information to the other in violation of the proprietary rights of any third party.

9.   Return of Company's Property. All materials (including, without limitation, documents, drawings, models, apparatus, sketches, design and lists) furnished to Contractor by Company, whether delivered to Contractor by Company or made by Contractor in the performance of services under this Agreement (the "Company Property") are the sole and exclusive property of Company or its suppliers or customers. Contractor agrees to promptly deliver the original and any copies of the Company Property to Company at any time upon Company's request. Upon termination of this Agreement by either party for any reason, Contractor agrees to promptly deliver to Company or destroy, at Company's option, the original and any copies of the Company Property, and certify in writing that Contractor has so returned or destroyed all such Company Property.

10.   No Conflict of Interest; Warranties. During the term of this Agreement, Contractor will not accept work, enter into a contract, or accept an obligation, inconsistent or incompatible with Contractor's obligations, or the scope of services rendered for Company, under this Agreement. Contractor warrants that, to the best of its knowledge, there is no other contract or duty on its part inconsistent with this Agreement. Contractor agrees to indemnify Company from any and all loss or liability incurred by reason of the alleged breach by Contractor of any services agreement with any third party. In addition, Contractor warrants that Contractor has the right, power and authority to enter into and perform this Agreement without violating or infringing any third party rights, including, without limitation, intellectual property rights.

11.   Term and Termination.

   11.1   Term. This Agreement is effective as of the Effective Date set forth above and will terminate on [completion of the Project Assignment specified in Exhibit A] unless terminated earlier as set forth below.

   11.2   Termination by Company. Company may terminate this Agreement, with or without cause, at any time upon five (5) business days prior written notice to Contractor. Company also may terminate this Agreement immediately in its sole discretion upon Contractor's material breach of this Agreement and/or upon any acts of gross misconduct by Contractor directly affecting this Agreement or the independent contractor relationship.

   11.3   Termination by Contractor. Contractor may terminate this Agreement for extraordinary cause, such as medical disability, preventing Contractor's performance of the services, upon written notice to Company.

   11.4   Survival. Sections 4, 5, 6, 7, 8, 12, 14, 15, 16, 17, 18, and 19 will survive any termination or expiration of this Agreement, as well as any terms which by their meaning or sense are intended to survive.

12.   Noninterference with Business. During this Agreement, and for a period of two years immediately following its termination, Contractor agrees not to interfere

with the business of Company in any manner. By way of example and not of limitation, Contractor agrees not to solicit or induce any employee or independent contractor to terminate or breach an employment, contractual or other relationship with Company.

13. Successors and Assigns. Contractor may not subcontract or otherwise delegate its obligations under this Agreement without Company's prior written consent. Subject to the foregoing, this Agreement will be for the benefit of Company's successors and assigns, and will be binding on Contractor's assignees.

14. Notices. Any notice required or permitted by this Agreement shall be in writing and shall be delivered as follows with notice deemed given as indicated: (i) by personal delivery when delivered personally; (ii) by overnight courier upon written verification of receipt; (iii) by telecopy or facsimile transmission upon acknowledgment of receipt of electronic transmission; or (iv) by certified or registered mail, return receipt requested, upon verification of receipt. Notice shall be sent to the addresses set forth above or such other address as either party may specify in writing.

15. Governing Law; Forum. This Agreement shall be governed in all respects by the laws of the United States of America and by the laws of the State of California, as such laws are applied to agreements entered into and to be performed entirely within California between California residents. All disputes arising under this Agreement may be brought in the Superior Court of the State of California in San Mateo County or the United States District Court for the Northern District of California as permitted by law. Developer consents to personal jurisdiction of the above courts.

16. Severability. Should any provisions of this Agreement be held by a court of law to be illegal, invalid or unenforceable, the legality, validity and enforceability of the remaining provisions of this Agreement shall not be affected or impaired thereby.

17. Waiver. The waiver by Company of a breach of any provision of this Agreement by Contractor shall not operate or be construed as a waiver of any other or subsequent breach by Contractor.

18. Injunctive Relief for Breach. Contractor's obligations under this Agreement are of a unique character that gives them particular value; breach of any of such obligations will result in irreparable and continuing damage to Company for which there will be no adequate remedy at law; and, in the event of such breach, Company will be entitled to injunctive relief and/or a decree for specific performance, and such other and further relief as may be proper (including monetary damages if appropriate).

19. Entire Agreement. This Agreement constitutes the entire agreement between the parties relating to this subject matter and supersedes all prior or contemporaneous oral or written agreements concerning such subject matter. The terms of this

Agreement will govern all Project Assignments and services undertaken by Contractor for Company. This Agreement may only be changed by mutual agreement of authorized representatives of the parties in writing.

20.   <u>Counterparts</u>. This Agreement may be executed in counterparts.

IN WITNESS WHEREOF, the parties have executed this Agreement as of the date first written above.

[Company]   [Contractor]

By:_____   By:_____

Name:_____   Name:_____

Title:_____   Title:_____

Date:_____   Date:_____

Exhibit A

PROJECT ASSIGNMENT

Services:

[Description of services]

Completion Date:

[Negotiated Completion Schedule]

Payment of Fees:

[Amount agreed upon]

IN WITNESS WHEREOF, the parties have executed this Project Assignment as of the date first written above.

[Company]   [Contractor]

By:_____   By:_____

Name:_____   Print Name:_____

Title:_____   Title:_____

ASSIGNMENT OF COPYRIGHT

For good and valuable consideration which has been received, the undersigned sells, assigns and transfers to Company, and its successors and assigns, all copyrights in and to the work performed pursuant to this Project Assignment, and all of the right, title and interest of the undersigned, vested and contingent, therein and thereto.

Executed this_____ day of_____, 20_____.

[Company]   [Contractor]

By:_____   By:_____

Name:_____   Print Name:_____

Title:_____   Title:_____

Approvals

Contractor's Name: _____

Address: _____

_____

_____

SS#: _____

Dept. Working In: _____

Start Date: _____

Contractor's Signature: _____

Manager's Signature: _____

VP's Signature: _____

Figure 17.7 Example of a work-for-hire agreement.

Qualifying Questionnaire

Another document that I mentioned in the last chapter is one that I often use to gather information about a project during the initial consultation. I call it a *new project questionnaire*. Granted, I may be going a bit overboard with the organization on this one, but I find that keeping this information handy helps me develop a client database as well as keep track of incoming projects, due dates, and what price I quoted for what work in case I need to reference it in the future. Though it's not a legal document, I feel that showing an example of it here might give you some ideas about how to develop your own questionnaire or ways to better keep track of the many, many clients you will eventually have. So here it is, in Figure 17.8.

New Project Questionnaire

Date:

Client Information

Company/Contact Name:	Address:
Phone/Fax:	E-mail:

Project Information

Start Date:	End Date:
Description of Work:	
Final Delivery Format:	Price Quoted:
Notes:	

Figure 17.8 New project questionnaire.

Glossary

This glossary is designed to be a quick reference for the digital audio terms introduced in this book. Like most words in the English language, many of these terms have multiple meanings. Their definitions have been tailored to the specific subject matter and as they are referred to in this book.

AC. Alternating current.

ACIDized WAV. ACIDized WAV files are regular WAV files that have additional metadata added to them that expresses certain properties about the content of the file, such as pitch, tempo, and the location of stretch markers. When an ACIDized WAV is imported into a compatible software program, you can change certain behaviors of the file, such as tempo and pitch.

active. Describes a device that is self-amplified.

A/D. Analog-to-digital.

ADSR. Envelope generator with Attack, Decay, Sustain, and Release parameters.

AIFF (format). Audio Interchange File Format. An audio format for storing audio on a computer. Compatible with both Mac and PC; however, AIFF is more commonly associated with the Mac platform. The AIFF file extension is .aif.

algorithm. A computer program designed to perform a specific task. In the context of effects units, algorithms usually describe a software building block designed to create a specific effect or combination of effects.

ambience. The result of sound reflections in a confined space being added to the original sound. Ambience may also be simulated electronically by some digital reverb units. The main difference between ambience and reverberation is that ambience doesn't have the characteristic long delay time of reverberation—the reflections mainly give the sound a sense of space.

amplifier. A device used to increase, or amplify, the volume of a signal that is passed through it.

amplitude. The magnitude of a soundwave.

analog. Describes a device that uses continually changing voltage or current to represent a signal.

Apple Loop. An audio loop encoded with additional data, or meta tags, that contain time-stretching, publishing, and musical information. Commonly AIFF-formatted. An Apple Loop is similar to an ACIDized WAV file except that the metadata can be accessed through compatible programs on a Mac only.

application. A computer program.

artifact. Momentary unwanted noise in an audio file caused by editing and processing. Usually in the form of a click or a pop.

ASIO. Audio Stream Input/Output. A computer protocol for digital audio that provides a low-latency, high-fidelity interface between a software application and the computer's soundcard.

attack. The time taken for a sound to achieve maximum amplitude.

attenuate. To reduce the amplitude.

AU. Audio Units. A system-level plug-in format provided by Core Audio (Mac).

audio buffer. Temporary RAM memory used in some computer operations, sometimes to prevent a break in the data stream when the computer is interrupted to perform another task.

audio frequency. Also known as *audible frequency*. Defined as frequencies that are within the range of human hearing. Typically 20 Hz to 20 kHz. Frequencies that exist below 20 Hz are typically more felt than heard.

aux. A control designed to route a portion of the channel signal to the send effect outputs.

backup. A safety copy of software or data.

balance. The perception of equal proportion between the left and right channels and/or across the stereo field.

band-pass filter (BPF). A filter that removes or attenuates frequencies above and below the frequency at which it is set. Frequencies within the band *can* be emphasized, but it's not always the case.

bass. Tones of low frequency or range.

bell. Refers to an equalization filter curve in which the center frequency is at the top of the curve, allowing the equalizer to operate smoothly across a range of frequencies.

binary. A coding system that uses a series of only 1s and 0s to express numbers. Computers can interpret binary digits as data.

bit. A binary digit, which can either be 1 or 0.

boost. An increase in amplitude or value.

bouncing. The process of mixing two or more recorded tracks together and consolidating them to a new track. Bouncing can also be the process of rendering real-time effects to a single track.

BPM. Beats per minute. The measurement of the tempo of a song.

brickwall (limiting). A compression setting with a very high ratio (typically 20.1 or greater) and a fast attack to ensure that a signal *never* exceeds the set threshold. Also called *hard limiting*.

broadcast wave (BWF). A neutral audio file format that is widely compatible with most nonlinear digital systems, Mac and PC alike. It is used mainly for motion picture and television production and contains additional metadata identifying file attributes, publishing information, and coding history.

bus. A common signal path along which signals carrying the stereo mix, groups, PFL signal, aux sends, and so on may travel.

bypass. A function that "turns off" a virtual device without removing it from the signal chain, allowing the audio signal to pass through it unaffected.

CD-R. A recordable type of single-use compact disc. CD-Rs cannot be erased and reused.

channel strip. A single strip of controls in a mixing console relating to either a single input or a pair of main/monitor inputs.

click track. An audible metronome pulse that conforms to the project tempo to assist musicians with playing in time.

clipping. A severe form of distortion that occurs when a signal attempts to exceed the maximum level threshold that a piece of equipment can handle.

clone. An exact duplicate or copy.

compander. Encode/decode device that compresses a signal while encoding it, then expands it when decoding it.

compressor. Device designed to reduce the dynamic range of audio signals by reducing the level of high signals or by increasing the level of low signals, bringing them closer in dynamic volume.

console. Alternative term for a mixer.

copy protection. Method used by software manufacturers to prevent unauthorized copying.

crash. A term relating to the malfunction of a computer program that prevents further use until the program is re-launched.

crossover frequency (multi-band processing). The frequency at which one frequency band meets another.

cut. To reduce.

cut/copy/paste editing. The ability to copy or move sections of a recording to new locations.

cutoff frequency. The frequency at which a filter begins to take effect.

cycle. One complete vibration of a sound source or its electrical equivalent. The pitch of sound waves is measured in cycles. One cycle per second is expressed as 1 Hertz (Hz).

daisy chain. Term used to describe a serial connection between effect plug-ins.

damping (reverb). The gradual reduction of the size of oscillation, vibration, or signal intensity by the removal of energy through altering the properties of virtual reflective surfaces.

data. Information stored and used by a computer.

data compression. A system used to express the same amount of data that represents an audio signal with a smaller number of bits, usually by discarding audio information that is being masked by more prominent sounds. Lossless data compression allows the exact original data to be reconstructed from the compressed data so that the sound quality isn't degraded.

DAW. Digital Audio Workstation. A computer designed to record, edit, and play back digital audio.

dB. Decibel. A unit of measurement used to express the amplitude level of sound.

DC. Direct current.

decay. The progressive reduction in amplitude of an audio signal over time. In the context of an ADSR envelope filter, decay occurs as soon as the attack phase reaches its full amplitude. In the decay phase, the signal level drops until it reaches the user-defined sustain level.

decibel. See *dB*.

de-esser. A plug-in or virtual device for reducing the effect of sibilance in vocal signals.

digital. Electronic system that represents data and signals in the form of binary digits (1s and 0s).

DirectX (plug-in). A plug-in format based on Microsoft's Component Object Model. PC only.

disc. A term used to describe vinyl discs, CDs, and MiniDiscs.

dither. A system of adding low-level noise to a digitized audio signal to mask re-quantization errors that may occur during a bit-rate reduction.

driver. A software application that allows communication between the host application and a hardware peripheral.

dry. A signal that has had no effects added.

DSP. Digital Signal Processing. The manipulation of digital audio data.

dubbing. The act of adding audio material to an existing recording. Also known as *overdubbing*.

dynamic range. The range, measured in decibels, between the loudest (highest) part of an audio signal and silence.

dynamics. The varying volume levels that occur in a piece of audio material.

EAN code. European Article Number code. Part of a barcode system used worldwide to identify a retail product.

early reflections. The first reverberations of a sound, after it bounces off a reflective surface, such as walls, floors, and ceilings.

edit. The act of modifying prerecorded audio material.

effect plug-in. An auxiliary program for modifying an audio signal in a creative way—i.e. delay, reverb, chorus, flange, phaser, vibrato, tremolo, distortion, and so on.

enhance. To improve.

enhancer. A plug-in or virtual device designed to improve certain characteristics of the audio material.

equal temperament. Standard Western tuning that divides each octave into 12 mathematically equal parts.

equalizer. Device for selectively cutting or boosting the selected frequencies of audio material.

exciter. An enhancer that works by synthesizing new frequency harmonics and adding them back to the original signal.

expander. A plug-in or virtual device designed to decrease the level of low-level signals and increase the level of high-level signals, thus increasing the dynamic range of the signal. An expander is the opposite of a compressor.

fade (in/out). A gradual change in amplitude from an audio signal's normal level to or from silence.

fader. A slider that is positioned on the mixer channel strip and is used to manually control volume.

far-field (monitors). A set of loudspeakers for playing back audio at a distance of typically 10 feet or more.

feedback (delay). A control parameter that sets the number of repeats that occur in a delay effect. Also describes the loud squeal heard when a channel is receiving its own output.

filter (equalization). A shape used in equalization to emphasize or attenuate a specific range of frequencies. Shapes include low-pass, high-pass, low-shelf, high-shelf, band-pass, and notch.

flanging. Modulated delay effect using feedback to create a dramatic, sweeping sound.

frequency. An indication of how many cycles of a repetitive waveform occur in one second. The fewer the cycles that occur in one second, the lower the frequency. A waveform that has a repetition cycle of once per second has a frequency of 1 Hz.

frequency band. A range of frequency classified by its position in the frequency spectrum. Common classifications are low frequency (LF), high frequency (HF), midrange (MID), low midrange (LM), and high midrange (HM) bands.

frequency range. A measurement of the frequency range that can be handled by a specific piece of equipment.

FX. Effects.

gain. The amount by which an audio signal is amplified. Measured in decibels.

gate. A plug-in, hardware, or virtual device that mutes low-level signals below the user-defined threshold in an effort to reduce unwanted noise during pauses in the wanted audio material.

glitch. An unwanted momentary corruption of an audio signal or the unexplained short-term malfunction of a piece of equipment.

graphic equalizer. An equalizer with predetermined frequencies, controlled by (virtual) faders that are arranged from left to right and that, when adjusted, visually depict the EQ curve being applied to the signal.

ground loop. A common electrical issue in which the wiring of multiple ground connections causes an audible hum to be picked up through the audio device. Also known as *earth loops*.

group channel. A channel in which a collection of tracks can be routed to provide overall control with the use of a single channel strip and fader.

hard knee (compression). A compression parameter that reduces gain abruptly on any signal exceeding the set threshold.

harmonic. A component frequency of an audio signal that is an integer multiple of the fundamental frequency.

harmonic distortion. A means of creating harmonics that were not present in the original signal.

headroom. The margin, in decibels, between the highest peak signal being passed by a piece of equipment and the absolute maximum level the equipment can handle without distortion.

high-pass filter (HPF). A filter that passes high frequencies and attenuates frequencies below its cutoff point (frequency).

high-range/HF (frequency). The range of frequency that typically exists between 6.5 kHz and 20 kHz in the frequency spectrum. Also referred to as *highs*.

hiss. Noise caused by random electrical fluctuations.

hum. Audible signal contamination caused by the addition of low frequencies.

Hz. Short for Hertz, the unit of frequency.

insert. A virtual port on an individual track that is a means of routing an effect to a track or channel.

insert effect. An effect that has been routed through an insert. Insert effects only affect the audio in the channel on which they are inserted.

interface. A device that acts as an intermediary between two or more other pieces of equipment. A GUI, or *Graphical User Interface,* is a set of graphical controls that allows you to interact with a software program, plug-in, and so on.

I/O. Input/output, or the part of an audio device that handles inputs and outputs.

ISRC. International Standard Recording Code. An international standard code used to uniquely identify sound and music video recordings.

JAN. Japan Article Number. A barcode standard for identifying retail products.

key commands. Specific keystrokes that execute a program action.

kHz. 1,000 Hertz (Hz).

level. A general term for volume or amplitude.

limiter. A plug-in or virtual device that controls the gain of a signal to prevent it from exceeding a preset level. A limiter is essentially a fast-acting compressor with a high compression ratio.

link. A function of a software program that allows you to virtually group two or more channels together so that any change applied to one channel in the group will be mirrored by all "linked" channels.

locator. A bookmark for a location within the project timeline.

loop. A repeating section of audio.

load. To recall a previously saved file, such as a preset or a project.

loudness. Perceived volume.

low-pass filter (LPF). A filter that passes low frequencies while attenuating frequencies above the set cutoff point (frequency).

low-range/LF (frequency). The range of frequency that typically exists between 20 Hz and 700 Hz in the frequency spectrum. Also referred to as *lows*.

makeup gain. A parameter that allows you to add gain to an audio signal in order to compensate for any volume lost during compression.

mastering. The phase of audio production that occurs after mixing and before replication. This phase is meant to enhance the sound quality of a final mix and make it ready for mass duplication.

MB. Megabyte. Approximately one million (actually 1,048,576) bytes of data.

menu. A list of choices presented by a computer program.

midrange/MF (frequency). The range of frequency that typically exists between 700 Hz and 6.5 kHz in the frequency spectrum. Also referred to as *mids*.

millisecond. A measurement of time equating to one thousandth of a second.

mixdown. To "bounce" or consolidate the multiple tracks of a final mix down to a single, two-channel stereo track.

mixer. A device or virtual device for combining two or more audio signals.

modeling. A process that imitates the sonic characteristics of a specific instrument or device by creating a virtual replica of the circuits and components of that device.

monitor (display). Display for a computer.

monitor (speaker). A reference loudspeaker used for mixing.

monitoring. The action of listening to audio signals.

mute. Used to silence an audio signal during playback.

near-field (monitors). A set of loudspeakers designed for listening at distances of 10 feet or less.

noise. Any unwanted sound that exists in an audio recording.

noise reduction. The reduction of unwanted noise that may be present in an audio signal.

noise shaping. A system for creating digital dither such that any added noise is shifted into those parts of the audio spectrum where the human ear is least sensitive.

normalization. A process that detects the loudest peak of an audio signal and raises it to 0 dB while raising the entire signal by the same amount to achieve a relative volume increase overall.

notch filter. A band-stop filter with a high Q value that that affects a very small range of frequency while leaving all other frequencies unaffected.

octave. When a frequency or pitch is transposed up by one octave, its frequency is doubled. The pitch at which the doubled frequency exists is the octave pitch. If a frequency is divided in half, the pitch will be an octave below the original pitch.

offline. Process carried out while a recording is not playing in real time.

operating system. The basic software that enables a computer to load and run other programs.

output. A port or virtual port from which audio is routed to another device or virtual device. The *main output* is a port or virtual port through which all audible signals are passed to the final monitoring destination.

overdub. To add audio to a recording or to replace one of the existing parts.

overload. To exceed the operating capacity of an electronic or electrical circuit.

pad. Resistive circuit for drastically reducing signal level.

pan (control). A control that allows the user to change the left or right positioning of an audio signal across the stereo field.

panning. The act of movement across the stereo field.

parallel (effect). A means of applying an effect by cloning the audio material, affecting it, and blending it into the original signal until the desired effect is achieved.

parameter. A variable value that affects some aspect of a plug-in, device, or virtual device's performance.

parametric EQ. An equalizer with separate adjustable controls for frequency, bandwidth, and cut/boost.

passive. A circuit with no active elements. Therefore, it requires an external power source.

peak. The highest signal level in any section of program material.

PFL. Pre-Fade Listen. A system used within a mixing console to allow the operator to listen in on a selected signal, regardless of the position of the fader controlling that signal.

phase. The timing difference between two waveforms expressed in degrees, where 360 degrees corresponds to a delay of exactly one cycle.

phaser. An effect that combines a signal with a phase-shifted version of itself to produce creative filtering effects.

pitch. Musical interpretation of an audio frequency.

pitch shifter. A plug-in or virtual device that changes the pitch of an audio signal without changing its duration.

plug-in. A computer program that interacts with the host application to provide a specific function, extending the host program's capabilities.

post-production. All stages of production that occur after the original audio material has been captured.

PQ coding. Process for adding pause, cue, and other subcode information to a digital master disc in preparation for manufacturing.

pre-delay. The amount of time before the first reverberations of a signal are heard.

preset. A set of saved parameters for an effect or virtual device that can easily be recalled.

processor (effect). A plug-in, device, or virtual device designed to treat an audio signal by changing its dynamics or frequency content. Examples of processors include compressors, gates, and equalizers.

project. A digital audio "document." Also called a *session*.

project folder. A designated folder on your hard disk where a project's audio files are stored.

Q/width (equalization). A measure of the resonant properties of a filter. The higher the Q value, the narrower the range of frequencies that will be affected.

RAM. Random Access Memory. A type of memory used by computers for the temporary storage of programs and data. All data stored to RAM is lost when a computer's power is turned off. For that reason, work needs to be saved to a hard drive in order to be preserved.

ratio (compression). A mathematical representation of proportional relation. In compression, a ratio of 4:1 means that for every 4 dB that the input level increases, the output level increases by only 1 dB.

real time. An audio process that can be carried out simultaneously as a signal is being recorded or played back. The opposite is offline, where the signal is processed in non–real time.

reduction. The amount by which something is lessened or diminished. For example, a −2-dB gain reduction means that the amplitude of the audio material will be decreased by two decibels.

release (compression). The amount of time it takes for an audio signal to return to its original amplitude once it drops below the set threshold level of the compressor.

release (envelope). The last phase in an ADSR envelope that begins at the end of the sustain phase. Gradually reduces the amplitude of the signal from the set sustain value to silence.

re-quantization. The reduction of data word length, or the action of expressing what is perceived as the same amount of data with a smaller number of bits.

resolution. The accuracy with which an analog signal is represented by a digitizing system. The more bits that are used or the more samples that are captured, the more accurately the amplitude of each sample can be measured.

reverb. Acoustic ambience created by multiple reflections in a confined space.

ReWire. A software protocol designed to allow remote control and data transfer between two or more independent digital audio applications.

RTAS (plug-in). Real Time Audio Suite. A plug-in format developed by Digidesign. Mac or PC.

safety copy. A duplicate or clone of an original piece of audio material for use in case of loss or damage to the original.

sample (content). A prerecorded piece of audio material that is used to supplement an original composition.

sample (measurement). A single unit of measurement that represents the momentary amplitude of an audio signal. If a sample rate is 44.1 kHz, it means that there are 44,100 samples that occur per second.

sample rate. The number of samples per second that are captured by a digital system.

sample/wave editor. An application for manipulating digital audio.

SDII (format). Sound Designer II. The second incarnation of an audio format developed by Digidesign. It is used almost exclusively with Pro Tools software.

send. A port or virtual port that allows multiple audio tracks to be routed to a single effect.

send effect. An effect that is inserted on a send output. A send effect can be routed to multiple tracks within the project and applied to each with varying mix levels. However, if you change any parameter of the send effect, it will affect all tracks that are routed to it.

sequencer (software). A program for recording, arranging, and replaying audio/MIDI data, usually in a multitrack format, allowing complex compositions and arrangements to be created in a nonlinear fashion.

shelf (equalization). An equalization shape that increases or attenuates the level of a wide range of frequencies by a fixed amount. A high shelf affects frequencies above the user-defined frequency. A low shelf affects the frequencies below the user-defined frequency.

sibilance. High-frequency whistling or lisping sound that affects vocal recordings, due either to poor mic technique or to excessive equalization.

signal. Electrical representation of sound.

signal chain. The path along which an audio signal is routed. A common signal chain is one that begins with the input signal, which is routed to an effect, which is routed into another effect, and so forth until the affected signal passes through the main output. The order in which effects exist in the signal chain has a direct impact on the way that the original signal is affected.

signal-to-noise ratio. The ratio of maximum signal level to the residual noise, expressed in dB.

slave. A software application that is controlled by a host program.

SMPTE. Time code developed for the film industry but now extensively used in music and recording. SMPTE is a real-time code and is related to hours, minutes, seconds, and film or video frames, rather than to musical tempo.

soft clip. A plug-in processing feature that allows a signal to clip in a subtle way, creating intentional harmonic distortion and thereby providing warmth. Most often found on compressors, limiters, and volume maximization plug-ins.

soft knee (compression). A parameter of a compressor that gradually reduces gain on any signal that exceeds the set threshold.

solo. A function of a software program that allows a piece of audio material to play back alone while the other tracks in the project are silenced.

soundcard. A computer expansion card that facilitates the input and output of audio signals to/from a computer under control of computer programs.

SPL. Sound Pressure Level. Measured in dB.

stereo. Describes an audio signal or recording that consists of both a left and a right channel.

sub-bass. Frequencies below the range of typical monitor loudspeakers. Also called "Perceived Bass."

sub-group. A group of channels that exists within another group.

surge. Sudden increase in voltage.

sustain. The duration of time in which a sound is held before it becomes inaudible.

sustain (ADSR). The third phase of an ADSR envelope that determines the level at which the sound will hold before the release phase begins.

sweet spot. The optimum position for a listener in relation to monitor loudspeakers.

sync. The act of making two or more pieces of equipment or software run synchronously with each other.

TDM (plug-in). A plug-in architecture, exclusive to Digidesign Pro Tools|HD systems, that lightens CPU load by performing signal processing on DSP chips rather than on the computer's internal processor.

tempo. Tempo is the speed of a musical composition. BPM is a way to measure tempo. If 120 beats occur in evenly spaced intervals over a period of one minute, the tempo is 120 BPM (beats per minute).

test tone. A fixed-level sustaining tone that acts as an audible reference when matching levels between speakers.

threshold. The level (usually measured in decibels) at which an effect will "kick in" and begin to affect the audio being passed through it.

track (performance). A piece of prerecorded audio meant to be played as part of a live performance. Sometimes called a *backing track*.

track (sequencer). Refers to audio material or MIDI data that is contained on a discrete channel.

tracking. The act of recording live audio performances into a digital audio workstation.

transient (waveform). The individual peaks in a graphic waveform.

transparent. Subjective term used to describe audio quality in which the high-frequency detail is clear and individual sounds are easy to identify and separate.

transparent (plug-in). In regards to plug-ins, if a plug-in is transparent, it means that it affects the audio without coloring the tonal characteristics of the original signal.

transpose. To shift a musical phrase by a fixed number of semitones.

treble. In a simple equalizer, treble is a control that adjusts audible high frequencies of an audio signal.

tremolo. An effect that produces amplitude (volume) modulation.

undo. A function within a software program that allows you to revert a document or project to its previous state.

UPC. Universal Product Code. A barcode standard used for identifying retail products.

USB. Universal Serial Bus. A means of connecting compatible devices to your DAW computer.

vibrato. An effect that offers pitch modulation.

volume. The amplitude or loudness of a sound.

VST (plug-in). Virtual Studio Technology. A plug-in format developed by Steinberg. Mac and PC formats, but more commonly PC.

VU meter. Meter designed to interpret signal levels in roughly the same way as the human ear, which responds more closely to the average levels of sounds than to the peak levels.

WAV (format). Short for *waveform*. An audio format for storing audio on a computer. Compatible with both Mac and PC. The WAV file extension is .wav.

waveform. A graphic representation of the way in which a sound wave or an electrical wave varies over time. Multiple individual samples are captured and strung together to create a graphic waveform image.

wet/dry mix. A parameter used to control how much of an effect is mixed in with a dry, or unaffected, audio signal.

white noise. A random signal with an energy distribution that produces the same amount of noise power per Hz.

write. To save data to a digital storage medium, such as a hard drive.

zero-crossing. The point at which a signal waveform crosses the zero axis.

Recommended Reading

Finding out what others have to say on the topic of digital audio can be a very enlightening experience. No one knows everything, but through reading, listening, and understanding varying opinions on the subject, we can assemble ideas about different ways to approach digital audio in our own studios. This section provides some recommendations on books and websites to help further your digital audio and post-production education.

Books

There are many books available on the topic of digital audio production and post-production in general. I've provided a short list of books that I've found to be helpful as an educational resource. Of course, if you need information on specific digital audio software programs, you can always turn to the music technology titles offered by Course Technology Cengage Learning.

- Berg, Richard E. and David G. Stork. *The Physics of Sound, Third Edition*. Benjamin Cummings, 2004.

- Clark, Rick. *Mixing, Recording and Producing Techniques of the Pros*. Thomson Course Technology PTR, 2005.

- Katz, Bob. *Mastering Audio, Second Edition: The Art and the Science*. Focal Press, 2007.

- Olson, Harry F. *Music, Physics and Engineering*. Dover Publications, 1967.

- Owsinski, Bobby. *The Mastering Engineer's Handbook*. ArtistPro, 2000.

- Owsinski, Bobby. *The Mixing Engineer's Handbook*. Thomson Course Technology PTR, 2006.

- Shepherd, Ashley. *Plug-in Power!: The Complete Audio DSP Reference Guide*. Thomson Course Technology PTR, 2005.

Websites

Ah, the Internet. The Internet is our friend. It connects us to a universe of information on almost any subject we can dream of... *and* digital audio! There are thousands and thousands of websites out there that offer information on digital audio production. But there are some that I've found to be particularly helpful. Many of these online magazines also have print counterparts that I encourage you to explore. Here are some recommendations for different sites that can help accelerate your digital audio education, in no particular order. (Well, okay, in alphabetical order.)

Information and Education

- *DigiZine.* Both a print and an online magazine centrally focused on features related to Digidesign hardware and software. A great resource regardless of whether you're a Pro Tools user. DigiZine can be found in the News section of the Digidesign website. www.digidesign.com.

- *Electronic Musician.* Even though it has the words "Electronic" and "Musician" in the title, it's related to much more than simply one or the other, or even the sum of the two. You can find audio-production articles and tutorials, as well as information on digital audio products and technology. www.emusician.com.

- **Gearslutz.** A great community forum where many professional engineers converse about everything from software and equipment to production techniques and critiques. www.gearslutz.com.

- **Harmony Central.** Harmony Central has a great resource section containing many "how to" articles written by industry professionals. You can find information on everything from audio editing to mastering. www.harmony-central.com.

- **KVR Audio.** A massive plug-in and software database. Also offers related news and forums. www.kvraudio.com.

- *Mix.* Another fine print and online magazine for professional audio production that provides many tutorials, as well as information on recording, live audio, post-production, equipment, and education. www.mixonline.com.

- *Sound on Sound.* Purportedly "The world's best music recording magazine." And it just may be. *Sound on Sound* is both a print and an online magazine that provides a wealth of information about digital audio, production techniques, and related products without all the paid commentary. www.soundonsound.com.

- **WikiRecording.** WikiRecording is a free online audio recording guide that is composed of articles submitted by various users—the articles can be edited by pretty much anyone. The idea is a free exchange of information. There is a lot of great information here, but not all the articles have been verified. If any information on WikiRecording hasn't been verified, it will be indicated in the article itself. www.wikirecording.org.

Software

There are hundreds of different digital audio software developers out there. I've provided a list of web addresses for the ones mentioned in this book and a short description of what they were mentioned for. When you visit their sites, you'll quickly notice that almost every developer does much more than simply a single software application. So be sure to browse around—you may find more that interests you.

- Ableton. Creators of Live. www.ableton.com.

- Apple. Developer of Logic for the Mac. www.apple.com.

- Bias, Inc. Peak, Deck, SoundSoap, and Master Perfection Suite. www.bias-inc.com.

- Cakewalk. Developer behind SONAR, Sonitus:fx, and more. www.cakewalk.com.

- Digidesign. World-renowned Pro Tools and many supported plug-ins. www.digidesign.com.

- Free Audio Plug-Ins. The name just about says it all. Virtual instruments and effects offered in many different formats. www.freeaudioplugins.com.

- IK Multimedia. T-RackS, Classik Studio Reverb plug-ins, and more. www.ikmultimedia.com.

- iZotope. Developer of great plug-ins, including iZotope Ozone. www.izotope.com.

- McDSP. Professional processing plug-ins. www.mcdsp.com.

- Propellerhead. Learn more about ReWire and Rex files. www.propellerheads.se.

- PSPaudioware. Quality plug-ins for mixing and mastering. www.pspaudioware.com.

- Roxio. Creator of Toast for the Mac, as well as other CD-burning software and utilities. www.roxio.com.

- Smartelectronix. A collection of both practical and oddball effects produced by independent developers. www.smartelectronix.com.

- Sonnox Oxford Plugins. The amazing Oxford plug-ins. www.sonnoxplugins.com.

- Sony Creative Software. Developer of Sound Forge, CD Architect, and Noise Reduction 2.0. www.sonycreativesoftware.com.

- Steinberg. Cubase, Nuendo, and WaveLab. www.steinberg.net.

- T.C. Electronic. The T.C. PowerCore DSP system and compatible plug-ins. www.tcelectronic.com.

- The Sonic Spot. Another resource for free plug-ins to help get you started. www.sonicspot.com.

- Tweakbench. Some handy sound-design plug-ins. Who knows what you might use them for? www.tweakbench.com.

- Universal Audio. The UAD-1 DSP card and plug-ins. www.uaudio.com.

- Voxengo. Great plug-ins. And some free ones too! www.voxengo.com.

- Wave Arts. Some rather dandy plug-ins. www.wavearts.com.

- Waves. Monster plug-in bundles! www.waves.com.

Index

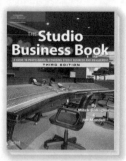

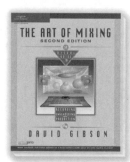